McPHEE GRIBBLE/PENGUIN BOOKS

STAINING THE WATTLE

Verity Burgmann was born in Sydney in 1952. After studying and working at the London School of Economics and Political Science she returned to Australia and completed a Ph.D from the Australian National University in 1980. Since then she has worked at the University of New South Wales, University of Melbourne and Deakin University. She is currently a lecturer in politics at the University of Melbourne. She lives in Elwood with her husband and son.

Jenny Lee was born in 1953 in Tamworth. She went to university in Canberra. Since then, she has continued to study and write history, and work as labour archivist at the University of Melbourne Archives. She has been editor of *Meanjin* since February 1987. She lives in Coburg with her husband and two daughters.

Other titles in the series

A Most Valuable Acquisition
Making A Life
Constructing A Culture

STAINING THE WATTLE

A People's History of Australia since 1788

EDITED BY VERITY BURGMANN & JENNY LEE

McPHEE GRIBBLE/PENGUIN BOOKS

McPhee Gribble Publishers Pty Ltd
66 Cecil Street
Fitzroy, Victoria, 3065, Australia

Penguin Books Australia Ltd,
487 Maroondah Highway, P.O. Box 257
Ringwood, Victoria, 3134, Australia
Penguin Books Ltd,
Harmondsworth, Middlesex, England
Penguin Books,
40 West 23rd Street, New York, N.Y. 10010, U.S.A.
Penguin Books Canada Ltd,
2801 John Street, Markham, Ontario, Canada L3R 1B4
Penguin Books (N.Z.) Ltd,
182-190 Wairau Road, Auckland 10, New Zealand

First published by McPhee Gribble Publishers
in association with Penguin Books Australia 1988

Typeset in Baskerville by Bookset, Melbourne
Made and printed in Australia by
The Book Printer

National Library of Australia
Cataloguing-in-Publication data

Staining the Wattle : a people's history of Australia since 1788.

Bibliography.
Includes index.
ISBN 0 14 011058 5.

1. Australia – History. 2. Australia – Social conditions. I. Burgmann, Verity, 1952– . II. Lee, Jenny, 1953–

994

Contents

Acknowledgements vii

Introduction ix
VERITY BURGMANN AND JENNY LEE

Big Brother is Watching You 1
ALASTAIR DAVIDSON

Conflicting Loyalties 13
CHRIS McCONVILLE

The Ties that Divide 27
ELLEN McEWEN

A Nordenfelt at every Woolshed 48
ANDREW MOORE

Only the Chains have Changed 66
PATRICIA GRIMSHAW

The Making of Homosexual Men 87
CRAIG JOHNSTON AND ROBERT JOHNSTON

Escaping the Well of Loneliness 100
LIZ ROSS

Divided We Fell 109
VERITY BURGMANN AND STUART MACINTYRE

The Beat of Weary Feet 132
CHARLIE FOX AND BRUCE SCATES

From Convicts to Communists 150
PETER LOVE

A Hundred Flowers Faded 164
PETER BEILHARZ

Preventing the Plunder 173
JACK MUNDEY

Cryin' Out for Land Rights 181
HEATHER GOODALL

Teaching Whites a Lesson 198
GARY FOLEY

War Against War 208
CHRIS HEALY

Power to the Young 228
BARRY YORK

Stop the Drop 243
BRENDAN CARINS

Fragmented Visions 254
JOHN MURPHY

Notes on the Contributors 265

Notes on the Chapters 269

Picture Sources 289

Index 291

Acknowledgements

We are grateful to Michael Daffey, Andrew Milner and our assorted offspring, who bore the brunt of the emotional and physical side-effects, and the phone calls. Michael Daffey was also of practical assistance with the more complex aspects of computing. Peter Love was a co-editor in the early stages of the project. Stuart Macintyre performed many functions, from errand-boy to chief adviser at moments of crisis and despair. Mark Richmond did much more than duty demanded as archivist at the University of Melbourne Archives, and kindly read proofs. Frank Strahan and the rest of the Archives staff took the project to their hearts and gave invaluable assistance, especially with the photographs. Sharon Ayre Fell was the best word processor we have ever come across. Carmel Shute located some illustrations for us. Sue Janson helped compile the index. Other people who assisted include Meg Arnot, Marian Aveling, Peter Beilharz, Meredith Burgmann, Joan Fox, Eric Fry, Marilyn Lake, Ken Norling and Lynne Wrout. McPhee Gribble were a lovely bunch of publishers to work with, and they played a creative role in the evolution of the project.

The University of Melbourne History Department gave us $600 (and more stamps, envelopes and photocopies than they'd like to know about) and the Faculty of Arts gave us $1,600. This was our total budget.

For permission to reproduce the illustrations in this volume, we would like to thank the Communist Party of Australia, Pat Counihan, Pat Fiske, the Herald and Weekly Times Ltd, Alban Johnson, the La Trobe Library, the Mitchell Library, the National Library of Australia, David Spratt, Frank Strahan, the Tasmanian

Wilderness Society, the University of Melbourne Archives and Barry York.

Finally, we have to thank the contributors themselves, for showing enough faith to sit down and write, and for being so tolerant of our editorial aberrations. It was their effort, their supportiveness, and their political commitment that gave us the heart to persevere with what at times appeared to be an impossible task.

Introduction

VERITY BURGMANN AND JENNY LEE

It has been said that war is the continuation of politics by other means. It could just as easily be said that politics is the continuation of war by other means. The core of politics is conflict – not just the rituals of parliamentary debate, but the day-to-day conflicts that run through a society where power and wealth are unequally distributed. To understand politics, we have to discard its bland, dictionary definition 'as the art or science of government' and look at the many contests between those who command the sites of power and those who do not.

Common to all oppositional movements is the participants' exhilarating realization that those who are powerless as individuals can change the world if they work together. Most of this volume deals with the actions of people who have made that mental leap, whether they are workers, women, Aboriginal people, unemployed people, gays, environmentalists or anti-war activists. It is through such movements of protest and dissent that people who were not born to power have made history, even if not under circumstances of their own choosing.

But trying to change the world is a struggle against the odds. It is difficult to point to any Australian popular movement that has achieved all of its stated aims. We should recognize the achievements of these movements, and the barriers that have confronted them but, we must also look at the mistakes they have made and the blinkers they have worn.

The first part of *Staining The Wattle* considers some of the most obvious barriers. It outlines how formal institutions have limited the scope of popular political action. This has partly been achieved by the blatant use of physical or legal force (the law being redefined, where necessary, to keep activists behind bars). It has also involved subtler processes – the evocation of a 'common interest' based on locality, race or nation, the use of token concessions to defuse dissident movements, and the inculcation of ideas of respectability, discipline and conformity that leave little scope for a radical review of the social order.

The second part points to the diversity and richness of the history of popular struggle in this country. It also investigates why so many popular movements have petered out. An interesting issue in that history is the relationship between dissenting movements and the labour movement, which is unique in having risen from a popular base to hold the reins of government. The labour movement, and especially its parliamentary wing, appears repeatedly as an obstacle to change. The Labor Party has tried to keep the lid on any left-wing activity that might damage its electoral chances. In power, it has adopted many of the bad habits of the old ruling élites. The ideal of solidarity has degenerated into intolerance and cronyism; it has been said of the party's New South Wales branch that 'when they call you "mate", it's like being kissed by the Mafia.'

Yet the successes of popular movements have mostly depended on labour support. This is the dilemma of our times, one made sharper by the power of conservative opinion within the labour movement of the 1980s and by the rising danger of economic and ecological crisis. During this century, the popular movements have redrawn the map of politics, opening up new spaces for action and debate. It may soon become difficult to defend these spaces against the pressures being applied by the international market. On this count, the most obvious 'lessons of history' are about what *not* to do. There is no blueprint. But to develop an understanding of the present and a strategy for the future, it helps to take into account the history of those who have already been brave enough to embark on the task of building a new society within the shell of the old.

Why a People's History?

This is not a general history. It does not pretend to be comprehensive. It starts from the assumption that 'comprehensiveness' can never be more than an illusion. The web of historical narrative is only a thin tissue of approved knowledge about a complex and contradictory social universe. We have tried to unpick some of the strands in that web and follow them through, one by one, in the hope that they will lead us closer to an understanding of the past. Each chapter looks at one particular subject, following it through, discussing how it has changed over time, assessing its influence and outlining the forces that have impinged on it. In many instances this overview is fleshed out by exploring a particular case study in more detail. Readers who would like to follow a subject further should consult the bibliographical essays at the back of the volumes and check the indexes for outlying snippets of information.

The idea of assembling a people's history of Australia grew out of a conversation between Eric Fry and Peter Love in the bar at the University of Warwick after the Commonwealth Labour History conference in September 1981. Peter Love discussed the possibilities with Jenny Lee later in 1981 and they together persuaded a somewhat sceptical Verity Burgmann to become involved in January 1982. From this point on the project took shape as a thematic rather than chronological history. We chose the themes that should constitute the chapters, then thought of appropriate people to ask to write about them. The response was generally enthusiastic. Many historians were dissatisfied with the proposed structure of the official bicentennial history and worried that it would emerge as a sophisticated form of celebratory history. We also sought, where possible, to enlist people who were not professional historians. Peter Love resigned for family reasons in the middle of 1984.

The editing of the chapters, which started coming in from 1983, was a long and painful process. To suit the overall purpose of the project, we remodelled each chapter to varying degrees, carefully re-typed it, and sent it back to the author/s for approval (or in a small number of cases, disapproval and then negotiation).

Studying history is like looking through a window. What you see depends on which window you decide to look through. You might settle yourself down in the 'best' room, where there is a pleasant view, framed by curtains and shrubbery. You look out onto other houses and other people presenting their best faces to the street. The view from the kitchen or laundry is a different matter. There, you might have a patch of straggling tomato plants, a line full of washing, bulging rubbish bins and all the evidence of living and working.

Its choice of windows is one of the things that makes people's history different from conventional history. Its touchstone is the experience of everyday life – what we are taught to think of as the 'private' domain, as opposed to the high-powered, high-profile, 'public' spheres of government, industry and culture. The writing of this kind of history has a long tradition in Australia, stretching back to those early settlers who penned memoirs as a way of warning others what to expect in the new colony. In the last couple of decades, however, it has risen to challenge orthodox ideas of what the domain of history should be.

In 1970, during the bicentenary of Captain Cook's landing, Bruce Petty joked that Australia was re-enacting more history than it was making. In the years since it has certainly been writing more history than it is making. Organizations large and small, from the federal parliament to the local primary school, have put money into producing histories to mark one birthday or another. These histories are a key part of the public celebrations that have reached a climax with the bicentenary of the British invasion of 1788. They go along with the fancy-dress parades, the speeches and the fireworks. As such, they are expected to endorse the aims of the organizations that sponsored them; it is hard for them to offer even gentle criticism.

It is clear that a history which concerns itself with the actions of well-heeled, white, Anglo-Saxon males can only tell a small part of the story. Now, its blank spots, its silences, are being punctured by new, insistent voices. We have tried to bring some of these dissenting voices together here. This history aims to recapture and review the experience of those who were neglected in conventional histories – Aboriginal people, women, members of ethnic or racial minorities and the working class in general. The intention is not merely to compensate for past neglect, but to assert that we can only understand Australian history by analysing the lives of the oppressed.

This history is critical not celebratory. It rejects myths of national progress and unity. It starts from a recognition that Australian settler society was built on invasion and dispossession. Here we have to emphasize that we, too, are dealing with only a small part of the continent's human history. Held up against the millennia of Aboriginal experience, the last two hundred years seem but a brief, nasty interlude. To underline our belief that white Australians urgently need to appraise and compensate for the damage that has been done to the Aboriginal people and the land that was stolen from them, these volumes do not only tell the victor's side of the story.

This leads us to question the nature of this transplanted, hybrid society. The settlers' languages, the economic order that shaped their lives, the dominant cultures within which their very thoughts were cast, all were originally imported. Australia has inherited old inequalities and developed new ones of its own.

Inequality is a dominant theme in this history. Although inequality has weighed most heavily upon the working class, it has many other facets. Serious social inequalities are also based on gender, race or ethnicity, and age. Half of the Australian population owns ninety-two per cent of the country's wealth. The other half who have to get by with only eight per cent includes disproportionate numbers of women, Aborigines, certain ethnic groups, old people and children, along with members of the 'traditional' working class. The people about and for whom this history has been put together are predominantly of the working class but not exclusively so. They are the vast majority of Australians who, on balance, have had the pattern of social relations weighed against them.

This history aims to encourage people to think critically about the imagined community of the Australian nation. In portraying how our society has developed, the contributors have queried the assumption of a common 'national interest' that informs so much of the political rhetoric of our age, an age that has produced 30,000 millionaires on the one hand and two million people living below the poverty line on the other.

One especially pressing question is how far peole who are outside the magic circles of power and influence have been able to assert control over their own lives. We believe that people are not powerless victims of their position; they are able to change or at least improve their condition. They have 'agency', and their attempts to assert themselves against the dominant class have been a major force in shaping Australian society. It is important to recognize that people have mobilized collectively with some success. Among other things, they have bettered their working and living conditions, induced governments to withdraw from unpopular wars and achieved legal equality for women. But here, too, it is essential to keep one's critical faculties alive. Many popular movements have petered out after making only token gains; others have come to act as power bases for self-interested cliques. When it comes to the small matter of achieving social justice, some of the popular movements of the past are now part of the problem, not part of the solution.

We hope that readers will find in this history some ideas that suggest new ways of exploring the past, comprehending the present, and making the future. The social relations around us and their attendant forms of knowledge are not part of some immutable natural order. The aim of this history is to suggest that we can not only interpret the world in new ways, but also use that knowledge to change it.

Perhaps when we go back into that 'best' room, we will begin to see it rather differently. We won't kid ourselves that this is all there is to life. We will be aware that there are other stories, other histories, that have an equal claim on our attention. And we'll be able to see something of where the best room came from – the labour that went into making it and keeping it clean and tidy, the nostalgia it embodies for a mother country on the other side of the world, the absurdity of that English garden scorching in the Australian sun. If we think about it for long enough, we might decide to get rid of that precious furniture, open up the doors and windows and let in a bit of fresh air.

Big Brother is Watching You

ALASTAIR DAVIDSON

Beggars, vagabonds, illiterate workers, strolling players and demobilized soldiers roamed incessantly around England in the eighteenth century. They were part of everyday life. They lived on what they could find: occasional work, begging, staying in the refuges provided by the religious orders, or helping themselves to anything on their way. Since many came from Scotland, Wales and Ireland, they often spoke Gaelic or Welsh. Over the eighteenth century the population rose rapidly, and with it the numbers of nomads. Throughout Britain, tenants had been thrown off the land they were used to occupying. By 1800 the wanderers numbered between a tenth and a fifth of the population. Increasingly, their presence was regarded as a social problem.

As private property became more important, the old habit of helping oneself was gradually turned into a crime. Pilfering along Thameside, poaching wild animals (which had once been fair game for anyone) and smuggling goods in through the south coast to avoid customs and excise all caused vast losses to property-owners and to the state.

The problem the rulers faced, however, was to work out a way of controlling the wanderers' depredations. In former times the law had functioned only intermittently, haphazardly and brutally, to punish the most extreme offenders. There were no police. When crimes were committed, the victims had to catch the offenders themselves and bring them before the assizes, which only came around occasionally to each provincial centre. Once brought before the assizes, the offender could count on a very harsh punishment.

At first the growth of crime in the eighteenth century was met by extending this old legal tradition. Soon there were 200 hanging offences on the books. Any person over the age of seven could be hanged, and children were hanged regularly for stealing small amounts. Worse crimes could be punished more terribly, by boiling people alive in oil, tearing them apart with horses or burning them.

These measures did not curb crime. People were reluctant to prosecute or convict minor offenders when the penalty was death. And the offenders were not deterred; from their point of view, it was as well to be hanged for a sheep as for a lamb. Some members of the ruling class began to question the way in which the state was attempting to maintain law and order. They were influenced by the ideas of Cesare Beccaria, whose book *Crime and Punishment* argued that punishment should be prompt, sure, inevitable and fitting to the crime. They began to argue for the establishment of a police force and for reform of the prisons, which previously had been nothing more than places where offenders could be kept out of the way until someone worked out what to do with them.

Most prominent in the debate on prison reform was Jeremy Bentham, who argued for a type of prison in which offenders would not just be punished but also reformed. This he called the Panopticon. It would be built around a central tower from which a guard could see into all the cells at a glance without being seen by those he watched. The prisoners would never know whether they were being observed or not. In time, they would become obedient to avoid getting on the wrong side of the invisible, all-seeing watchers. Bentham and his supporters wanted this principle to be applied widely in schools, hospitals and factories. His ideas had their opponents and were not implemented until early in the nineteenth century. It was not long before there was general agreement, however, that the state should aim to educate, cleanse, discipline and punish its citizens so that they would all be obedient and reliable without having to be too closely policed by the forces of law and order.

We can analyse this as a shift from the use of repression towards the establishment of hegemony. It was this shift that marked the beginning of the modern state. State rule was no longer to be based mainly on the use or threat of force. Its presence was much less obvious but, at the same time, more pervasive. In simple form, the term 'hegemony' refers to the practices through which conflicting interests in society are resolved and their potential for change defused. Force alone cannot do this.

The real strength of the modern state lies in its ability to find ways of influencing the way people think about themselves. This involves a process of isolation – making sure that they are engaged in some repetitive work in a particular location so that their horizons are limited. From where they are, they cannot make the connections that are needed to arrive at a total criticism of the existing social system. Force and consensus are combined in such a way as to be indistinguishable.

Unfortunately for Bentham, his ideas came a little late. Already the jails of England were over-crowded. Prisoners were being kept in disused warships, or 'hulks', which were found all along the coast. For well over a hundred years, the English had been getting rid of the surplus by transporting convicts overseas, to the West Indies and the United States. But the American revolution of 1776 put a stop to that. The government began to look for alternatives and finally decided that New South Wales would be a suitable place for a convict settlement. So when Australia was settled in 1788, the people who stepped off the boats were a combination of convicts from the nomadic tribes of the British Isles and members of the new reforming ruling class.

The latter aimed to reform the convicts by a mixture of punishment, surveillance and discipline, turning them into cleansed and educated citizens who would no longer pose a problem to the state or to the system of private property. A system similar to Bentham's was set up in Australia from Governor Phillip's time onwards, particularly under Governor Macquarie in New South Wales and Lieutenant-Governor Arthur in Van Diemen's Land (Tasmania). From the moment the convicts were put on the ships to carry them to Australia they were under surveillance. Files were kept on their conduct and, on arrival, these files became the property of the government, which added further reports each year. As Geoffrey Blainey has said, Australia was the first police state. The convicts quickly discovered that it was hard to escape the watching eyes. The Aborigines and the outback were hostile; police, guards and informers were everywhere. Every little offence was carefully recorded and drastically punished.

Convicts were marched to church on Sunday. The authorities made strenuous efforts to teach them obedience and punctuality and to get them used to settled habits of work, whether they were in public work gangs or on assignment to private employers. At all times, those in authority compiled reports on them, rewarded those who showed signs of reformation and punished those who did not.

The convicts not only had to be taught how to work. They also had to be taught to wed. In late eighteenth-century Europe, most people without property did not marry in our sense at all. As the masses were forced off the land, relationships among them became increasingly transient. Families meant nothing. Even when couples did marry, their relationships were short-lived. Children were thrust on wet-nurses, thrown into foundling homes and generally expected to fend for themselves from an early age.

Marriage was an important part of the process of disciplining the dangerous classes. On the one hand, it gave greater control over population growth; provided that a balance was kept between production and reproduction, the labour power of the population could become an economic asset and bring increased wealth. On the other hand, marriage was an important part of the process of subjecting the people to the authority of the state. It brought duties and prohibitions, and it allowed the state to keep tabs on people. To marry legally in Britain after 1753, a couple had to dwell for at least a month in the parish where they would marry. So they could not be nomads. They had to give their 'true Christian names and surnames' and the address where they were living, and legal records of this information had to be taken and preserved for public use.

In the convict colonies, marriage was particularly important for disciplining the female convicts. The men were tamed through labour. But women assigned to private employers often entered into sexual relations with them; in modern terms, assignment meant prostitution. Because there were far fewer women than men, women's sex gave them power. They were always reported as being the most incorrigible of the convicts. The female factories set up in New South Wales and Van Diemen's Land did not succeed in reforming them by teaching them stable work habits. Marriage was the only answer.

It was an important arm of state policy from Phillip's time. While in Britain the Church of England had the power to decide who could marry, in the colonies the governor had direct control. He could make marriage easier by reducing the cost of the licence (as Macquarie did); he could permit Catholics to be married by their own clergy; he could offer inducements for convicts to marry.

The emphasis on promoting marriage was especially strong from 1824, under Darling's governorship. Darling gave married men an extra day off each week so that they could work on their own account, and bent over backwards to make sure that married convicts were able to live with their spouses. Married couples were also offered land for their own use. Though many of those who married were not faithful to their partners and resisted moral reform, marriage did gradually increase, and the care of children began to pass from the state to the family. From 1837, too, family migration was encouraged, and in 1840 Gipps offered a bounty for married couples to come to the colony. By the middle of the century, the conventional family was firmly established.

The convicts also gradually bowed to the discipline of work. After a few revolts and several attempts to maintain their ways of living, they learnt to play the system. Those who continued to resist found themselves in places of secondary punishment, hell-holes like Norfolk Island and Port Arthur. It was easier to keep your head down and eventually settle on the small plot of land you would be granted at the end of your sentence.

How far the convicts had been tamed became apparent when the emancipists (ex-convicts) began to make themselves heard in politics. They looked back to ideas that were familiar to them from their homeland. They demanded no more than that British law and order, and its corresponding rights, should be established in Australia. They were in fact calling for a considerable change in the authoritarian system that had been set up by the first instructions issued to the governors. The governors had been placed above the law and were able to exercise powers wider than those of the British monarch. The governor could act as accuser, judge and executioner, and he did.

These demands also gained support from the free immigrants who began to arrive in larger numbers in the 1830s. Many of the people who migrated with government help came from much the same social background as the convicts. Like the convicts, they were expected to prove that they were industrious by working hard on the big landholders' properties. And, like the convicts, they were then expected to take up little farms close to the towns and work hard to improve them.

At first the wealthy local elite resisted the demands of the lower orders. They became known as 'exclusives', because they believed that the ex-convicts were not sufficiently reformed to be allowed to take part in politics. By 1840, however, they had begun to change their minds and look to co-operation with the ex-convicts for the sake of securing greater local autonomy. By that stage there were a considerable number of wealthy, moderate emancipists who were prepared to abide by the law and maintain the system. The first proposals for independent constitutions were drawn up by associations of emancipists and exclusives, and in 1842 New South Wales obtained its first semi-elective legislature.

From then on it was really only a matter of time before full self-government would be granted. The British government tended to stonewall, reluctant to lose Colonial Office control. It argued that there were still convicts going to Van Diemen's Land and suggested that the colonies were not rich enough to pay for themselves. But by 1850 even the British had been persuaded that they had nothing to fear. Between 1850 and 1855, the Australian colonies were granted self-government by the constitutions that today rule over the states of New South Wales, Victoria, Tasmania and South Australia. Each of these constitutions allowed for an elected assembly, and in practice all adult men were entitled to vote. But each also provided for a legislative council, which would act as a final guarantee of the large landholders' rights.

Britain's interests were also safeguarded. To keep colonial autonomy within bounds, the British made sure that they retained paramount and overriding rights over the colonial legislatures. The governors were given extraordinary powers, and there was no suggestion that Australia was to have responsible government; the governors did not have to confine themselves to acting on the instructions of the elected majority in the lower house. In 1865 the British parliament brought in new laws to protect its position further. These laws clearly stated that no Act of an Australian parliament would be legal if it were repugnant to British legislation. And the governors made it clear from the early days that they did not feel obliged to listen to the instruction of the local legislatures. Denison in New South Wales was one of many governors who insisted that they were there to keep a close eye on the colonials' activities.

The pastoralists had a strong presence in both the upper and lower houses. They were strongest, however, in the legislative councils, and they organized a series of reforms to revamp the upper houses. In Victoria, for example, they changed the method of appointing the legislative council. Rather than being nominated by the governor, the legislative council was to be elected by property-owners. The danger with a nominated upper house was that, if the governor acted on the advice of the elected government, he could threaten to stack the upper house with new members, and so force it to accept the government's policy. In New South Wales, a number of reforms were carried through in this way. An upper house elected on a limited franchise served the interests of the squatters far more effectively. Victoria, however, was left without any machinery for resolving conflicts between the two houses. This was to lead to constitutional crises in the 1860s and 1870s, when reforming governments ran up against the opposition of the upper house.

In such circumstances it was difficult for a party system to emerge in Australia. Political alliances would arise around particular issues, such as land legislation, trade policy or state aid to church schools. But they did not crystallize into permanent parties. Instead, members of parliament acted mainly as brokers

The *Bulletin* in the 1880s lampooned the Legislative Councils as havens of privilege.

for their electorates. They sold their votes quite openly in return for roads, bridges, schools or railway lines and changed allegiances with remarkable speed. The largest political conflicts did not take place within the lower houses but involved clashes between the landed interests dominating the upper houses and reforming governments with strong support in the lower houses. And repeatedly the upper houses were backed up by Britain's overriding prerogatives.

In 1865, for example, the Victorian lower house attempted to introduce tariffs. It tacked the necessary legislation to the supply bill, which meant that the upper house could only block the tariffs by rejecting supply and leaving the government without funds. The tactic failed. Twice the upper house rejected supply, even though there was an increasing majority in the lower house in favour of the bill. Eventually, the government tried to get around the block on supply by encouraging people to sue it to recover the money they were owed. It indicated that it would pay them out without a legal contest. This was not permitted under British law, however, and when it was pointed out that such actions were illegal, the lower house tamely accepted the decision. This incident showed not only that local political initiative was really very limited, but also that the local legislatures were unlikely to try to extend their powers. The system had nothing to fear from such law-abiding citizens.

The state was boastful about the extraordinary speed with which a criminal nation had been rehabilitated. It did not, however, stop with the gains it had already made. The goldminers of Eureka, the bushrangers in the 1860s and the nomadic rural workers who humped their blueys across the countryside reminded the rulers that the process of organizing and disciplining the populace had to be extended to meet new problems. This was brought home especially by the influx of gold diggers in the 1850s. In Victoria, the police force was already stronger than in any other country in the world, but the state extended its activities even further. Drawing on earlier schemes for small-scale settlement, it used land policy to defuse the danger of social disorder. Victoria's Selection Acts were to encourage a slow, rational and orderly settlement of small landowners. In all the colonies, as the chapter on land has already outlined, selection was to encourage the myth that anyone who was prepared to work could make it in Australia. This national ideology was the cement of a national consensus. Taking it as a

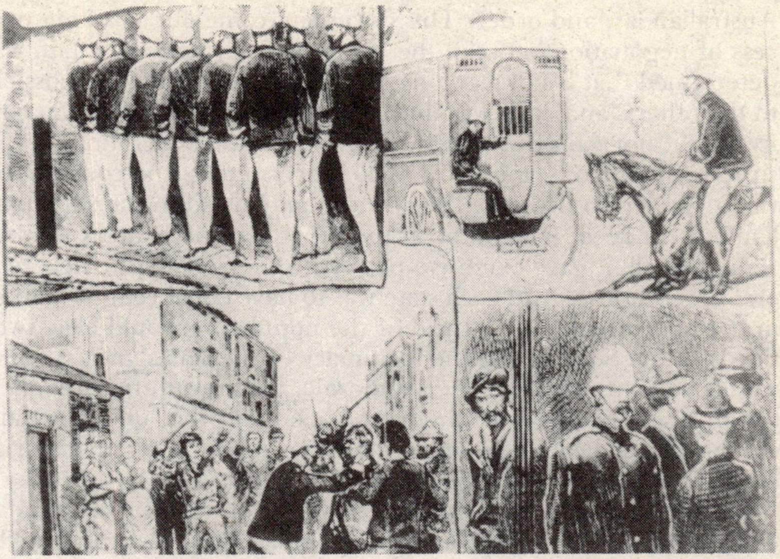

Police 'keeping the peace' in Melbourne late in the last century.

starting point, it was possible to make further moves towards responsible government. This was to be done by consolidating the system, not by setting up any new basis for the Australian state.

During the last two decades of the nineteenth century, the problems of having a single continent split into six separate colonies became increasingly pressing. French and German expansion in the Pacific was threatening Australian interests there, and at home the lack of free trade between the colonies was creating all sorts of anomalies. The depression of the 1890s gave the federation movement added urgency. Tariff barriers were slowing industrial recovery. It also seemed likely that federation would restore the colonies' overseas credit, which had taken a battering during the depression.

But this was not a mass movement. The federationists had no popular support before 1893, though in 1891 they had already drawn up the document on which the Australian constitution would be based. Samuel Griffith from Queensland, who was extremely influential in drafting the constitution, was a lawyer. So were many of the other founding fathers. They drew up the constitution as lawyers would, to entrench the accepted tradition of British law and order, though now, of course, they wished it to be

Australian law and order. This document came out of a long process of negotiation between the colonies. Each petty chieftain was determined that his own colony should sacrifice as little as possible to the others, and each was intent on making sure that the majority would not gain the upper hand in the new federation. While supposedly introducing responsible government, the constitution was amended to preserve the system that existed in the state parliaments. Indeed, it could be argued that it made matters worse.

First of all, it gave extensive powers to the Senate, the new federal upper house. And each state was to have equal representation in the upper house. One-third of the population would elect two-thirds of the Senate, and the legitimacy of the states' own systems would be confirmed. At the same time, the constitution retained the prerogative power of a governor-general who, under certain circumstances, would be answerable not to the elected majority but to the Queen.

More important, this constitution was given the seal of popular endorsement. After 1893, a bogus 'popular' movement was deliberately constructed in favour of federation. Where the old colonial constitutions had always been open to criticism from a radical, democratic, nationalist standpoint – after all, they had been drawn up by the squattocracy in its own interest – the new constitution was harder to assail. It appeared to have popular backing, and the conventions that agreed on the constitution were surrounded by great fanfare. But this was really a movement led by the prosperous middle classes. The whole legalistic process was remote; it did little to inspire mass enthusiasm. If the constitution was eventually approved by referendum (after failing to get enough votes the first time around), it was more out of weariness than active support.

Radicals raised their voices against it. They set up a new paper specifically to oppose the proposed constitution. Their sense of imminent danger was apparent from the name they gave their journal: *Tocsin*, meaning alarm-bell. They argued that the constitution was undemocratic and would be almost impossible to amend. To accept it was to take an irretrievable step backwards: it would so shackle Australia that there would be no hope of peaceful political change. They were, of course, dismissed as ratbags. Federation was sold to the populace as a business deal: it would bring the prosperity and progress that had been so conspicuously lacking in the last decade.

The constitution was carried to London, where it was further watered down by the British government. Britain needed to preserve its own interests, and these differed from Australia's. British citizens (and powerful ones at that) also had investments that needed protecting. The British government not only tried secretly to corrupt and influence members of the Australian delegation in England but also insisted on altering key clauses to maintain a power structure that might otherwise be whittled away. One clause in the constitution, for example, made the Australian High Court the final court of appeal. This was changed so that appeals could still be made to the British Privy Council. English notables, not Australians, would have the last word on contentious issues. When finally the constitution was established, it was by a British Act of Parliament; the constitution was only a schedule to one article.

On the first day of the new century, federation was officially declared. Surveying the enthusiastic crowds from his panopticon, Bentham would have felt a glow of satisfaction. Here was a state that had produced the right sort of people, in spite of its unpromising origins. Well scrubbed, well combed and well clad, accustomed to an orderly family life, schooled to discipline, they had

Elaborate ceremonial arches put up for the federation festivities in 1901.

learnt the virtues of work and of the Australian way. They had no choice in the matter. They would play by the rules, even if those rules left them no room for autonomy or a sense of self.

The small but urgent voice of dissent was drowned out. Today, however, the applause has died down; we can take a place in the panopticon, vicariously at least, to review the past. And the notes of the *Tocsin* can still be heard. The rules laid down in 1901 have formed the basis for a conservative state. They did not establish responsible government, as the dismissal of the Whitlam government in 1975 made clear. They have been a bonanza for lawyers, a millstone around the necks of reformers. It has proved impossible to change them significantly from within. And they carry with them a powerful inheritance of laws designed to keep the population beavering away in an orderly manner, oblivious to the possibility that there might be other ways of using their time and space.

Conflicting Loyalties

CHRIS McCONVILLE

The sense of place is extremely powerful in politics. At the most basic level, politics usually becomes a question of 'us' against 'them', and its entire texture depends on who is defined as 'us' and who as 'them'. People who identify themselves primarily as members of a social class, for example, will act very differently from those whose principal loyalty is to their own family, to their club or to the place where they were brought up.

Often these loyalties are so tangled together that it becomes difficult to see a distinct role for either class, locality or the family in shaping political action. Take the case of Geoff O'Connell, the former mayor of the inner Melbourne suburb of Richmond. When he was asked to explain why so many members of his family had jobs on the council staff, O'Connell pointed out that he was not ashamed of any of this:

> The boys have been on the council for that many years ... Richmond is a close-knitted city. You see, a lot of kids, when they grow up want to follow in their father's footsteps. (*Age*, 8 August 1981)

It was not only a strong sense of local identity that explained the council's being used as a family employment bureau. There was also the question of class loyalty. In his words, O'Connell was 'an ordinary working man', even if he did have his own demolition business. And, after all, it was the business of Labor councils to help the ordinary working man.

Sometimes local loyalties have had a positive side. They have at times been important in defending the rights of the poor and marginal within particular communities. But perhaps more often they have become a convenient mask behind which the propertied and powerful have been able to pursue their own interests in the name of advancing the interests of their compatriots.

Localism became a force in Australian politics long before the O'Connells took over municipal government in Richmond. It was apparent in Australia's first organized political movements – the campaigns for colonial self-government during the first half of the nineteenth century. Britain's attitude to the colonies in their early days was summed up by one observer of Tasmanian life who commented that 'a company of exiles, overawed by a dissolute soldiery, interspersed here and there with a few persons of a superior class could only be governed by despotism'. The agents of that despotism were the colonial governors. Against them, the squatters and other wealthy colonists asserted the need for self-government.

Their protests were based on a firm notion of the 'rights of Englishmen' – but not the kind of rights that would be of use to the working class. The rights they held dear were those that men of property and substance would expect to have if they were in England or Scotland. As Governor Darling remarked, 'The people are taught by the papers to talk about the rights of Englishmen and the free Institutions of the Mother Country ... the evil of this place is the passion which exists that New South Wales should be the counterpart of England.'

Political reform was gradual. In 1824 a Legislative Council was set up to advise the governor of New South Wales. Its seven members were appointed by the governor, and he could still enforce laws against the council's wishes. Four years later, the Legislative Councils of New South Wales and Van Diemen's Land were enlarged to fifteen members, but the governors could still by-pass them in various ways. Even the reforms of 1842, which allowed for twenty-four members to be elected and twelve nominated by the governor, did not shift the balance of power. The governors could dissolve the councils and refuse to consent to their laws until the British government approved them. Still the pressure for reform did not abate. In 1850, Victoria and South Australia were granted similar legislative councils. And in 1852, these councils, which were dominated by the squatters, finally won the right to control crown lands. Over the next four years, the four colonies achieved self-government, with elected legislative assemblies and governor-appointed legislative councils.

Although they might at times defy the governors or rail against Earl Grey, the 'Autocrat of the Colonial Office', the men of property who supported self-government were far from being Australian nationalists. They were localists in the sense that they mainly wanted to escape the red tape of the distant Colonial Office and secure a form of government that would be more amenable to their influence. If they used the language of democracy, the kind of democracy they wanted was a very limited one. Their essential aim was to defend their property rights.

The defence of property rights is a theme that crops up again and again in demands for local autonomy. Even before the struggle for self-government had finished, the New South Wales Legislative Council was moving to set up local government authorities in Sydney and Melbourne. It looked to Britain for its models.

The form of local government in Britain had recently changed. A new Municipal Corporations Act had been passed in 1835 as a response to the social problems that had arisen in the new industrial cities. The Act set up larger local government bodies to provide badly needed urban services, so defusing criticism of the central government. At the same time, it placed control of the new municipalities in the hands of substantial local property-owners. What could be more natural than for the colonies to imitate this example?

In 1842, the Legislative Council passed laws allowing for town councils in Sydney and Melbourne. Sydney was to become a city and Melbourne a town, because the former village was the seat of an Anglican bishop and the latter was not. In their early days, these councils were the scene of a ludicrous political sideshow. Melbourne Town Council, for example, seems to have been little more than a stage on which groups of Orangemen and Irish Catholics could act out the religious squabbles of their homeland. The councils had little power or funds and, as only a minority of the population could vote, few dissenting opinions were heard in the council chambers.

During the 1850s, however, rapid urban growth produced real problems. The councils had a hard job providing services to the expanding population. Land values were higher in the areas with municipal services than in the shanty towns that sprang up on the fringes of the cities, and there was greater competition for municipal facilities. But this did not lead to a sharpening of conflict within the central councils. Rather, it produced demands for the creation of new, smaller municipalities.

In Melbourne, each of the new suburbs created in the 1850s became the home of a movement for local autonomy. In 1854, local committees in Prahran and Emerald Hill (South Melbourne) petitioned for their own councils. Many of the members of these committees appear to have been local land developers. Similar committees of propertied men were to be found in Collingwood, Fitzroy and Richmond. Usually they based their claims on the assertion that the central government could not provide roads, bridges or railways. In Collingwood, local businessmen objected to council attempts to stop the tanneries and fellmongeries from polluting the Yarra. Local control meant bolstering the local

The *Bulletin's* design for a new corporation seal

economy and local land values by providing better transport or more freedom for local manufacturers.

The land booms of the 1880s reinforced this pattern. The leading land boomers became local heroes. In cities and country towns all over the country, land developers won the support of local land associations or railway leagues, many of which were dominated by small businessmen who expected some of the profits of the boom to come their way. In a working-class suburb such as Footscray, labour leaders also backed the local manufacturers' campaigns for council elections. If freedom from interference was good for the shopkeeper or tannery owner, it also meant more work for the labourer.

In many localities, power remained in the hands of the property developers and manufacturers throughout the twentieth century. The land boomers of the nineteenth century would have been thoroughly at home on the Queensland Gold Coast in the 1970s or 1980s. Most conservative local aldermen were happy to see council affairs as 'non-political' – concerned only with good housekeeping and prudent management. Of course, this was not true. Councils were always making political decisions in the widest sense, whether they were putting up war memorials, deciding who should get permits for new businesses or zoning their municipalities to keep workers' housing and smelly, noisy factories out of the areas where the well-to-do lived. From the 1920s, local businesspeople were also able to press their claims through progress associations, which lobbied for tree plantings, electrified transport and other measures that improved the quality of their environment – and, of course, the value of their properties.

The 1890s depression, however, had produced a new force in local politics. In a haphazard sort of way, candidates began to stand for councils 'in the labour interest'. In Port Melbourne, for example, local wharfies and members of the Victorian Socialist Party took seats on the council. Similarly, in New South Wales, Billy Hughes was active on the Paddington Council, and the Balmain Labourers Union established a strong presence in local politics. They and others began to contest the manufacturers' and landlords' right to represent the working class at the municipal level.

Occasionally, local labour politics took a dramatic turn. One such case was in the north Queensland port of Townsville. Townsville's tradition of municipal socialism went back to the

1890s, when the townspeople had elected the flamboyant Ned Lowry to the council. In the early twentieth century, the workers in the sugar industry and on the waterfront had elected men to the left of the Labor Party. During the Second World War, with Townsville becoming a major port, the waterside workers became more important in local politics. Communist Party and left Labor influence was strong on the council at the end of the war. This council promoted a version of municipal socialism. It brought the city a publicly controlled fruit and vegetable market, for instance, free shopping trolleys and free child-care centres.

But this was exceptional. For the most part, Labor candidates worked within clearly defined limits. In the inner suburbs of Sydney and Melbourne, the main labour parties had begun to imitate their conservative opponents by the turn of the century. Labour men got into politics by old-fashioned means. They were active in local benefit societies and sporting clubs, they had links with local publicans and shopkeepers, and they promised to work for better roads or water supplies. If they did gain power, they usually tried to improve wages and conditions for municipal workers. Few went any further than that: there was no serious attempt at municipal socialism, no urge towards social change at the local level.

In the process, Labor councillors perfected the art of municipal corruption. Local politics has always had more than its share of back-room deals, and undoubtedly there was cause for concern in conservative suburbs as well as in the Labor strongholds. But in the inter-war years, when Labor took control of many urban councils, A.L.P. mayors and aldermen won a special reputation for graft and double-dealing. Some of this was a crude attempt to play Robin Hood – to sting developers and industrialists for the benefit of the local workers. Usually, however, there was a trade-off. The workers were expected to keep on rolling up to vote Labor men in, and to let them enjoy the perks of office – whether these were jobs for their relatives, or cash payments for turning a blind eye to breaches of local by-laws. In Sydney, for example, Civic Reform opponents of a Greater Sydney Bill claimed in the 1930s that Labor candidates in areas such as Pyrmont were buying votes for 'a jug of beer'. A similar pattern of local control seems still to be in force at present in the inner western suburbs of Sydney, especially Balmain.

Nevertheless, Labor's successes in New South Wales state politics meant that the networks of patronage and graft were less strongly focused at the local level than in Victoria. In Melbourne, complaints about local political corruption centred on Collingwood. This was partly because of its association with John Wren. However, Wren was not the only influential Labor figure there. For several decades, real influence on the council lay with Robert 'Sugar' Roberts. Roberts and his colleagues from the Collingwood 'tote' had managed to turn the council into something of a private theatre by the 1930s. It was claimed that his group disrupted council meetings at every chance, even turning out the lights and assaulting opponents in the dark.

Roberts and his kind represented a particular male working-class tradition of the inner city. They were the last in a long line of Collingwood larrikins. They brought the culture of the street into the town hall, ridiculing the council's proceedings and the other aldermen's pretensions to respectability. They had their links with the liquor and gambling industries, and enjoyed the support of the semi-criminal fringe that flourished in a city where off-course betting was illegal and pubs closed at six o'clock. But they did not set up great political 'machines' to milk big business, as their American counterparts did. Their politics was one of demonstration rather than of action. Having gained power at the local level, they had little idea what they could do with it.

The Collingwood lads' capers earned them the hatred of middle-class moralists. Their culture was also very different from that of many more radical Labor figures, who were inclined to see the publican and the bookie as enemies of the working class. The radicals' teetotal bent hardly fitted with the casual, unreflecting class identity of the people who backed men like Roberts in Collingwood, or the O'Connells and Loughnans in Richmond.

Despite their assaults on respectability in the council chambers, these councillors were quite capable of indulging in an exaggerated nationalism when the occasion demanded. Whenever the left-wing Movement Against War and Fascism asked to use the Collingwood football ground for meetings in the 1930s, for example, Roberts and his supporters would oppose them in the name of patriotism. Roberts boasted of his son's war record, and accused the anti-fascists of wanting to hand Australia over to Hitler! A purely local working-class culture could produce only a very limited political consciousness.

At the same time, from beyond the city, places like Collingwood seemed to stand for all that was evil in the chaos of urban life. Australia inherited from Britain a romantic tradition of anti-urbanism. This found expression at many levels in the colonies.

Guides to immigrants portrayed Australia as a land of wheat, sheep and kangaroos; they did not mention that the rural areas were forming the hinterland to the fastest-growing and most concentrated urban society in the western world. The romantic image of the self-sufficient small landowner was also a powerful force in nineteenth-century radical politics, as Alastair Davidson and Andrew Wells have outlined in their chapter on land in the first volume of this history.

The 1890s depression gave still more force to visions of rural innocence. If the land booms of the 1880s had made the capital cities a source of wonder and pride, the crisis that followed turned eyes back to the bush. In May 1893, the *Pastoralists' Review* greeted with satisfaction the news that most of the colonies' banks had crashed, commenting: 'The town populations of Australia have been spoiled children. They have now met with the usual fate of spoiled children and must come down to the realities of this work-a-day world.'

Working-class politicians at the turn of the century attacked the spread of the cities in much the same language as the pastoralists did. Though the inner city areas of Sydney and Melbourne gave the Labor Party its first successes, the party also established a strong base in the countryside during the 1890s. The powerful Australian Workers Union, which dominated the rural branches, became increasingly influential within the political labour movement. With its rise, Labor moved away from a politics based on class to one based on the idea of a populist alliance of labour and small business, with strong anti-urban overtones. For many years, Labor was *the* party of anti-urbanism, especially in New South Wales. In the state elections of 1920, for example, a Labor candidate topped the poll in Tamworth after a campaign in which he characterized Labor as a party of primary producers and described Sydney as 'a huge cancerous growth upon Society'.

The clearest sign of the force of anti-urbanism, however, was the rise of the country parties. There had been farmers' groupings in the colonial parliaments since the 1880s, but the pastoral interest had remained aloof. Competition between the squatters and farmers was still too strong, and memories of the bitter conflicts over land in the 1870s too fresh, for any wider alliance to be formed.

Around the turn of the century, this began to change. The struggle for land was over, and farmers and pastoralists began to look on each other as potential allies rather than enemies. It also became clear that a conservative political movement could be based on the rural electorates, which had long been suspicious of the way the state governments spent their money in the cities. The Kyabram Movement in Victoria and the People's Reform League in New South Wales rose to prominence during the early years of the new century, both pressing for radical reductions in government expenditure.

Nevertheless, the emergence of a distinct Country Party was a slow process. Though farmers' organizations were endorsing candidates in elections before the First World War, it was not until after the 1922 elections that a Country Party grouping was formed in the federal parliament. In state politics, too, the new party had mixed fortunes, being plagued by defections to the Nationalists, the main conservative party. In its early years, the Country Party still embraced some of the radical notions that Labor had made so much part of the rural political scene. It had a strong romantic, populist, anti-monopolistic streak.

But this was gradually eclipsed by hostility to the cities and the trade unions. Landowners in Australia had long been strongly opposed to the trade-union movement. Envisaging themselves as the most deserving of all producers, they saw the demands of shearers, transport and meat industry workers as threats to their independence. The bush was also the source of much of Australia's moral conservatism. It was not long before the new party had shifted the balance of power substantially towards the conservative side of politics.

The Country Party had considerable success in promoting the interests of the country against the cities. Certainly, it was instrumental in diverting state funds away from the inner-urban areas. Ironically, its rise was assisted by some of the inner-city Labor figures. John Wren himself apparently arranged Labor support for Albert Dunstan's Victorian Country Party government and supposedly helped the Country Party to get its act together in federal politics. The short-sightedness of his brand of labourism was never more obvious.

Although differences between localities, and between the city and the bush, have always been important in social values and in politics, they often hide more significant conflicts. In all places there are inequalities of power and class. The strength of rural mythology in Australia has masked these differences and the conflicts that emerge from them. The strongest of urban traditions, like that brought into politics by the leaders of the inner-city working class, has not been reflective or potent enough to challenge the grip of the rural myth.

In the 1970s and 1980s. a new and militant form of anti-urbanism has emerged. The National Party of Joh Bjelke-Petersen has led the fray, but his populist rhetoric is echoed by a multitude of lesser right-wing organizations. Once again we see the city being depicted as the source of all evil. In Queensland and the Northern Territory, especially, conservative governments have long been in the habit of blaming agitators from the south for any social conflict. The cities are not only the havens of socialism, feminism, homosexuality, and so on; they are also despatching stirrers – environmentalists and land rights activists – to create disharmony in the north. The image of a pure countryside being polluted by the influence of the cities has been taken to its logical conclusion.

The influence of the conflict between city and country has extended beyond the day-to-day business of parliamentary politics. The romantic image of a pure, uncontaminated bush has long dominated much of Australian thinking. The country, in this mythology, is not only the principal source of real wealth (in a nation that 'rides on the sheep's back'), but is also what makes Australia different from other nations. It is central to conventional ideas of national identity.

Yet even with its rural bias, Australian nationalism has not always been a conservative force. The *Bulletin* writers of the 1890s and the people who formed their audience proudly claimed to be part of a radical nationalist tradition. And in the late nineteenth century, when the Australian colonies deferred to an imperial power in London, nationalism could easily appear radical. Faith in the unity of the Australian working class merged into faith in the Australian people and hostility to the imperial connection – especially to the squatters, fat city bankers and merchants who were caricatured as London's loyal supporters in Australia.

Indeed, it was true that, by the latter part of the nineteenth century, a love of empire was often wedded to an anti-labour stance in politics. The campaign for self-government had achieved most of its aims. The local capitalists had a firm hold on political power at home and close links with the mother country abroad. British money and markets had made them wealthy. British society and its customs were their cultural models. They looked on with pride as the British Empire entered a new phase of expansion in the 1870s and 1880s. It was inconceivable that anyone would want to stop being part of an enterprise that brought so much plunder and profit to those of British stock. Indeed, as Stuart Rosewarne's chapter in volume one has already outlined, when it came to questions of British expansion in the Pacific, they were more aggressive than their British mentors.

In this context, it was understandable that those on the other side of the political fence should adopt a nationalist banner. Theirs was a radical nationalism, hostile to the political power that Britain held over the colonies and determined to prevent Australia from becoming like the Old World, with its massive inequalities. These ideas readily combined with socialism to become the creed of the emerging Australian labour movement.

The writer Joseph Furphy was one of many who exhorted the working class to stand up against economic exploitation by supporting a national movement for equality and democracy. Furphy derided working-class men and women who 'vote Conservative, work scab' and remained loyal to Britain; he tagged them the 'deserving poor': they deserved their poverty. Another proponent of radical nationalism was Henry Lawson, who saw an Australian nation as the only way to prevent working people finding 'the good old English gentleman over them, the good old English lord over them, the good old English aristocracy rolling around them ... scarcely deigning to rest their eyes on the common people who starve and rot for them and the good old English throne over them all'.

Yet the nation that was formed in 1901 fell far short of the radicals' aims. The new constitution put the radical nationalists in a quandary. Some labour moderates supported it, arguing that half a loaf was better than no bread. Others were inclined to fight. But they were paddling against the stream. The parish-pump politicians who had drawn the constitution up had successfully taken the wind out of the radicals' sails.

Nevertheless, moderate socialism and nationalism remained closely entwined until the First World War. It was the war, and more especially the anti-conscription campaigns, that forced a decisive change. The conscription issue drew a new line of conflict through Australia. The left became increasingly wary of nationalism, seeing that it could be used to justify militarism. Before the war the only strong advocates of internationalism had been the minority of socialists who were influenced by the Industrial Workers of the World (I.W.W.). But during the war much larger sections of the labour movement became internationalist in orientation. From the bitter experience of war, they had learned that the workers of each country had more in common with each other than with their rulers, who had so blithely sent them out to die.

At the same time, the character of nationalism was changing. By the end of the war, there was little trace of the nationalist idealism of the 1890s. Nationalism had lost its anti-imperial tinge. Gone were the jibes at the English aristocracy and the fawning local money-bags; gone, too, were the dreams of an independent nation of equals. Nationalism now ranged itself against new enemies. First in line were the pacifists and socialists who had opposed the war. In the 1920s Australian nationalism became a plaything of empire loyalists. It drew in businessmen and church leaders who had supported the war. And it cast all who wished to break the link with England or reform Australian society as Bolsheviks, enemies of a nation made great by all the blood it had shed to preserve the empire.

This conservative nationalism was closely linked with a faith in national development and material progress. And here the old suspicion of the inner cities began to play a role once more. In the 1920s and 1930s, anti-urbanism, a strict anti-libertarian morality and a desire for 'national progress all came together in developing the ideal of the garden suburb. Leading nationalists took up the cause of 'national efficiency', proposing garden suburbs and zoning laws as part of the effort to build a healthier nation and put it on a better footing in the event of another war.

The suburban ideal was remarkably durable. During the long boom after the Second World War, it underpinned Australia's self-image as a 'Lucky Country'. A powerful ideology of national progress was built around the home, the garden and the car. Even in the 1970s and 1980s, when the suburban ideal has been threatened, the state has made every effort to shore it up. To do anything else is to risk electoral disaster in the crucial 'mortgage belts' that ring the capital cities. With the extension of home ownership, the desire to defend one's own turf has acquired an added political force. It has become one of the great constants in Australian political life, and an enduring barrier to social and political reform.

Over the last few decades, however, there are important signs of change. In particular, a new kind of localism has emerged that seeks to challenge the rights of capitalists rather than uphold them. And a kind of ruralism has developed that questions whether property-owners have a right to do whatever they like to the environment. The material progress brought by capitalist expansion has lost some of its gloss. It is now seen to bring, not only new homes and new cars, but also pollution, poverty, unemployment and the likelihood of nuclear disaster.

Many of these movements are discussed elsewhere in this volume, and I will not go into their history in any detail here. It is worth pointing, however, to the major changes. The first is the development of an environmental movement that has called into question the ideology of 'development at all costs', which was so strong in Australia during the post-war boom. The Green Ban campaigns of the early 1970s, as Jack Mundey outlines in a later chapter, involved new forms of local action. Their successes inspired other local endeavours. More socially critical voices began to be heard through local residents' action groups and local councils. More voices began to demand that local politics be concerned with justice and social utility rather than profit alone.

In the countryside, the environmental movement has made less headway. Country people have long regarded conserving natural resources as the kind of luxury that they can never quite afford. And at times the new conservation movement has seemed to be in danger of being absorbed into an older style of anti-urbanism. Yet it has nevertheless brought a new kind of politics into the rural areas.

It is not by chance that groups such as Greenpeace have an international membership. Nor is it a coincidence that 'green' politics has become allied to another international movement, the anti-nuclear campaign. These movements pose a challenge to the politics of nationalism. They also take localism more seriously than radical movements have done in the past. One slogan commonly seen in peace banners and murals is, 'Think globally, act locally.' Together these demand a re-thinking of old identities and policies. For all the contradictions in these movements, they set a pattern which will no doubt be followed in other radical politics. Much will depend here on the labour movement's reaction. Developmentalist ideas still have a strong voice in the Labor Party, and the unions have recently moved away from the kind of politics that the green ban campaigns developed. Nevertheless, there are many in the labour movement who are alert to the possibilities of new forms of action, and who recognize that the chances of social reform depend heavily on creating a new sort of localism that goes beyond the interests of private property and is misled neither by the superficial politics of city versus country nor by the dangerous myths now attached to Australian nationalism.

Australia has reached its bicentenary as a society that is becoming more unequal. Sometimes the inequalities are expressed locally – a short drive from the bicentennial celebrations' site on Sydney Harbour to the depressed industrial centres of Wollongong and Newcastle would bring that home to anyone. Yet, even as these contradictions become more acute, they are masked by nationalist rhetoric. Local identity, based on clear socialist goals rather than on the old networks of patronage and family ties, is one important part of the defence against this corrupt form of patriotism.

The Ties that Divide

ELLEN McEWEN

In the early 1980s politicians and public servants were in the habit of christening every second government welfare agency a 'community' service. Their message was a conservative one. They hoped to conjure up images of harmony and co-operation, to bring back to life old feelings of personal responsibility, mutual aid and local initiative. In so doing they were trying to sidestep social tensions and divisions. They were also ignoring some of the nastier features of the close-knit traditional 'communities' they idealized – their rigid inequalities, their intolerance and their blood feuds.

The language of 'community' had been used in the 1970s by counter-culture groups to criticize all kinds of social institutions for being 'too distant, too remote and too bureaucratized to be responsive to the needs of people'. With their rejection of urban industrial society, these groups too had a conservative slant.

Even in the writings of left-wing historians 'community' has often appeared as something which is universally desirable. But the way the term is evoked by conservative and radical alike makes it clear that 'community' does not exist in the large cities where most Australians live today. What it does not tell us is what 'communities' and local organizations were like in the past. These are the questions I want to ask here, surveying different localities at various times: did communities ever exist, who was in control of them, and when did they start to disappear?

Concern for 'community' among middle-class professionals began with the work of Ferdinand Toennies and other nineteenth-century sociologists. Toennies contrasted the traditional agricultural societies, with their sense of belonging based on kinship, neighbourhood and long acquaintance, with the cities into which people were migrating. In the cities, he believed, family ties had been lost. Instead, people relied on formal voluntary associations.

Australia was founded at a time when industrial and urban growth were fostering voluntary organizations in Europe. Workers moving from town to town banded into friendly societies that would provide medical help and a decent burial if they should die away from kin. These were the starting points for the trade unions. The new dissenting religions of the sixteenth and seventeenth centuries were also voluntary associations. Their members had actively decided to leave the established Church of England and join the new churches. The cornerstone of the Wesleyan Church was the class meeting, where ordinary members could take a greater part than they did in traditional church services. Voluntary associations also prospered among the middle class who gathered in the cities.

Charitable organizations, schools, refuges, and societies devoted to 'good works' abounded. Town councils of worthy burghers sought to improve city living. In many ways traditional ties were also strengthened. New arrivals depended on kin for food, shelter and even to get them jobs until they were established. But going to Botany Bay on the other side of the world was a different matter.

The transportation of convicts to Australia broke up ties of kinship and affection. The settlers had no traditional leaders to take responsibility for making decisions, and voluntary associations were weak. Prisoners became the responsibility of the state. If a convict fell sick, he was treated at the government-built hospital. If a woman found herself with child, she gave birth and nursed it in the Female Factory. The government built churches, fixed wages, allotted servants and made roads. Convicts had little time for organized leisure activities. In a spare moment they might put a bet on the result of a cockfight, but little more. The voluntary societies that were to grow up around team sports were things of the future. Music was provided by the state as late as the 1840s. Each town garrison had a regimental band, which meant there was no need for other musical groups to play at dances or for general enjoyment.

As free settlers and time-expired convicts came to figure more largely in the population, they established the same kinds of voluntary associations that flourished among the uprooted in the new towns of the Old World. Clergymen arrived and offered their services to prospective congregations. At Windsor, north-west of Sydney, on the Hawkesbury River, a Wesleyan class meeting was held from 1812. When the Hawkesbury flooded in 1817, leaving many settlers in distress, the local magistrate and 'other gentlemen' raised 500 pounds to tide them over until harvest time. In 1819, help became more ordered with the founding of the Hawkesbury and District Benevolent Society. Assisted immigrants brought working-class institutions. Trade unions and friendly societies grew from the 1830s.

In European terms, Windsor and Parramatta, west of Sydney, were no more than villages at this time. Yet in both places the vehicle for getting things done was the formally organized group, not the family or neighbourhood. This is not to deny that there were growing networks of kin. Whole families would gradually migrate, a few at a time, providing support for each other on arrival, in times of sickness, unemployment and sorrow. By the 1840s, also, a second generation of children had been born in the colonies. Yet it was still a society in which most children would never see their grandparents. In Pat Grimshaw's words, the wrench of immigration meant that the Australian family was 'born modern'. So too was the wider network of social relations, with its emphasis on formal associations over family groups. In any case, the immigrants were mainly city people who by this time were used to more than church organizations, friendly and benevolent societies, and local councils. They looked to sporting, literary, musical and political clubs for their enjoyment, education and political expression.

Power and authority in the new associations were at first in the hands of the well-to-do. Those attending the first meeting of the Windsor benevolent society included two officers in the New South Wales regiment, four early free settlers, a clergyman and a doctor. Four were Justices of the Peace (J.P.s). Even the Wesleyan Church was manned by the propertied, the leading laymen in the 1820s being almost entirely local small farmers. The friendly societies of the 1830s had more working-class members. William Sibson, a shoemaker, was instrumental in founding a Manchester Unity lodge at Parramatta. The important decisions, however, rested with men of wealth, education and social standing. The Windsor District Council included William Cox, a pastoralist, Josiah H. Betts, a merchant, Francis Beddek, a solicitor, and Dr Thomas Arndell. The only members with questionable credentials were Thomas Tebbutt, a dealer, and Robert Fitzgerald, a well-educated ex-convict who had quickly risen to the post of superintendent of convicts and received a land grant.

Over the ranges the Shire Council of Mudgee, formed at the squatters' instigation in 1843, was entirely in their hands. All its members used convict labour. One, G. H. Cox, had tenants farming the flats of the Cudgegong River on his Burrendulla property. He had a finger in every local pie. A trustee of St John the Baptist Church, he was also on the hospital and mechanics' institute committees and the school board. He had a separate school at Burrendulla for his tenants' children. The homestead he eventually built was a large, two-storey structure, its main staircase lit by a stained-glass window bearing the Cox crest and monogram. His fellow councillor, Nicholas Paget Bayley, owned 14,000 acres and, although a trustee of the Church of England, displayed his patriarchal concern for all by giving 500 pounds to the Mudgee Wesleyan Church. He was also on the inaugural committee of the Pastoral and Agricultural Association, founded in 1846. Cox, Bayley and several other squatters made up the Mudgee bench of magistrates, where they sat in judgement on their tenants and employees. In 1858, Cox was elected to the new Legislative Assembly.

Into this squattocracy poured free settlers with money made on the goldfields, a feeling that they were as good as any squatter and a hunger for land. They resented the wealthy, conservative squatters' hold on town life. Literate and self-confident, they set up a variety of new organizations and infused new life into the old. They were not frightened to put forward their own political candidates and, with the advent of manhood suffrage, they had the numbers at the polls. In Armidale, in northern New South Wales, only one-fifth of local adult males had been qualified to vote in 1856, and over a quarter of the electors held pastoral runs. In 1858, a ten-pound householder franchise let the urban middle class in. They successfully put up their own candidate, a Sydney solicitor by the name of Hart. Next year, 1859, came the first election fought under manhood suffrage. Hart won again by two votes. At Mudgee the conservative Cox did not feel confident enough to stand again under the new rules, and S. H. Terry was elected on a liberal platform.

But the backlash came when the squatters found themselves forced to share the fruits of office in the local courts as well as in parliament. In October 1859, a large number of J.P.s were appointed on the recommendation of the new members of parliament. Although there was nothing new in this, the conservatives were outraged. They attacked the education, social standing and morals of the new appointees. One had the fact that he had offered a bribe when he was eighteen years old dragged up against him. Another was objected to because during the gold rushes he had gone into business as a storekeeper. Myles Hartle Lyons of Mudgee, an Irishman and Catholic, faced the charge of having once been a policeman. The *Goulburn Herald* reported, however, that he had been a lawyer in Ireland and had upset the Mudgee bench by advising defendants before them on points of law. Almost to a man the Mudgee bench resigned. Dissatisfied benches in other districts followed their example. At Goulburn two-thirds of the bench resigned. At Armidale five squatters resigned after two storekeepers and a labourer were appointed.

Refusing to be bullied, the government accepted these resignations. None of the old guard was re-appointed. In many areas the squatters admitted defeat and retired from public life. In Armidale, for instance, liberal candidates continued to win elections to the assembly, and the bench by 1863 was almost wholly in the hands of the townsmen. The regular attenders were storekeepers and a surveyor.

In Mudgee the squatters did not retire so gracefully. Lyons, whose appointment had caused such a storm, sat on the bench with the police magistrate, the mayor, and squatters Thomas Cadell and Edward Marley. Town and district were split along liberal/conservative lines. The town council included among its aldermen a number of prominent liberals. The more conservative squatters had secured their own municipality of Cudgegong. Bayly and Cox were on the Cudgegong council, Cox being the mayor in 1859. At the 1860 election S. H. Terry was put up again as a proponent of unlocking the squatters' estates. James Martin stood against him for the conservatives and lost 541 to 80. There was also division between the town and the squatters on the question of state aid to religion, with the Church of England squatters favouring state aid and the townspeople opposing it. Even so, the squatters did not completely withdraw from town society. While some organizations such as the Mudgee Building and Investment Society and Mudgee Union Benefit Society were 'town' associations, run largely by town council members, Cox and Bayley stayed on the mechanics' institute committee and school board.

In April 1861 the squatters had a stroke of luck. Their arch-enemy Lyons was dismissed from the magistracy for libelling the mother of one of the ex-magistrates. He also lost office, was removed, or resigned from the committees of other town organizations. This did not mean complete victory for the squatters. Only some of the J.P.s who had resigned were reappointed, and not more than one from each family. At the next commission of the peace Andrew McAuley, townsman and contractor, who had already sat on the bench as mayor, was allowed a seat again without opposition. Cudgegong and Mudgee councils continued their separate paths. Lyons did not slink away. He remained on the council for his term of office and did not resign from the hospital. Significantly, these were the organizations with the most townite, that is liberal, middle-class members.

Meanwhile, the same battle for control over the administration of local justice was being played out in parliament. Amid growing alarm at the quality of bench appointments, the conservative James Martin was elected in 1864 on a platform including the revision of the commission of the peace. His new, cleansed commission of August 1864 produced equally loud howls of political favouritism. Whole families of conservatives remained while honest, competent liberals were excluded. The return of squatters who attended less regularly meant numerous courts of petty sessions were too short-handed to do business. This pleased no one. By January 1865, the liberals were back in office, and the most qualified among the liberal J.P.s were gradually re-appointed. The small man was here to stay.

The acceptance of ordinary townsmen – storekeepers, auctioneers, millers and surveyors – to the bench opened the way for their ascendancy in town life. Closer settlement increased their role. There were now large numbers of small to medium farmers and graziers without the time or money to take a leading part in local life. The squatters, while they did not disappear completely, no longer dominated. The pastoral families of the Hunter Valley, for example, where there were many small holdings, were absent from town councils, voluntary associations and social assemblies. In no way did they dominate religious organizations, politics or the magistracy. Indeed, pastoral families were rarely seen in town, for they did most of their shopping and spent most of their leisure time in Sydney.

Except in smaller towns and villages, the squatter by the 1880s was a figurehead who might be persuaded to lay a foundation stone or cut a ribbon and, with any luck, to make a fat donation. Increasingly, however, these services were performed by the mayor's wife. The age of squatter domination had gone, but the bourgeois establishment that replaced it was just as strong.

In the Victorian country towns of Wodonga, Coleraine, Bairnsdale and Colac, 80 per cent or more of office-bearers in local government and voluntary organizations in the 1880s were from the upper middle class of businessmen, professionals and civil servants. Until one looks at who ran the friendly societies, the working class seems invisible. In Bairnsdale, tradesmen were only 8 per cent of office-bearers in other voluntary associations but 45 per cent of friendly society office-bearers. In Warracknabeal, a wheat town, they were 96 per cent of friendly society officials but only 11 per cent of those in other voluntary associations. Not only did the upper middle class run town life. They ruthlessly excluded their inferiors. Tickets for the Bairnsdale St Patrick's Day sports were ten shillings and sixpence a double, enough to exclude stockmen, hop pickers and employee tradesmen, who would take several days to earn that much. The committee made quite certain the riff-raff were kept out by reserving the right to refuse admission. Similarly, those invited to the Philharmonic Society's first meeting in May 1888 decided that members would have to do more than pay a subscription. Applications would be put to a vote and those with a third or more votes against them would be rejected.

The discrimination against whites from the wrong side of the tracks was nothing compared with the treatment of the Chinese and Aborigines. Subject to an unofficial apartheid, they were fringe-dwellers. Only where they had gathered in large numbers, as at Cairns, did the Chinese have their own quarter in the built-up area of the town. In most places they congregated in camps inside town boundaries but on inferior, poorly drained ground. At Herberton they were excluded from the township altogether. They were also kept out of certain jobs. The Herberton miners' association voted to force the permanent exclusion of Chinese from tin mining because they knew too much about it. In 1888 the Cairns Municipal Council passed a motion stopping the Chinese from securing any tender over which it had control.

The Chinese and Aborigines were socially accepted only when they were of entertainment value. At Alexandra in Victoria, a local donated one guinea for a boomerang competition among the local Aborigines who agreed to amuse the white population by showing their skill. Bairnsdale residents always included a special 'Chinese Race' at their sports days, which gave them much amusement. It is hard to see why a group of Chinese running should be any funnier than a group of whites. It must be remembered, however, that nineteenth-century Chinese dressed in the Chinese style of the times. At the Boxing Day races held at the Rocky River goldfields near Armidale, in 1856, the Chinese were to compete in a 'Pagoda hat race'. There was much speculation about the fun there might be if their wide trousers got inflated and lifted them into the air. Larger groups of Chinese also provided spectacle and pageantry when they celebrated their festivals. In Cairns the white population gathered to watch the New Year celebrations with their processions, Chinese bagpipes and firecrackers being let off to exorcise evil spirits.

If the Chinese asserted themselves too strongly and expected to be treated like whites, townsmen reacted swiftly. Whites at Cairns were happy to watch the New Year celebrations but drew the line at giving permission to hold the associated feast in the Divisional Board Hall. In Bairnsdale, the evidence of a Chinese in court was dismissed by the defence as 'only the unsupported testimony of a chinaman'. When a Shepparton resident leased land to one Wah Kee for a Chinese garden, a group of citizens bought the land to keep him off it. In Wodonga, white publicans sold liquor after hours without being arrested. A teamster, however, thought nothing of drawing police attention to a Chinese running a sly grog shop on the outskirts of a town, and he was promptly jailed. Compulsory school attendance was fought strenuously. In Albury, a six-year-old Chinese-Australian boy was refused admission to the Roman Catholic school because he was wearing a pigtail. He and other children from the Chinese camp were let into the public school but faced much prejudice and opposition from European parents.

The middle class established the same grip on local life in the city suburbs. Aldermen were upper middle-class professionals, shopkeepers, factory-owners and proprietors of transport firms. Predominantly working-class areas, such as the inner Sydney suburbs of Newtown and Balmain, did not automatically elect working-class representatives. In the last quarter of the nineteenth century, 67 per cent of Balmain electors were manual workers but, in 1888, nine out of ten aldermen were professionals, manufacturers or builders. Churches, local hospitals and charities were largely in middle-class hands. It was only in strongly working-class areas that there were sporting or religious organizations with predominantly working-class membership. In Balmain, half the members of the rugby and bicycle clubs whose occupations are known had manual jobs. And invariably there would be another football or cricket club with a very different class composition. In Newtown, the Rugby Union Football Club had no working-class members. Most were upper middle class. By contrast, the Oxford Club had no upper middle-class members and at least a quarter were workers. Certain sports such as tennis and sailing were too expensive for manual workers. Bowling clubs at both Newtown and Balmain were middle-class organizations. Religions were stratified on lines similar to those outlined by Marc Askew in his chapter on religion in the previous volume. In Balmain, upper middle-class professionals ran the Church of England, while the middle class generally controlled the Presbyterian Church. Half the prominent Wesleyans and 78 per cent of well-known Catholics, however, did manual work. Voluntary organizations dominated by the working class were separate from the middle-class associations, where they existed at all.

Today local organizations rest in the hands of much the same groups they did a century ago, even though many of them have changed their focus. A 1944 study of the needs of Victorian country towns by A.J. and J.J. McIntyre included a lot of information about power and status in rural areas. Local government was still important and still failed to represent the working class. Country people scarcely participated in town affairs. Friendly societies drew their members from middle and lower income groups. Large landholders provided patronage as distinct from leadership. The working class was either barred from sporting and social activities or forced to organize its own. Apex and Rotary, by constitution, had to include leading townsmen. This usually meant the well-to-do. The McIntyres forgot to add that Aborigines were still fringe-dwellers while the Chinese, thanks to the White Australia policy, were dying out.

The outstanding difference between the late nineteenth and early twentieth centuries was the rise of youth and women's groups. The former were not autonomous organizations of young people. They were usually run by adults who wished to do something to and for youth. They were of no importance for the local power base. Women's groups, however, reflected the same status divisions as men's, and even more sharply. They were led by the wives of school-teachers, bank managers, clergymen and big tradesmen. High subscriptions were used to exclude the socially undesirable. In any case, most women avoided groups involving contact with women of different classes on the grounds that they would feel uncomfortable. Clearly they knew their place.

Since the Second World War, the middle class has continued to dominate country town life. Indeed, there is little evidence of change in the social hierarchy. In R.A. Wild's 1974 study of Bowral, a country town south of Sydney, the social structure that had emerged was not greatly different from that of the Victorian rural service centres of the 1880s. At the top of the tree in both cases were the large landowning families. In Bowral, which is just within commuting distance of Sydney by car, modern transport had produced a second wealthy group which Wild called 'Grange-ites'. These were well-off retired people and commuters enjoying the pleasures of country life while living within reach of the city. This group has no nineteenth-century equivalent. But it was not these groups who ran things in the town. The motive force in local politics and in voluntary societies was the group Wild called the 'bosses', the employers and professionals who were already dominant in the 1880s. Below them were the shopkeepers, clerks and skilled tradesmen, then the manual workers. At the bottom of the ladder were the people Wild called 'no-hopers', a latter-day version of the casual workers, drunkards, deserted wives, Chinese and Aborigines whose presence in nineteenth-century towns can usually be detected only by reading the records of the courts of petty sessions.

In suburban areas, local government and local voluntary associations have been losing their sway over local life since the end of last century. Improved transport meant that people no longer had to seek leisure locally. Throughout the 1880s there were many recreation clubs in Sydney based on work groups in the central business district; for instance, there was a drama society in the Government Printer's department. It was also possible for people in one suburb to join a voluntary association in another. The Leichhardt Mutual Improvement Association officially described itself as a 'purely unsectarian body of male and female residents of Leichhardt and other places'. For the same reason, friendly societies also lost their local identity. Workers who travelled to the city for trade-union meetings might also attend lodges there. The Sydney United Labourers Society operated only at the city centre. Others joined lodges miles from where they lived. W. J. Rose, secretary of the Iron Duke Lodge of the United Ancient Order of Druids at Redfern, lived 10 kilometres away at Kogarah.

The average Sydney suburb was up to ten times the size of a country town. Sporting clubs multiplied to cope with those eager to participate. As a result a team's victory or defeat meant considerably less than in a country town where everyone identified with one team. The large number of peripheral religious organizations had the same effect. Choirs, literary, debating and charitable societies proliferated along religious lines. At Newtown the St Joseph's Literary and Debating Society belonged to the Church of England; the Presbyterians set up their own literary society. The local mechanics' institute, administered by town notables, was just one of many such groups, and the notables themselves were spread across religious groups.

In country towns, small size meant that everyone knew everyone else's business, and everyone helped each other. The various denominations helped each other by subscribing to organ and building funds or attending and sewing for bazaars. Any denomination that put on a good show attracted an audience beyond its adherents. At the Wodonga Church of England Harvest Thanksgiving, pride of place was given to a large loaf of bread made especially by Peter O'Connor, a pillar of the Catholic Church. In strongly Presbyterian Bairnsdale, there was a public holiday for the St Patrick's Day Sports. But in the suburbs, when churches needed help, they turned to nearby members of the same denomination, not to other local churches. When Burwood Presbyterian Church got up a bazaar, it sought help from Presbyterian churches in other suburbs. 'Strathfield and Homebush', 'Enfield and Concord', 'Croydon and Ashfield' and even 'Saint Leonards and Manly' were blazoned across the stalls. Just as significant was the fact that they held the bazaar at the Sydney Town Hall, not at Burwood.

The rising cost of public utilities was also eroding local involvement. It was simply not feasible for individual suburbs to arrange for their own water supply and sewage disposal. The state governments increased their own hand in local government through statutory authorities on which local council representatives sat with government appointees. The constitutions of bodies such as the Melbourne and Metropolitan Board of Works or Sydney's Water Supply and Sewerage Board reduced participation by the municipalities. The Sydney Board took control of water supply and sewerage from the City Council in 1886. In March 1888, aldermen chose two men from the City Council and twenty-three suburban municipalities to represent their interests. The president and most other members were government appointees, and construction was in the hands of the Minister of Works. The board had extensive powers. For instance, it could tear up local streets as it pleased.

Local hospitals were also swallowed up as they changed from charitable institutions to scientifically based, government-funded places of healing. By the 1880s, accident victims from all over inner Sydney were taken to the Royal Prince Alfred Hospital at Camperdown. Those with infectious diseases were despatched to the Coast Hospital miles away at Little Bay. Balmain was an exception, with its own cottage hospitals lovingly tended by the council, drama society and friendly society lodges.

Entertainment also became commercial, overshadowing local voluntary societies. Steamer companies offered excursions to beaches and bays and up rivers to residents from all over Sydney. In the western Sydney suburb of Ashfield, the commercial Recreation Grounds were open every evening and Saturday afternoon. They boasted the largest skating floor in the southern hemisphere and had special buses to meet every train that pulled into Ashfield station. At the southern seaside suburb of Coogee, the Palace Aquarium, baths and pleasure grounds provided a centennial carnival on 25 January 1888, including a Grand Centennial Circus and music by the Centennial Band. The baths were open to all who wanted to use them, and the seals and fish were fed at 10.30 a.m. and 4.30 p.m. With attractions like these, who wanted to stay at home and organize a sports day or Sunday School picnic?

Big business and big government further encroached on local bourgeois control in the twentieth century. Child endowment and other welfare payments replaced the local benevolent society. Radio, television and gramophones made it unnecessary to work together to produce entertainment.

The local bourgeoisie's control was not only threatened from above. Working-class urbanites could travel beyond where they lived to the central business district where they maintained trade unions, friendly societies and bands, often based on the work group. As a result they could develop a sense of loyalty to other members of the working class, regardless of where they lived.

Generally, small population centres tended to be dominated by the local middle class while in modern cities local identity tended to disappear. But there have been exceptions. These are the mining and industrial centres that have often been dominated by the working class and seem to resist absorption into a larger urban mass. Even in these places, however, working-class dominance is by no means inevitable.

One distinctive feature of mining last century was the large number of men employed by each company. Although factories and workshops in the city rarely employed more than a hundred hands, the Australian Agricultural Company's Sea Pit off the coast at Newcastle was employing 700 to 800 men in 1900. The mining companies, through their managers, had a golden opportunity to

Moonta mines in the 1920s

assert their dominance over the mining towns. Their employees were far below them on the social ladder. As mines are invariably established in rural or isolated areas where towns have to be built from scratch, there was a strong tradition of paternalism. Of necessity, the companies had founded schools and mechanics' institutes, provided houses and given liberally to the churches.

By the late nineteenth century, a mining town such as Moonta, in South Australia, seemed to belong to a bygone age of land-owner dominance. Moonta's miners had been brought over from Cornwall. They were housed on mine property. Any offence to the manager, Captain Hancock, including failure to go to church, meant eviction as well as dismissal. As tenants on unincorporated property, miners could not even vote in local government elections. Any initiative the miners took to improve their lot could be put down. Because of the long walk from the mines to the town, a few of them had started a co-operative store, buying in bulk from Adelaide. When the Moonta storekeepers complained, Hancock posted notices stopping the co-operative on pain of eviction. He played God in the fashion of an eighteenth-century squire, talking of 'his' town and 'his' people. He laid the foundation stones of most churches and presided over most town social occasions, which the miners did not attend. He was superintendent of Moonta Mines Wesleyan Sunday School and, along with most senior officials, a Justice of the Peace. He was president of the

Agricultural, Horticultural and Floricultural Society and insisted on judging the Cornish Pasty section personally. If the squatters had retired, Hancock had not. Significantly, he also sent his children to the local school, in contrast to the squatters who patronized the elite private schools in the capital cities.

Hancock did not have control at Moonta township. The townspeople ran their own voluntary associations. Among the town leaders, doctors, lawyers and merchants, Hancock's biographer has noted that he was much sought after for his humorous speeches. This side of him never surfaced when he was dealing with the carters, labourers, miners and masons on the mines; there, he assumed a 'mantle of omniscience'. So Moonta township, where few miners could afford to live, was much like any other Australian country town – bourgeois dominated, with the largest landowner sometimes condescending to visit. Out at the mines, however, the men remained under Hancock's thumb.

In Newcastle, where a distinctive working-class town did emerge, the ruling ideology and the patterns of land ownership were very different from those at Moonta. In the villages of the Newcastle Coalmining District, 56 per cent of the male workforce were miners and 86 per cent tradesmen, miners or labourers. The better off coalminers were the dominant occupational group in the municipal councils and mechanics' institutes. With other manual workers, they dominated the committees of most organizations, including the friendly societies.

By the late 1880s, Newcastle was changing from a district dominated by the colliery manager to a society led by the working class. Mine managers were still powerful and respected figures in the colliery townships, but they no longer ran them. From the start company housing, the main means of social control in the English coalfields, was either non-existent or a failure. Most companies cut up part of their properties as township allotments. These were bought not only by business people as intended, but also by miners. A tenant miner, then, might be renting from a shopkeeper, baker, or fellow-miner instead of from his employer. Many people also squatted on the crown land near the townships. Though they had no security there, they did not have to depend on the whims of the managers.

Freedom from company housing gave the miners the opportunity to follow their own interests. Co-operative stores did much better than elsewhere in Australia, and colliery managers did not interfere on behalf of the storekeepers. Trade unions were already strong in north-eastern England, from which many of the miners came, and took early root in Newcastle. Virtually all the hewers were union members throughout the late nineteenth century. By contrast, the Cornish miners of Moonta had no strong tradition of unionism and did not set up a proper union until 1889.

Experience in working-class self-help organizations gave the miners confidence to organize voluntary movements. Towns were incorporated against the wishes of the colliery companies. Although mine managers might donate large sums to local causes, they did not hold the initiative. Nor was their patronage essential. The towns could get government grants for schools, hospitals and mechanics' institutes. Through membership of local councils, especially the mayoralty, miners won respectability and got themselves on to school boards and the local bench. The tradition of patronage was strained by industrial conflict in the 1880s. In 1885 Thomas Croudace, a more than usually paternalistic colliery manager, helped to arrange a horticultural show only to have it ruined by a strike at Lambton Colliery. In 1886 he wrote to his directors: 'It really seems to me the more you do for workmen and the better you pay them the more ungrateful they are.'

Although the managers became less willing to bestow patronage, the miners became less willing to accept it. The miners had seen their wages fall sharply, the managers becoming intransigent and the companies contributing as little as they could to the localities. All this fitted in very well with the newly arrived European socialist idea that the interests of labour and capital were incompatible. The miners were not upset when the colliery managers began to withdraw from municipal councils. Indeed, it must have been a relief that there were no managers on the council during the 1888 coal strike, which featured the use of troops and many arrests for riot and unlawful assembly. Among those arrested were at least three miners prominent in local voluntary associations and on municipal councils. Where the working class managed its own affairs, it was much more willing to challenge the established order.

Newcastle in the nineteenth century was the precursor of Broken Hill in the twentieth. Yet most of the Barrier's early settlers were Moonta copper miners who voted with their feet rather than striking for higher wages in the South Australian depression of the 1880s. So it is not surprising that working-class participation in local life was weak in the early years. In 1886, the local branch of the Amalgamated Miners' Association celebrated its first anniversary with a picnic and demonstration. Not only were the mine

The new mining settlement of Broken Hill in the late 1880s.

managers invited, but they took a major part in organizing the proceedings. Then again, the union had cheerfully elected a committee with no working miners on it. There were two coaching agents, an auctioneer, a bank manager, an assayer, a chemist, a sharebroker and a storekeeper. The first patron was a Broken Hill Proprietary (B.H.P.) director. When the union secretary, a miner, stood for a vacancy on the improvement committee in 1886, he polled only seven votes. On the other hand, mine managers were prominent on the hospital committee and as magistrates. When a committee was formed to set up a mechanics' institute in 1888, it consisted of two clergymen, several businessmen and some professionals. By late 1888, the working class had begun to get a clearer idea of how to pursue its interests. Two union officials, both mine workers, were elected to the first municipal council. But the mayor was Richard Piper, a mine manager formerly at Moonta, who had put pressure on Broken Hill South miners to leave the union.

Broken Hill's working-class hegemony developed over two decades, from the 1890s to the First World War. It had more to do with the Labor Party and European socialism than early British trade unionism. By 1896 the town had its first 'Labor' alderman who, when he eventually became mayor, was confident enough to challenge B.H.P. over its failure to pay rates. In Newcastle the *Miners' Advocate* had been crucial in developing civic-mindedness among coal miners in the 1870s. At Broken Hill the Labor Party's organ, the *Barrier Truth*, urged readers to vote in municipal elections. A drive for compulsory unionism in 1913 and 1914 got rid of the itinerant non-unionists who had been used as strike-breakers. And as the mines declined and jobs became scarcer, the itinerants stopped coming to Broken Hill. The union became involved in local and state politics, welfare, health and educational reform.

Meanwhile B.H.P. gave nothing. Eventually it came into contact with the policies of enlightened self-interest followed by welfare capitalists in the United States. In 1919 it appointed Gerald Mussen from New Zealand as a 'consulting industrialist' to organize reforms. But in a militant town Mussen's sweet reasonableness and charm were a red flag to the union bull. The company's overtures were branded as an attempt to 'chloroform the worker', and the miners went on strike for sixteen months. Industrial action secured a thirty-five hour week underground, an investigation into the incidence of lung diseases among Broken Hill miners and compensation for those already afflicted.

Many writers have emphasized the importance of kin and neighbourhood in producing working-class militancy in isolated towns or districts. But these seem less important than working-class dominance of local government and voluntary associations. Where this dominance was achieved, the working class was not only able to mount powerful industrial actions: in Broken Hill

The dining room in a mine manager's house at Broken Hill.

and Newcastle the local working class established its hegemony over the middle-class residents of the towns.

The one-industry towns that have grown up since the Second World War have shown no such tendencies. The new localities have more in common with nineteenth-century Moonta than twentieth-century Broken Hill. An example is the Western Australian asbestos mining settlement of Wittenoom. The mine work was underground contract work, which is usually seen as producing high job involvement and solidarity, spilling over into after-hours friendships and club memberships. Yet in its twenty-odd years of life, there were only weak and sporadic attempts to improve working and living conditions at Wittenoom. Nor was there any major strike. The single men's quarters remained in such an appalling state that in 1965 the regional health inspector reported: 'I seldom see such squalor, even among the dozens or so Native reserves that I visit. That such conditions exist in Australia is rather amazing.'

Wittenoom was a company town in an old (or new) tradition. As well as running local government, the mine managers were also the magistrates, ran a store and cinema and provided the single men's quarters. Although the state government built the houses, many saw the company as the effective owner, as it collected the rent, carried out any maintenance and charged for water and power. People ran up hire purchase debts of up to $5,000 at the company store, so they were further locked into company control. In her study of Wittenoom, Lenore Layman argues that any challenge to the company would probably have failed, but adds that few contemplated it. Most simply left: over half left within six months, and less than a quarter stayed more than a year. More than half the workers were non-English speakers from such a variety of countries that it was impossible to provide sufficient interpreters in such an isolated area. Italians did the underground face work. Most were former rural workers with no experience of mining. When they arrived, it was the foreman, not their fellow-workers, who showed them how to do their job. There was none of the solidarity of hewers in other mines who shared skills and experience. Unlike the underground miners of old, who were the aristocracy of the mine workforce, the underground miners at Wittenoom were despised.

Since 1950, mining has grown rapidly in Australia's isolated tropical third. The mining companies have had to provide water, housing and other facilities to attract labour in an era of unprecedented comfort in the cities. Drawing partly on the Cornish antecedents of so many who manned base metal mines in Australia, partly on early twentieth-century American strategies, welfare capitalism became common in mining centres. Geoffrey Blainey has claimed: 'The mines triumphed over tensions, pioneering a brand of industrial relations that was so advanced that the new social benefits conferred by parliament often seemed mean or irrelevant.'

It was not just that the workers were bought off. Layman's study of Wittenoom shows that conditions were by no means ideal, even disregarding the terrible long-term effects of exposure to asbestos. The workers were not well equipped to fight paternalism. They had no union tradition, no common language, no commitment to the place itself. The conservative Australian Workers' Union, which covered Wittenoom, was not likely to try to help them find their voice. They remained incapable of any collective action.

A glance at the town of Whyalla is enough to show that welfare capitalism has never been a strong point of B.H.P., Australia's largest company. Whyalla, on the western side of Spencer Gulf in South Australia, owed its existence to its role as a port for the iron ore mines at Iron Knob. From 1930 to 1950 it was a classic company town. B.H.P. supplied water, electricity, roads and housing.

Whyalla during the 1950s

But by the 1960s, the South Australian government had taken over most of these tasks. The South Australian Housing Trust built 7,000 houses. With little contribution from B.H.P., the state financed roads, railways, the airport, schools, the hospital and tertiary educational institutions. It also paid the assisted passages of its largely immigrant workforce.

But B.H.P. has remained in control because it is overwhelmingly the largest employer. The company holds the town's future in its hands. It has avoided paying taxes on its rateable property, handing over only $15,000 to $20,000 a year, about 2 per cent of what it would normally pay. Many businesses and smaller industries are dependent on B.H.P. Embarrassing stories about the Big Australian are never printed in the local newspapers. Doctors and other professionals at the apex of local society prefer to stay out of local affairs, spending their spare time in palaces of conspicuous consumption and expensive private pastimes. Most are overworked by the need to provide certificates for sick B.H.P. workers. Several general practitioners and specialists receive most of the company referrals in return for giving worker's compensation reports that favour the company.

B.H.P.'s employees do exhausting work and obligatory overtime. They have little time for outside activities. Many are immigrants who are effectively silenced by the language barrier. Union organizers cannot move around the works freely, and workmen who leave or are sacked are blacklisted. The company liaison officer also encourages new arrivals to buy on credit or hire purchase. For fear of losing their jobs, they buy housing trust houses and then have to go heavily into debt furnishing them. They are tied to Whyalla and B.H.P. until they pay off their debts. There is a company credit union, but if men who are in debt to it lose their jobs they lose all their money. Wages, holiday pay and superannuation are taken to pay off the loan. The work-place is heavily supervised, and good work and initiative never acknowledged. Nor is excellence in a trade. Pliable rather than good workmen are promoted; the traditional working-class hierarchy in which skill, high wages and status go together does not exist in Whyalla. Leisure centres around falling asleep in front of the television, fixing old cars and gardening in brighter moments.

B.H.P.'s welfare programmes, although they might impress outsiders, have little impact on the town. Commenting on its donations to a variety of clubs and societies, one local government official told Roy Kriegler: 'Instead of providing something lavish, like a large recreation centre for the city, B.H.P. prefers to make these small hand-outs. It gives them a finger in every pie and of course it's good propaganda.'

Workers will often go out of their way to avoid borrowing from the credit union because it will tie them to B.H.P. Contrary to Blainey's impression, generosity and benevolent paternalism have not played a great part in establishing ruling-class dominance in these recent one-industry towns. Whyalla's lack of a strong working class owes more to shiftwork, the language barrier, a lack of union tradition, private leisure pursuits and thinly disguised manipulation by the Big Australian.

When you search through the history of white Australia, it is hard to find much evidence of the harmonious, united communities that today's power-brokers so confidently evoke. Formal associations rather than family and neighbourhood have been the best means of getting things done. And 'communities' have very seldom been united. If at times they may speak with one voice, that has often been because the majority of their people were silenced. Only in a handful of mining towns has the working class been able to participate actively in shaping the urban environment, and even there the wheel has turned full circle today, with the companies back in the driver's seat. Meanwhile, in the cities, the sense of local identity has been broken down by new patterns of work and recreation. To people who live in one suburb, work in another, visit parents in a third and go to concerts or sporting matches all over the city, the idea of 'community' has become obsolete.

A Nordenfelt at every Woolshed

ANDREW MOORE

My dream for this district is a Gifford gun beside every bed, and a Nordenfelt at every woolshed. Then we who own the land will feel secure in our possession of it once again.

Part of a fictional address delivered by a retired major-general during the 1890s shearers' strike

The year after the British invasion of Australia the French Revolution shook the European ruling classes to their foundations. At this time there was little chance that a convict uprising would succeed in storming any of the scrub Bastilles of Port Jackson, where military governors held near-absolute power. Nevertheless, the calls for liberty, equality and fraternity that echoed around Paris were not lost entirely on the colonial lads and lasses.

The rulers of the colonies were nervous by disposition. Back in Britain, their class was in the midst of a major struggle to keep tight rein on a disorderly, dispossessed working class. They knew that the distance between discontent and mutiny was not very great. Their siege mentality was magnified by ignorance, distance, isolation and fear of the unknown, the 'ghastly blank' of the Australian continent.

Fears of uprisings by the lower orders lay deep in the consciousness of the dominant class. Occasionally, their nightmares became real. This occurred in 1804 at Castle Hill; two decades later, Ralph Entwistle led an armed rebellion in the Bathurst district and, in 1834, there was a rebellion at Norfolk Island. After 1850 there was much concern about Fenian conspiracies, bushrangers and the first stirrings of working-class interest in mass political action. The Aborigines' determined resistance, the miners' revolt at Eureka in 1854 and the campaign of guerilla warfare conducted by Ned Kelly all gave evidence of formidable opposition to 'social order'.

As Australian capitalism developed, it spawned its own adversaries. A reserve of unemployed or under-employed labour and an increasingly assertive working class threatened the social ascendancy of the bourgeoisie. The 1890s brought bank crashes, revealing just how fragile some of capital's seemingly impregnable institutions were. There was also industrial turmoil, providing a glimpse of where it all might end – the hell fires of socialism. This prospect again raised its head in 1917 and during the depression of the 1930s. Even though the ruling class owned most of the guns, it was hard to relax while radicals like Billy Lane were proclaiming in 1888: 'We shall not be truly safe until we realize the aspiration that found a voice at Eureka and hoist the starry cross above a free and united Australia'. Later, in 1929, Lane's former colleague Senator Arthur Rae called for the socialization of production, arguing that communism aimed at establishing 'the very highest form of society'.

This chapter is concerned with explaining why Australian capitalism did not fall into the hands of such devils. Its focus, however, is not on the failings of people on the labour side. It is concerned with those on the top of the pile and how they stayed there. Over the years, the Australian ruling class used a variety of tactics against potential threats. They have defended their position and privileges by the use of force; they have mobilized in new ways in politics and industry; they have won over influential people from within the labour movement and fostered division among workers; and, when they had no other choice, they have made strategic concessions to working-class demands. It was in times of crisis, such as the 1890s and 1930s, that the ruling class was inclined to show its mailed fist. When economic conditions were more buoyant, there was room for a more subtle approach and a certain amount of accommodation. But there were long periods of time, between 1788 and 1842 and again between 1910 and 1941, when the ruling class made very few concessions, even when economic conditions made it possible for them to do so. The actions of the ruling class depended on the changing balance of political and industrial forces as well as the state of the capitalist economy. The contours of the argument are best followed in historical sequence.

The Australian ruling class was not present at its own formation. Its members were all in London, in the Pitt Ministry and the East India Company. At Sydney Cove in 1788, their agents were carried from the boats; men of such station could not be allowed to get their fine clothing wet. Officers' salaries and capital from official sources laid the basis for a primitive capitalist economy. Control of the government store, a monopoly over various commodities, including rum, and land seizures yielded wealth to a small elite. The new colony soon had its own entrepreneurs, including emancipists like the 'Botany Bay Rothschild', Samuel Terry. In 1821, 60 per cent of all the alienated land in New South Wales was owned by eighty people. A colonial gentry swiftly established itself, erecting homes that resembled garrisons, socializing together, inter-marrying, and dispensing patronage. As British Prime Minister Gladstone said, the move to the colonies brought the new elite an 'intoxicating augmentation of wealth and power'. Exploration helped master the vastness of the Australian continent, and the state sponsored explorers to ensure that 'respectable government' could rely upon effective 'land communication'. Artists and writers, still living in the British dreamtime, began to smooth over the worst of Australia's jagged imagery.

Nevertheless the ruling group recognized that their hold on power was precarious. In 1810-11 a commercial crisis nearly wiped out the first generation of traders. Economic growth was held back by a lack of capital for investment, by the rum trade and by an intractable labour force.

The early colonial years have a special place in the history of the Australian ruling class. Its members constituted a cohesive group who shared common objectives and views of the world. They saw themselves as providing the cement necessary to subdue and civilize a rough and brawling society. United in their commitment to accumulating vast private fortunes, they worked to establish a Protestant ascendancy and a plantation-style economy based on exporting primary products to England. They also enjoyed an unusual degree of autonomy. For in the early years of settlement, the British were primarily interested in New South Wales as a jail and a strategic outpost in the South Pacific, rather than a frontier of capitalism. This meant that people such as John Macarthur and Samuel Marsden were allowed reasonable scope for independent initiatives. Their activities were of little interest to London, except when they arrested governors.

When it became apparent that there was money to be made in this inhospitable outpost, however, British capital began to play a more active role. From the 1830s the local ruling class's autonomy dwindled. For the next 150 years, Australia hardly possessed its own ruling class. The strategic sectors of the Australian economy were invariably dominated by foreign capital. With certain exceptions – such as the sugar and mining industries – local entrepreneurs were largely content to act as accomplices and agents of overseas capital. The rewards for doing so were often very generous. Other local businessmen carved out private niches in less central sectors of the economy, such as retailing, brewing and publishing newspapers. Again the rewards could be considerable. The Hordern family became almost unimaginably wealthy by operating retail emporiums after 1838 and then diversifying into pastoralism and other activities.

As the pastoral industry and the finance sector expanded, the ruling class grew larger. Yet it remained exclusive. For a while Governor Macquarie tried to encourage equality between ex-convicts and free men, and both he and William Bligh attempted to help small farmers. But these experiments were abruptly stopped by the Bigge report in 1821. Social mobility was brought to an end. As the historian Stuart Macintyre has commented: 'The class division between propertied wealth and labour hardened and became overlaid by a social division between the exclusivist and the emancipist.' The Bigge report also cleared the way for Australia to become a vast sheep run. J. T. Bigge and other shareholders in the British-owned Australian Agricultural Company could rejoice as pastoralism ran riot and agriculture was retarded. Ordinary folk were less excited. It took until the late 1840s for the colonies to be self-sufficient in grain.

Convictism was at the one time appallingly, yet also appealingly, one-sided. In this sense, from the ruling-class perspective, things have gone downhill since the end of transportation. Convict society was strictly hierarchical and splendidly deferential, though the brave and the foolish might offer plenty of cheek. The lower orders could be ruthlessly subjugated and disciplined at the point of production. The relationship between the state and the ruling class was generally unambiguous. There were internal conflicts – manifested most clearly in the military coup of 1808 when Governor Bligh, a stickler for the rules, refused to play along with the Rum Ring's organized corruption; for the most part, however, the state and ruling class were one. State terror could be practised without the faintest suggestion of impropriety. At Castle Hill in

1804, members of the New South Wales Corps opened fire on the rebel convicts and then hanged their leader without trial. The judicial process paid scant attention to the rights of free Englishmen; the criminal court established at the colony's foundation took the form of a court martial. Notions of 'justice' mattered so little that palaces for stabling horses were built before court-houses. It was not until 1827 that the Supreme Court building was opened in Sydney, recreating the gloom of the Old Bailey. In the bush it was common for court sittings to be held in the graziers' houses, and the Australian Agricultural Company constructed court-houses and police stations in several towns throughout its vast fiefdom in the north and north-west of New South Wales.

The state soon began to rely upon prominent citizens to help maintain 'law and order'. In 1800, Governor Hunter called on the services of the surgeon and landholder, William Balmain, to organize the Sydney and Parramatta Loyal Associated Corps in the face of rumoured disaffection and revolt among the Irish convicts. 'Sedition' was controlled by public order legislation based on British law but made even more repressive. Assemblies of more than twelve people were forbidden. Provision was made for up to 1,000 lashes to be administered to anyone judged to be involved in 'any seditious purpose'. A police force was established in 1811 with D'Arcy Wentworth as police superintendent. The new police regulations kept 'prisoners and labouring persons' without reasonable cause out of the streets between 9 p.m. and daylight.

This was a society built upon force, where the ruling elite's first resort was resistance and repression. Martial law could be declared when the convicts looked like staging an insurrection, or so that explorers and settlers could shoot Aborigines with impunity in the interior. The Georgian symmetry of public building architecture and town planning made it easy to watch the streets from above. Military garrisons were strategically placed in central areas. Other measures paralleled the responses of the European bourgeoisie in the age of revolution. The surveyor-general T. L. Mitchell received letters from Britain urging that 'a precise and decided spirit be shown to put down the Radical Associations', and himself feared 'flooding revolution' by the 'most depraved part of the population'. Apparently influenced by the counter-revolutionary preparations after 1789 in Paris, he set out to re-design Sydney's streets to speed the passage of troops, with wide streets on a grid plan and numerous unassailable watch towers.

Maintaining order was a paramount goal. In 1823 the British government provided the governor with a small legislative council. But it did not want to make it hard for him to take decisive measures in an emergency. If rebellion broke out, if the governor thought a popular rising was imminent, counter-revolutionary measures could be set in train even if opposed by every member of the council. From the outset the ruling class was able to dominate political debate; its members sat cheek by jowl in the elite council. Never again would the colonial grandees enjoy such power without challenge. Governor Bourke in the 1830s, like Governor Macquarie before him, drew the fury of the exclusive elite by showing favour to the emancipists. And the abolition of convict assignment to private masters in 1839 took away the landed gentry's cheap labour supply.

From the 1840s the ruling class had to compete for power against other forces. A new liberal bourgeoisie rose to prominence and challenged the aristocracy in a number of areas, including land legislation. The governing class lost its unity. An element of diversity over such issues as trade and land policy would become the norm. Nevertheless the disjuncture should not be emphasized too strongly. The convict period left many legacies. One was the flogging tradition. It was singularly appropriate that in 1890 the son of a Norfolk Island jailer, Colonel Tom Price, could order his troops to 'fire low and hit them in the guts', though in this case it was striking unionists, not convicts, that were in the rifle sights. The withdrawal of the British Army did not instigate the formation of a state apparatus committed to the ideals and aspirations of Australian working people. The state remained in the pocket of the ruling class. Though the Australian bourgeoisie was fond of proclaiming its commitment to individual effort, its position was very much dependent upon the state. It became accepted that the state's proper role was to create conditions under which private enterprise could prosper. In particular, the state provided transport and other basic facilities for pastoral and then industrial development. The police and military were also expected to defend the rights of property.

Nevertheless the emergence of a 'free' labour force brought significant changes in the style of labour discipline. The cat-o'-nine tails was no longer appropriate, especially when working people began to form unions. The problem was how to maintain a comparable control. 'Responsible' government after 1856 afforded the illusion of democracy. For the newly ascendant bourgeoisie, parliamentary structures and the fiction of liberal democracy were vital. Yet 'democracy' might get out of hand. The 'mob' might take over.

With rule by consent at least a partial reality, the ruling class was obliged to become more sophisticated in its management of the hired hands. Force had to be tempered and concessions granted to the better organized sections of the working class. In convict society troublemakers could be hanged. But with wage labour, the surplus of workers' labour power needed to be expropriated for profit. This was difficult to arrange if one was dealing with corpses.

In typical fashion the Australian ruling class entered this new era of social relations looking back over its shoulder. To contain the labour force industrially, employers harked back to the legislation of the convict period – the 1828 Masters and Servants Act. As Adrian Brooks's chapter on work relations in volume three has suggested, however, many workers were also able to use the Act against their bosses. Politically the new parliaments conferred great legitimacy and proved to be excellent arenas for sorting out differences of opinion on issues such as protection or free trade. Membership of institutions such as the Victorian Legislative Council was confined to males who held freehold property of 5,000 pounds and suffrage rights were severely curtailed. There was never any doubt that 'responsible government' would be responsible to the bourgeoisie.

Earlier chapters of this history have outlined the ways in which the bourgeoisie entrenched itself: by establishing a consensus about land reform, by making marriage and family life more routine, and by mounting an offensive on many fronts against an unruly working-class culture. Members of the bourgeoisie were under no illusions that rule by consent, or democracy itself, could be permanently maintained. They needed further guarantees that their authority would not be upturned. Force, or the threat of force, underpinned social relations from the picket line to the school-room. In 1850, a private group known as the Society for the Protection of Life and Property was formed in Sydney. The permanent military forces were re-organized. From the 1860s, prominent grazing families raised their own militia units. Equipped with Nordenfelt machine guns, these units were designed to carry their weapons across country at high speed. As the historian Michael Cannon has suggested, they were formed 'supposedly [at] the prerogative of the Queen' but in reality were 'a private defence against proletarian revolt'. These units were incorporated into the permanent military forces. In 1861, the Sydney Volunteers performed guard duty while the permanent garrison tried to keep order in the anti-Chinese riots at Lambing

Flat. In the early colonial years there had been fears that the marines might side with the convicts, who were of similar social origins; the increasing number of soldiers coming from the 'right' sort of families by the middle of the century must have been a source of some satisfaction.

Fear of the working class merged with apprehension about the Irish. Anti-Catholic Orangemen were invariably in charge of the military forces. The repressive apparatus of the state consisted of the colonial police forces in the frontline, the military behind them, and in the rear irregular groups such as the secret force raised by Sir Henry Parkes in 1867 to liquidate the Clarke gang of bushrangers in the Braidwood district. Together they ensured that the bourgeoisie would not give up power in any open conflict. Throughout the latter half of the nineteenth century, bourgeois resistance was helped by technological changes in transport, communications and weaponry. The steam train and the telegraph became valuable weapons. Improvements in rifle technology, in particular the development of the Martini-Henry breech loader, repeating rifles and machine guns ensured that the state would have the upper hand in any encounter with subverters of internal order.

The events of the 1890s put these arrangements to the test and shattered the illusion that Australia would enjoy a long, golden summer of class harmony. For some time before 1890, the large pastoralists had been growing increasingly restless about the growth of the big bush unions. W. E. Abbott of the Pastoralists' Union, known in the radical press as 'Wing 'em', described the labour leaders as 'a pack of hungry dingoes' who needed to be exterminated.

In 1890, the so-called maritime strike brought work to a halt on the wharves, the coalfields and in the pastoral industry. Panic-striken, members of the bourgeoisie reacted like drunken pugilists in a bar-room brawl. Unsure whether a wild hay-maker or a boot to the ribs might be the best way of subduing the strikers, they tried everything and anything. To them this strike, and those that followed between 1891 and 1894, were the beginning of civil war and 'mob rule'. Anti-combination laws and riot acts, conspiracy trials and kangaroo courts supplemented the military might of the police, special constables, the mounted infantry, and a militia composed mainly of station owners and their employees armed with Nordenfelt and Gatling guns. Correspondents of conservative newspapers agitated repeatedly for the letting of proletarian blood. Horace Trozer, the Queensland colonial secretary, circulated a manual to all justices of the peace and police instructing them to shoot on sight any person suspected of committing a felony or carrying fire-arms. Even the quiet men of high culture and refinement participated. The eminent portraitist, Julian Ashton, was among the special constables in Sydney in 1890. At the same time his friend and fellow artist, Arthur Streeton, wrote to Tom Roberts:

> I am afraid the strike will be [a] serious matter, wish it would come to a head, even if they fight about it, much the best ... I think if it comes to riot and serious strife the military and police would be insufficient. The public would then have to defend their property etc.

The rule of capital nevertheless emerged intact. The claret at the elite Union Club began to lose its bitter taste. Some members of the ruling class were unrepentant, but others emerged from their blind fury to realize that they had behaved rather poorly. This ushered in a period of accommodation.

With the acquiescence of some sectors of capital, the state intervened to establish industrial tribunals. The conflicts of the early 1890s had pricked the liberals' conscience and produced a parliamentary Labor Party lobbying for concessions. Bourgeois charity had been shown to be inadequate by the widespread unemployment and impoverishment accompanying the 1890s depression. Moves were made to improve the conditions of working-class life in a variety of ways, by laws to regulate factory conditions and public health, the increased subsidization of private charities and a range of social welfare policies, including the introduction of old-age pensions. Under Major-General E. T. H. Hutton, attempts were made to democratize the composition of the standing army. The police also tried to improve their image by shedding some of their militaristic trappings and stressing their function as an impartial, professional and civilian arm of the law that could be identified as an 'agency of the community'. This was helped by increased state meddling in family relations, especially between 1895 and 1910. Truancy became a matter for police concern, giving the police a chance to become friendly custodians and soften their image as hired guns of the ruling class. Yet cultural persuasion was not always effective. The policing of truancy hardened working-class hatred for the 'traps': truant officers (usually lapsed teachers) were universally loathed.

Between 1890 and 1910 employer federations, chambers of commerce and manufactures blossomed. The bourgeoisie was putting forward its class interests in more sophisticated ways. Fed-

Old-fashioned liberalism is overtaken on both sides as class lines are drawn during the first decade after federation.

eration gave it an ideal opportunity to deny the existence of class conflict: the new nation's natural leaders would lead the country away from the disrepair of Barcaldine and Clermont towards stability, security and class harmony. In the years after federation, the bourgeoisie's political forces went through a long process of realignment, leading in 1907 to the fusion of the liberal and conservative factions into a single parliamentary party.

Stability proved to be short-lived. Not only did industrial tensions re-surface, as in the 1912 Brisbane general strike, but by the end of 1914 the nation was at war. Enthusiastic imperialists, the members of the ruling class launched an ideological offensive, quickly latching on to the ethos of Anzac and identifying themselves with the war effort. Yet it was mainly workers' blood that was spilt on the fields of France and the shores of Gallipoli. Occasionally, the well-heeled citizenry found a cushy job for themselves in intelligence rather than offering their bodies to 'God, King and Country'. Intelligence work usually meant staying at home, spying upon domestic radicals, far away from any physical danger. Moreover, sections of the Australian capitalist class were supplying the enemy. There were long-standing connections between German finance capital and important sectors of the Broken Hill base metal industry. Both B.H.P. and the Collins House Group continued these connections during the war, revealing a most ambiguous commitment to conventional ideas of patriotism.

There was much internal dissension in the war years. The activities of the Industrial Workers of the World (I.W.W.), the Great Strike of 1917 and other disputes, and the revolution in Russia, made the bourgeoisie fear that Sydney was on the brink of becoming another Petrograd. They began to wonder whether a democracy could possibly defeat 'a great autocracy' like Germany, and spoke of sending parliament and parliamentarians to the 'right about'. With the wartime emergency as an excuse, Australia went back to its colonial origins. It became a police state. As the commonwealth solicitor-general, Sir Robert Garran, later put it: 'John Citizen was hardly able to lift a finger without coming under the penumbra of some technical offence under the War Precautions Regulations.' Repression, particularly against the I.W.W., was ruthless, systematic and effective.

The bourgeoisie also strengthened its hold at the point of production, as outlined by Peter Cochrane's chapter in the second volume of this history. Some welfare schemes were stepped up, but this was accompanied by the introduction of 'scientific management' of the worker and the work-place. The war also saw the high water-mark of employer-sponsored 'bogus' unions. On the waterfront, and in the railways, in the steel, soft-drink and chemical industries, scab unions tried to draw workers away from the existing structures towards more 'sensible' company-run organizations. On top of that, a split in the Labor Party saw such people as Billy Hughes, the former Balmain firebrand and pioneer union organizer, cross to the bourgeoisie's parliamentary annexe. This was not the last time that a Labor 'rat' gave the bosses a valuable propaganda victory. Encouraging labour leaders to change sides was an enduring feature of ruling-class strategy. Thanks to such measures, the Great War saw the comfortable classes ascendant in two areas of warfare: in the internal struggle against the working class and on foreign battlefields against the Kaiser.

Despite these successes, at the conclusion of the war, it seemed that the ruling class had secured only a Pyrrhic victory. In 1919, Australian capitalism was in a parlous state. Disruptions in shipping had interfered with the flow of trade, raising prices and creating unemployment. The political dissensions of the war had wrought havoc on rule by consensus. There was widespread social and industrial turmoil. The dynamic of colonial capitalism had been broken.

Australian capital had to increase industrialization in order to survive. Its profits needed to be established on a new economic and social basis, which revolved around manufacturing and industrial capital. This involved stepping up labour discipline within the factories and vigorous state repression. Managers such as Essington Lewis prowled around B.H.P.'s plant on the lookout for less than assiduous workers. Policemen such as General Sir Thomas Blamey and W.J. MacKay, both enthusiastic pugilists, were also part of this new order of ruling-class control. Though the military became less willing to intervene in industrial disputes, the police periodically forgot their manners, most glaringly during a lock-out at Rothbury in 1929, where a police ricochet bullet killed an innocent bystander, Norman Brown.

Rarely was there a conservative government so finely attuned to the ruling class's interests as that led by S. M. Bruce between 1923 and 1929. Bruce's policy of developing 'men, money and markets' was deeply satisfying to the Australian bourgeoisie. Bruce lost no opportunity to attack the labour movement. In 1925 he introduced an immigration bill that set up procedures for deporting anyone born outside Australia who was convicted of an offence against the industrial or trading laws of the commonwealth. In 1926 he amended the Crimes Act to 'deal with industrial extremists' and changed the Commonwealth Arbitration Act to give the arbitration court greater powers to enforce its awards. But 'Spats' Bruce overplayed his hand. In 1929 the government was defeated in the House when it tried to repeal the Commonwealth Conciliation and Arbitration Act. A few months later it was swept from office at the polls.

This was a moment of truth for the ruling class. Worse was to come. Not only had they lost Bruce and been forced to deal with 'disloyal' Labor governments, but the onset of the Great Depression was deeply unsettling. The socialist pamphleteers were not the only ones who believed that depressions were the death-knell of capitalism. J. T. Lang, premier of New South Wales, commanded massive working-class support with his tirades against 'Money Power' conspiracies. His plans to repudiate interest payments to British bondholders struck right at the heart of the imperial cosmology of the Australian ruling class. There were hints that an expanding body of unemployed workers might strike back at the expropriators. The communists were widely regarded as a well-organized and substantial threat: they were biding their time, waiting in the shadows until 'the day' arrived when they would storm the temples of capitalism in Pitt and O'Connell, Swanston and Collins Streets. The bosses had good reason to believe that their ship was sinking. Never in Australia's history had bourgeois hegemony been more endangered. Never was rule by consent more in peril.

The ruling class had many elder statesmen who had weathered the storms of the 1890s. Some of them shared the brawling nature of the early colonial worthies. Appropriately, it was Sir Philip Goldfinch, grandson of the colonial governor Philip Gidley King, who occupied a central position in the bourgeois resistance during the depression. As general manager of Australia's largest private company, Colonial Sugar Refining Co. (C.S.R.), he used his business acumen to ensure that even though sugar consumption dropped dramatically, shareholders still received substantial dividends, and a strategic component of capitalist enterprise survived the hard times. The sugar king was also a major manipulator and financier of capital's newly formed parliamentary mouthpiece, the United Australia Party (U.A.P.). The U.A.P. was formed after another 'good' Labor man, J. A. Lyons, had been seduced into crossing sides. But Goldfinch's most telling commitment was in the area of counter-revolution. He was the principal figure in the secret army known as the Old Guard, which was set up by the ruling class to ensure that 'law and order' would prevail if the military and the police were overwhelmed. When he spoke privately and optimistically of the 'possibility of a dictatorship', he was no doubt influenced by sentiments imported from fascist Italy

The lone fighter, left after the slaughter by the banks of Labor Governments in Australia, is taken in the rear at the moment of victory.

and Germany, for such sympathies were widespread among those of his class and social position. He may also have been harking back to the days when his grandfather had presided over a colonial autocracy.

The difference between the 1890s and the 1930s mobilization was largely its sophistication. A capital strike was organized to erode the financial stability of Lang's New South Wales government. The Government Savings Bank was sabotaged. Pressure was placed on Sir Philip Game, the governor of New South Wales, to dismiss the rebel premier from office. Ultimately Game was placed in such an invidious position by the intrigues of the bourgeoisie that he had no other course to follow. A war of ideas was unleashed in the conservative press. Attempts were made to ban working-class literature. Violence remained a fundamental tactic. The special constables of the 1890s became the 'peace officers' of the Old Guard in the 1930s. The petit-bourgeoisie, attacked on both sides by big business and organized labour, flocked to the ranks of the New Guard, one of whose leaders was Major-General J. M. Antill, the grandson of Governor Macquarie's aide-de-camp.

Members of such paramilitary organizations and police frequently bashed unemployed workers and radicals. The military brushed up its plans for maintaining 'internal security'. Aircraft and tanks would serve the same ends as more rudimentary technology had in 1890-1. The murderous threat of Colonel Price hovered over the working class like an evil ghost.

Despite the rebel chorus, the blood did not stain the wattle. Capitalism survived another ordeal. Wage cuts placed the burden of economic recovery on broad proletarian shoulders yet again. Growing demand for wool to supply the Japanese army revived the wool trade. The ruling class began to regain enthusiasm for parliamentary democracy. In November 1935, Sir Philip Goldfinch took on a new job – he became a member of state parliament while concurrently holding down his 'man-sized job in civil life'. Goldfinch proceeded to use parliament as a forum to defend C.S.R.'s profits and criticize unemployment relief and other welfare schemes. It was a rare and largely pointless exercise. For the most part, big business could leave parliamentary politics to the political specialist – the lawyers and professionals who went into parliament grateful for a chance to represent business interests.

The respectable section of the community in full display at an international Rotary convention in 1935.

Never again would the parliamentary and business wings of the ruling class lie in such close proximity.

The rest of the 1930s was spent gearing up for the highly profitable exercise of war. C.S.R. opened an annexe to produce explosives. General Motors-Holden was lucky enough to have the specialized technology to produce 25 lb howitzers. In October 1936 G.M.H., Imperial Chemical Industries (I.C.I.), the Collins House companies and B.H.P. combined to form the Commonwealth Aircraft Corporation to build combat aircraft.

With British imperialism waning, Australia businessmen turned to the rising sun. Japanese capital was particularly vital in the pastoral sector. After the Japanese attack on Pearl Harbour, this economic dependence on Japan raised questions about the patriotism of leading Australian businessmen. Labor's Eddie Ward was the first to raise the allegation in Parliament that highly influential political, business, military and security figures had made a deal with the Japanese to establish a 'Brisbane Line', with the northern part of Australia to be handed over to a Vichy-style puppet state in the event of a Japanese invasion. The details of this plot were naturally well hidden, but enough leaked out about it to make the principal culprits, particularly their parliamentary wing, thoroughly unpopular with the great mass of working people. R. G. Menzies, the prime minister who as attorney-general in 1938 had wanted to export pig iron to Japan, lost power in temporary disgrace.

Nevertheless, the Curtin A.L.P. government showed that it was possible to learn to live with Labor. It was rule for, if not by, capital, an acceptable administration to foster class harmony and encourage working-class participation in the war effort.

As far as internal 'subversion' is concerned, the ruling class has been largely able to rest on its laurels since the 1930s. If it was a football team, its coach might be telling it not to become too confident. The anti-communist hysteria of the Cold War was largely an exercise in shadow boxing. It was partly inspired by the substantial growth in membership of the Communist Party of Australia, but also by the need to placate the United States. It certainly did not signify any genuine threat from below. The working-class challenge of 1890 to 1910 has never been repeated. Subsequent economic 'malfunctions', such as the 1961 credit squeeze, or the stagflation of the 1970s and 1980s, have not produced the disturbed social conditions of the 1890s or the 1930s. Nevertheless, the Australian ruling class has continued to try to turn back the clock. Prime Minister Menzies's attempts to ban the

Communist Party by legislation and referendum in 1950 and 1951 were compared with the fascist measures of Nazi Germany. But it could be argued equally that Menzies was as much a colonial autocrat born a hundred years too late as Adolf Hitler in antipodean disguise.

With the exception of the 1949 miners' strike, the military might of the capitalist state has been less necessary to contain the working class since the Second World War. The long boom of the 1950s encouraged a certain social quietude. Accommodation rather than resistance was the mainstay of bourgeois strategy. Wage concessions, profit-sharing and other incentives have been progressively introduced to co-opt and demobilize the working class. The welfare state became more embracing. Weapons of bourgeois warfare such as the motor car have become democratized. Consumerism built upon usurious help from hire-purchase firms has taken hold in working-class households. The working people have become increasingly fragmented. Proletarian solidarity has been broken up as factories have been moved to outer-suburban districts and the inner-city working-class communities dismantled.

These processes were part of the re-casting of Australia after the Second World War, according to a new framework determined by United States capital. The shift has brought substantial changes in the nature of the Australian ruling class. Corporate liberalism has taken hold and changed both its structure and its outlook. Foreign ownership has increased. Fewer of Australia's bosses reside in Australia. The relationship between business and political leadership has become less direct. The interconnections of capital have become more complex. The beaming television images of modern managers of Mammon reflect massive self-confidence and self-congratulation.

This is despite the emergence of a new chorus of dissent, as later chapters in this volume will show. In the 1960s the sons and daughters of the bourgeoisie turned against their parents, conscription and the Vietnam war. In May 1969, more than one million workers around Australia downed tools in support of tramway unionist Clarrie O'Shea's stand against the penal powers of the arbitration court. Six years later, the man who jailed O'Shea again precipitated a potentially explosive situation when, as governor-general of Australia, he dismissed the Whitlam Labor government from office. The echoes of November 1975 still resound in Australia. And to some extent the peace, feminist, gay, land rights, residents' action and conservation movements all represent threats to the ruling class's preferred scheme of things. They make it difficult to expropriate surplus value 'with the minimum of fuss' and expatriate it 'home' to the United States, Japan, Great Britain and West Germany.

To ensure that these threats do not get out of hand, police forces have been increasingly militarized and the secret state – principally A.S.I.O. – expanded at a time when welfare services are increasingly contracted. Sections of the ruling class have also forged links with a new ally – the A.L.P. government of R.J. Hawke. The fear that surrounded the A.L.P.'s emergence and lasted until the 1930s has finally been allayed. Cowed into silence by the events of November 1975, Labor governments maintain business links and pursue policies that the conservative parties might envy. This could be seen as destroying the prospects for social change. But perhaps modern Labor's frank and unqualified support for the values and aspirations of the ruling class will finally lay to rest the illusion that there can be a parliamentary road to socialism. It has certainly encouraged the left to re-group. After 200 years, maybe the Australian people will begin to make, as well as to write, their own history.

Only the Chains have Changed

PATRICIA GRIMSHAW

From 1969, Australians became increasingly aware of the women's movement. Insistent voices were arguing that women must gain equality with men. Throughout the country groups of women responded to the new feminist demands in a variety of ways. The paths that led women into the movement can be illustrated by looking at the experiences of two women who became involved at this time.

Ann Curthoys was a postgraduate student in Sydney when she first heard of the women's liberation movement. During an anti-Vietnam march late in 1969, she was handed a simply produced leaflet. On the front was a drawing of a woman in chains, with the caption: 'Only the Chains have Changed.' Inside was the bald statement: 'TO BE A WOMAN IS TO BE OPPRESSED.' The leaflet went on to argue that, while Australians paid lip-service to the notion that all people should be free and equal, in fact half of the population was denied the right of full participation in society from birth. Women were forced into a 'woman's role' as good wives and mothers, obedient followers of the *Women's Weekly*, regardless of their interests and abilities. Femininity meant being 'sweet, attractive, submissive, understanding, dependent and defenceless'. The women's liberation movement offered a way of breaking those chains. The struggle would not be easy, the pamphlet warned. No group in society could be free while capitalists held the real power:

The same powerful class of business tycoons who profit from women's cheap labour, who pressure women to pay them high prices for cheaply made goods, and who decide that our resources should not be spent on welfare but should be spent on arms – this same class is leading the war in Vietnam!

The pamphlet announced a women's liberation meeting early in the new year. Ann decided to go along. She had not viewed women's status in quite this light before. The daughter of left-wing intellectuals, she had been attracted to socialism and put her energies into the anti-Vietnam war movement. She had soon discovered that some of the women in the movement were unhappy with the way the 'New Left' treated its female members. Liberationist groups in other countries, especially in America, were placing more emphasis on personal freedoms. Yet they did not apply this thinking to women. The women who joined these movements were seen as followers rather than as leaders. Male members were preoccupied with the problems of class at home and imperialism abroad and were inclined to laugh at women's issues. Ann responded to the women's grievances. Like hundreds of others all around the country, she threw in her lot with the women's liberationists. She was drawn by their determination to share personal experiences of sexism, to shape new theories and to work out ways of sharpening society's awareness of the need for revolutionary change in gender relations.

Avidly reading feminist theory, Ann worked with a collective based in the suburb of Glebe to found a journal, *Mejane*, to spread the views of women's liberation more widely. There were small groups with different goals and activities; but, understanding that 'the personal is political', the women stressed the need to share experiences as a basis for developing theory. Dozens of 'consciousness-raising groups' sprang up throughout the country. No one knew how many adherents the movement had. Women's liberation had an anarchist style and set its face against the usual trappings of formal organizations – membership lists, office-bearers, hierarchies of power and status. Sisterly co-operative groups would show society better ways of working together towards humane goals.

Joyce Nicholson came to the feminist movement two years after Ann. Joyce was in her early fifties, married with four children, and living with her professional husband in the comfortable Melbourne suburb of Hawthorn. In April 1972, she went to a meeting of a new feminist organization, the Women's Electoral

Lobby (W.E.L.). The year before, Joyce had read Australian-born Germaine Greer's radical review of women's status in *The Female Eunuch.* The book had an enormous impact on Joyce. She began to look back on her own experience in a new light. There had been her years as a dutiful daughter, basking in her father's praise for doing well at her private school and at Melbourne University. Then there had been the early years of marriage, when she had loathed being tied down to home and children and had shut herself off for stolen moments to write. Later, she had spent some time back in paid work, running her father's publishing business, but found her enjoyment marred by the guilty struggle to do the right thing as a wife and mother.

Reading *The Female Eunuch* was a revelation. The tensions she felt were not personal, she realized; they were structural, the result of 'sex-role conditioning', which forced women into a subordinate place in society and left men free to monopolize the spoils. When Joyce saw a notice in the local paper announcing a meeting of the Women's Electoral Lobby at the 'Women's Centre' in the city, she immediately decided to go along.

W.E.L. was only two months old. One Sunday at the end of February 1972, Beatrice Faust, a freelance journalist, had convened a meeting of ten women at her home to discuss an article on feminist political lobbying that had appeared in the American feminist magazine, *Ms.* The article had described how American feminists had rated presidential candidates according to their attitudes towards key feminist issues. The women who attended Faust's meeting, mostly professionals in their early thirties, were impressed. They decided to form themselves into a pressure group to lobby candidates for the federal election due later in 1972. Their aim was to advise women which candidates were most likely to represent their needs. 'Make Your Vote Count', they would urge; 'Think W.E.L. Before You Vote'.

Beatrice Faust had attended women's liberation consciousness-raising sessions, but they had left her cold. What was the use, she asked, of sitting and talking about personal experiences when you could be out pressuring those in power to change conditions by changing the law? As W.E.L.'s first pamphlet argued, there were no women in the House of Representatives, even though women had had the vote for seventy-five years:

> Women are discriminated against at work, at school, and in the home. Married women suffer many anomalies in tax benefits, medical and welfare payments. Single women are discriminated against through credit,

home loans and insurance.

All women suffer from laws which deny them the right to control their biological destinies by adequate sex education, inexpensive contraception and elective abortion – THESE THINGS MUST CHANGE.

The April meeting that Joyce attended had been convened to discuss the adoption of a constitution. To her amazement, a number of women got to their feet and walked out when the constitution was proposed; they were completely opposed to structures such as constitutions. In other ways, the meeting was typical of what was to come. As Joyce, looking back, descibes it: 'Everyone late, everyone doing too much, everyone tired, everyone arguing, talking at once, but, full of enthusiasm, determination, excitement.' The media gave W.E.L. close attention, and the organization quickly spread nationwide. Joyce's previous business experience stood her in good stead. She became involved in the co-ordinating committee and in editing the *Broadsheet*; she gave interviews in the media, planned questionnaires, wrote submissions, collated information, attended marches. W.E.L. campaigned for women's issues across party lines: not for them the radical rhetoric of the Women's Liberation movement.

These were two facets of a movement that went on to impress, educate, astonish, repel and horrify people all over Australia. The movement was many-sided. It drew on diverse political ideas and appealed to women of all classes. Though its numbers were not large, it was highly influential. It suggested ways of achieving a fairer future. It gave many women a new sense of purpose and taught them to view the world in new ways.

Yet the women's movement itself was far from new. It had its first birth in the 1880s. The feminists of this era had fought a long and hard civil rights campaign against great odds. Their immediate aim had been to win legal equality for women, but they also had a broader goal: to change people's ideas about what women could do, and about their right to have a public presence. As the 1970s feminists soon realized, the massive efforts of these 'first-wave feminists' had been lost to memory because they had been ignored by those for whom men, and only men, made history.

This first feminist movement drew much of its inspiration from Britain, where feminism had a long history. At the time of the French Revolution, Mary Wollstonecraft had pleaded that women, too, should be included in the struggle for liberty, equality and fraternity. Her *Vindication of the Rights of Women*, published in 1792, spurred several decades of debate about the status of women in British radical circles.

But it was the liberal philosopher, John Stuart Mill, who gave the new European women's movement its strongest stimulus with the publication of *The Subjection of Women* in 1869. Mill argued that sex was the most obstinate barrier to the progress of women and hence to the development of humanity in general. The old forms of dominance were breaking down, yet the subjection of women persisted. It was hard to overcome because it was a peculiar form of oppression: it gave every last member of the male sex the liberty to dominate the person nearest to him. Meanwhile, the oppressed sex could not join together to fight for equality. Each woman was isolated in her separate household. Furthermore, women were educated to be emotional and inward-directed; their assertive, rational qualities were left undeveloped. They were reared like plants with half their roots in the hot-house, the other half in the snow. Man then looked at the woman he had created and marvelled at her 'naturalness'. But who could say what her true nature was? To escape their oppression, women had to be able to participate in public life. They should receive full civil rights, ranging from equality under the marriage laws to the right to vote and stand for parliament.

Mill's message reached Europe and America as well as Britain. It was received enthusiastically by small but dedicated groups of middle-class women. Industrialization was already changing the lives of many western women. As household production gave way to capitalist industry, working-class women were taking the skills they had learnt at home into the mill and the factory, where they worked for meagre wages, many taking on the double burden of work at home and in the world outside.

Middle-class women, in a sense, had the opposite problem. Their servants freed them from household work, yet they were shut off from most paid labour and from public life. Men of their class put them on a pedestal, romanticizing their moral virtue and spiritual superiority. Yet legally and socially women were subordinate.

Mill's reform agenda fell on fertile soil. Armed with their new ideas, unmarried middle-class women sought entry to higher education and professional employment. Their married sisters, who had long been active in religious and charity work, began to find themselves a role in more politically effective organizations. In scattered groups, small and large, feminists began to lobby for women's emancipation.

In 1869, Mill had suggested to Catherine Spence, a South Australian feminist, that there was unlikely to be organized protest in the Australian colonies because so many women were married and busy at home. Clearly, he saw the British movement as being powered by single, middle-class women's urge to gain a place in public life. But for once Mill was proved wrong. Ideas and literature moved quickly from Britain to Australia. A small but lively women's movement emerged in the colonies, and much of the feminist programme made rapid headway. Colonial women gained legal and political rights ahead of their sisters in the mother country.

The women's movement in Australia was shaped by several factors. First of all, those who joined were not only educated women with an intellectual attraction to feminism. There were also a large number of Protestant evangelicals, who came to the women's movement by way of social reform movements, particularly the temperance movement. Feminists also gained considerable influence on public opinion by linking feminism with a developing local myth: that of the pioneer woman who had struggled valiantly against great odds to mother a new nation. And the feminists' goals were wide-ranging and progressive by the standards of their time. If their vision stopped short of full equality, they nevertheless achieved most of their aims before the First World War.

It was one remarkable organization, the Woman's Christian Temperance Union (W.C.T.U.), that brought the Australian women's movement its grass-roots activists. The W.C.T.U. had begun in the American west during the 1870s. Bands of praying women invaded grog shops and bars, entreating men to stop drinking and publicans to stop selling liquor. It had soon grown into a lobbying organization of formidable strength. Under the influence of Frances Willard, an outstanding college lecturer with leanings towards feminism and Christian socialism, the W.C.T.U. had encouraged women of diverse backgrounds to gain a broad understanding of women's social position.

By the 1880s, the movement was strong enough to look overseas. American envoys helped to set up an Australian equivalent in 1887. Within a few years, the W.C.T.U. had picked up a membership of several thousand in the colonies, with branches in

Rose Scott

many city suburbs and country towns. Most members belonged to the Methodist, Presbyterian and Congregational churches. Most were middle class, coming from the families of shopkeepers, small businessmen and clergymen.

The union's watchword was 'For God, Home and Humanity'. Its central goals were to persuade drinkers to sign the 'pledge' and to persuade the public that alcohol was such a destructive drug that its sale and use should be strictly regulated by the state. It might seem a large step from campaigning against drink to campaigning for women to get the vote. But a change in gender relations was a significant part of the temperance women's vision of a reformed society. They were genuine feminists: they saw men as holding an unfair and often oppressive power over women, and they fought publicly to remove women's disabilities.

The link between temperance and feminism was understandable. As David Dunstan has discussed in an earlier chapter, masculinity and drinking were almost inseparable in colonial Australia. Whatever the joys of drinking, women knew few of them. Women did, however, bear the brunt of the ill-effects. It was they and their children who were physically abused, they who watched the next week's rent disappear into the pub till.

The women who joined the temperance movement developed new political skills through their campaigning. At the same time, they discovered just how powerless they were to press women's interests against the organized resistance of a large, lucrative, cynical industry. The way was open for a wider, though still cautious, feminist analysis.

The W.C.T.U. women were not the only advocates of the women's cause at the time. There were other feminists who stayed apart from the union. Some of these were educated women of social standing and influence in liberal political circles. Outstanding among them was Rose Scott, a woman of affluent family and enormous ability. With Lady Windeyer, wife of a Supreme Court judge, Scott formed a Women's Suffrage League in Sydney in 1891. She identified herself publicly with feminism and was also involved in a number of other reform campaigns.

In Melbourne, a Women's Suffrage Society had been formed before the W.C.T.U. came on the scene. Several forceful and intelligent women were active in the movement. Among them were Harriet Dugdale, Annette Bear-Crawford and Vida Goldstein, who produced a journal called the *Woman's Sphere* and was later to become the first woman to stand for the Senate under the new federal constitution.

Most of these feminists were rather more intellectually sophisticated than the average W.C.T.U. member, though they too were often Christians and opposed to alcohol. Most of them worked through very small groups, but they also helped to form alliances that brought together representatives of all the organizations sympathetic to women's suffrage. Temperance leaders such as Elizabeth Nicholls in South Australia and Marie Kirk in Victoria were prominent in these alliances. In spite of the differences between them, the temperance and non-temperance feminists had very similar policies, strategies and goals.

There were also a number of feminists with labour sympathies, among whom Louisa Lawson was one of the most notable. Her women's journal, *Dawn*, was founded in 1888; her 'Dawn Club' gave women a chance to acquaint themselves with the new feminist ideas and discuss ways of broadening women's participation in public life. Lawson spoke with a fresh voice. She pointed out many of the ways in which men set the boundaries of women's lives. A woman, she noted, could not bear a child without its being delivered by a male doctor and baptized by a fat old parson. Furthermore, she wrote:

> A girl goes through life obeying laws made by men; and if she breaks them, a male magistrate sends her to a gaol where a male warder handles her and locks her in her cell at night... If she gets so far as to be hanged, a male hangman puts the rope round her neck; she is buried by a male gravedigger; and she goes to a Heaven ruled over by a male God or a hell managed by a male devil. Isn't it a wonder men didn't make the devil a woman?

Years of hardship rearing four children alone in Sydney made Lawson intensely aware of women's economic subordination. She was also influenced by contact with like-minded people in local radical circles. Her social critique ranged widely. She wrote of women's exploitation both as workers and as consumers and spent a lot of time ridiculing the culture that was foisted on the housewife by manufacturers keen to expand the market for new pieces of frippery.

There had long been links between the women's and labour causes. The early socialist movement in Britain had included many advocates of women's rights. In 1884, Friedrich Engels had set out a Marxist position on women's emancipation in *The Origin of the Family, Private Property and the State*. He argued that, under capitalism, women needed full civil rights and wage equality to make them equal to men; but women's true liberation would take place when they worked with men to bring into being a socialist society in which there would be no exploitation based on sex or class.

Many labour leaders, however, paid little heed. They were mainly interested in protecting men's jobs and viewed women's emancipation as a threat. The labour movement's apprehensiveness can be seen in this comment made in the *Worker* newspaper in 1903:

> Women's organizations in Australia seemed inclined to plead the cause of the woman who competes with the man in the wage mart, and to forget the claims for sympathy of the woman who stays at home. Justice for the Homeworker should be a plank in the women's platform.

Yet there were many individual socialists, both men and women, who firmly championed women's rights within the Labor Party and the union movement. Bertha McNamara, for example, was a leading figure in Sydney's Social Democratic Federation and later a Labor Party supporter. Her battle for social justice included advocacy of women's rights as well as support for socialist causes.

The character of the socialist women's platform is made clear in an address given in Melbourne during 1893 by Rose Summerfield, women's organizer for the General Labourers' Union. At the Trades Hall, Summerfield argued that woman had to be freed from 'economic thralldom', to be 'permitted to take her place as the mate and equal of man'. She also issued a 'call to her sex'. Did not working women toil for others' comfort? Had they not brains to think with, hands to work with, strength, energy and concentration? Then, she urged, they had 'a right, the indispensable right to fair and just compensation'.

Socialist women continued to press this right in the early years of the twentieth century. Middle-class feminists were also pressing for changes in the work-place. They called for protective legislation to safeguard women's health at work and argued that women who had to earn their living deserved better pay. The socialist feminists' emphasis was different. They argued that any woman had a right to a secure place in the workforce. They campaigned not only for higher wages but also for the widening of job opportunities. Their demands were couched in terms of the wider class struggle. Women's union activists saw organizing women in the work-place as an essential first step towards mobilizing them politically.

The labour movement was slow to respond. Differences began to emerge among socialist women. Some insisted that the only way to make gains was to continue working within the male-dominated structures of the Labor Party and the unions. Others looked outside, to an alliance with other feminists. The issue came to a head in Victoria in 1913, during a campaign for equal pay. Some women's union activists had lent support to a non-party equal pay rally, while others opposed any alliance with non-Labor women. Bitter dissension followed, giving hostile elements on the Labor executive an ideal excuse to get rid of the Women's Organizing Committee, which had been the main focus for women's activities inside the party. This was only one instance of a problem that would plague women in the labour movement.

All advocates of women's rights had to contend with the entrenched idea that 'woman's sphere' was in the home. 'We do believe in women's rights. We do', declared the *Australian Women's Magazine and Domestic Journal* in May 1884. 'We believe a woman has a right to a good home, a devoted husband, and a baby she is sure is the handsomest baby that ever was, and we believe she should have 'em!' Femininity was associated with caring for home, husband and children; women were very often regarded as passive, dependent, emotional and stupid. The Victorian version of femininity was more positive, emphasizing the purity, moral force and spiritual leadership of the 'good' mother and wife. And this was also the feminists' starting point. Few of them took to heart Mill's subtle arguments about the way ideals of femininity were constructed. Women, they insisted, *were* different from men. It was by manipulating this idea that they justified extending women's sphere into public life.

Their basic argument was that women needed opportunities to spread their moral influence into the public as well as the private sphere. The world must become a home, a family. Of course women needed to vote and engage in public life, declared the *Dawn*. Men's ways of reasoning and acting were material, physical and passional; women's sympathies and intuition led them towards higher goals. And 'the two united constitute both strength and beauty and the perfect *one*'. As long as there were sick, orphaned and erring people, said the *Woman's Sphere*, there would be 'a need for women's acumen and women's sympathy' in the public sphere. 'Public life has suffered from want of her.' Or, as a temperance feminist put it, women had struggled too long to fit their sons for the world; they needed now to fit the world for their sons.

The colonial feminists' approach here was broadly similar to their English sisters'. The model they drew on to give their arguments force, however, was not the English 'angel of the home', but the local myth of the sturdy, independent 'colonial helpmate'. The 'colonial helpmate' was courageous and practical; she could cope with any challenge. Had she not borne the new generation that had transformed the colonies? Had she not built up a home and livelihood in the wilderness? Had she not brought the comforts of civilized living to the frontier, taming male roughness and violence with her gentle hand? How could anyone deny such a vital person civic equality?

As the W.C.T.U.'s *White Ribbon Signal* asserted, it was not in the interests of the race to degrade women by making them slaves for men's service or dolls for men's amusement. Woman must be 'an equal, a companion, a co-partner, and a co-worker in all departments of life'. Their appeal struck a sympathetic chord in some men. As one Victorian Member of Parliament put it when he spoke in favour of the women's vote:

> We were just what our mothers made us very often. We talked of men going out to battle and taking their lives into their hands ... but we knew that in every case a mother took her life in her hands in the birth of her offspring. A woman had to stand by her home and brave many dangers of life, and it was really she who built up the nation, and performed many important duties which went to make up the strength of the nation.

From the 1880s until the First World War, the feminists campaigned on this basis. They held public meetings, churned out pamphlets, wrote to newspapers and lobbied politicians. It was a civil rights campaign of genuine significance.

The fight for the vote was their most visible and controversial struggle. 'Are Women Citizens?' asked the Victorian Women's Suffrage Society. 'Yes! when they are required to pay taxes. No! when they ask to vote ... Does law concern women? Yes! when they are required to obey it. No! when they ask to have a voice in the representation of the country.' But the vote was not the only item on the feminists' agenda for reform. Vida Goldstein's Women's Political Association listed a long string of aims: equal marriage and divorce laws, equal parental rights over children, equal rights to bequeath property on death, equal pay for equal work, the appointment of women to a range of public offices and their election to local councils. In a wider context, feminists campaigned for peace and arbitration, for new liquor laws, for reform of child welfare legislation, for pure food and milk supplies and for educational reform.

The feminists upheld the primacy of marriage, but strove to equalize women's position in the family and in the world outside. If marriage was to be honourable, it had to be freely chosen, not based on economic dependence. So women needed better education, better work conditions and access to a wider range of jobs, including professions such as law and medicine. And if women were to be faithful to their husbands, men should abide by the same rules. Feminists fought Contagious Diseases Acts that required prostitutes to submit to health inspections but let their customers go scot-free. They pointed to the absurdity of society ostracizing unwed mothers but not the men who seduced them. They also argued that wives should have rights over their own bodies within marriage and should be able to control childbearing by regulating their sexual contact with their husbands. Every wife had the right to 'voluntary motherhood'. 'Wives have a right to demand of their husbands at least the same consideration that a breeder of cattle extends to his stock,' stated one feminist bluntly; unlike most, she favoured artificial contraception. Deliberate efforts to limit family size contributed to the transition to a low birth rate in the 1890s and early 1900s.

The feminists were remarkable for their perception of women's social disadvantages. But their vision had its limitations. It stopped short of a class awareness that might have liberated working women; and it stopped short of any transformation of what Kate Millett was later to term 'sexual politics'. Civil rights for women did not solve the central problem of women's economic dependence on men. Only isolated feminists within the socialist movement had embraced Engels's argument that women could not be independent when thrown into lifelong dependency on men to bring in an income. Feminists had applauded motherhood and domesticity while arguing that women's sphere should not be confined to the home. But for most wives, even with smaller families, domestic life would continue to be restrictive. The feminists were listened to only because they were moderate enough to appeal to at least a substantial minority of men. More radical voices fell on deaf ears.

Women were given the vote in South Australia in 1894, in Western Australia in 1899, in federal elections in 1902, and in all remaining states by 1908. The central goal having been won, the movement splintered. It did not, however, die away. The vote gave women influence on issues that affected them closely. Enfranchised women became important to the political parties, and women's groups formed on both labour and anti-labour platforms. The Australian Women's National League, formed in Victoria in 1903, was one organization that married a commitment to equal rights for women with a conservative political outlook. The Australian Labor Party established women's auxiliaries where women could help support the party and promote women's interests. There were also many small non-party feminist groups, most of them short-lived.

Feminists were seriously divided in their attitudes to the First World War. Pacifist women opposed the war. Had women's status not been promoted on the basis of their superior qualities as nurturers and peacemakers? Many feminists, however, went along with the militarism of the time, creating bitter conflict. But the story was not only one of political division and fragmentation. The National Council of Women was set up in 1896 as an umbrella organization, with delegates from a wide range of women's groups, including religious and charitable groups as well as others of a more feminist bent. An Australian Federation of Women Voters was formed in Western Australia by Bessie Rischbieth in 1921. It was decidedly feminist in its aims, and it soon incorporated a number of other organizations, including the Women's Service Guilds of Western Australia, the League of Women Voters in Victoria and South Australia, and the United Association of Women, which was the brainchild of Jessie Street, another notable feminist. The federation's main goals were to promote women's representation in politics, on juries and on government boards and commissions. The federation split during the Second World War, with Bessie Rischbieth objecting to Jessie Street's pro-Labor and pro-Soviet sympathies. Yet, despite such divisions, many women continued to agitate for greater equality into the 1950s.

Their battle was a difficult one. Australian society was becoming increasingly complex. Public rewards went to those with legal and organizational skills, money, connections, self-confidence and assertiveness: in other words, to men. The 'feminine' virtues of kindness and unselfishness won few races. Women were excluded from positions of power and status. Occasionally, a successful man's mantle might fall upon a female family member. Thus Enid Lyons, wife of premier Joseph Lyons and mother of twelve children, became the first woman to gain a seat in the federal House of Representatives in 1943. But for the most part women were subordinate in politics and took a secondary place in all other fields of public life.

Not even those women who were most favourably placed in terms of wealth, education and class were taking an equal place with men. Most of the formal barriers to women's equality had been removed, with the crucial exception that women were far from having access either to equal pay or to equal work. In the eyes of employers and the arbitration courts, men were the breadwinners; they had to earn enough to support their families. Women did not; their wages supposedly went only to support themselves or to supplement the man's earnings, so they needed to earn less. At the same time, men still took the lion's share of opportunities for training and employment. In the labour market as well as in the home, the work women did was mainly the work that men did not want to do. The gender division of labour changed during wartime, when women were needed to do jobs that had traditionally been reserved for men. But when the wars ended, employers, trade unions and the state lost no time in restoring the old order. The achievement of civil rights had clearly failed to solve the 'woman problem'.

It was to tackle this problem that women began to reappraise their position in the second wave of feminism that began in the 1960s. Again, many of their ideas were drawn from overseas, though this time it was women rather than men who were articulating them and Americans rather than Europeans who led the debate. In America, as in Australia, the new women's movement

An equal pay demonstration in Melbourne during the 1950s

was divided. On the one hand was the National Organization for Women (N.O.W.), which was formed by Betty Friedan in 1966. Three years before, Friedan's *The Feminine Mystique* had presented a forceful analysis of the problems experienced by women confined to the home. Her solution was clear-cut: women needed to find work in the public arena, where they could find the same satisfactions as men and make the same contribution to society. To this end, Friedan formed N.O.W. as a lobby group for women's causes. In particular, N.O.W. set out to take full legal advantage of the Equal Pay Act of 1963 and the 1964 Civil Rights Act, which promised to expand women's opportunities for employment.

On the other wing of the American movement were women who had been involved in, and influenced by, the liberationist groups of the 1960s, especially the black power movement and the campaign against the Vietnam war. The organizations that these women began to form in 1968 were very different from N.O.W. in style and focus. They began to formulate a radical feminist position. Their central texts were Kate Millett's *Sexual Politics* and Shulamith Firestone's *The Dialectic of Sex*, both published in 1970; the British New Left feminist Juliet Mitchell's *Woman's Estate* was also influential.

For Millett, patriarchy was a dominant feature of western society. The reins of power were held by men. Women were kept down chiefly by being made to conform to stereotypes of femininity. Even the most intimate relations between the sexes were shaped by male power. This point was reinforced by Germaine Greer in *The Female Eunuch*. Greer took a combative approach, especially in interviews. To a *Playboy* interviewer in 1972, she said, 'We've been castrated. It's all very well to let a bullock out into the field when you've already cut his balls off, because you know he's not going to do anything; that's exactly what happened to women.'

Shulamith Firestone gave greater emphasis to biology as the basis of male power. She argued that Marxists, while emphasizing class relations arising from production in the public sphere, had neglected the class relations arising earlier within the household from the process of reproduction. Juliet Mitchell also criticized Marxists for concentrating on production to the neglect of the family, where human beings first acquired their identity. All these writers looked to the establishment of democratic socialist states, though they did not believe that socialism alone could solve the problems of gender relations.

The different strands of feminist theory came to be classified as liberal feminism, radical feminism and socialist feminism. Liberal feminists sought equity for women within capitalist society, although they often criticized the excesses of consumer capitalism and showed concern for welfare issues. Radical feminists viewed the domination of men over women as the primary constraint on all women's lives, though they also recognized that it would eventually be necessary to end a class society. Socialist feminists, by contrast, continued to maintain that class was the main determinant of all people's lives, and sought to incorporate feminism within a Marxist theoretical framework. For many women, however, these distinctions were not important; what was important was the fundamental challenge that all feminists posed to the social relations between the sexes.

There were many reasons why feminist ideas were making sense to a sizeable minority of western women in the late 1960s and 1970s. Women's economic roles were changing. The notion that 'woman's place was in the home' was becoming increasingly irrelevant. The boom after the Second World War had seen a rapid expansion of employment in manufacturing and service industries. Both these sectors had long employed a lot of women, though mainly at the bottom of the job ladder. At the same time, capitalism was increasingly invading the 'private' sphere of family life. A multitude of mass-produced goods streamed out of the new factories into homes throughout the western world.

In Australia, as elsewhere, there were rising pressures for married women to stay on in paid work, or return to work after their children started school. Not only was there plenty of work available, but the lure of earning money to buy the new consumer goods was strong. No amount of careful money management could earn enough to buy that second car. Married women's employment rates climbed, helped along by improved methods of birth control. In 1921, only 9.2 per cent of women in the paid workforce were married; by 1970, the figure was over 53 per cent. Most worked of necessity rather than choice; married to working-class men, often to migrants who were discriminated against at work, they had to bridge the gap between their husbands' earnings and their families' needs. But there were also those who worked because they wished to do so, whether to escape the confines of the home or to assert their economic independence. The possibility of finding a role in the public sphere stimulated younger women of the student generation to accept new political and social agendas.

Out of these changes the modern Australian women's movement emerged. The radical groups were sparked off by the movement against the Vietnam war, while the formation of W.E.L. in 1972 owed much to the exciting prospect of Labor's gaining power at the federal level for the first time in twenty-three years. The radical and reformist wings had different styles, different political bases. But in practice their reform goals overlapped, and their paths of development ran parallel through the 1970s and early 1980s.

The radical groups challenged accepted ideas about sexuality, family relationships and consciousness of gender. They also challenged the power of the state and the structure of economic life. The early radicals attacked on a wide front. The Canberra feminist group, for instance, began in 1970 with about twenty or thirty women meeting in a student household. They used a poster of Freud as a dart-board; they formed numerous consciousness-raising groups, and discussed all facets of women's lives – sisterhood, sexuality, childcare, education, housework, employment,

International Women's Day in Melbourne, March 1978

communal living. As Susan Magarey recalls:

> We saw ourselves as feminist revolutionaries, committed ultimately to the total transformation of our whole society, indeed of all societies. Our struggle against the power of men over women, of masculinity over femininity, was also, simultaneously, a struggle against any element in society having power over another – employer over worker, white over black, native-born over immigrant, teacher over student.

The Sydney feminist Barbara Levy described the movement as having its tone set by the example of the anti-war student movement, its model in the black power movement. These were educated women; they expected to be able to enter elite occupations; their resentment grew when they realized that they were being thwarted. They were also, she argued, women without too much to sacrifice in their struggle. They were mainly used to an independent life, without husbands or children, and did not share most single women's stereotyped ambitions to find a good man and settle down.

But the revolutionary stance proved hard to sustain. After the first year or two, radical groups began to develop a range of practical programmes. By 1974 the Melbourne movement, for example, included a women's health collective, a half-way house for battered wives, a women's abortion action group, a rape crisis group, groups concerned with non-sexist writing for children and feminist music and theatre, and a 'grapevine' through which women could learn from each other about subjects ranging from car mechanics to women's sexuality. To support such a range of operations, even with a large amount of volunteer labour, it was necessary to apply for government money. Most detested having to do this, fearing that the movement would be swallowed up by the male political system.

After 1976, with the conservative political parties in power, there was some loss of hope. Divisions within the movement also became more serious. There were splits between socialist, anarchist and radical feminists, between lesbian and heterosexual feminists, between those who continued to reject structured organizations and those who were beginning to speak of the 'tyranny of structurelessness'. Some of the radicals began to look anew at the feminine stereotypes of nurturing, friendliness, peace-making, unselfishness. There was support for separatism and interest in the works of such writers as Mary Daly and Adrienne Rich, who argued that even if women's lives had been constrained by male power, their qualities still deserved to be celebrated.

The W.E.L. feminists had begun from quite a different starting point and were greeted with suspicion by the radical groups. W.E.L. fought to offer women a fairer share of the fruits of a wealthy capitalist society. They lobbied for better jobs for women, for child care, for more women in public office, for legal changes that would end many forms of discrimination. W.E.L. included many professional women who brought a wide range of skills to the task – in the law, the media, education and government.

This moderate brand of feminism stood to gain from the Whitlam Labor government. Indeed, among his earliest acts as prime minister, Whitlam supported the introduction of equal pay in the Commonwealth Public Service, appointed an adviser on women's affairs and began to subsidize the cost of the contraceptive pill. Though the main thrust of W.E.L.'s activities was to lobby the federal government, they also scored successes elsewhere. In Victoria, for example, Rupert Hamer's Liberal government was sympathetic enough to take a number of initiatives, such as passing anti-discrimination legislation, opening up the higher divisions of the public service to women and reviewing married women's access to superannuation.

But from 1976, the moderate feminists became less active. This was partly owing to the economic recession and the fall of the Whitlam government. It was also partly a result of members dispersing into new fields. Many who had been housewives went on to further education or to work; others found careers in the public service or in politics. Voluntary workers were hard-pressed, partly because W.E.L., like the liberationists, found itself dealing with women's personal, welfare issues as well as its lobbying work. Numbers dropped and the scope of activity diminished.

Increasingly, women who had been exposed to feminist ideas were moving into new arenas. One significant change was women's increased participation in the trade union movement, including the white collar unions. Over the 1970s the A.C.T.U. inched towards adopting a working women's charter, though with no great enthusiasm. Women activists in several unions succeeded in placing issues such as child care, maternity leave and equality of opportunity on the industrial agenda. If these reforms fell short of restructuring relations at work, the gains were nevertheless considerable. The most startling indication of women workers' increased industrial militancy was the seven-week strike by Victorian nurses late in 1986, which resulted in the nurses at last gaining a commitment that their status as professionals would be recognized within the health system.

In the late 1970s, Joyce Nicholson reluctantly stopped playing a prominent part in W.E.L.; she felt she had spent her energies, and her job was putting her under pressure. Ann Curthoys also withdrew from active involvement in 1981 after a serious dispute with other members of the collective that brought out the journal *Refractory Girl.* But neither stopped supporting women's issues, and a core of feminists remained to keep the organizations running. Both women had seen their cause make its mark, in legislation, in consciousness, and in the transformation of some women's lives. Yet neither could feel fully satisfied.

Feminists spoke persuasively of equal rights and equal opportunities. Yet they did not have the means to achieve equality of outcomes or equality of esteem. Poor women, Aboriginal women, migrant women, needed more than the feminists could offer. Even feminists' success in improving the lives of middle-class women had been incomplete. They had not been able to overcome the rigidity and inequality of a labour market that advantaged the full-time male worker with a wife at home to care for him and support his career. A gender division of labour that continued to place women's primary responsibility in the home inevitably limited what women could achieve outside. There could be no drastic change of gender stereotypes without a drastic re-ordering of productive work and class relations. The women's movement offered a brilliant critique of Australian society; stubborn forces still thwart the realization of that vision.

The Making of Homosexual Men

CRAIG JOHNSTON AND ROBERT JOHNSTON

Even before he sailed with his fleet to invade Australia, Arthur Phillip wrote the first words on male homosexuality in the colony. Discussing the proposed conduct of the expedition and treatment of convicts, he said:

> There are two crimes that would merit death – murder and sodomy. For either of these crimes I would wish to confine the criminal till an opportunity offered to deliver him as a prisoner to the natives of New Zealand, and let them eat him. The dread of this will operate much stronger than the fear of death.

This extravagant hostility to sodomy and sodomites sets the tone for subsequent attitudes within Australian white society. Despite this broad hostility, however, there has been a profound change in the perception of homosexuality over the years. Phillip and those who followed him were expressing shock at certain sexual *acts*, particularly anal intercourse, which were seen as 'unnatural'. At this early stage there was no perception of the homosexual as a distinct *person*.

Indeed, homosexuality as a concept, and even as a word in the language, is only a century old. The emergence of the word itself reflects changes in social attitudes. A hundred years ago, the homosexual was someone who indulged in perverse physical acts; now homosexuality is seen as a matter of leading a particular gay way of life. This change occurred both in Europe and in Australia.

The transformation was closely tied up with exploring the relationship between sexual practice and gender identity: trying to discover what we mean by 'masculine' and 'feminine'. In the nineteenth century, there was not such a clear distinction between sexual practice and gender identity. As a result, people with homosexual interests would imagine themselves as having changed gender – hence the strong 'traditional' association between homosexuality and dressing in the clothes of the opposite sex. Likewise, men who appeared 'masculine' and women who appeared 'feminine' could avoid being identified as homosexual, while still indulging in the physical act.

Towards the end of the nineteenth century, social scientists began to try to identify homosexuals as a distinct 'species'. Homosexual practitioners were presented as gender *inverts*. By the 1950s inversion was being distinguished from perversion. Inverts were seen as 'true' homosexuals – 'feminine' men and 'masculine' women. Perverts were 'pseudo' homosexuals: they were 'masculine' men and 'feminine' women who for some strange reason chose partners of the same sex. In each case it was assumed that the 'masculine' partner took the active role in the sex act.

Homosexual sub-cultures evolved within the framework of these dominant ideas. At first these sub-cultures could be found in social enclaves that tolerated such practices as cross-dressing. The development of sub-cultures accelerated after the Second World War, but it was not until the 1970s that people who identified as homosexual began to make a clear distinction between sexual orientation and gender identity. This was part of a social/political movement that contested the inferior position of homosexual and gender non-conformist practices. The movement brought together 'communities' of gay men and lesbians fired by a positive identification.

The history of homosexuality in Australia is mostly a history of the sexual practice. This practice has had an important connection with the wider phenomenon of homo-eroticism, or the development of loving relations between people of the same sex, not necessarily involving sexual acts. Homo-eroticism is closely bound up with the Australian myth of mateship, and through it with the national ethos. A history of Australian homosexuality must also explore the development of a people with a distinct identity. Within that identity, homosexuals have moved from acceptance of inferiority to the affirmation of 'ethnic' pride. This is the history of homosexuals themselves.

The Australian colonies were off-shoots of the most dynamic capitalist society in Europe: a society where the growth of large cities, the breakdown of extended family ties and the emergence of mass cultural forms encouraged the development of minority sub-cultures. In direct contrast, the Aboriginal population was supported by hunting and gathering and enjoyed a social organization based on extensive kinship networks. The structuring of Aboriginal society did not allow for the emergence of self-conscious homosexuals. That there are Aboriginal homosexuals today seems mainly to result from their incorporation into non-Aboriginal society and acceptance of European gender roles. This particular difference between Aboriginal and European society at the time of the invasion reflects a contrast between capitalist and pre-capitalist societies.

If there were no homosexuals as such in Aboriginal society, there is evidence to suggest that there was nonetheless a place for homosexual acts and a strand of homo-eroticism. This evidence, however, must be treated carefully. Our own particular cultural viewpoint can lead us astray in interpreting activities of another culture, and we have to rely on accounts written by observers who were often blinded by their own prejudices. When Carl Lumholtz, after extensive travels in North Queensland in the 1880s, described Aborigines as 'gay and happy', we can be sure he is not using the word 'gay' as we might today. Even when as assistant protector of Aborigines in Victoria, James Dredge writes, in 1845, 'In the licentiousness of their lives, they are as the men of Sodom, sinners exceedingly', are we right to assume that he is speaking of homosexual practices?

Geza Roheim's studies of Aboriginals in Central Australia provide the strongest argument for the existence of homosexual practices. He believed homo-erotic tendencies were displayed in the initiation period of the Aboriginal man. In his *Children of the Desert*, Roheim states that homosexuality was institutionalized among the Nambutji tribe. After initiation young men became the boy-wives of their future fathers-in-law, adopting the female role in sexual activities. The Aranda people allowed a man to have homosexual relationships with his wife's brother, since he belonged to the same marriage class as the wife. But individuals might resist an attempt to form such a relationship. 'If a man tried to do that to me, I would pull his penis out and then spear him,' one Aranda man told Roheim.

Roheim refers to other instances of homosexual practices. Pitjentara men masturbated each other before setting out on a blood-avenging mission. In the Kimberleys he found that men of seventeen or eighteen would take boys as lovers as a temporary substitute for marriage. And he writes of a women's corroboree in which the participants rubbed each other's clitoris with their legs and called to the bell bird to fetch home their male lovers.

Other observers contradict these impressions. Catherine Berndt reports that the Arnhem Land Aborigines believed sodomy to be rare among their people. She argues that the open association between the sexes in Aboriginal society made it difficult for unorthodox sexual practices to become establisned. Sexual intercourse held a central position within their social structures; in religious ceremonies it signified the renewal of human existence and the continuity of community and family life.

Whatever their attitudes to homosexual behaviour, the Aborigines had no concept of sexuality as obscene. The British invaders, however, brought vastly different attitudes. Colonial authorities had persistent problems dealing with homosexual activity. The greater number of men than women, first in the original settlements and subsequently on the expanding frontier, was the mainspring of their troubles.

From Van Diemen's Land, for example, it was reported that the scarcity of women led to four capital crimes: rape, carnal knowledge of girls under ten, homosexuality and bestiality. The dreaded jails at Macquarie Harbour and Port Arthur were renowned for the incidence of 'unnatural offences' among their inmates. In the early 1840s, Lieutenant-Governor Eardley-Wilmot wrote to the secretary of state for the colonies, expressing his concern over the extent of a 'nameless crime' within his domain. The last execution for sodomy in that colony took place as late as 1863.

The state moved early and consistently to suppress homosexuality. Given that the first colonies were penal settlements, institutionalized homosexuality should come as no surprise. But having established the conditions that favoured it, the state sought to prevent the practice. It cannot be argued, however, that it was merely a product of the convict system. In 1861 a select committee of the New South Wales Legislative Assembly found that in the prisons of Sydney and the Cumberland District were committed 'practices grossly obscene' and 'unnatural crimes of the deepest dye'.

The segregation of the jail and the isolation of the frontier both established a milieu in which homosexual acts were frequent among men. In *The Australian Legend* Russel Ward suggests that, in the absence of wives, the bushmen appeased their desire for close companionship by a sublimated homosexual relationship with a mate of their own sex. The isolation of their life provided both a practical and emotional need for such companionship. Later the sexual imbalance on the various goldfields around the continent reinforced this tradition of male bonding. Homo-eroticism became one of the pillars of Australian mateship, finding a range of expressions, from the loyalty of the Kelly gang to the writings of the bush bards.

Nevertheless it was from the city that the homosexual first emerged. The official response was hostile. The Australian colonies followed the lead of the British Criminal Law Amendment Act of 1883, punishing the 'abominable crime of buggery' with a maximum sentence of life imprisonment.

The hostility of the state and a society that encouraged rigid gender roles placed homosexuals in a position of double deviance. Men suffered from stereotypes just as constricting as those imposed on women. It was a constant struggle to attain the desired standard of masculinity. Some men signalled their refusal to play this game by acknowledging their own 'effeminacy'. The most obvious characteristic of Australian male homosexuals has been this double deviance.

A police raid on a boarding house in central Sydney in 1916 gives one example of how this double deviance worked in practice. Neighbourhood gossip that there was something strange about the house brought police surveillance. The police concluded that the boarding house was inhabited entirely by men. Each room was occupied by a male couple, posing as 'man and wife'. Offensive behaviour charges were laid when police observed some of these men embracing other male friends in George Street.

Police commentaries on this particular case pointed out that such offenders were often people with influence in high places. This suggests that homosexual sub-cultures were basically middle class. Although convicts, pastoral workers and miners may have practised homosexuality frequently, it seems to have been within the middle class that the sodomite evolved into the homosexual. No longer just an aberrant sexual practice but a distinct identity, homosexual sub-cultures began to reverse the gender roles of patriarchy, mirror-like, for each sex. As a result transvestitism took on a different meaning. In 1851, in Sydney, clashes occurred between police and sailors after some drunken tars were arrested for attending church dressed as women, for a lark. By the end of the century, such cross-dressing had taken on a new meaning: it indicated a distinct sexual orientation.

The First World War threw large numbers of men together in the barracks and the trenches. And after the war feminism, psychoanalysis and modernism all began to have influence. Niches were opening up in which embryonic sub-cultural life could develop. The homosexual became a recognizable type. Certain styles of clothing were associated with homosexuals, as writer Jack Lindsay found in the 1920s when his unconventional attire roused the hostility of the Woolloomooloo push and he was accused of being a 'queen'. The physique and mannerisms of homosexuals also became standardized in the popular mind. Dacre Esme Eugene in Christina Stead's 1934 novel *Seven Poor Men of Sydney* had a 'fluty' voice, and another character was described as possessing small manicured hands, fine wrists and pink and powdered cheeks. Now recognizable, the type was clearly socially unacceptable. The only sympathetic treatment of a homosexual in a novel of this period is found in Kenneth Mackenzie's *The Young Desire It* of 1937; and it is not until Elizabeth Riley's *All That False Instruction* in 1975 that such a treatment appears again.

The contempt heaped on such effete characters is clearly displayed in Lawson Glassop's *The Rats in New Guinea*, published in 1963. Set in a Second World War army camp, it introduces readers to 'well-known actor and radio announcer' John Hemilton who, fellow-soldiers joke, played the female lead in *Rio Rita*. When he approaches, the cry goes up from one soldier: 'Knock, knock, who's there? Baxter. Baxter who? Backs to the wall, here comes John Hemilton.' After this display the newly arrived corporal thinks to himself: Surely Hemilton was not a queen. That was one thing you feared – having a queen in your section.

By the 1920s, male homosexuals were firmly established as effeminate men who wore women's clothes. Heterosexual men were hostile. But a sub-cultural way of life had become accepted within bohemian circles in the largest cities. At the same time police activities against homosexuals continued, at its most vigorous on the 'beats', the public places where many men went in search of sexual adventure.

Between the wars a rare voice was raised timidly in defence of homosexuals. A Sydney doctor, Richard Storer, argued in his *Survey of Sexual Life in Adolescence and Marriage*, published in 1932, that humans were basically bisexual. Storer admitted that it would be difficult to convince many people that 'homosexuality is an endowment rather than a vice, and unmoral rather than immoral'. Yet he speculated that in the near future society would come to tolerate homosexuality, as having children became less important. Storer maintained that social hostility towards homosexuals prevented innocent people from expressing their normal sexual conduct. For speaking out, Storer had to endure an obscenity prosecution against his book.

Australian ideas about the psychological aspects of homosexuality were derived from European and North American sources, but they sometimes took on new form during the transfer. *The Book of Life*, published by *Health and Physical Culture* magazine in the early 1930s, critically examined what was termed the 'cult of effeminacy'. The authors, whose magazine extolled the virtues of sunshine and vigorous exercise, were troubled by the growing numbers of effeminate men in Australia. They traced this development back to the war years. As they saw it, when fathers enlisted in the army, the masculine influence vanished from countless homes. This encouraged an unnatural bonding between mothers and sons. The result was the homosexual, and the authors told readers what to look out for: 'One is able to see them on all sides, easily recognizable for their habit of referring to each other as 'she', for their quiet, decorous, almost feminine voices, and for their rather effeminate style of dress and of dressing their hair.'

If the upheavals that flowed from the First World War encouraged homosexual sub-cultures – though for different reasons from those suggested by *The Book of Life* – then the impact of the second global conflict was even greater. By the late 1940s the popular press was publishing sensationalist stories about male homosexuals, which suggested that there was a significant sub-culture. Despite this press attention it remained an underground network, with members actively trying to keep things quiet. Typical of the exposés popular at the time was a 1949 article in *Truth* that spoke of men with silver screen drag names such as Vivien Leigh, Victoria Lester and Merle Oberon and described the running of 'Queen of the Pansies' beauty contests.

A few years later the Australian press reported with interest the indecent assault convictions obtained against Montague of Beaulieu and John Gielgud. A comment on these cases appeared in *A.M.: The Australian Magazine* in November 1953, which attempted to give an objective picture of male homosexuality without the usual sensationalism. The anonymous author, described as a Sydney psychiatrist, discussed the homosexual clubs that existed in Sydney, the grapevine among mercenary and casual homosexuals, and the constant 'warfare' between police and homosexuals. The writer's comments clearly indicate that there was a complex male homosexual sub-culture. It had extensive social and gossip networks (which among other things passed on information about police activities), a high awareness of its own illegality and vulnerability and included a minor strand of male prostitution. The sub-culture still has these strands today; what has changed in the meantime has been their extent and openness.

New approaches emerged in the 1950s with growing scientific and medical interest in understanding homosexuality. Gender identity was at last being distinguished from sexual practice. Transsexuals and transvestites were recognized as distinct groups. Later, this would allow men to be homosexual without having to be 'effeminate' and women to be lesbian without imitating men's dress and behaviour. The *Health and Physical Culture* magazine of the 1930s could never have envisaged homosexuals taking on such new identities.

Meanwhile governments were tightening the rules in an attempt to suppress homosexuality. In 1955 amendments to the New South Wales Crimes Act made offences of acts of indecency with a male and procuring and soliciting a male. Speaking in support of these amendments, Attorney-General William Sheahan said: 'The government has acted because it considers that the homosexual wave that has struck this country – though not to the extent of continental countries – must be eradicated.' The attorney-general described homosexuals as pests and soliciting between men as an evil. He echoed the arguments of the 1930s, observing that the growing homosexual trend was caused by the enforced absence of so many fathers during the war years. To highlight the problem, he referred to one of the city's most fashionable hotels where the manager was regularly forced to call the police to remove homosexuals from the premises because their behaviour offended guests. It must be acknowledged, however, that comment was not uniformly bigoted. In the same debate a member of the Liberal opposition argued that the amendments would be ineffective and showed a familiarity with the more enlightened ideas contained in the 1948 American best-seller, *Sexual Behaviour in the Human Male*, by Alfred Kinsey.

The New South Wales government returned to the question of homosexuality in 1958. It established a special committee in June of that year to examine the causes and treatment of the phenomenon. In the same month the state's police commissioner, C. J. Delaney, had publicly warned that homosexuality was Australia's greatest menace. The committee comprised a psychiatrist, two priests and two prison officers. They apparently visited Cooma jail, where 70 per cent of prisoners sentenced for homosexual offences were housed. This unique policy of segregation provided the committee with abundant captive subjects for study. Their labours extended over five years. By mid 1963, a report was ready for release. Dubbed 'controversial' by the *Sydney Morning Herald*, it has never seen the light of day. At the time there was speculation that the report was rejected because it tried to discuss the subject rationally and presented recommendations of a 'mature and tolerant' kind, in line with those suggested by the British Wolfenden report of 1957.

Throughout the 1950s and 1960s the popular press continued to look for sensational headlines. The Wolfenden report itself fell victim to this treatment. The heading in *People* magazine of October 1957 was typical: 'Shock Sex Report.' And at the time there was a lot of activity to report, as relations between the state and homosexuals continued to be aggressive and confrontationist. These were the days when gays resisted police raids on a Kings Cross bar, when police raided private parties ('The boys in frocks shock the cops'), when a purge was held at Puckapunyal army camp, when police provocateurs hung around well-known beats, and when it was claimed that organizations dealing with young males were the centre of a vice ring.

At the same time, however, a more inquiring and dispassionate response to homosexuality began to emerge. The movie, *Tea and Sympathy* in 1956 broke fresh ground with its examination of masculinity, and *Victim* in 1961 bravely addressed the subject of the vulnerability of homosexuals in a hostile society. In the written word new perspectives emerged from a variety of directions. Between 1959 and 1961 Roger Casement's diaries were published, an enlightened article appeared in *Popular Medicine*, and customs bans were lifted on certain books, including D. J. West's *Homosexuality*. Such magazines as *Life*, *Time* and the *Bulletin* later began to treat the subject with more sensitivity. On another front, in May 1967 the General Assembly of the Presbyterian Church in New South Wales called for the decriminalization of male homosexual acts between consenting adults. By the mid 1960s it was clear that the surge of hostile popular opinion was ebbing, and that opportunities were opening for a more liberal response.

On 27 July 1969, the Australian Capital Territory Law Reform Society was established. The society's aim was the amendment of the statute regulating male homosexual behaviour in the Capital Territory. Although it was a civil liberties group and not a homosexual political organization, its creation signalled the beginning of organized resistance to official views and practices on homosexuality.

The years 1969 to 1978 saw the first phase of that resistance: they were the years of the 'gay movement'. Almost immediately the Daughters of Bilitis/Australasian Lesbian Movement appeared in Melbourne, and in September 1970 the Campaign Against Moral Persecution began in Sydney. In a few years the latter group became a national organization and published *Camp Ink*, the first political publication for homosexuals. Gay Liberation groups associated with the New Left and the counter-culture sprang up in many cities after 1971. As the decade progressed, the range of organizations broadened and the movement set up its own publications. Organizations, newspapers and magazines were run by homosexuals for homosexuals. They raised political demands and opposed oppression and discrimination. They also affirmed homosexuality as a part of the normal continuum of human sexual expression and rejected the idea that it was simply gender inversion. These militant homosexuals actively confronted the regulators: not only the police, a traditional enemy, but also behaviourist psychiatrists who claimed to be able to 'cure' homosexuality by aversion therapy. That some homosexuals were seeking such therapy indicates that the experience of being homosexual often embraced guilt, self-hate and fear. As the Sydney physician Herbert Moran said of lesbian Eugenia Falleni in the 1920s:

> Falleni knew nothing of the literature of her own malady – nothing of Lesbian luxuriousness in high places. All she did realize was that her behaviour was unusual. She understood that most people loathed it. She was always afraid, terribly afraid of discovery.

It was this experience that gay liberation contested: the gay liberationists invited fellow homosexuals to make their own history.

The controversy surrounding the death of George Duncan in Adelaide in 1972 provided the impetus for South Australia to become the first state to decriminalize male homosexual acts. The federal parliament gave support in October 1973 when the House of Representatives passed a resolution that expressed the view that 'homosexual acts between consenting adults in private should not be subject to the criminal law'. Since then most of the states have followed this lead. In the early 1980s, several legislatures also made it an offence to discriminate against homosexuals.

The first phase of resistance brought changes in sub-cultural life. The political gay movements of the 1970s grew out of the broad political contests of the 1960s and early 1970s. They drew life from the radical intelligentsia. At first they were far removed from the existing camp sub-culture, which had been produced by many decades of painful oppression. Secretive and self-absorbed, this camp sub-culture was preyed on by organized crime; underworld personalities firmly controlled gay venues, particularly in the Kings Cross district of Sydney. Beats, such as Sydney's Hyde Park, which had a continuing history going back to the turn of the century, declined in importance as new meeting places emerged in the hotels, with their more liberal trading hours.

Gay activists add a note of their own at a Melbourne anti-uranium demonstration, March 1978.

At the beginning of this first phase of resistance, homosexuals identified themselves as 'camp'. The American term 'gay' was known but little used. The political movement changed the terminology. It rejected the idea of being 'camp', with its overtones of gender inversion. As 'gays', homosexuals could show their pride in what they were, just as the American blacks had shed the term 'Negro' to announce that 'black is beautiful'. The political movement eventually started to influence the established sub-culture. By the late 1970s, armed with this new pride and openness, the commercially oriented section of the sub-culture began to expand. At last the commercial homosexual press's coverage of the political movement's activities ended the movement's isolation from the sub-culture.

Australia's largest gay event, the annual Mardi Gras in Sydney, was first held in 1978. From then on the resistance entered its second phase: the formation of distinct gay communities. These communities accepted that homosexuality had evolved historically from an act to a state or condition and took it one step further to create a style of living ('be gay, think gay, buy gay').

The victories of the late 1970s and early 1980s were won at a price. In accepting the categories 'homosexual' and 'heterosexual', the gay communities relinquished the ideals of the radical founders of Gay Liberation groups – the attainment of general sexual liberation. They also signalled their retreat from radical ideals by their failure to go beyond the class, sex and race divisions of Australian society. The gay communities were a political victory for the middle classes, for the highly educated professionals of the post-war generation and the small businesspeople and hoteliers who serviced their leisure demands. It is not surprising that they were also predominantly white and male.

With the massive assaults on native cultures since the British invasion, the involvement of Aboriginal Australians and Melanesian Australians in the homosexual world has been on European terms. Those few blacks who identify as homosexual have an ambiguous relation to both worlds: a 'past' where homosexuals did not exist and a homosexual scene that is part of a white culture that oppresses blacks.

For lesbians, problems of relating to the most recent development of gay communities have focused on the ambivalence about the category 'homosexual'. Until recently in Europe women were assumed to have no sexuality of their own. The 'romantic friendships' of the Victorian era among bourgeois women were probably rarely expressed in physical terms. Women who were struggling to develop an independent sexuality could adopt the label 'homosexual', and many did. In establishing an independent sexual identity, some of them also adopted a non-conformist gender-identity. Both 'Bill Moran' and Eugenia Falleni are examples of women who lived large parts of their life as men. Lesbians generally mixed socially with men, and sub-cultural groups and venues usually attracted only a small female clientele.

Feminist lesbians have sought to deny that male and female homosexuality can necessarily be equated with one another. Attracted by the second wave of Australian feminism after 1970, they have been the backbone of many feminist projects. Their primary concern has been the development of feminist politics and women's communities rather than the homosexual political movement.

The insistence by feminist lesbians that their struggle will not simply be the other half of the struggle of homosexual men affirms the principle that resistance movements have to be independent. It stresses that they are movements of self-affirmation and self-definition. For male homosexuals the definitions tend to come from the state, whether it is Arthur Phillip's cannibal remedy for sodomy or liberal legislators conferring 'minority group' status on homosexuals by passing anti-discrimination laws.

These definitions have changed over time and are developed in uneven ways. Thus in the mid 1980s there was a revival of the nineteenth-century 'medical model' of homosexuality as a sickness. Certain critics in the church and the press strongly attacked homosexuality after unprotected anal intercourse was identified as having a high risk of transmitting the Human Immunodeficiency Virus (H.I.V.). The appearance of the Acquired Immune Deficiency Syndrome (A.I.D.S.) in many gay men also revived the religious fundamentalists' notion of homosexuality as a sin ('The wages of sin is death').

Notions of homosexuality have not been static, and the activities of sodomites, inverts and gays have contributed to this evolutionary process. This explains the survival of gay communities in Australia's major cities after the advent of A.I.D.S. These communities have used the positive self-identification of gay men, the network of gay-oriented institutions, and even the resources of the liberal state, to care for the victims of the virus and to continue the celebration of their distinctive way of life. The decolonization of sexual identity is still going on.

Escaping the Well of Loneliness

LIZ ROSS

Until the late nineteenth century, it was customary for women friends to walk around arm in arm and to embrace each other frequently. This was considered normal, and men did not object to it. Attitudes changed, however, when increased job opportunities for middle-class women enabled many women to live independently of men, and first-wave feminism began to challenge male domination. The accusation of lesbianism was often thrown at the women's movement, to counter the attempts of women to emancipate their sex. And sexologists such as Havelock Ellis, who was widely read in Australia in the 1890s and early twentieth century, wrote books about the horrors of lesbianism.

In the face of these sorts of attacks, the women's movement and the international 'sexual rights' movement of the day supported lesbians' right to their sexual preference. Radclyffe Hall's famous 1928 novel *The Well of Loneliness* has a central lesbian character lamenting:

> There are so many of us – thousands of miserable unwanted people who have no right to love, no right to compassion because they are maimed, hideously maimed and ugly. God's cruel; He let us get flawed in the making.

But the overall theme of the book was a positive argument for lesbianism. This was why the conservative forces of the time took action against it. Other writers such as Gertrude Stein, Renee Vivien and their 'circle' in France lived openly as lesbians and wrote novels and poetry about lesbian sexuality.

Nonetheless it took until the 1970s for a self-conscious and proud lesbian movement to develop, which argued for liberation not just acceptance. This chapter is an attempt to integrate a personal history with an outline of the recent history of lesbianism in Australia.

The story starts in Canberra in 1971. Germaine Greer's *The Female Eunuch* had just been published and had an electrifying effect on thousands of women all over the world. Greer's book was a revelation to me also. After years of confusion, the world suddenly made sense. I realized that private personal solutions, such as psychotherapy and a good job with a future, were not enough. I began to think in terms of seeking a collective political solution to the discrimination I had suffered. The Canberra Centre for Continuing Education was running a women-only course on 'Women and Society', so I attended this course and was exposed to more ideas on women's liberation and introduced to the notion of gay liberation.

In the period leading up to the 1972 federal election that brought the Whitlam Labor government into office, Canberra was a stronghold of the Women's Electoral Lobby (W.E.L.). But I joined the more radical women's liberation movement. Sisterhood. It was frightening, euphoric, wonderful, awesome and real. It offered an analysis and tactics; it suggested both a theory and a practice. There was so much to learn, so many meetings to go to, so many books to read. The movement related women's lives to existing political issues and created new political questions. Above all, it gave us the means to fight for change. Lesbians were actively involved in the women's liberation movement right from the start. And right from the start they bore the brunt of raising lesbian issues, confronting attempts to ignore and exclude lesbianism and lesbians from the movement. For instance, the coverage of lesbian issues in feminist publications was often minimal.

The issue erupted in a big way at the third national women's liberation conference held in Canberra in January 1973. This was a conference full of controversy, but the most contentious paper came from the Hobart women's liberation movement. It was entitled 'Sexism and women's liberation or ... why do straight sisters sometimes cry when they are called lesbians?' It began by stating:

> Just as women in left-wing movements became dissatisfied with waiting in the wings until the socialist revolution solved everyone's problems, lesbians have become increasingly dissatisfied with the women's liberation movement that demands the same of them.

The paper went on to criticize the way some structures of women's liberation – consciousness-raising groups and the concept of sisterhood – often excluded lesbians. It concluded:

> Women's liberation has so far failed to come to grips with sexism either inside or outside the movement and in fact there are signs that it is moving further away from grappling with this problem to (perhaps) up dated stereotypes of masculinity/femininity ... [By] merely attempting liberation through attacking some of the symptoms of sexism evident in patriarchal society, they have avoided basic questions and a commitment to basic ideology.

This paper sent reverberations throughout the women's liberation movement in Australia, shaking us from the comfortable notion that we only had to fight issues 'outside' the movement. Lesbianism became an issue within the women's liberation movement.

Before this conference, my feelings about my own sexuality were repressed and confused, and I was less involved in the women's liberation movement. Coming to terms with my sexuality on a personal level proved to be an easier process than coming to terms with lesbianism politically. That has been a much more drawn-out process, the theory following a long way behind the practice. I became very active in the women's liberation movement, helping to organize the march and other activities for International Women's Day in 1973, contributing to and helping to put out the women's liberation newsletter, while living in a lavender and black room in Women's Liberation House. Canberra lesbians moved about uneasily between the women's liberation movement and the gay liberation movement, occasionally meeting separately but not on any concerted basis. Within the women's liberation movement, they had been experiencing the problems outlined in the Hobart paper at the 1973 conference. So when Charlotte Bunch delivered her paper on 'lesbian separatism' at the International Women's Year Conference in Canberra in 1975, she struck a responsive chord.

The feminism and sexuality conference in Melbourne in 1976 was a major attempt to bring the issues of lesbianism, sexuality and sex roles to the fore of both women's liberation and gay liberation. I presented a paper that argued that all the scientific research so far undertaken into homosexuality should be rejected because its aim, explicit or implicit, was to turn gays into heterosexuals. But the first national gay conference, in August 1975 in Melbourne, was a greater landmark in homosexual politics and history in Australia. Many of the issues we are still discussing were first raised at this conference. Papers at this conference came under four main headings: 'How homosexuals are oppressed'; 'Why homosexuals are oppressed'; 'Homosexuality and Feminism'; and 'Homosexual movements – past and present'. Both women and men at the conference confronted the sexism of homosexual men and raised the general issue of sexism.

By the end of 1975 there was a lesbian separatist discussion group as well as a lesbian feminist group in Melbourne. There was no separate lesbian publication, but at last the gay liberation publications from all states and the women's liberation publications from South Australia, Victoria, Tasmania, the A.C.T. and New South Wales were covering lesbian issues. I moved to Melbourne at this time, a stimulating experience that exposed me to many of the debates over lesbian issues and also to the questions raised by the issues of class and race in relation to both women's and gay liberation. Involvement in active liberation movements is a very good education.

A lesbian conference was held in Melbourne in February 1976, and a lesbian political action group was formed as a result. This group was short-lived, a common problem with lesbian groups, as the activists easily become overcommitted because of their involvement in women's liberation, gay liberation and now lesbian action. Lesbian organization mushroomed nonetheless. There was a lesbian mothers' group, a lesbian consciousness-raising group and a lesbian resource centre. In March 1976 a lesbian newsletter appeared. This newsletter attacked 'heterosexism' and supported the rights of lesbians at work and to information on lesbian sexuality. Lesbian was seen as a political definition, not just a sexual one. It was at this time, too, that a gay liberation radio programme, the first in Australia, began on the Melbourne community radio station 3CR.

Lesbian separatism continued to be one of the major issues of lesbian politics. Lesbian separatism means the separate organizing of lesbian action groups, without either heterosexual women or gay men. I think that how lesbians organize, whether separately or not, is a tactical question. The answer can vary from one period to another, depending on your organizational strength and the strength of your allies. The decision made has to be the best one at the time for building a movement. While the women's liberation movement was strong, it was appropriate that lesbians organize separately. But separatism as it developed became more than a tactic for the moment; it turned into an ingrained practice and theory, a religion almost, that was reactionary and limiting in its effects. When the down-turn in general political activism came in

A new spirit of assertiveness marked the rise of lesbian politics, 1978.

the late 1970s, separatism became an inward-looking response to decline.

As the political climate changed, the need for joint rather than separate action became more pressing. It was necessary both to win short-term objectives and to bring about change in the whole society, clearing the way for further advances. I believed that it was no longer possible to bring about complete liberation for lesbians without overthrowing the entire system. After all, lesbianism challenges the traditional family set-up, which is such an important economic and social unit. Lesbian separatists seemed to be living in a fantasy world, out of touch with reality.

It was in the years 1977 to 1979 that left-wing political parties were most active in the homosexual movement, though left-wing activists had also been the founders and leaders of both the gay and women's movements. The first socialism and homosexuality conference was held in Sydney in July 1977, and a socialism and homosexuality newsletter started appearing around this time. Unfortunately, it didn't last long, and gay socialists had to turn once more to overseas sources for developments in the theoretical debates. The effect was that more people in the liberation movements began to link the position of gays and women with that of other oppressed groups and to become more aware of the issue of class.

After the fourth national homosexual conference in 1978, the Melbourne Lesbian Action Group was formed. It became the largest group of lesbian activists, and it formed several subgroups. It effectively replaced women's liberation as the political priority of many women. It met weekly, and lesbian politics flourished in Melbourne. The lesbian newsletter continued and grew in circulation and influence, and there was an active radio group broadcasting on 3CR.

The first open organizing of homosexual groupings came with the anti-Festival of Light campaign in 1978. This campaign was probably most effective in Victoria, but it had Australia-wide effects. The Festival of Light had invited the right-wing morals campaigner Mary Whitehouse to tour, to publicize their organization. They hoped the tour would help develop a strong right-wing backlash to the 'left' reforms of previous years such as abortion law reform, equal pay for women and homosexual law reform. But the campaign against the Whitehouse tour succeeded in exposing the Festival of Light as a small bunch of puritanical busybodies who believed they had a God-given right to dictate how other people ran their lives. The Festival of Light acknowledged that the campaign against them had made the tour a financial flop that left them thousands of dollars in debt.

Partly in response to the success of this campaign, 1978 was also a year of concerted police attacks on and arrests of lesbians and gay men in Sydney. These attacks continued for some time after, though not on the scale experienced in 1978. Lesbians and gay men, along with some left-wing parties and civil rights groups, campaigned actively and successfully to get these charges dropped.

The anti-Festival of Light campaign continued as the Campaign Against Repression, and it survived in this form until the fifth national homosexual conference in 1979. Its main target was the 'International Year of the Child', which opposed a woman's right to abortion and keenly supported traditional family structures, with all the limitations this posed for 'children's rights'. The Campaign Against Repression worked actively for recognition of children's rights. A pamphlet, *Young, Gay and Proud*, was published by a collective from the Gay Teachers and Students Group in August 1978, and the Campaign Against Repression actively supported its distribution to schools and bookshops. Right-wing pressure groups attempted, unsuccessfully, to have *Young, Gay and Proud* banned in schools. It was in this anti-child 'International Year of the Child', 1979, that Young Gays had their first meeting.

A look at *What's On* for October 1979 shows that lesbians were still actively involved in non-separatist organizations such as 3CR and 3RRR, La Donna Disco, Women's Liberation Bookshop, International Women's Day meetings, Gay Teachers and Students, *Gay Left* journal, Women Writers, Summer Offensive Campaign Committee, Gay Health and Welfare Workers, Gay Solidarity Group, Women Behind Bars, Women Against Rape, Women's Massage, Women and Labour Conference Collective and Gay Solidarity Group. And there was separate organizing, too, in the lesbian consciousness-raising group, Lesbian Action Group, and a lesbian health group, which held two very successful lesbian health days. In the lead-up to the fifth national homosexual conference in 1979, there had been considerable debate about whether to organize separate lesbian and gay male conferences. Eventually the Lesbian Action Group did organize separately, which I thought was a divisive step that only weakened activist organization.

The conference newsletter continued as *Gay Community News*, and is now published as *Outrage*. Initially this was a publication for activists, but it now focuses on literature and living, as well as some activist news from Australia and overseas. As a publication it has fairly accurately reflected the changing nature of gay politics in Australia. Lesbians and gay men have turned away from activist politics towards the pursuit of lesbian or gay male pursuits. The *Lesbian Newsletter*, which is still being produced, reflects much the same concerns.

In 1980 the Lesbian Action Group was debating issues such as religious guilt, the right-wing backlash, coming out, prostitution and drugs, and the long-running questions of lesbian separatism and lesbian feminist politics. Sport also became a subject of political debate and an area of active involvement, too. The lesbian newsletter published articles about these issues and commented on the state of the movement. It also discussed the issue of class. Di Otto wrote in *Lesbian Newsletter* in October 1980:

> We make the mistake of assuming that lesbianism, in itself, is a radical position. This has led us, in the past, to supporting a whole range of events, ventures, political perspectives, etc., just because it is *lesbians* who hold those beliefs or are doing things. It is as ludicrous as believing that every working-class person is a communist. Whilst it is important for us all to have a positive image of lesbians, it is conservative to ignore differences such as class and political perspective.

Her comments were prophetic, for the political differences among lesbians became apparent in the 1980s. In Sydney alone, for instance, there were strong groupings of anarchist lesbians, socialist lesbians and lesbian separatists. Many socialist lesbians turned their attention to organizing within the work-place. The Australian Social Welfare Union, for example, had a very open lesbian and gay male presence, at both leadership and membership levels. It was one of the first unions to take an actively pro-gay stance. Other unions, such as the Teachers, Plumbers, and Federal Public Service Clerks began to oppose discrimination, under pressure from their gay and feminist members. I was involved in work among unemployed workers, in building up a fight-back against the Fraser government.

But lesbian separatism was gaining strength. This grouping was brought together in an organized fashion by a forum on 'Womyn, Patriarchy and the Future'. The spelling of 'women' indicated the influence of the American lesbian writer, Mary Daly. Her book *Gyn/Ecology* became the bible of lesbian separatism. It was a kind of feminist *Pilgrim's Progress*, with awful stories of women as victims of rape, mutilation and murder; stream of consciousness ravings; and an exhortation to weave webs to solve the world's problems. The real world was necessarily male-dominated, according to Daly, so she recommended complete withdrawal from it. It was no wonder that the Rockefeller Foundation gave Daly an enormous grant to write the book. What better way was there to derail women's fighting potential than by encouraging them to isolate themselves in a world of fairytale solutions? The reactionary nature of lesbian separatism became the major focus of debates among lesbians, particularly for those who were trying to build a different way forward towards socialism.

Unfortunately for the socialist lesbians, the left-wing political parties such as the Socialist Workers' Party scaled down their involvement in gay liberation, encouraging their members to move into growing movements such as the anti-uranium movement. Their decision may have been right, as the liberation movement had lost much of its radical dynamic. By 1983 my only purely lesbian activities were social ones, as I preferred to work within activist political organizations, making sure that lesbian and gay issues were raised.

Lesbians still organize today, but much of the public organization is around social events. Many are active around issues such as equal pay in their unions, at beauty queen protests, in the nurses' dispute and in opposition to apartheid. The last national gay conference overwhelmingly passed a motion, moved by a lesbian activist, to support the Builders Labourers' Federation in its struggle against deregistration. One lesbian activist recently won her right to work as a teacher in Victoria, after the government attempted to prevent her teaching again.

There is no activist gay liberation movement now, and women's liberation has met a similar fate. The political and economic situation has changed dramatically since the heyday of these movements. Every oppressed group is now fighting to maintain past gains rather than to demand new rights. And as society moves rightward and the recession continues, these changes are reflected within the gay community. Splits between lesbians and male homosexuals, socialists and non-socialists, have become more clearly defined. Sometimes there has been co-operative, collective action, but often there has been total separation. The most obvious feature of the lesbian movement has been the retreat inward to personal solutions rather than outward to political ones. This has been partly a symptom, but also a cause, of its decline. Whether it can revive depends upon its moving outward and establishing new alliances.

Divided We Fell

VERITY BURGMANN AND STUART MACINTYRE

In 1905, when Bill Morrow was seventeen, he and his father were working as labourers on the Queensland railways. A locomotive ran over Bill's father and took his leg off. Bill recalled: 'The pain was awful. I could hear him moaning then screaming. They took him up to Chillagoe. They were crude in those days. We could hear them sawing the bone off while we waited outside.' His father was off work for eighteen months. One day Bill came home and found 'this slimy looking cow talking to my father, and my father was smoking a cigar'. This was the company man trying to persuade Bill's father to settle out of court for the cigar and fifty pounds. Bill and his brother had to offer to throw the man over the verandah before he would agree to 300 pounds. But Bill's father had to make his own wooden leg with an auger, file and rasp, using a broken bottle as a plane. He shaped the wood into a leg, carved out an ankle, then inserted springs into the ankle and toes. He made more wooden legs for all the workers around who'd had similar accidents. 'On Sunday mornings you'd see all the one-legged fellows coming around for fitting more of father's legs. They were made of willow – a good job. He'd make them for other people and never charge them.'

Young Bill became a life-long labour activist, struggling to make working and living easier for other wage-earners. The labour movement is made up of such individuals banding together in common endeavour; the movement expresses their common interests and loyalties. They have to work together, because their efforts as individuals would be useless. In Australia, as in all capitalist societies, employers have a clear interest in paying their workers as little as possible and making them work as hard as possible, in order to maintain or increase profits; and when workers are killed or maimed in the process, employers are not instinctively generous with their offers of compensation. It is only by combined efforts that workers can hope to get reasonable pay and working conditions. The Amalgamated Shearers' Union rules stated boldly in 1890:

> Experience has shown that all the privileges the working classes now enjoy have been gained through and by their Trade Unions. As disunited individuals they are at the mercy of their employers, but united they can obtain all that is just and right.

Unions prevent the employers from having it all their own way. In doing so, unions protect the interests of most Australians, who are wage or salary earners, against the interests of the small

The labour movement's vision of hope in 1917

minority who are employers. It is the dog-eat-dog nature of the capitalist system that makes unions necessary and encourages their development. 'It throws workers together in large numbers making collective organization possible and creates the deprivations which spur them to combination.'

The labour movement is made up of people in action. It represents their interests in the broadest sense – the common interests of those who work for a boss. But to people like Bill Morrow the labour movement is more than a mere interest group. It is a crusade for justice, a set of ideals, a force for the common good; it is a 'movement' in the sense that it is working towards something positive, a more equal society. The movement has to take an organizational form, but it is not just an organization. If it allows organizational needs or limited, sectional interests to take precedence, then it loses the impetus that makes it a movement. It is this moral and ethical aspect of the labour movement that explains the extraordinary loyalties and emotions it generates and the superhuman sacrifices that so many of its members make. It was not for the sake of a vested interest that striking shearers in the 1890s endured three years' jail on a daily diet of sweet potatoes 'always over-ripe, stringy and fibrous, and boiled to a glue-like substance which we were forced to eat or go hungry' when they might have been let out early if they said they were sorry and wouldn't do it again. Nor was it for the sake of a vested interest that Bertha McNamara continued to speak in the Sydney Domain in 1931 when she should have been at home in bed; she died as a result. These people were acting for the sake of a movement that fired their emotions and imaginations, seeing in it the means to make society more equal.

Bill Morrow was just one of thousands who have devoted their lives to this movement. But in 1953 he was expelled from the Labor Party. He had opposed things the party was doing, including the Chifley Labor government's use of troops to break the miners' strike in 1949. Bill's story highlights some of the tensions and contradictions that often make the labour movement appear to be more divided within than united against the outside world. This is so precisely because it is made up of real people with different needs and aspirations and very different ideas about what the labour movement should be.

The labour movement constitutes and renews itself through its collective memory. Bill Morrow's life has meaning for us because of his contribution to this common store of struggles, defeats and victories. Looking back, we can see how wealth and power have rested in the hands of a minority. But we can see also the challenges that have been mounted, the improvements that have been won. Were it not for such historical insight, the same costly lessons would have to be learned over and over again. Worse, we would be denied the power that comes from knowledge of our own traditions. We therefore commemorate particular successes: the anniversary of the winning of the Eight Hour Day is still marked by a public holiday. We honour those who made sacrifices: in Fremantle, for example, there is a monument to a unionist killed on the picket-line during a strike in 1919. With words and symbols we draw on the past to express and renew our loyalties.

As well as these uses of the past, there are formal, written accounts of the labour movement, usually known as labour history. Labour history often presents a 'smooth' version of the past, ironing out the fundamental tensions and contradictions within the labour movement, celebrating its achievements and turning a blind eye to its failings. In this chapter we ask whether the labour movement has really lived up to its members' expectations. We also ask how effectively the labour movement has represented the interests of workers in general. In capitalist societies like Australia, workers are not equal: at one extreme, there are reasonably well-paid, highly skilled, Anglo-Australian male workers in secure jobs; at the other extreme, there are unemployed people, and badly paid, unskilled, immigrant women workers who don't know whether they will be working from one week to the next. Between these extremes there is a vast range of sorts and conditions of workers. One of the reasons why capitalism has survived is that it has kept workers divided and at odds with each other. In particular, capitalism entrenches divisions based on skill, gender, and race or ethnicity. So we need to ask whether the labour movement has been able to bridge these divisions.

The white settlement of Australia occurred as part of an economic and social upheaval in Britain, which was the first country in the world to pass through a transition to industrial capitalism. Among the ranks of the convicts who were dumped here were men and women who directly resisted the ruinous changes. Some had been convicted because they agitated for political rights; some had banded together against rapacious landlords; some had taken action against the new machines that were destroying their livelihood; some, like the agricultural labourers of the village of Tolpuddle, were transported simply for belonging to trade unions. The convicts were not permitted to organize or negotiate for better conditions, and any attempt to do so brought down the full weight of repression. Sometimes convicts did win improvements by collective action, but for the most part they were isolated and ground down.

By the 1830s it was becoming easier for workers to organize collectively. More free immigrants were coming in, and growing numbers of ex-convicts and free-born colonists were selling their labour to earn a living. These men and women from the other side of the world brought with them the possibility of a movement to defend the interests of working-class people. And the colonists secured some basic civil rights, including the right to free speech and to form associations and freedom from arbitrary arrest. At last working people could begin to band together for the common purpose of improving wages and conditions of work.

As it turned out, however, the early trade union movement was more interested in preserving distinctions within the workforce than achieving a common purpose among workers. Unions, or 'trade societies' as they were called, were first formed in Sydney in the 1830s and in Melbourne from 1840 among craftsmen – engineers, coachmakers, carpenters and joiners, plumbers, painters, drapers, tailors, shoemakers, plasterers, stonemasons, shipwrights, bakers, saddlers, compositors, bookbinders, and similarly skilled people. Their members were skilled workers who identified themselves as tradesmen (and trades*men* they always were) in a particular occupation. They were as much concerned to protect the 'privileges' of their trade against less skilled workers as to take a stand against employers.

'Tradesmen' were several cuts above 'labourers'. In 1835 Governor Bourke, conducting a rough census of the workforce, counted a tradesman as equal to two or three labourers. The tradesmen were acutely aware of their superiority to labourers, and they preferred to keep it that way. They were 'craft conscious' rather than 'class conscious'. Trade societies often permitted 'masters' to join, but never labourers. There were good reasons why they felt closer to masters than labourers, for skilled workers could easily become employers themselves in unmechanized trades such as carpentry, printing or food-processing, where a workshop was indeed no bigger than a shop. It was easier for a tradesman to become an employer than for an unskilled worker to become a tradesman. So tradesmen could rise occupationally and socially; and their exclusiveness prevented them from falling to the level of less skilled workers. The trade societies controlled entry to the craft. They made sure that only qualified men who had completed apprenticeships were allowed in and carefully limited the number of apprentices so that their skills would always be in short supply. They laid down the rates for which members worked and called on them to withdraw their labour if the rates were not paid.

Often these trade societies were also 'friendly societies', providing benefits such as relief to widows and insurance against loss of tools. To do so, they required their members to pay high subscriptions, which helped to keep them exclusive. And in the help they gave their well-off members they reinforced the social distinctions of the time. One of the most important benefits commonly available was funeral expenses; to respectable, thrifty unionists, nothing was more important than avoiding the indignity of a pauper's burial.

There was, moreover, a considerable overlap between these trade societies and other voluntary organizations – friendly societies, building societies, co-operatives, mechanics' institutes, temperance organizations and even the local churches. The purposes of these organizations varied. Friendly societies provided assistance in sickness or some other calamity; building societies lent money so members could buy their own homes; the co-operatives were usually retail stores owned and run by members; mechanics' institutes offered libraries, classes and recreational facilities; temperance groups fought the demon drink; and the churches performed good works as well as saving souls. Regardless of function, such bodies had some distinctive common features. They were *voluntary* in that one chose to become a member; *self-supporting,* since members paid to support their activities; *mutual* in the sense that they were based on collective endeavour and exhibited a common concern; *improving* in that they placed strong emphasis on moral uplift. None of the organizations was exclusively working class, and in many cases the office-bearers were shopkeepers and small businessmen. Their appeal was generally restricted to workers who were better off than, say, general labourers. Even so, they became an important extension of working-class organization, strengthening workers' capacity to control their own lives.

Trade societies were based on a single locality. The term 'union' was first used to describe the union of several societies from different localities, a development that began in the middle of the century. These 'craft' unions catered for the skilled tradesmen or craftsmen of the old societies but covering a wider geographical area. For example, societies in Melbourne, Geelong and Ballarat might form a Victorian union in their particular craft, perhaps later in the century aspiring to establish an Australian union with their counterparts from other colonies. During this period, the colonies passed Acts modelled closely on those passed by the British parliament in 1871 and 1875, which declared that trade unions were legal, responsible only to their members and could own property, and that picketing in the course of industrial disputes was permissible though intimidation was not. South Australia was the first colony to pass such legislation in 1876, followed by New South Wales in 1881, Victoria and Queensland in 1886, Tasmania in 1889, and Western Australia in 1902.

Craft unions also set up regional bodies to promote co-operation between different unions and resolve differences between them, such as demarcation disputes over which union's members should do a particular type of work. Sydney's Trades and Labour Council was set up in 1871 and Melbourne's soon after, though Melbourne had had a Trades Hall committee since 1856. The next step was to hold a series of inter-colonial trades union congresses, to discuss and develop policy on matters pertinent to trade unionists, such as the law relating to trade unions, factories and workshops. The first was held in Sydney in 1879, the second in Melbourne in 1884, the seventh and last of its kind in Ballarat in 1891. It was not until the sixth, in Hobart in 1889, that unions of unskilled workers were represented.

The best known achievement of this early craft union movement was the Eight Hour Day, which was won by stonemasons in Melbourne in April 1856 and extended to most skilled trades by the end of the year. But this 'victory' was neither complete nor final. Some craft unions, such as the bakers, missed out. Others had to fight to keep the Eight Hour Day, especially in periods of recession and unemployment. Moreover, the 'boon' was not shared by all workers but was the privilege of a minority. Most wage-earners continued to work nine, ten or more hours. In the rare instances where labourers also got the Eight Hour Day, it was either as government employees or because they worked side-by-side with craftsmen. The annual celebrations of the Eight Hour Day 'victory' became displays of craft-conscious pride and exclusiveness. Instead of bending their resources and energies to extending the Eight Hour Day to all workers, skilled and unskilled, the skilled tradesmen preferred to keep it as a symbol of their greater worth and even to cherish the fact that it was not widespread.

The period between 1861 and 1891, when craft unionism

Craft union members march under their banner on Eight Hour Day at Broken Hill in 1908.

expanded rapidly, is often referred to by historians as the 'first long boom'. Yet in a recent article in the journal *Labour History*, Jenny Lee and Charles Fahey have rightly raised the query: 'A boom for whom?' They point out that those who write of the prosperity of this period have relied on estimates of average income and consumption, which reveal nothing about how wealth and income were distributed. Moreover, the argument that the working class had high living standards rests on data about wage *rates* (that is, the daily or hourly wage offered by the employer) and not about *incomes* (that is, the actual earnings of real, live workers). For even a good wage rate is of little use to a worker who is regularly unemployed or under-employed, and this was what happened to a large proportion of the workforce in this period. Unskilled workers in particular suffered great insecurity of employment, often going for months at a time without a wage. This was especially true in rural areas, where there was a very clear seasonal pattern of employment. But it also affected urban workers, as many manufacturing concerns had distinct 'dull' and 'busy' times and passed this problem on to the employees by simply laying them off or putting them on short time. In general, winter was a slack season in both town and country, the time of discontent for the unemployed, as Charlie Fox and Bruce Scates will describe in a later chapter in this volume. According to Lee and Fahey: 'The great divide within the work-place was between permanent and temporary hands.' Who was treated as permanent, and who as temporary, was strongly influenced by race, gender and ethnicity. Most of all, the distinction accentuated differences based on skill.

Up to 1890, therefore, it is difficult to talk of an Australian labour 'movement'. Labour organizations covered only a small minority of workers and their outlook was shaped by sectional interests. They shared many of the beliefs of the society at large. Organized labour subscribed to the great Victorian faith in progress – the material progress of bricks and mortar, and the moral progress of order, sobriety and self-discipline. The Australian unions liked to believe that the New World could avoid the poverty, injustice and inequalities of the Old, that every *man* should be able to enjoy modest comfort as a result of his own efforts. They believed strongly in the dignity of labour – 'The labourer is worthy of his hire' was a favourite maxim. This meant taking a stand against the unscrupulous boss. The unions, however, saw no reason why a decent employer should not treat his men fairly, since both parties stood to benefit from mutual respect and co-operation. Together, they would maintain the standards of the trade. Equally, unionists believed that their political interests could and should be served by an alliance with liberals. So it was that a spokesman reviewed the progress of organized labour in a *History of Labour and Capital* published in 1888:

> The strength of labour in Australia is not to be measured by the violence and frequency of isolated agitations, but by the strong compelling interest which its combined constitutional and often undemonstrative action has had upon the legislation of the country, and by the part it is now taking in the moulding of its future destinies. There can be no doubt that if the forces of Australian labour are wielded with the same moderation for legitimate ends in the future as they have been in the past, its political power will be increased, and its social status thereby maintained.

But within two years the unions were embroiled in a nation-wide conflict that ended in their utter defeat. The bitter strikes of the 1890s had their roots in the growing difficulties of the Australian economy, especially of the export industries. The most powerful group of employers, the pastoralists, were trying to cut costs, taking a firm line against shearers and other pastoral workers. These workers established new unions that included the unskilled and sought to make employers take only union members so that the employers could no longer exploit docile non-unionists. The dispute spread from pastoralism to transport, and later to mining and other industries. In every case the employers were backed up by the state – the police, the judiciary, even the defence forces were brought in to break picket lines and harass unionists. And in every case the employers won. The onset of widespread unemployment in the depression of the 1890s made it impossible to hold ranks against non-union 'scab' labour. Many unions went out of existence. The surviving ones sued for peace.

But if the great strikes of the 1890s ended in defeat, they left an enduring legacy for the labour movement. After capital triumphed over labour, the victorious employers went on to reduce wages, increase hours and re-organize the work process. Even the most privileged workers felt the effects. The earlier divisions among workers began to yield to a common identity and a common antagonism to the boss. The earlier expectation of mutual respect between master and man yielded to the new polarization of 'them' and 'us', and a corresponding sense of working-class solidarity. The events of the 1890s took on an epochal significance in the folklore of the labour movement. As the labour movement consolidated itself, however, other limitations became more apparent. Of these, the most important was its masculinity.

One delegate to the inter-colonial trades union congress in 1891 claimed that Australia was not a paradise for the working man but 'a tolerably complete working model of hell'. It was certainly hell for the working woman. Like unskilled male workers, women faced the problem of irregular employment, but they were worse off: women earned only half the male rate, and their conditions were worse than for unskilled men, as Raelene Frances has already discussed in volume two. Unionism was urgently needed for women workers, but it was slow to develop. Labour historians have frequently blamed the women, concocting theories about women's natural passivity and their lack of interest in public affairs. But the fault was not theirs: it lay with the nature of their employment and the fact that male unionists resisted their initial efforts at unionization.

The most common forms of paid work for women were domestic service and the clothing trade. Both required skills that were widespread throughout the female population, and there were plenty of women desperate for employment, so employers were not likely to be distressed by the threat of strikes. Moreover, most women

Female Confectioners were one of the few women's unions to participate in Eight Hour Day on their own account, *c.* 1922–5.

worked in their own homes, or in other people's. Capitalism did not bring women workers together, as it did male workers, in large-scale units where they could share their experiences of exploitation collectively. Organization was therefore extremely difficult. The early women trade unionists should be regarded as especially heroic. They had to battle against odds that male unionists never encountered, and against male unionists as well.

Why were these male trade unionists so unhelpful? They often explained their opposition to women workers on economic grounds. Since women were paid less than men, the men argued that employers used them to drive down wage levels. Of course, there was more than one solution to this: male unionists could have welcomed women and encouraged them to insist on equal pay instead of opposing women's entry. Occasionally unions did support equal pay but as a device to make women's labour less attractive to employers.

For alongside the economic argument there often surfaced arguments based on notions of male dominance. The labour leaders frequently affirmed their belief that a woman's place was in the home and that the man should be the breadwinner. They claimed – it was a self-fulfilling prophecy – that women could not endure the rigours of doing 'men's work' and could not stand up to the boss. The very ethos of independence and self-reliance they proclaimed was a masculine ethos. Thus, the 'malestream' trade union movement frequently opposed both female employment and female unionism. The New South Wales Typographical Association, for example, was determined to prevent women working as compositors and refused them entry to the union. Its first strike, in October 1880, was against the employment of four women compositors in a newspaper office. Later in the decade, the association tried to sabotage Louisa's Lawson's feminist newspaper, the *Dawn*, because her ten compositors were all female. The Trades and Labour Council carried the motion without debate. But when an association official ventured into the *Dawn* office to harangue the staff, he had a bucket of water thrown over him by Louisa Lawson.

Male unionists even connived with employers to stamp out female unionism. In 1899, for example, the Cigar Makers' Industrial League in New South Wales agreed with one employer that, if he recognized their union, they would keep his female workers out of the union. Again the Trades and Labour Council supported the union's action. An outraged letter from 'Jemima Jorkins' appeared in *The Worker* of 25 March 1899:

> They made a big mistake in agreein' with the employer not to countenance the formation o' a Union among his female operatives. It's time they knew that the men's battle is the wimmin's, an' that if the wimmin 'as ter werk fer next to nothin' they'll take the men's billets, an' they're qualifyin' fer it nearly every department o' werk. It ain't right ter slight the female sex; it can't be did to eny great extent without recoilin' on the offender's 'ead.

The arbitration system reinforced the distinctions between men and women, as Diane Kirkby has already outlined in her chapter on arbitration in volume two. In 1907 Mr Justice Higgins brought down his celebrated Harvester judgment: men should be paid a 'family wage', sufficient to keep themselves, a wife and three children in frugal comfort. This judgment was used to keep female rates of pay about half those of men, until the principle of equal pay began to be recognized in the 1960s. It had been an uphill battle for women unionists for decades.

Sara Lewis was one of these battlers. She became secretary of the Female Hotel, Club, Restaurant and Caterers' Employees' Union in 1910. Lewis recognized that women workers had special needs because of the greater incidence of outwork, long hours, overcrowding and poor hygiene in factories and workshops, and especially in the need for equal pay. Her goal was to secure autonomy for women in the labour movement so that they could 'stand shoulder to shoulder with our brother unionists, confident of our strength, better fitted for the fight and more hopeful of success'. But the Melbourne Trades Hall Council treated Lewis as 'an unco-operative troublemaker', and early in 1913 it instructed her to 'fall in line with the suggestions of the men's union ... in the interests of unionism'. As Lewis wrote in *Labor Call* of 28 August 1913: 'In a perfectly illogical manner the T.H.C. seek to show women that they are entirely dependent by seeking to crush any independence shown by them.' As Melanie Raymond observes in her biographical sketch of Lewis's career, Lewis's campaigns brought out the male unionists' 'inherent resentment and suspicion of the effect of women's political and economic demands', which were threatening a balance of power in which male workers' interests were paramount.

Male union officials were especially threatened by the appointment of women union officials. Shortly after the First World War, May Brodney and Lesbia Harford, who were on the executive of the Clothing Trades Union, wanted to have a woman engaged as an organizer for the union. Alf Wallis, the secretary of the union, dug his heels in. He described his ideal type of union official: a tall man with dark, curly hair, well dressed and with good manners. Brodney and Harford gave up arguing and turned to ridicule. They suggested that the union should only appoint a man with dark, curly hair, of well-dressed appearance and with good manners. Wallis finally gave in, and Lilian Whitford got the job.

Attitudes have not improved much since. Irene Bolger, secretary of the Victorian branch of the Royal Australian Nursing Federation, discovered during the 1986 nurses' strike that the sexism of the Trades Hall Council and the A.C.T.U. was 'quite extraordinary'. She said it was so marked it took her completely by surprise. She was continually pressured behind the scenes by the men of the Trades Hall and the A.C.T.U. to keep quiet and let them fix things up for the nurses. They seemed to be offended that there was no man leading the strike, just as the media kept trying to work out which men were really behind Bolger. And union men did not treat Bolger with the respect they normally gave other union leaders, just as the media kept trivializing her statements and actions. Rank and file nurses were also enraged by the men who run the union movement. One nurse on the picket line at the Royal Melbourne Hospital described them as 'the greatest bunch of chauvinists ever', who were affronted by Irene Bolger because she was so articulate and ran rings around them. Even after this strike was won, which should have taught male union officials a few lessons, the Trades Hall Council kept on putting nurses' motions so low on the agenda paper that they were not debated at council meetings. It is not surprising that Bolger has responded by describing the council as a men's club where men get up and blow a lot of hot air.

Women have had to fight within the Labor parties as well as the unions. Male dominance in the union movement has created Labor parties unconducive to the equal participation of women. One labour historian has commented that in the A.L.P. 'women have played an unspectacular and relatively inarticulate role ... in the local branches and in the arduous but unpublicized work of campaigning and local fundraising, women have been towers of Labor strength'. In other words, women have worked extremely hard for very little reward. Often they have suffered abuse, especially if they showed any tendency to stand up for women's rights. Sara Lewis earned the wrath of the Victorian Labor Party executive because her union participated in the campaign for equal pay along with non-Labor groups. Even the Women's Organizing Committee of the party, of which Lewis was a prominent member, accused her of breaching party loyalty. Not all members of the Women's Organizing Committee shared Lewis's determination that Labor women should press for greater autonomy and influence in the party.

In general, women's committees have been formed in state Labor branches, not to represent the separate interests of women, but to mobilize the female vote for the A.L.P., despite its unimpressive record on women's issues. It is true that Labor governments did introduce maternity benefits and child endowment: the 'baby bonus' of five pounds was brought in by the Fisher Labor government of 1910-13, and the Curtin Labor government during the Second World War broadened the provision for child endowment. But both these reforms reinforced the idea that women belonged in the home, bearing children. As such they cut against women's moves to achieve equal pay. Labor governments remained evasive on this issue until the Whitlam Labor government of 1972-5 supported equal pay for women in the Commonwealth public service. Whitlam also greatly increased funding for child-care centres, one of the few reforms that has encouraged women to combine motherhood and paid work.

From its beginnings, the Australian labour movement proclaimed a strong national identity, as Chris McConville has outlined earlier in this volume in his chapter entitled 'Conflicting Loyalties'. At a time when much of Australia's economy was owned and controlled from Britain, this nationalism was only to be expected. Even so, nationalism had a darker side. The unions were strong supporters of the White Australia policy, which was a prominent plank of the A.L.P. programme from the time of its creation. With notable exceptions, unions and the A.L.P. were as hostile to Aborigines as were other sections of white society, and Labor governments proved as racist as non-Labor governments. Labor also encouraged the creation of Australian defence forces and supported the introduction of compulsory military training in 1910. Paradoxically, the fear of a threat to this white outpost in South-East Asia led the A.L.P. to seek closer ties with Britain, and it was a leader of the federal Labor Party who pledged Australia's last man and last shilling to the support of Britain at the outbreak of the First World War. When it became clear during the Second World War that Britain could no longer defend Australia, a Labor Prime Minister transferred dependence to the United States. In the 1980s, the Hawke Labor government maintained the A.N.Z.U.S. agreement, provided bases for the United States military and allowed American nuclear vessels to visit Australian ports.

Against this sorry record of bigotry, there has always been an internationalist current. The international ideals of the labour movement express the common interests of all workers regardless of nationality; they assert that workers should stand aloof from the conflicts engendered by capitalism and militarism, and work instead for peace and co-operation. In the late nineteenth and early twentieth centuries, this was the goal of the Second International of working-class movements, to which sections of the Australian movement were affiliated. Labor critics opposed the preparations for the war of 1914–18. They opposed conscription for overseas service during the war, and rallied the labour movement into defeating the proposal. In the 1920s and 1930s these advanced sections of the movement supported national independence movements in Asia and Africa and opposed the fascist threat to peace. A highpoint of the Australian labour movement's international record was its support for Indonesian independence at the end of the Second World War. When the Dutch attempted to re-impose control over their colonies, and used Australian

Melbourne Trades Hall during the anti-conscription campaign of 1917.

ports as military bases, the Australian unions boycotted Dutch ships and denied them help. During the 1950s and 1960s it was again the labour movement that led the opposition to Australia's military support for right-wing regimes in Malaya, Korea and Vietnam.

The labour movement's narrowness and its frequent complicity in racism and imperialism forces us to reconsider the questions with which we began this chapter. Clearly, organized labour has usually paid most attention to the interests of those who carry the most clout. It has not adequately represented workers at the bottom of the pile – the unskilled workers of the nineteenth century, women workers since, or 'ethnic' and Aboriginal workers at any time. Moreover, those who most need to be championed – old age pensioners, single-parent families, the unemployed, the disabled, un-unionized and badly paid workers – have received secondary consideration, at best.

Again, from selfishness and fear, the A.L.P. has done little to support workers and subject peoples elsewhere in the world. All these failings suggest that crucial aspects of a genuine labour movement are missing: sectional interests have prevailed over forward-looking vision and robbed the labour movement of momentum.

Why have the thousands of working people who have given their lives to the labour movement been so sadly frustrated? The chief institutions of the labour movement – the parliamentary parties and the trade unions – seem peculiarly resistant to the movement's declared goals. The labour movement has brought trouble upon itself through its own representatives. The full-time union officials and M.P.s are no longer the servants of the movement, as they were originally intended to be, but its masters. There are endless conflicts between pragmatism and principle; there is a constant battle between opportunists in positions of power (or aiming to be) and purists who aren't and won't be. The movement set up structures that were not suitable to carry out its aims. These structures prevent it from operating effectively as a 'movement' towards a more equal society.

One of the most striking contradictions within the movement is the contrast between the Labor M.P.s with their professional privileges and the relatively impoverished people who elect them. Labor M.P.s are supposed to represent the interests of working-class people, but in reality the traffic goes the other way. Politicians transmit to working-class electors the needs and interests of the 'nation', cajoling the working class into 'tightening their belts' in the 'national interest' (which is always shorthand for 'employers' interests'). They insist that they would like to redeem their pledge to implement the movement's policies, but the time is not ripe. The time is never ripe.

In a similar way, trade union officials communicate the bosses' wishes to the workers as well as the workers' to the boss. Since the formation of the A.C.T.U. in 1927, the trade unions have become increasingly bureaucratic. Full-time officials increasingly carve out trade-union careers without ever having experience of the shop-floor. Their power within the unions is, however, only part of the problem. Even officials and unions with a strong commitment to keeping contact with the rank and file find that an organizational structure grows up between the union member and the operation of the union. A concern with organizational needs makes it harder for ordinary members to participate. Thus one successful and progressive union recently introduced a system where dues were paid by mail instead of being collected by shop stewards. It did this for the sake of efficiency, but the effect was to remove an important point of contact between rank-and-file members and their elected representatives.

In a broader sense, union leaders mediate conflict between labour and capital. They settle strikes rather than win them outright, they persuade their members to accept less than they really want on the grounds that no more can be reasonably expected from employers. It was trade union officials who persuaded workers to accept the Accord, which reduced workers' living standards. And the most compelling argument put forward in defence of the Accord was the supposed importance of electing a Labor government and keeping it in office in order to prevent a more savage attack on working conditions and wages. For the labour movement, representation is a double-edged sword that harms those who seek to use it to reform society.

'We have come into this House to make and unmake social conditions,' declared George Black on behalf of the thirty-five Labor M.P.s who took up their seats in the New South Wales parliament in 1891. The trade union activists who had worked so hard for the new party were jubilant. The *Australian Workman*, the Trades and Labour Council newspaper, announced that the election day would be remembered as the day on which the workers of New South Wales 'cast off their shackles'. Militant workers throughout Australia were confident that Labor in politics was a winner, and much was expected of it. They saw parliamentary representation, not as a substitute for trade-union activity, but as an additional weapon to secure a fair deal for workers and to make society more equal. They believed that as soon as Labor formed a government anywhere, workers there would cease to be exploited and oppressed.

Over the next two decades, the Australian Labor Party was built, and it achieved rapid success. The Queensland Labor Party, formed in 1890, already had four M.P.s a year later; and South Australian Labor obtained three in 1892. Victorian Labor got off to a shaky start in the 1890s, and in Western Australia and Tasmania, Labor parties were formed in 1900 and 1903. In 1899, when the British Labour Party had not even been established, Queensland had a Labor government – a short-lived minority one, but the first in the world, nonetheless. By 1914 Labor had held power in the commonwealth and all but one of the states. Labor was also active at the municipal level, and had achieved significant results. During the same period the industrial wing of the labour movement was rebuilt: union membership grew from a lowpoint of about 50,000 in 1896 to more than half a million by 1914. Not the least achievement of the labour movement in these years was the way it empowered its members. In the union meeting, the party branch and other spheres of activity, men and women met and deliberated, made and implemented decisions. Even a poorly attended meeting in an ill-lit hall gave the participants a sense of their own capacity. The open-air meeting on the street corner, where speakers mounted the soap-box to denounce capitalism and explain a socialist alternative, could grip the imagination of the listeners. Activists could see tangible results, and they could envisage a better future. By 1945, when the first majority Labour government was formed in Britain, Australia was experiencing its seventh federal Labor government. Moreover, the separate Australian states were also governed periodically by Labor administrations.

Labor governments presided over some legislation that improved social conditions: the Fisher government between 1910 and 1913 raised and extended the old age pension and introduced invalid pensions; the Curtin government brought in widows' pensions and unemployment, sickness and funeral benefits; the Chifley government increased funding for low-cost housing; the Whitlam government introduced Medibank and the Hawke government re-introduced it.

Activists in the movement, however, expected much more than welfare measures. They anticipated that Labor governments would change the way that society was organized, 'make and unmake social conditions'. It was not merely that Labor governments did too little; activists had cause to object violently to some of the things they did. The Scullin government during the depression gave in to employer pressure to institute a 10 per cent cut in real wages. And in 1949 Chifley capped the state Labor governments' record as strike-busters by sending in troops to break the big miners' strike, the action that led to Bill Morrow's exit from the party he had worked so hard for.

But these deficiencies fade in significance when compared with the record of the Hawke government. From the time it was elected it began breaking its promises and defying party policy. Pledges to maintain social welfare were compromised; commitments to students in schools, colleges and universities were broken; child-care funding was cut; environmental protection was sacrificed to miners and woodchippers. In the field of foreign policy, the people of Timor were abandoned to the Indonesian invaders; uranium mining and sales were permitted; the needs of the American military took precedence over all else. The government boasted how far it had gone in removing public controls over the economy, it stood by idly while media monopolies strengthened their stranglehold on the press and television, and embarked on the sale of public assets into private hands. The cornerstone of its industrial policy was the Accord, which restricted unionists' right to press for higher wages and better conditions. And after Labor came to power, Australia became an even more unequal society: the proportions both of millionaires and of people living in poverty have increased.

As early as 1903, the Victorian labour movement paper, *Tocsin*, noted sadly: 'The tendency of Labour movements in politics has been to yield very soon to the dissolving influence of quasi-public interests, corporate power and party manipulation.' George Dale, an activist in the Amalgamated Miners Association at Broken Hill for several decades, lived to regret Labor's venture into politics. He wrote in 1918:

> Those who for their personal gains exploited our leisure hours and energies in stumping the country in order to return them to well-paid billets have in the hour of our direst needs deserted not only us who breathed political life into their evil-smelling nostrils, but have trampled upon every principle they ever professed, and have acted generally in a manner that would put to shame Judas Iscariot.

A former private secretary to the New South Wales Labor premier just after the First World War attempted to analyse the process by which Labor M.P.s become remote from their supporters.

> The fact is that, possessed of a substantial salary, a gold pass on the railways and other privileges, and surrounded with the middle-class atmosphere of Parliament, the workers' representative is liable to get out of touch with the rank and file that put him in the Legislature, and to think more of keeping his seat and scoring political points than of carrying out the ideals he was sent in to give effect to.

Nowadays, free travel on Australian Airlines and chauffeur-driven government cars have replaced the gold rail pass. The description remains basically accurate. These privileges turn Labor M.P.s into middle-ranking executives who carry their briefcases from meeting to meeting, delegate the menial jobs to their staff and quickly learn to fob off unwelcome questions at branch meetings on the rare occasions they turn up.

Some Labor politicians resist the pressures of the parliamentary club and middle-class way of life. But they are few, and they rarely get anywhere within the party. Mostly, they are isolated, sometimes even ostracized. As George Petersen, a longtime backbencher and left-winger in the New South Wales parliament has observed of Labor M.P.s: 'Those who do take up radical causes find themselves regarded with at best toleration, at the worst hostility. As numerous examples show we either go right, or go cranky.' An M.P.'s power within the party rises as his or her loyalty to the movement's desire for radical change diminishes. Always, those who start on the conservative or pragmatic wing of the party or who drift in that direction have at their disposal the argument that radicalism loses votes.

If this is true, then parliamentary politics is clearly bad for the labour movement as a movement for reform. The basic unit of the parliamentary system is the electorate and its M.P. The electorate is a geographical division. Electorates do not divide the population up according to occupation and economic interests. Most elections are decided by the way a small proportion of voters in marginal seats respond to the campaigns of the respective parties. These election-deciders are a mixed bunch of people by occupation, but they are generally more affluent than the needy people for whom Labor is meant to act. Pollsters and party strategists warn against offending these swinging voters or alarming them with talk of social change. For this reason, electoral politics encourages a softpedalling of any policies that would make society more equal for fear that redistributive policies would cause panic among this group of people. Labor in politics, though it started life as a form of working-class mobilization, has become a powerful influence in the demobilization of the working class.

To sum up, there are four main reasons why parliamentary representation has failed to realize the labour movement's expectations that it would 'make and unmake social conditions'. Two of these reasons affect M.P.s as individuals: there are psychological pressures, such as the mores of the parliamentary club; and there are material inducements, such as the good salary and the perks. The other two reasons affect M.P.s as a group, as a government or as a potential government: there are electoral considerations, the fear that reforming policies will lose votes; and there are serious structural constraints, the fact that powerful but non-elected people, notably businessmen and top public servants, can dissuade Labor administrations from taking any course they might find threatening. As the Labor premier's private secretary put it, after resigning in disgust from the Labor Party: 'To avoid giving offence to middle-class supporters Labor governments have followed a vacillating policy and have tried to govern in the interests of all classes instead of standing up boldly in defence of the one class which put them in power.'

The failures of the unions and the sorry record of Labor in politics call into question the labour movement's ability to secure its objectives. It is hardly surprising that many socialists refuse to be in the Labor Party at all. At the outset we suggested that a labour movement gains its momentum by moving towards the goal of a better, freer, more equal society. To this extent, the labour movement is like a bicycle – you have to keep moving forward or you fall off. For the best part of a hundred years labour activists have drawn their inspiration from socialism. They have been able to imagine a social order where wealth is shared collectively rather than being held in private hands, where economic exploitation is impossible because no one profits from the labour of another, and where other forms of exploitation and oppression can therefore be eliminated. The labour movement has not lived up to the expectations of its rank-and-file activists. Nor has it always done as much as it could to bridge divisions within the working class.

The course of events in this century has not been kind to socialist ideals. We have seen revolutions overthrow capitalism only to reproduce new inequalities and forms of exploitation. We have seen capitalism itself survive deep crises and widespread hardship only to renew itself in new ways. The ideal of co-operation and peace between the workers of the world has been mocked by two major and many minor wars, and the existence of human society is now threatened by nuclear weapons. Subject peoples have thrown off their colonial status only to reproduce inequality and surrender their formal independence to the dictates of international capitalism. In this country the Aborigines have become understandably impatient with the idea that they will achieve equality by forming links with white workers. The women's movement has good cause to doubt that its aspirations will find expression within a socialist tradition that has been insensitive to women's needs, at the very least. Those who fear for the environment doubt that socialism will save it.

All these movements have an energy that increasingly makes the labour movement look tired. Each of them has its own viewpoint and strategy, and each has registered valuable achievements. Even so, it is clear that Australia continues to be dominated by wealthy, white males, and that the forces opposed to them are weakened by their isolation from each other. Is it possible for them to come together on the basis of common values and objectives? There are good reasons for thinking that the interests of workers are compatible with the interests of the social movements. All share a common objective of liberating humanity from oppression, inequality and ultimate self-destruction. If the labour movement is to renew itself, it will need to renew its goals and open itself up to these other concerns. It will need also to forge new organizational forms appropriate to new strategies. In this it can find assistance in an unflinching inspection of its past record as well as in a critical analysis of its present condition. Most of all it needs to imagine its future.

The Beat of Weary Feet

CHARLIE FOX AND BRUCE SCATES

On a drizzly winter morning in August 1890, a crowd of 7,000 unemployed assembled on Queen's Wharf, Melbourne. After some fiery speeches bemoaning the want of work in the colony, the agitators produced a crude effigy of Premier Gillies and doused it with kerosene. The crowd then set off for Flinders Park, a popular haunt for Melbourne's left and an appropriate place for the cremation of a premier. On the way a man named Mahoney, dressed in cabbage tree hat and flaming red necktie, danced with the effigy. His drunken swagger and lewd remarks mingled festivity with protest. As the crowd approached the Yarra, a group of constables came forward to save Gillies' image from destruction. As the *Bull Ant*, a radical weekly paper, reported: 'Four of the diabolical incendiaries were promptly arrested ... and ... a few other inflammatory persons ... clubbed on the head and ... kicked for falling by the ever zealous ... constables on duty.'

The *Age* of 7 August 1890 saw the scene somewhat differently: a 'riotous mob' was threatening to push the city's protectors into the Yarra; the capture of the 'counterfeit premier', however, restored a sense of order to the troubled metropolis. But on one point the *Ant* and the *Age* were in agreement: the unemployment agitation of winter 1890 was larger and more dangerous than any that had preceded it.

Before 1890 agitation by the unemployed had never posed much of a threat. Fuelled by massive overseas investment, the colonies had enjoyed a long period of relative prosperity. Unemployment was mostly seasonal in character, coinciding with the end of the harvest or regular trade fluctuations; agitation among the unemployed was short lived and localized. Workers laid off for the slack season congregated in the cities each winter, where they were able to lobby colonial governments for relief. Their demands were not very far reaching. They urged the government to curb immigration, extend tariffs or expand programmes of public works. Their tactics were also moderate. Processions of men would march to Parliament House where their delegates were received by one or other of the ministers. Usually the government would agree to some increase in government works, though often less than the unemployed had hoped for. The crowds would disperse, and no more would be heard of the organizers until the next slack season came, when the performance would be repeated.

Such an exercise fell well within the bounds of peaceful parliamentary protest. Indeed, deputations were often introduced by sympathetic liberals, who used the grievances of the unemployed to further their own interests. The moderate unemployed movement of these early days also found support within the labour movement. There, too, it was a marriage of convenience. Providing work for the unemployed protected the wages and conditions of those still in work. Of course, this early wave of unemployment agitation was concerned only with male unemployment. Unemployed women had no voice in these campaigns. Indeed, it was not accepted that women could *be* unemployed. The pick-and-shovel work offered for unemployment relief was directed exclusively towards men. In their tactics and objectives and, above all, in their cheerful assumption that the state would bail them out, these unemployed movements functioned effectively as wings of the mainstream labour movement or props to the liberal political factions in parliament.

The 1890s signalled an end to this. With the onset of the depression, unemployment was no longer a seasonal aberration. By 1893 the average term of unemployment was measured in months rather than weeks, leaving many families and communities in a state of near-starvation. The collapse of rural markets and the onset of drought in the late 1890s dashed any hope of finding relief in the countryside. As one casual worker complained, he had 'carried his drum from Melbourne to the Darling and from the Lachlan to the Paroo', seeking work but never finding it. The effects of the depression were felt practically everywhere. Unemployment afflicted skilled and unskilled, in the city and in the country. One typographer told his union that he

Unemployed men march in Sydney in 1892.

had 'not enjoyed the luxury of a breakfast' as long as he remembered. Once the elite of colonial craftsmen, typographers were among the many skilled workers who suffered severely in the 1890s from the combined effects of technological change and general depression.

Public relief works were curtailed or abandoned as the crisis deepened. Intent on balancing their budgets, governments were no longer prepared to cushion the effects of unemployment. Nor did they see it as their duty to do so. Deputations to various premiers were met with lectures on the virtues of thrift and independence. As Patterson, the Victorian Minister for Works, explained to one such party: 'What would become of the colony if all its citizens became suckers on the state?' He advised the unemployed to follow his own example as a youth and 'hump their blueys' with stoic self-reliance.

But many were not prepared to leave their families for the uncertain chance of finding work in the country. It was these people's protests that were heard in the unemployment agitation of 1890–8.

This agitation differed from the earlier campaigns in several ways. It went on longer and involved more people. Crowds varied in size from a few hundred to several thousand people. Even Adelaide, small by comparison with Melbourne and Sydney, hosted large and 'rowdy' demonstrations. Unappeased by hostile governments, the unemployed met regularly for several months in succession. In Sydney, Melbourne, Adelaide and Brisbane, the unemployed formed their own associations, some of them lasting for several years. Socialists and anarchists were important within these organizations.

The involvement of radicals meant that the 1890s demonstrations were more politicized than the earlier ones. Through much of 1892, speeches on 'socialism, anarchy, democracy, capitalism, dynamite, one-man-one-vote and other social reforms' were carefully recorded in the diaries of the Melbourne police. That same year, in Sydney, a meeting of 4,000 unemployed affirmed that the 'only rational solution [to their difficulties] would be nationalizing the land, machinery and all ... the instruments of production'.

But the politics of the unemployed movement invariably had a practical application. Chummy Fleming, a Melbourne anarchist and a leader of the unemployed agitation, attributed the plight of the unemployed to conspicuous consumption on the part of the wealthy: 'If the rich of the city had not hearts as hard as stones they would give up useless rooms in their mansions for the housing of the poor.' Failing that, tenants should refuse to pay rent and the homeless demand accommodation in the Exhibition Buildings. Fleming fused political polemic with practical demands.

Arguments such as these had an obvious attraction. While press and government spoke of the laws of the free market, radical rhetoric offered immediate solutions. Moreover, it shifted the blame away from the individual failings of the unemployed or abstract economic forces to the greed of bankers, capitalist landlords and 'other well-fed loafers'.

The unemployed adopted tactics as radical as their rhetoric. The old strategy of deputation and petition gave way to a more confrontationist approach. Processions by the unemployed were no longer orderly or predictable. Demonstrations took over the streets in Sydney and Melbourne. Detours through depressed inner-city suburbs added to their numbers. Bearing banners by day and torches by night, they made the city an arena for social conflict. Often they marched in military formation, a brisk whistling of the *Marseillaise* lending rhythm and bravado. In May 1892, 'the second Victorian regiment' tried to storm the steps of parliament, only to be pushed back by a cordon of police. On other occasions, demonstrators forced their way through the bishop's gardens, marched on the governor's residence and harangued representatives of the Chamber of Commerce and the Salvation Army. Such targets were carefully chosen; church and state, business and charity were noted for their hostility and indifference. And in each case, the demonstrators took over space from which they had previously been excluded, destroying the complacent isolation of middle-class society.

The challenge to law and property was real and symbolic. In the Sydney suburb of Surry Hills, bread carts were toppled and their contents distributed among the destitute. In March 1892, a Salvage Corps was founded in Melbourne. Its purpose was to rescue goods or furniture confiscated in lieu of rent or repayments. Through the winter of 1892, it battled with bailiffs and police. In the depressed inner city, tenants united against landlords, workers against capitalists, people against the state. In the view of one contemporary, only 'the vigourous use of batons' saved the city from the 'mob'.

These campaigns involved women in a way they had seldom done in the past. Demonstrations outside St Paul's Cathedral in the winter of 1892 attracted 400 people, over fifty of whom were women. Three female speakers 'portrayed cases of poverty'; their stories of struggling to make ends meet were a powerful indictment of charity and government. That May they took to the streets, a procession of 200 'wives and mothers', pleading for work for their 'husbands and sons'. Many carried babies in their arms. The 'public sphere' of politics and the 'private sphere' of homemaking and child-rearing intersected for once through the women's protest. In September they took up banners they had made themselves, turning their domestic skills to political ends.

Women did not only protest at the loss of male breadwinners. In June 1892, a 'female assemblage' numbering over 400 streamed along Russell Street in Melbourne, 'tapping rather heavily with their umbrellas at the glass windows and doors ... of

Chinese laundries', which were making inroads into a predominantly female industry. Every Chinaman they passed en route was 'loudly groaned at'. The demonstration outside St Paul's ended with a 'stroll' through the central business district. Women, like their menfolk, accosted shopkeepers and demanded employment. Despite their unfortunate racist overtones, occasions such as these gave women a sense of their power as women by challenging the traditional notion that women should be passive and ignorant about political matters. They also initiated women into the radicals' ranks. Several sought membership of unemployed associations, and in September 1892 a Mrs Brazill in Melbourne formed an autonomous women's organization. Affectionately dubbed the Brazillian League, it aimed at organizing a workforce long overlooked by male unions.

Unemployed politics were about survival as well as protest. The Active Service Brigade (A.S.B.), founded in Sydney in 1893, is a good example. A coalition of anarchists and socialists, it was probably the most militant of all the unemployed organizations. As 'Ringleader 27' wrote: 'The Social Question is really one of war – war to the knife between the robbers and the robbed ... The lean mob ... must expect no quarter and should give none.'

Most of these battles took place on the hustings at election times, the brigade disrupting public meetings in the name of 'the swindled people of New South Wales'. In a typical episode, crowds of angry unemployed heckled a conservative political candidate and ousted him from the platform. Triumphant, they passed a resolution in favour of the social revolution and concluded the proceedings with a lusty rendering of the *Marseillaise*.

But much of the Brigade's time and energy was devoted to practical help. The A.S.B.'s 'barracks' in Castlereagh Street offered shelter to the unemployed without the stigma of charity. Bed, breakfast, a wad of tobacco and leaflets could all be obtained for sixpence. By 1895, 'a plunge bath or shower' was provided for 'the great unwashed'. The brigade set up 'foster families' for those without a sixpence to spare. Those evicted from their homes or 'stripped bare ... by the commercial system' often sought its help.

Previous demonstrators had petitioned the government for work, but the brigade was an exercise in self-reliance. Its labour exchange sought 'remunerative employment' for 'tradesmen and workers of all sorts'. The brigade also created work when there was little to be had. In 1895, its offshoot, the Australian Order of Industry, began a co-operative mine at Wentworth. Digging for 'socialistic coal' became the only way for many to make a living.

Given the vitality and diversity of this agitation, why did it collapse? The most obvious reason was the severity of state repression. Unemployed activists were imprisoned on any pretext, from conspiracy to disturbing the peace. The movement's leaders were thrown into jail. Police agents infiltrated the 'barracks' to spy on the inmates. Mass processions, the most powerful medium of protest, were also the most vulnerable. Mounted police turned their batons against the people. Indeed, one A.S.B. member dubbed this period 'the reign of terror'.

The state policy of dispersing the urban unemployed also weakened the movement. Though reluctant to provide relief works, colonial governments gave the unemployed rail passes to the country. There they were forced to wander from station to station in the hope of work or hand-outs. Many perished in the wilderness. All were immortalized by Lawson's depiction of the Sundowner, of men 'half crazed' with loneliness and hunger.

What work the government did provide was a punishment in itself. The unemployed had to drain swamps in winter, break rocks for roadworkers, clear scrub and widen rivers. They were employed half time, their wages scarcely enough to feed them. Victoria also set up a number of labour colonies. These were dubbed 'work houses' by contemporaries, places where the unemployed received 'the minimum of nourishment for the maximum amount of labour'.

Village settlement served a similar purpose. In all the eastern colonies, groups of unemployed and their families were sent from the city to farm blocks of land in the countryside. There they were expected to regain the virtues of thrift and independence, achieving the colonial dream of an independent yeomanry. But the reality was different. The land they were allocated was often unsuitable for settlement, and 'stonemasons and carpenters' were not well qualified to farm it. Abandoned by the government, few escaped their old condition of poverty and dependence. Village settlement, the *Bulletin* concluded, did 'not put heart into men but ... deprive[d] them of the last vestige of spirit remaining in their bodies'.

Private charity was also manipulated to break the spirit of the workless. Those who took part in demonstrations were denied relief as punishment. Agitators, it was argued, were 'undeserving' of help. Political meekness thus became the price of survival. As one member of the Active Service Brigade lamented, the unemployed 'had lost their manhood'.

A final reason for the demise of agitation in the 1890s was the lack of support from the mainstream labour movement. As the depression deepened, so did the conflict of interest between those in and out of work. Few unions could provide relief for those unable to keep paying their dues. Falling membership and industrial defeat drained the coffers of those unions that provided for their unemployed members. For their part, the unemployed were unable to find work at union wages. Business and government were keen to exploit such differences. Unemployed men were offered rail passes to break strikes at Broken Hill in 1892 and in the shearers' strike of 1894.

The interests of the mainstream labour movement and the organized unemployed became more and more irreconcilable. Groups such as the Active Service Brigade were revolutionary organizations. Intent on changing the social system, they damned 'the toadies ... crawlers and fencesitters' who looked to parliament for salvation. Labor leaders, by contrast, feared that rowdy processions would jeopardize their chances of election. They preferred the timid tactics of 'soup kitchens' and petitions. Using their influence within the labour movement, Labor leaders were able to out-manoeuvre militant unemployed organizations and to discourage workers from supporting them. Demoralized and divided, the mob that had threatened Gillies with destruction was eventually tamed and conquered.

The pattern in the 1930s was similar. Australia was struck by another depression in 1929. To distinguish it from other depressions, historians labelled it the Great Depression, not because it was worse than earlier ones, but because it was more international, affecting all capitalist societies. In Australia, unemployment began its alarming rise, above the usual 5 to 8 per cent, in late 1928. By 1929 it had reached 11 per cent and continued to climb, reaching more than 20 per cent in 1930, 25 per cent in 1931 and 29 per cent at its peak in 1932. It declined to 25 per cent in 1933, 20 per cent in 1934, 16 per cent in 1935, returning to its predepression levels in 1938.

In many ways Australia in 1929 had changed little since the days before federation. Economic policy-making was still old-fashioned, and governments were unable to regulate the economy to keep the workforce fully employed. Except in Queensland, which introduced unemployment insurance in the early 1920s, the relief of poverty was still seen as a matter of charity. Notions of the work ethic, independence, thrift and sobriety infected the policies and practices of middle-class charity workers, as Rob Watts's chapter on welfare in volume two has shown.

Yet some things *had* changed. The infant Labor Party had grown up and had its turns at government both federally and in the six states. The trade unions had recovered from the 1890s and had developed considerable defensive strength. The arbitration system had given legal enforcement to a structure of wage regulation. Workers probably imagined that if another depression occurred they would be better protected than they had been in the 1890s.

Or were they more cynical? Unemployment existed to some extent throughout the period between the two depressions. Every winter there had been agitation on the part of the jobless. This unemployed movement had sometimes friendly, more often hostile, but always ambivalent relationships with the 'official' labour movement: the trade unions and labour councils, and the Labor Party. The radical ideologies that many unemployed had grasped so eagerly in the 1890s had hardened into the certainties of syndicalism and communism. By 1930, the unemployed had become persistent and aggressive, tarring Trades Hall and the federal Labor government with the same brush, as a bosses' movement.

It became obvious in 1930 that this time it would not be enough to rely on the private charities to relieve distress and provide irregular relief work for the unemployed. Therefore each state government set up its own relief system, paid for with special unemployment relief taxes (except in South Australia, which used money from its ordinary revenue). Each scheme combined relief work with a new measure – sustenance, popularly known as 'susso' or 'the dole'. This was usually paid in the form of an order on shopkeepers for goods (although in Western Australia it was part cash, part goods and later in New South Wales it was cash). It was family based, usually paid to the man of the household. Single men were sometimes given sustenance, sometimes food and bed tickets and relief work. Several governments set up special camps to control them, such as at the Exhibition Building in Adelaide and the Blackboy and Hovea camps on the outskirts of Perth. Single men were sent off to look for gold or to work on farms for a pitiful wage. Single girls were sometimes given sustenance or work in sewing centres but were more often completely ignored. Conservative governments thought single girls could and should find work as domestic servants.

These were not unemployment benefits in the strict sense, because you could be unemployed and yet get nothing. You were ineligible if any one member of your family earned an income above a certain limit and if you still had realizable assets apart from your family home. So never in any state did more than a small proportion of the unemployed receive relief. And the assumptions that underpinned the relief system were much the same as those of the old charity network. Applicants were investigated by private or government inspectors or the police. In Queensland they had to sign a declaration: 'I hereby declare that I am indigent'. In Melbourne, from 1932, they were forced to work for their sustenance to prove their 'genuineness'. Even when unemployment was at its peak, the jobless could not escape that suspicious inquiry: 'Are you really looking for work? Are you genuine?'

Plainly, the new relief systems had much in common with the old. They were used to control the behaviour of the destitute. The unemployed were made dependent, vulnerable and powerless. The old charity network had extended class domination into poverty relief. The new mass forms of relief in the 1930s institutionalized that domination. And the new relief networks were administered by the same people who ran the old, even down to the police who gave out relief in country towns.

In the 1930s, thousands of men, women and children experienced unemployment for the first time and were thrust into relationships they had never before encountered. But many understood that their subordination was a product of their isolation. Individually, they were supplicants, but together they could be powerful. And, ironically, it was usually the relief system that brought the unemployed together. It was at the local sustenance relief centres, at ration dumps, on the job at sustenance and relief work sites, at single-men's camps, and at labour bureaus that experiences were exchanged, the inadequacy of the dole condemned and the government's neglect exposed. It was here that new ideas about ideology and change were disseminated, the rudiments of organizations were laid, alliances formed and costs and benefits debated. An interesting parallel can be drawn with Marx's prediction that the factory system of modern capitalism would bring about working-class organization, as employed workers would be thrown together in factories to experience collectively their exploitation. The way the capitalist state treated unemployed workers also helped them to organize resistance.

Unemployed politics was extremely complicated, but for the sake of clarity it can be divided into radical, moderate and conservative streams. The radical stream was associated with the

Communist Party, and included groups such as the One Big Union of the Unemployed, the Unemployed Workers Movement, the United Fronts of Employed and Unemployed, and the Dole and Relief Workers Council. In 1933 a small Trotskyist group split off to form the Dole Workers Union in Victoria and the Unemployed and Relief Workers Union in Sydney. These radical organizations had branches in most capital cities and the big industrial mining towns.

The moderate stream was associated either with the Labor Party or local Trades Halls. The Central Unemployed Committee in Victoria was an affiliate of the Trades Hall; the Queensland A.L.P. rank and file committee was, as its name stated, allied to the state Labor Party. These were federated groups without interstate connections.

Then there were the conservative groups with no labour movement connections. These included organizations of unemployed returned soldiers. Another example was the Western Australian Relief and Sustenance Workers Union, which had links with the Douglas Credit Party. There were also many suburban and town groups who, hoping to impress conservative municipal councils, stuck to providing relief and odd jobs for members and steered clear of politics.

The boundaries between these streams, however, were never clear-cut. In the first place, there was a constant process of adjustment, alignment and re-alignment, as unemployed politics developed a chronic factionalism. In the Melbourne suburb of Richmond, for instance, seven organizations came and went in 1930. In the second, because most groups took their strength from their local communities, a solidarity developed across factional lines behind the backs of the sectarian leaders. It was most manifest during periods of intense activity such as eviction struggles, dole boycotts and sustenance strikes. By the late 1930s, in Melbourne and Sydney at least, sectarianism had so declined that moderates and radicals were able to merge fairly peacefully into those city's major groups – the moderate Central Unemployed Committee in Melbourne and the radical Council of Unemployed and Relief Workers in Sydney.

The aims of these organizations reflected their political connections. The Unemployed Workers Movement (U.W.M.) regarded itself as the Communist Party's 'bridge to the unemployed masses', and the C.P.A. itself was composed mainly of unemployed workers during this period. In accordance with C.P.A. dogma, the U.W.M. regarded Australia as 'rotten ripe' for revolution and saw the moderate labour movement as the principal barrier to revolutionary change. The moderate organizations generally took a left Labor Party line, opposing the timid 'Premiers' Plan', supporting left Labor leaders such as New South Wales Premier Lang, and campaigning for a general programme of bank nationalization. They also thought the U.W.M. was composed of desperadoes. One Melbourne leader described U.W.M. tactics as 'sporadic attempts to send out speakers to persuade the unemployed to pillage and maraud and then pass on to leave the C.U.C. to clean up'. An extraordinary amount of spite, bitterness and violence was spent between the various groups.

Sectarianism, however, was only one side of the story. Common to all unemployed groups was the desire to improve the range, quantity and quality of relief. Generally they sought full-time work at award wages and conditions or sustenance paid at basic wage rates. They wanted to stop the evictions of the homeless and the harassment of the unemployed by police. This was crucial, because police often used vagrancy laws to jail militants and a range of other laws to harass strikers, marchers and picketers. Police also tried to persuade state governments to pass new laws to suppress dissent. They were successful in South Australia, where the Hill Labor government passed a Public Safety Preservations Act.

Within these general aims were a multiplicity of specific campaigns with more immediate objectives. The range is huge: from agitation by itinerant unemployed men in north Queensland for decent shelters in country towns to fights with railway police in the Victorian Mallee District for a free ride on 'the rattler'; from the Adelaide Beef Riot in 1931 (a protest against government plans to replace beef with mutton in men's rations) to mass protests against evictions in the Melbourne suburb of Brunswick. Day to day, these groups fought constant battles with local councils over the right to use council premises and the right to collect relief. This too was crucial. Practically all unemployed groups, no matter how large or small, supplemented government relief through their own efforts. Not only was this necessary, but leaders well knew that producing extra relief meant more members. The reluctance of the radical U.W.M. to provide extra relief did much to undermine its appeal to the unemployed.

The tactics of unemployed groups varied greatly. The conservative groups did unpaid work for local councils. The moderate organizations with grander aims adopted peaceful and constitutional methods of protest: deputations, negotiations, peaceful

HOUSEHOLD GOODS figured largely yesterday in a clash between police and evicted unemployed men in Gisborne Street. The lower picture shows impedimenta piled in James Street, Fitzroy, after the eviction of 95 men from Fitzroy Street. Top picture shows the litter in Gisborne Street after police had charged the procession of men carrying the furniture towards Parliament House.
SH 1-8-33

An eviction struggle in Fitzroy, Melbourne, 1933

marches and rallies and, to show they were good unionists, strikes and black bans. The radical groups did all these things too, but with fire.

The distinction between moderates and radicals can best be seen in eviction fights. The moderates would collect the belongings of evicted people and dump them on the steps of the local town hall for the council to deal with; the radicals would fight the eviction itself. Hence there were pitched battles between police and U.W.M. members at Bankstown and Newtown in Sydney and Tighes Hill in Newcastle. And in Melbourne, houses in South Melbourne and Reservoir were burnt to the ground. The radicals led the way in major campaigns such as the four big dole strikes in Melbourne in 1933, 1934, 1935 and 1936. But unemployed politics was not all excitement. It was the same as any other form of politics, with periods of intense activity interspersed with long spells of routine administration and mundane organizing, a fairly constant round of meetings and fund-raising nights.

We can measure the success or failure of unemployed politics in the Great Depression in several ways. First of all, the various organizations never captured the permanent loyalty of all the unemployed. They constantly struggled against a chronic inertia. Nevertheless at times they could mobilize extraordinarily large numbers. For example, the entire sustenance workforce in Victoria struck for a week in 1935 to wring increased sustenance out of an unwilling government. Secondly, in countless individual cases, the unemployed movement forced concessions, withdrawal or retreat from local councillors, landlords, police, sustenance administrators, and others, who held the fate of the individual unemployed workers in their hands. Thirdly, large-scale agitation forced concessions from governments. In Victoria, for example, practically every improvement in government relief came about as a result of a specific agitation. The abandonment of a Victorian scheme to replace coupons with goods given in bulk was a result of a black-ban on the local depot by the unemployed of Richmond. The institution of an eight shilling a week rent allowance was the product of a sustained agitation against eviction. The two big increases in sustenance rates in 1933 and 1935 were granted after strikes by sustenance workers. One strike involved 3,000 men and lasted fully five weeks. The passage of legislation ending police harassment of street meetings came about after a campaign of civil disobedience in 1933. And a long agitation in 1932 forced the United Australia Party government to restore basic wage rates on relief works. Another strike by single men in 1934 forced the government to give them more relief work, which increased their 'wages' by 50 per cent.

On the other hand, there was no revolution in Australia, though the radical unemployed struggled hard for it. Even in their more immediate aims, the unemployed organizations did not have complete success. No government anywhere ever introduced full-time relief work at award wages and conditions or paid sustenance at the basic wage rate, or called off the police and the bailiffs. And just as there were countless little successes, so there were also countless little failures. But all this is practical politics. And in one sense the outcomes of the unemployed movements of the 1930s were less important than their role in developing a politics, a sense of consciousness, among the unemployed. The Great Depression was an experience that might have encouraged passivity, fear and inaction on the part of its victims, pushed out as they were by much of the rest of society. Yet a creative, often extensive and vigorous unemployed movement was born and sustained by the victims of the worst poverty Australia has known. Surely that is where the success story lies.

High unemployment returned to Australia in the mid 1970s. It lingered at about 8 per cent of the workforce until 1982–3 when it began to rise alarmingly. It has fallen since then to about 8 per cent again.

Old radicals who remember the 1930s sometimes ask why today's unemployed workers are so passive. Politics of any sort is a product of its time, and times have changed. Unemployment has not reached the dizzy heights of the 1890s and 1930s. But it resembles the rates between those depressions – excessive but not alarming to governments. City life has also changed. The close-knit working-class communities that spawned the strong and resilient local politics of the 1930s have gone. People's lives have become increasingly centred on their homes; street life and local entertainment have been replaced by the television and the video. The patterns of suburbia have also changed. It takes time to build social bonds; many of the newer outer suburbs are too young to develop a working-class consciousness. There is little left of the sustaining working-class culture that led people to help each other get through previous economic crises. Furthermore, the political agenda of the labour movement has changed a lot. Interest in the unemployed has been left to minor parties, the power and influence of which are small.

Employers have taken a very different tack when it comes to reducing the number of people they employ. Many unions have been powerful enough to negotiate the terms under which retrenchments will take place. This has generally involved a combination of early retirement schemes, severance pay for those who are sacked, and reductions in the number of new people taken on. Allowing the workforce to be reduced by 'natural wastage' creates less obvious trauma than suddenly sacking large numbers of people. But it also means that the people who are out of work tend to be those with the least access to the trade union structure. They tend to be people who, because of isolation or discrimination, have little social power. Ageing workers, school leavers, Aborigines and immigrants have borne the brunt of the labour market decline. There are also large numbers of 'discouraged' workers, mainly women, who would like to work but have given up trying to find jobs. They are not officially recorded as being unemployed; neither are the many people who are working part time because they cannot find full-time work. If these people are included, the real unemployment rate is considerably higher than the official figures suggest. But of course the government always prefers to use the lowest figures possible. In March 1987, for instance, the unemployment rate would have been over 12 per cent, if the figures included every person officially designated as unemployed and every other person who was seeking a job from the Commonwealth Employment Service. In addition, 259,000 of Australia's 1.4 million part-time workers want to work more hours.

The state also responds differently to unemployment and the unemployed. It offers unemployment benefits without insisting that the unemployed go through the humilitation of working at meaningless jobs to earn them (though both the major parties have considered reverting to the old practice of forcing people to work for the dole). It offers a wider range of support services such as re-training, an employment service and youth support schemes. It closely monitors the volume of unemployment and has a far greater degree of control over the direction of the economy than did the state in earlier depressions.

The unemployed are at least treated better now than they were before the Second World War. But this isn't to say that their situation is now fine. If they don't have to beg for charity, they are still forced to prove that they are looking for work to qualify for the dole. When there are no suitable jobs around, this can be a pointless, humiliating exercise. They have also been subjected to snooping by officers of the Department of Social Security, which now employs review teams who intrusively and brutally compete to see who is best at cutting people off the dole. The dole has been abolished for people under eighteen and replaced with a weekly allowance of twenty-five dollars. It is supposed to encourage students to stay at school. It won't, for kids alienated by the classroom will still leave when they can no longer stand it. Unemployed adults under twenty-one must now wait thirteen weeks before becoming eligible for benefits, and unemployed adults over twenty-five must now pass an assets test before they get their entitlement. The government also abolished the Com-

Where in earlier depressions governments had offered relief work, in the 1970s the Fraser government offered only cosmetic measures, including social centres to keep the young unemployed off the streets.

munity Employment Scheme. It is part of a re-orientation, it said, away from job creation to re-training. Extensive job re-training is necessary, but we must ask whether the government is serious when it spends so little on it, when it starves the state school system of money while financing the elite private schools, when it reduces general funds and re-introduces fees for higher education. The unemployed are still blamed repeatedly for their own plight by the media and the political parties, who find it a convenient way of covering up the fact they have no solutions to the problem. And the dole itself is completely inadequate. If the unemployed are better off, in absolute terms, than the unemployed of the 1890s or 1930s, they are also living in a vastly more affluent society. In relation to the general standard of living, their poverty is extreme. In a society where consumerism has become a way of life, and money is king, the poor are excluded more completely than they have ever been before.

In this context we should expect unemployed politics to have its own character. It is smaller and less influential. The media have an irritating habit of regarding social workers as the legitimate voice of the unemployed, and so the real voice of unemployed politics is not often heard. This politics is actually radical. One demonstration in Melbourne, for instance, concluded with rallies that damaged the Stock Exchange and the Melbourne Club. This assault on symbols of capitalism and privilege was reminiscent of the unemployed politics of the 1890s. The movement is also less dominated by men and demands for male employment than its predecessors. In its political ideologies there is a commitment to gender equality. The sheer number of women in the workforce makes the old masculine emphasis redundant. It also demands the right to a job, rather than a mere increase in unemployment benefits. And it is well aware that proposals to force the unemployed to work for their pitiful dole attack the unemployed as a whole. If the threat to introduce work for the dole becomes reality, the influence of the present-day unemployed movement will be finally put to the test.

From Convicts to Communists

PETER LOVE

Australia was founded on conflict. The convicts and jailers of Phillip's First Fleet established a society based on force. Settlers used violence to dislodge the Aborigines, jailers used violence to keep the convicts in line, men used violence against women. At the same time, conflict was expressed in subtler forms. Private entrepreneurs tried to wrest control of land and labour from the state. The colonial administration was often divided within and at odds with its superiors in London. In these circumstances, discontent was expressed in many forms, and radical ideas gained a wide following.

Most noticeably, it was the arduous condition of being a convict that provoked revolt. A good deal of resistance to the authorities was expressed through individual action: by insolence and idleness, 'bolting' or brawling. Sometimes, however, harsh conditions and old hatreds combined to produce a collective uprising. The Castle Hill Rebellion in 1804 involved some 300 convicts, mostly Irish. William Johnston, who had been transported for his part in the Irish rebellions of 1798, rallied his fellow-prisoners to the banner that for centuries had symbolized the Irish struggle for liberty. The rebels marched towards Windsor, a new settlement west of Sydney Cove, to inflict revenge on their British oppressors. But on the way they were met by a small, disciplined detachment of soldiers and civilians, who defeated them in a short and bloody engagement. The rebellion was an early example of a persistent theme in the history of Australian radicalism: the influence of overseas conflicts and ideas on local struggles.

There were also some free settlers who fought for justice and liberty. Edward Smith Hall came to Sydney in 1811 with a record of benevolent work among the poor back in England. He spent his early years in the colony building up his grazing properties and working to establish the Bank of New South Wales, but he did not prosper as a grazier or banker and had to spend his later years working as a public servant. In 1826 he and Arthur Hill set up the *Monitor*, a newspaper dedicated to the causes of civil liberty and political democracy. Through its columns Hall advocated representative government and trial by jury. He was particularly concerned with the treatment of convicts; he believed many of them had been 'punished contrary to law'. And he vigorously condemned Governor Darling's oppressive rule. Indeed, his frequent criticism of public administration, of prominent citizens and the clergy led to several convictions against him for criminal libel. His obstinate fight for a free press eventually provoked Darling to take vindictive action against him. Hall, however, had the last word when Darling was sacked by the Colonial Office for taking those actions. In the late 1840s, Hall joined forces with Henry Parkes, an association based on the broadly nationalist ideas held by both men. After Hall's death in 1860, he was remembered as a democratic radical and champion of the common people.

For most of the nineteenth century, and well into the twentieth, religion was a major source of conflict. The recurring struggles between the Church of England, non-conformist Protestantism and Catholicism often reflected national and class allegiances carried over from Europe. Ruling-class admirers of the Mother Country regarded the Church of England as one of the pillars of British civilization. Scottish Presbyterians linked an austere acquisitiveness to spiritual salvation. Many immigrant English workers added a religious dimension to their class consciousness in the practice of Methodism. Irish Catholics' faith affirmed their ethnic and class identity as well as their religious devotion. These differences sometimes became the focus of bitter disputes. For example, there was a sharp conflict over state aid to church schools. Although they appeared as doctrinal squabbles, many such disputes were also about the distribution of social power. Rarely, however, were they truly radical: they did not imply a fundamental change in the pattern of social relationships. Indeed, many radicals attacked the churches for distorting popular perceptions of wider social problems and encouraging the poor to wait for their rewards in the afterlife rather than attempt to improve the world around them.

The main preoccupations of nineteenth-century Australian radicals had nothing to do with religion. They centred around two related issues: political democracy and economic independence. There was nothing unique in this. Similar struggles were being conducted in Europe and other parts of the world at the same time. But the way these issues developed in Australia was distinctive.

Until the 1880s, radical movements tended to be short-lived and to focus on specific issues. For example, workers tried to exercise some control over the labour market. In the early 1830s the Society of Emigrant Mechanics agitated for a restriction on immigration to protect employment in the skilled trades. Later, during the economic crisis of the 1840s, a Mutual Protection Association was formed. It began in 1843 with an unsuccessful effort to have convict labour banned from public works projects, but it soon expanded its interests to include opposition to immigration, demands for small land grants and calls for government relief for the distressed. Although they were not immediately successful, campaigns of this sort were the forerunners of the movements that later produced more enduring working-class organizations. In the meantime, there were occasional victories, such as the achievement of the Eight Hour Day in 1856.

Many of the radical causes of the mid nineteenth century involved an alliance of workers and progressive sections of the middle class against conservative pastoralists. The anti-transportation movement that gathered momentum from 1848 is an early example of this alliance in action. Radical workers opposed convict transportation, because workers' bargaining position in the labour market was weakened by competition from convict labour. It was hard to press for higher wages when convict labour was available for practically nothing. Many urban businessmen and professionals hoped that the ending of transportation would undermine the economic and social dominance of the pastoralists, the chief employers of convict labour. Together, the progressives and radicals attacked transportation as a blight on the rising nation. They recruited enough mass support to help end transportation and so remove this prop of the landed ruling class.

This alliance was held together by a combination of moral principle and economic self-interest. It came into action again in the debates over 'self-government' in New South Wales. The squatters wanted an elitist, 'aristocratic' constitution, to represent property rather than people, and to confirm the pastoral industry's dominance. The alliance of radical and liberal activists wanted a more democratic system of government, to reflect the interests of an increasingly diverse economy. The politics of this alliance ranged from the more advanced opinions of the *People's Advocate*, the Political Association and the Democratic League, through the pragmatic radicalism of Henry Parkes's *Empire*, to the moderate liberalism of the New South Wales Constitution Committee. Despite some internal differences, they all agreed that the proposed squatters' constitution was an attempt to transplant the old English class system in Australia. A truly 'democratic' constitution should recognize other 'interests' in the colony – especially those of manufacturers, respectable workingmen and small farmers. If such people were included in the government, all legitimate interests would be recognized, and there would be political harmony and economic progress for all.

This coalition of 'the people' against the 'squattocracy' eventually won a form of self-government on a reasonably democratic voting system (as long as you were male), but only in the Legislative Assembly, the 'lower house' of parliament. The squatters retained effective control over the nominated Legislative Council, the 'upper house', which still had the power to restrain the lower house. In due course, the constitutions adopted by all the other colonies reflected this same balance of political power: all upper houses, whether elected or nominated, overwhelmingly favoured propertied interests.

The urban middle class had harnessed the momentum created by radical opinion to start the long process of wresting control of the state from the hands of the landed gentry. Many radicals hailed the new constitutions as a triumph of 'the people' against 'the monopolists'. That apparent victory, however, was to limit the forms of radical action in the future. Radicals increasingly had to act in ways that were acceptable to liberal opinion. The old radical causes of political liberty and economic independence, which led to popular uprisings such as the Eureka Stockade, became liberal issues to be pursued through the institutions of the state. Many radicals now began to see the state as an active agent that might be captured and used in the struggle for social power.

An early example of this tendency was the way the 1857–60 Land Convention looked to governments to solve their problems. The convention's programme called for the free selection of land, a more democratic electoral system, removal of the Chinese and an end to assisted immigration. Here the radical demand for greater social equality was transformed into a populist programme as a result of having to work within the framework of liberal ideologies and institutions. This populist programme aimed to unite 'the common people' against 'the monopolists' who wished to deprive the people of their right to a free and prosperous future. It was not until the last twenty years of the nineteenth century, when socialist ideas began to make headway in the emerging labour movement, that this kind of populism was seriously challenged as the leading form of radical expression.

Despite the hopes of the Eureka rebels, the members of the Land Convention and other mid nineteenth century radicals, Australia did not become a country of small, independent producers and yeoman farmers. The most profitable sectors of the economy – wool growing, mercantile trading, finance, transport and larger scale manufacturing – were dominated by a small number of British and Australian companies. Although wealth was more evenly distributed than in Europe, by the early 1890s more than two-thirds of the workforce earned a living by selling their labour for wages. The growth of an organized labour movement was a consequence of these economic relations.

The growth of the trade union movement has been discussed in the chapter by Verity Burgmann and Stuart Macintyre earlier in this volume. The main developments to note here are the expansion of the large industrial unions in the 1880s and the moves towards closer unionism with the development of trades and labour councils over the same period. As a result of these changes, the organized labour movement was in a better position to exert industrial 'muscle'. But it did not speak with a united voice. As a general rule, the older craft unions tended to seek piecemeal reforms by so-called 'responsible' means, while the newer industrial unions were more inclined towards militant action and more attached to the tradition of populist radicalism.

Socialist ideas only began to creep into the language of the labour movement in the late 1880s. They were first introduced by a few individual agitators armed with the latest European literature, who explained how workers were robbed by their bosses paying them less than their labour was really worth. This theory of 'surplus value', first elaborated by Karl Marx, came as a revelation to many radical workers. They saw it as the first 'scientific' explanation of the basis of class relations under capitalism. Through the formation of organizations such as the Australian Socialist League, by speeches on street corners and in work-places, and through articles published in the growing number of radical papers, socialism gradually found a wider audience. But the increasing influence of socialist ideas was not simply brought about by the persuasive powers of a few small sects and a handful of dedicated agitators. The steady decline of wages and working conditions in the late 1880s, followed by economic collapse and the 'great strikes' of the early and mid 1890s, provided a receptive audience for radical ideas. Yet the conditions created by mass unemployment and the ruthless suppression of strikes did not produce a uniform response. Some workers sought 'responsible' solutions through 'moderate' measures introduced with liberals' support; others were still attracted to populist 'conspiracy theories', which claimed that bankers were trying to destroy the labour movement; and an increasing number began to see that socialist theories made sense of the situation confronting them. As a result, those theories moved out of the journals and club rooms of socialist groups into the language of labour's peak councils.

So popular was socialism in the 1890s that the Brisbane-based agitator William Lane was able to persuade hundreds of people to join his utopian socialist community in Paraguay, which lasted in some form or another from 1893 until early this century. Lane and those who followed him had despaired of seeing Australia transformed in a socialist direction. The thousands of socialists who remained were more optimistic. Socialists took a leading part in building the new Labor parties around the turn of the century. Most of them harked back to the older radical tradition. They imagined that, if they could win power in parliament, they could use the state to build the foundations of a socialist society. But although they spent much energy in argument and organization, these state socialists soon found that parliamentary politics was fundamentally hostile to socialist strategies for change. Union and party conferences made bold declarations of socialist objectives, and rank and file party members believed ardently in the need for socialist policies, but the balance of power within the Labor parties always favoured the pragmatic labourists who looked merely for minor reforms within the capitalist system.

It did not take very long for the more perceptive socialists to identify their dilemma. Since the Labor Party held the loyalty of most of the working class, socialists either had to squander their energies trying to turn it into a truly socialist party, or work outside it and risk political isolation. In practice, they tended to adopt one of three main options. Some, such as the brilliant socialist orator Harry Scott Bennett, struggled within the party to win it round to a socialist objective and force its politicians to accept that objective. Others turned their back on politics and looked to the unions to develop industrial strategies that would pave the way for socialism. The third option was to establish an alternative party, as visiting British union leader Tom Mann did when he established the Victorian Socialist Party in 1905–6. The same approach was used later by organizations such as the Australian Socialist Party and the Socialist Labor Party before the First World War and the Communist Party after the war. These were the standard responses to the socialists' constant dilemma: should they 'bore from within' or 'batter from without'?

In the early twentieth century, the strategy of aiming for socialism by industrial rather than political means found its most popular expression in the Industrial Workers of the World (I.W.W.), often referred to as the 'Wobblies'. This organization started in the United States in 1905 and established itself in Australia from 1907, providing yet another example of the importance of foreign influence on Australian radicalism. The I.W.W. was utterly contemptuous of parliamentary politics. The Wobblies advocated a syndicalist strategy: the working class should organize itself into bigger, more powerful industrial unions and eventually into One Big Union of all workers, which would seize control of the means of production and build socialism. Despite great dedication and an unswerving commitment to their cause, they were never able to mobilize the mass support they needed for their revolution. But they were very effective – and often witty – propagandists, who attracted a great deal of attention.

Unfortunately, some of this attention was of the wrong kind. During the First World War, they became easy targets for Prime Minister Hughes, whose War Precautions Act was used ruthlessly to suppress them. This did not, however, put an end to the influence of syndicalism. Immediately after the war, trade union and A.L.P. conferences jostled for control over the labour movement, and one of the central issues in that struggle was the question of the One Big Union. In the end, syndicalism and socialism both lost out. The A.L.P. adopted a weak 'socialisation objective' in 1921 and then began immediately to water it down even more. The final indignity came when the conservative Australian Workers Union claimed that it was the One Big Union.

True syndicalism had flourished during the First World War, because the war created profound social tensions within Australian society. There was a sharp decline in living standards almost as soon as the war began. By 1916 a series of events brought those tensions to the point of widespread strife. There were massive casualties on the western front in France, and people were beginning to understand the full horror of war. Australia's Irish Catholics reacted angrily to the British government's brutal suppression of the Easter rebellion in Dublin. The conscription referenda split

TOM MANN

As the Capitalists wish to see him.

Socialist activist Tom Mann was jailed for his role in the Broken Hill miners' strike of 1908–9.

the A.L.P. and the entire population into two bitterly hostile camps, as Chris Healy describes in his chapter on anti-war movements in this volume. In 1917 a general strike in New South Wales went very close to civil war. In the midst of this, news began to filter through a heavily censored press that a socialist revolution in Russia had succeeded. For Australian socialists of all persuasions, this was the most significant event in modern history. At last, the question of socialism had been removed from the realm of speculation. A revolution in the name of Marxist socialism had actually happened somewhere, even if only in a backward feudal state on the other side of the world.

After the war, the Soviet Union formed the Comintern, an organization designed to help spread the Bolshevik revolution into other countries. In Australia, various socialist parties vied for official Comintern recognition, each claiming to embody the revolutionary spirit of the Australian working class.

When a communist party was formed in 1920–2, it had to meet a set of criteria laid down by the Comintern before it could be recognized as the only legitimate Communist Party of Australia and take its place in the organizations of the international revolutionary movement. This had profound effects on the new party. For a start, it was committed to policies determined by a foreign organization that had little or no local knowledge. Overseas influence in Australian radical affairs was now taking an extreme form. Furthermore, according to Comintern instructions, Australia was to have a communist party organized along the lines of the Russian Bolshevik Party. It was also to denounce all reformist elements in the socialist movement that did not accept its claim to lead the working class. The English historian Eric Hobsbawm once remarked: 'Each communist party was the child of the marriage of two ill-assorted partners, a national left and the October revolution.' The Australian party was no exception. Tension between the instructions from Moscow and the inclinations of Australian communists was to be a continuing theme in the party's history.

The connection with the Comintern was to commit the Communist Party to a series of policies that often isolated it from the mainstream of the Australian working class and the organized labour movement. Occasionally compromises were worked out. In 1921, for example, the Third Comintern Congress introduced the 'united front' policy, by which communist parties would work in 'friendly collaboration' with other sections of the labour movement. In Australia this meant the unions and the A.L.P. To the

One Enemy, the Employing Class
DIRECT ACTION
VOL 2 NO. 28. Registered at G.P.O. Sydney. SYDNEY, MAY. 1, 1915. ONE PENNY

Direct Action was an appropriate title for the newspaper of the Industrial Workers of the World.

Communist Party this looked like the old 'bore from within' strategy, so many leading members such as Jock Garden chose to continue working within the A.L.P. and the union movement in an effort to capture them for the communist cause. But really, Comintern policy was not to convert existing organizations to communist policies but to steal their support within the working class and then destroy them. This led to all manner of confusion, both inside the Communist Party and the A.L.P.

For a short time, there appeared to be some success. In 1923 the Communist Party was granted provisional affiliation with the New South Wales Labor Party. But when it was realized that Comintern policy aimed at destroying the A.L.P., and that affiliation therefore meant taking a viper to its bosom, the A.L.P. promptly expelled the Communist Party. Now isolated from the mainstream of the labour movement, the Communist Party lost support. With the economic climate improving, the party almost disappeared. When it openly challenged the A.L.P. in the 1925 New South Wales election, it suffered a humiliating defeat.

In the late 1920s, as the capitalist world began to slide into the Great Depression, and as Stalin began to get complete control of the Comintern, a new policy was announced. Capitalism, it was declared, was entering a 'third period' of major crisis. Proletarian revolutions would occur in most of the developed countries. In the context of deepening depression and revolutionary ferment, the social democratic and labour parties would become the working class's worst enemies, because they would attempt to convince workers that the system could be rescued and thus delay mass insurrection. These same parties would be supported by capitalists in the early stages of the crisis, because they were trying to save the system. Ultimately, however, they would fail, and overt class war would erupt. At this point the bourgeoisie would turn to fascism as a means of suppressing the revolution. The role played by the social democratic and labour parties in this process was termed 'social fascism'. Communist parties were therefore required to sever all links with such parties and concentrate their energies on exposing 'social fascist treachery'. Obediently, the Australian Communist Party followed instructions, with disastrous results. The venom and self-righteousness with which many Australian communists denounced the members of the Labor Party turned temporary suspicions into bitter and lasting hatreds. As a result, the party remained on the margin of Australian politics at a time of great social tension, when it might otherwise have expected to command growing support. Most radical opinion

The Communist Party saw the U.S.S.R. as the main force opposing Hitler's fascism. Noel Counihan drew this cartoon as 'Cunningham' for the *Workers' Voice* in 1934.

swung behind New South Wales Premier Lang, who was busy reviving labour's old populist tradition with spirited attacks on the bankers and monopolists, who, he claimed, had caused the depression. One of the ironies of 'third period' communism in Australia was that it drove many of its potential supporters into the arms of the so-called 'social fascists'.

The Comintern, however, did have some policies that were more appropriate to Australian conditions. During the 1930s the strategy of the 'united front from below' proved to be much more successful. It marked a turn away from 'party politics' to a strategy of making direct contact with workers on the job. Groups of communists, or nuclei, would be set up in factories and other work-places to organize the workers under Communist Party leadership, but secretly, because Communism had become so unpopular during the preceding period. In this way, party workers gained considerable influence in particular industries, most notably in mining, transport and on the waterfront. For many years this industrial strategy was to be one of the cornerstones of Communist Party policy. It also gave the communists a far greater influence in the labour movement than their numbers warranted. Moreover, the 'united front' policy was to extend beyond the work-place into 'progressive' organizations that were regarded as 'fraternal'. These 'front' organizations, as they were widely known, succeeded in building bridges between the party and a number of popular movements. The standard method was to set up or take over outfits whose policies were broadly in line with party views. Among the more successful of these were the Unemployed Workers' Movement, the Movement Against War and Fascism, and the Friends of the Soviet Union.

Perhaps the most stark example of the Communist Party's difficulties with its Comintern connection was the case of the Second World War. In the late 1930s it had been following the Comintern line on the popular front against fascism. In doing so, it had won a measure of support from a number of thoughtful left liberals. It had been among the first in Australia to sound the alarm about the rise of fascism in Europe, and developments in the mid 1930s confirmed its position. As events unfolded, the party gained a good deal of respect for its stand and built up a degree of moral authority.

But all this good work was dashed with the signing of the Nazi–Soviet Non-aggression Pact in August 1939. Australian communists were stunned and confused. They had to work out their position without the Comintern guidance on which they had increasingly come to rely. After a study of the Leninist position on war, the party eventually decided that it was an 'imperialist war'. In the words of Jack Blake, it was 'a war between two conflicting groups of imperialist powers for world supremacy'. Communist theory was adapted to suit Russian national interests. The party was banned by the Menzies government in June 1940. Almost immediately, offices and homes were raided, literature was confiscated and some members were jailed for 'illegal activities'.

When the German army invaded Russia on 22 June 1941, however, the party had to perform another somersault. Almost overnight, the conflict became the 'great patriotic war'. Communist union leaders who had been insisting that there be no erosion of working conditions, no surrender of civil liberties, and that the right to strike be exercised as in peace time, were suddenly transformed. Now, everything had to be subordinated to the war effort. Communists were among the most vociferous in denouncing strikes as unpatriotic; there was a maniacal enthusiasm for productivity and a constant call for the Allies to open a second front in Europe to relieve the pressure on 'our great and glorious Soviet allies'. The ban on the party was lifted by the Curtin government at the end of 1942.

The party's inconsistencies were apparent to all, and there was some well-deserved cynical comment. By that stage, however, there was almost unanimous support for the war among the Australian people, a mood only strengthened in 1942 by the Japanese threat to the nation's security. In these conditions, communists became the most vigorous advocates of an all-out war effort. Their dedication to the cause, coupled with reports of the heroic sacrifices being made by the Russians in their struggle with the forces of Hitlerite barbarism, served to increase the party's popularity. By the end of the war it was at the peak of its power. Through its leadership of numerous unions, it could call on the support of more than a quarter of the organized labour movement. Its electoral support, although still small, was higher than it ever had been, and it had some 23,000 members on its books. But its strength owed more to the temporary popularity of the Soviet Union than to working-class commitment to the struggle for communism in Australia. Once again, foreign concerns were intimately linked with the forms and fortunes of the Australian left.

A Hundred Flowers Faded

PETER BEILHARZ

The left's fortunes in the post-war period were less favourable than before 1945. No sooner had the grinning mug of the victorious Marshal Stalin graced the cover of the *Women's Weekly* or the Red Flag flown over Sydney Town Hall than the balance of forces worldwide began to shift against the left. Communism's newly won respectability was devastated, eventually to dissolve in the atmosphere of the Cold War. By 1949 communist leader Lance Sharkey was being jailed for pro-Soviet sedition. The Soviet Union had now served its purpose for the west: British Prime Minister Churchill and American President Roosevelt had met Russian leader Stalin at Yalta to divide the world into their respective spheres of influence. The Iron Curtain descended, and communism again emerged as public enemy number one. Anti-communism was to remain a major theme of political life for decades to come. The left was isolated, confused, persecuted and threatened with bans by conservative governments under Menzies and Fadden. Many on the left responded to this state of siege by becoming even more zealous and ridiculous in their defence of the Soviet model.

These were miserable times for those on the left who lived through them. Reduced to pariahs, they fought where they stood. The left and its friends, such as the historian Brian Fitzpatrick and Labor leader Dr H. V. Evatt, became major defenders of the civil liberties that others wanted to deny them. Public hostility was whipped up by the Petrov Affair, where Prime Minister Menzies used the defection of a minor Soviet Embassy official to claim that there was a 'nest of traitors' infecting the Labor Party and Australian political life. Leftists were compelled to change their political tactics and to stop issuing blatantly pro-Soviet propaganda. This was all for the best, but otherwise political persecution seriously demoralized the forces of the left in this period.

There were also economic reasons for the decline of the left at this time. In the post-war reconstruction, Labor governments had briefly gained legitimacy. But when the post-war economic boom began, socialist or reforming politics seemed less urgent than they had been, say, in the 1930s. The Labor Party lost what dynamism it had possessed in the 1940s, when increased state planning of economic life had briefly become fashionable, in Australia as in other capitalist societies. The enthusiasm for planning faded as the long boom accelerated. This period was the heyday of conservatism in recent Australian history. Anti-communism split the Labor Party in 1955, leaving it rudderless until Gough Whitlam emerged to modernize it a decade later.

In communist circles, there were two major developments in the 1950s. Communists' industrial tactics became closer and closer to those of the left of the labour movement. After the failure of the 1949 coal strike, in which they had played a leading part, communists became less enthusiastic about militant rank-and-file activity and more interested in winning positions in the trade union bureaucracy. Communist unionism developed within the mould of the trade unions' preoccupation with wages and conditions. Communist militants in the unions were 'good blokes' (and blokes they usually were). They delivered the goods to their mainly male membership, and they also knew how to blow the whistle on the ruling class when it indulged in blatant oppression overseas.

Meanwhile, the Soviet Union was losing its place as the sole political model. Some communists turned towards the Chinese model; others began to enthuse about developments in the communist parties in Western Europe. There was some interest in Yugoslavia, but the real fascination was with the Italian party, where the foundations of 'Eurocommunism' had already been laid by Togliatti. He argued that communist parties ought to pursue 'national roads' to communism, employing methods appropriate to each particular country but aiming at the same goal – socialism in the manner of the 'people's democracies' of Eastern Europe. By 1951, the Communist Party had adopted a policy of pursuing an Australian road to socialism, which was later approved by Russian leader Khruschev at the twentieth congress of the Soviet party.

Eventually, the attachment to new communist models overseas led to a series of splits. In 1964, the pro-Chinese left the Communist Party to form the Communist Party of Australia (Marxist-

The sober style of the old left: over 7,000 marchers attend the 1961 funeral of Jim Healy, communist leader of the Waterside Workers' Federation.

Leninist). In 1971, the pro-Soviets departed to form the Socialist Party of Australia. And, in 1984, some of the original enthusiasts for the Italian Communist Party's methods finally decided that the Labor Party's strategy was the closest thing to an Australian 'national road' and sought to become its think-tank by forming the Socialist Forum in Melbourne.

In the late 1950s, a 'New Left' emerged, consisting of various groupings of intellectuals and ex-communists, among them Ian Turner, Jim Staples and Helen Palmer. They rejected the accepted wisdom that you had to support either the U.S.S.R. or the U.S., without any third options. This New Left milieu brought together the fragments of the cultural and bohemian left that were so much a part of inner-city radical life in Sydney and Melbourne. These early New Left impulses had greater effect in the late 1960s. The journal *Arena*, as Andrew Milner has shown in his chapter on intellectuals in volume three, emerged as a major independent institution of the New Left. Politics at last returned to the streets and the newspapers, and it became more popular to distance the socialist project from its pro-Soviet image.

Though international forces helped to isolate the left here in the 1950s, events outside Australia also rekindled the local left in the 1960s. Of course, left activists – militants in the union movement, socialists in the A.L.P., members of communist or socialist parties, and radicals in social movements outside the parties – had not disappeared during the 1950s and early 1960s, but their audience certainly had. The experience of the Vietnam war and the huge anti-war marches helped change all that, as Barry York describes in his chapter on the anti-Vietnam movement in this volume. Conscription made the issue personal: not only longhairs but also shorthairs and their parents were goaded into action. So leftist politics became again more genuinely popular in this period, as they had from 1941.

This was the period when a hundred flowers bloomed on the Australian left. Student radicalism revived, with its mass meetings, megaphones, masturbation and Maoist clichés. The women's movement emerged as a particularly strong force, though the left, historically dominated by men, was less than responsive. On the whole, the men of the left preferred to believe they had nothing to learn from the women's movement and insisted that class alone explained all exploitation and oppression in capitalist society. They tended to rail against the conservative sections of the women's movement and ignore the left-wing sections of it.

Communist demonstrators dining out after an anti-nuclear protest in the late 1950s.

La Trobe University students outside Heidelberg Court in 1971, while Vietnam moratorium activists are tried inside.

The Communist Party tried to respond positively to the upsurge in left activity. It replaced the drab and dogmatic *Communist Review* with the more colourful and open-minded *Australian Left Review* in 1966. Theoretical debate flourished, though it was often drawn from debate on the British left, which was itself derived from the French. The party entered its so-called ultraleft phase. As John Sendy has noted, the 1974 congress political document used the words 'revolution' and 'revolutionary' fifty-four times in nine pages. Revolution seemed to be on the agenda. New forces were attracted to the party, but at the same time old allies and members were repulsed. Resenting these turns to the trendy, and astonished by stronger and stronger criticism of the Soviet Union, much of the remaining old guard left in 1971 to form the pro-Soviet Socialist Party of Australia.

Trotskyism became a substantial movement for the first time in Australian history during the late 1960s. Trotsky was the Russian revolutionary leader who was murdered in 1940 because of his opposition to Stalin's repressive rule. His image as a loyal revolutionary and oppositionist put him on a par with the Cuban revolutionary hero Che Guevara in the student imagination. While many others on the left still slavishly supported the Soviet Union, Trotskyists defended the Russian Revolution but were critical of the regime that emerged from it. They believed in 'permanent revolution'; they also identified with anti-imperialist revolutions in the Third World. Trotskyists were active against Australian involvement in the Vietnam war and gained support, particularly among young people. Trotskyism even secured a foothold within the Communist Party in the 1970s, and various Trotskyist parties were formed in this time such as the Socialist Labour League, the Socialist Workers' Party and the Spartacist League. By the 1980s, however, the Trotskyist groups were becoming less critical of the Soviet Union and were acting as publicity bureaus for different Third World outposts of 'socialism'.

Even the A.L.P. looked radical for a while. Jim Cairns had a charismatic effect. He was able to bring together apparently disparate issues such as anti-imperialism, the defence of civil liberties, and the values of an emerging 'new' politics, which did not just involve a critique of capitalism but opposed consumerist industrial society in all its forms.

A combination of events and circumstances elsewhere helped to spark off the New Left. The mass strikes and student insurrections of May 1968 in Paris raised again the question of how viable capitalism was. In the same year Soviet tanks invaded Prague, ousted the Dubček government and put an end to its reform programme, making it clear that the Soviet regime would not tolerate deviations. Governments of all kinds were discredited; grassroots movements and initiatives seemed to point the way forward, both on the factory floor and outside the work-place.

One exciting development was in the New South Wales branch of the Builders Labourers Federation (N.S.W.B.L.F.). As Jack Mundey discusses in his chapter on environmentalism in this volume, the N.S.W.B.L.F. popularized radical union politics in the push for 'Green Bans', in which the union refused to work on environmentally destructive development projects in Sydney. The union was supported by local residents and environmentalists. It extended the tradition of militant communist industrial action and took a broad view of communism to speak of 'socialism with an ecological heart'. Sadly, these new forms of union action ended with the collapse of the economic boom. In the face of crisis and mounting unemployment, unions returned to the pursuit of more short-term, traditional goals. Even so, the experience of the Green Bans had been an exemplary and exhilarating one.

The election of the Whitlam government in December 1972, the first federal Labor government in twenty-three years, was partly a result of the momentum the left achieved in this period. Yet during the Whitlam years the left retreated to the political fringe. Whitlam self-consciously identified social justice as a priority. At the same time, he presided over the A.L.P.'s emergence as a middle-class party. On the whole, the left responded to the modernization of the A.L.P. in a negative way. Many leftists damned the A.L.P. as a tool of capital or a right-wing wolf in reformist's clothing. Yet between 1972 and 1975 there was perhaps more potential than ever before to develop arguments for socialism and expand a socialist vision. The left's failure to respond to this opportunity partly explains its weakness today. Certainly, it could be argued that Marxist theory became more obscure in the 1970s. Writers such as Louis Althusser were incomprehensible to most people; they were a long way from the tradition of pamphlet tracts written for the people with the power and inclination to change society. Perhaps the irrelevance of much leftist politics in the Whitlam years has helped to weaken the left's ability to resist the staunchly conservative policies of the Hawke government and the union movement's acceptance of reduced living standards under the A.L.P.-A.C.T.U. Accord. The left in recent years has returned to the mainstream, but in the meantime the mainstream has moved to the right.

Historically, the left in Australia has tended to slide about between developing its own traditions and espousing the traditions of the other regimes that have been seen as socialist Meccas. Often the left tried to do both at once. For example, it can be argued that, although the left talked about a future modelled on the Soviet Union, its own practices were not very different from those of the mainstream labour movement. Certainly, the left has always been too easily impressed by developments on other shores. Yet there will always be points of continuity between local and overseas experiences. Perhaps the left's main problem has been the particular overseas models it has chosen to emulate. Some overseas influences have been positive, especially those that came from oppositional movements in other societies. The effect of the American-derived Industrial Workers of the World might be one example. Others might be the recent movements for workers' control or local self-organization, which drew upon British experiences; or the way the Green Party in West Germany is offering inspiration to sections of the left here. On the other hand, the influence of movements that are identified with foreign governments, such as the Soviet Union or Libya, has been harmful. Too often such movements promote the interests of that nation rather than the project of Australian socialism.

This fascination with overseas experiences, however, has now been replaced by a rejection of all foreign images and an enthusiastic embracing of the Australian past. This turnabout could have as many dangers as the process it is reacting against. There are few purely Australian traditions of thorough-going radicalism to draw upon. The shift can be witnessed within the Labor left, as the members of the so-called new Socialist Left reject the overseas associations of the old Socialist Left and present themselves as alternative managers of the capitalist crisis. Communism, meanwhile, is no longer an independent force in Australian politics, if it ever was. Leading communists, such as Laurie Carmichael, have emerged as advocates of the A.L.P.-A.C.T.U. Accord; others, such as Pat Clancy, have remained a little more distant; and rebels such as Norm Gallagher still live out the old position, though now from exile. The splits and splinters of the communist movement in the post-war years, and its eventual liquidation into the Labor party, have, in a sense, ended the tension between local and overseas influences. In supporting the Accord, communists and radicals have moved back into the local tradition. Among them are many of the workers who had traditionally been the most militant, such as those in the metal trades. The left has made it plain that it wants to secure a place in the house of power that earlier socialists had hoped someday to besiege or transform.

Rupert Lockwood is reputed to have observed that ex-communists formed the biggest party in Australia. Certainly, communists, radicals and socialists, ex-communists, ex-radicals and ex-socialists have contributed greatly to cultural and intellectual life in Australia, to its literature, art, industrial life and standards of living. Many hard-working people dedicated their lives to changing and improving the world. These include not only the better known stalwarts such as Ralph and Dorothy Gibson or Audrey and Jack Blake, but thousands of people, who sold newspapers, held pickets, organized locally – who dared to struggle. The Australian people have benefitted from these labours, at whatever remove.

The decline of communism in Australia and its return to labour and to Labor indicate something of the solidity and continuity of the national tradition that has underpinned local radicalism. It is the national tradition alone, with all its narrowness of vision, that now dominates the left's project. Young and old folk alike might scratch their heads and wonder how it can be that the left is still, after all this time, concerned with the pursuit of what William Lane a century ago called 'the workingman's paradise' – or at least its minimum programme, a wage-earner's welfare state. After all these years of struggle, the socialist project has come to this. Is there nothing better?

Preventing the Plunder

JACK MUNDEY

Environmentalism has been among the most significant political movements in Australia in recent years. Immediately after the Second World War, most people took no account of the price of rapid industrialization, with its unprecedented depletion of material resources and degradation of the environment. In both east and west the dominant idea was, 'Let us conquer nature and use nature for man's benefit.' There was to be development for development's sake, at any cost.

From the time the first Europeans arrived in this country, the vastness of Australia seemed to invite a belief that here was a country of infinite resources. White Australians in the nineteenth and early twentieth century thought of Australia as having the same productive potential as the United States, because of its similar size. Australia, however, is a much drier continent, with a water run-off only one-sixth of the United States. Beyond the Great Dividing Range, except in the occasional rainy period, much of the country is semi-desert. It is now much the worse for wear, thanks to two centuries of over-exploitation. Only one-quarter of the forests that were here in 1788 still remain today. As white settlement expanded, environmental considerations were totally ignored by governments, farmers, industry, trade unions, science and education – by all segments of society. The rare people who expressed concern for the environment were dismissed as 'crackpots' or 'weirdos'.

The destruction of the environment increased dramatically after the Second World War. The long economic boom, which lasted for about three decades until the mid 1970s, affected the natural and built environments in a way never before experienced. The technology developed for destruction during the Second World War was unleashed for peacetime production. There was a gigantic increase in the production of cars, refrigerators, washing machines and other consumer durables. The material living standards of practically all Australians, including the working class, improved substantially. American and Japanese capital became increasingly important, and the once dominant British influence began to wane. It was widely believed that science and technology were going to bring an ever-lasting Eldorado. Such thinking affected not only Australians, but people in all of the industrialized countries. Even the nations defeated in the war quickly rebuilt their shattered industrial base: in the late 1950s and 1960s, Japan and West Germany were lauded as 'economic miracles', with soaring production, consumption and living standards.

The rapid extension of industrialization in this boom period can be shown by just one set of production figures. In 1950 there were 50 million motor vehicles registered on the world's roads; in 1980 the number had increased to a staggering 400 million; and Toyota have released figures that predict that there will be about 551 million registered motor vehicles throughout the world by 1990. So, in a mere forty years, the population of cars has increased from 50 million to 550 million. Examples from other industries show a similar pattern. Moreover, the Eastern bloc countries also increased their industrial production, with environmental degradation similar to that in the west.

It was really only in the 1960s that environmentalists started to arouse public consciousness about the finite nature of the earth's resources and their rapid depletion, the alarming increase in the world's population (which will exceed six billion by 2,000 A.D.), and the myriad environmental problems caused by the outdated and predatory qualities of existing social systems. Among the books that alerted the public were *Silent Spring* by Rachel Carson, *Population Bomb* by Paul and Ann Ehrlich, and *The Closing Circle* by Barry Commoner. In Australia it was the Green Ban movement of the early 1970s that first brought environmental and ecological issues to the forefront. The controversy surrounding these struggles stimulated the development of an environmental consciousness in the wider society.

During the 1960s and early 1970s, our major cities underwent a transformation. Enormous amounts of 'hot' money, both from Australia and overseas, were poured into property development.

The construction of giant glass and concrete buildings changed the face of our cities. This was most evident in Sydney, much of whose charm and beauty were destroyed in the name of progress. Beautiful old buildings were razed, producing the bleak, windswept streets that are now inner Sydney. The New South Wales government under Sir Robert Askin slavishly followed the whims and wishes of the property developers. Construction was for profit, not for use. At one stage there were ten million square feet of vacant office space in Sydney's centre, while people looking for their first homes or flats could find nothing.

The New South Wales Builders Labourers Federation (N.S.W. B.L.F.) first raised its voice on environmental issues in 1971. The union argued that priorities should be reversed, and that the construction of flats, home units and working-class housing was more important than piling up empty or under-used commercial office buildings. This union claimed the right, indeed the responsibility, to intervene in the decision-making process and exert a degree of workers' control. The workers of the N.S.W.B.L.F. were determined to use their labour in a socially useful manner, and to express a social responsibility for what they produced. These connected issues of social usefulness and social responsibility were to be the central themes in the Green Ban struggles.

The Green Ban campaigns brought together an enlightened trade union in common struggle with other progressive segments of society, such as resident action groups, national trusts and environmentalists generally. The development ethos had begun to decline when people saw what was actually happening to their cities. They started to realize that they were powerless to express an opinion on how their cities should be developed. This anger and frustration spawned the resident action groups, which mushroomed as the developers became even more bold. By 1970 there were over fifty such groups in the Sydney metropolitan area alone. In 1971 a group of women from the fashionable suburb of Hunters Hill sought the help of the N.S.W.B.L.F. to try to save Kelly's Bush, the last remaining open space in that area. They were known as the 'Battlers for Kelly's Bush', and their appeal to the N.S.W.B.L.F. was a last resort. They had already been to the local council, the mayor, the local state member, even Premier Askin, all without success; they had read about my idea of social responsibility and felt there was a possibility of putting it into effect. So an unlikely alliance was born.

The N.S.W.B.L.F. was a very open union and believed in an egalitarian society. It had won wage increases that took its

The exuberant spirit of a B.L.F. march in the early 1970s

members up to the same rates as tradesmen. But it was not only concerned with wages and conditions. To combat entrenched bureaucracy in its leadership, it had a 'limited tenure' rule. Elected union officials could only stay in office for six years. After that, they had to return to the rank and file, and to the pick and shovel, for at least three years before being again eligible to stand for office. The N.S.W.B.L.F. was also the first construction union in the world to win women the right to work as building workers. The union had civilized a rough industry, winning dignity and respect for the workers, and making the work much safer. The openness of the N.S.W.B.L.F. ensured that the 'Battlers for Kelly's Bush' found a fresh and responsive executive committee when they arrived to seek support.

The union asked the Battlers to call a public meeting at Hunters Hill, to show that there was community support for the request for a union ban on the destruction of Kelly's Bush. Over 600 people attended the meeting, which formally requested a ban. The N.S.W.B.L.F. agreed to their request, and a union ban was put on Kelly's Bush, where Melbourne-based developer A. V. Jennings wanted to build luxury houses for the very rich.

The bans the union imposed were different from the Black

Bans that trade unionists everywhere have used to exert pressure on employers for better wages and conditions; the workers in the N.S.W.B.L.F. were not imposing these bans in their own economic interests. Indeed, in the short term, the workers were denying themselves work. In the long run, the workers could see that such a ban to save open parkland was in the interests of the entire community. So the new ban became known as a 'Green Ban', to distinguish it from a Black Ban. Green Bans contained an environmental element and a social element: they expressed the union's determination to save open space and to ensure that people in any community had some say in what affected their lives.

A. V. Jennings reacted by declaring it would build on the Kelly's Bush Park using non-union labour. Building workers on an office project of A. V. Jennings in North Sydney sent a message to Jennings, saying: 'If you attempt to build on Kelly's Bush, even if there is the loss of one tree, this half-completed building will remain so forever, as a monument to Kelly's Bush.'

This firm action by the Builders Labourers had a sobering influence not only on A. V. Jennings but also on the other developers and the Master Builders Association. It even reduced the aggressiveness of Premier Askin. The first Green Ban was successful, though it was not until thirteen years later that a N.S.W. Labor government finally dedicated Kelly's Bush as an open public reserve.

After this first success of the 'worker-resident' action alliance, frustrated resident action groups rushed to ask the N.S.W.B.L.F. to impose similar bans. The union won much support, because it always insisted that a ban could only be imposed *after* there had been an enthusiastic public meeting by the people concerned; the union did not set itself up as the arbiter of taste, and the leadership never attempted to impose bans willy-nilly. Three years after Kelly's Bush, forty-two Green Bans had been imposed, holding up well over $3,000 million worth of so-called development.

Some argued that we were denying workers employment. We replied by pointing out that, yes, we wanted to build buildings, but public buildings, kindergartens, homes for the aged and unemployed, community welfare housing; that we didn't want to build buildings for the get-rich-quick developers, with their superfluous concrete and glass canyons that were destroying much of Sydney's soul. What would we have said to the next generation? That we destroyed Sydney in the name of full employment? No, we wanted to construct buildings that were socially useful.

Jack Mundey addressing a meeting outside the Melbourne Trades Hall in 1973.

It is now history that over one hundred buildings considered by the National Trust to be worthy of preservation were saved by the Green Bans. And these Green Bans led to the New South Wales government bringing in tighter demolition laws. In the 1970s the N.S.W.B.L.F. was vilified by the Liberal government, the developers, the conservative press and much of the trade union movement. The New South Wales Trades and Labour Council attacked it for 'going too far beyond the prerogatives of unions'. But in the 1980s, the Green Bans have been vindicated.

Look at some of the Green Bans success stories. First there is The Rocks, the birthplace of European Australia, where over three million visitors go each year. Would anyone bother to go if it had been $500 million dollars worth of concrete and glass, as the developers had wanted? Then there is Woolloomooloo, which the Green Ban saved from $400 million dollars' worth of high-rise commercial buildings. Instead the Housing Commission, with contribution from local residents, has now built a prototype for attractive and useful inner-city re-development: a genuine socio-economic mix of residents, with a substantial number of working-class people, living in medium-density buildings with many trees and landscaped surroundings. And Centennial Park still exists.

Who would now dare to consider turning this beautiful 'breathing space' into a concrete sports stadium? No one, of course, but only twelve years ago that was the intention. Then there is the Sydney Botanical Gardens. Not even the most extreme motor vehicle lobbyist would propose that the Opera House carpark be built there. Attitudes have changed.

Even though the conservatives within the trade union movement let the union and Green Bans' originators be destroyed, the campaigns made an invaluable contribution to both the environmental and labour movements. After fifteen years of direct involvement in the environmental movement here and overseas, I find that the articulate, middle-class people who control and influence the environmental movement generally fail to understand the importance of involving the working class in the movement; and the trade union movement is still essentially concerned with wages and conditions. Of course, unions must fight for better wages and conditions – that is their main function – but with the great diversity of problems confronting people today, it is necessary for trade unions to broaden their vision. Trade unions must become more involved with environmental issues, and environmentalists must become more concerned with the importance of promoting trade union struggles for socially useful production and consumption. Too few people question the products we make.

An anti-uranium demonstration in Sydney, April 1978

The Green Ban movement was significant in that it forged a winning alliance between enlightened middle-class people in the environmental movement and enlightened trade unionists in the N.S.W.B.L.F. This was living proof that such alliances can work, and it must give heart to all those who believe that similar alliances must be built now and in the near future. For the ecological crisis must be solved, and our social order transformed, if nuclear war is to be avoided and a society come into being that can provide a decent standard of living without pillaging the world's surface and threatening the stability of the atmosphere.

All too often, environmentalists and workers are divided, when they should be natural allies against big business and insensitive bureaucracies (such as the Tasmanian Hydro-Electric Commission). Big business and conservative politicians often depict environmentalists as hippies, or as armchair activists with good middle-class jobs trying to stop ordinary workers getting on with the business of building dams and sawmills, mining uranium, and so on. Even in the great victory on the Tasmanian dams issue in 1983, the Tasmanian Hydro-Electric Commission was able to confuse the workers for a time. The heat was only taken off the conservationists when it became clear that alternative work opportunities would be made available. After that, the trade union movement influenced the Labor Party to take the positive stand it finally adopted.

Another compelling reason for conservationists to ally with trade unionists is that, so far, the achievements of the conservation movement have been only in the conservation of nature – the Tasmanian Wilderness, Fraser Island, the Barrier Reef, Kakadu Wilderness, for example. These are all very important, but success in the built environment is vital. After all, 90 per cent of the Australian population resides in urban areas, and half of it is in the Newcastle/Sydney/Wollongong or Melbourne/Geelong regions. Trade unionists are especially well placed to influence the construction of the built environment. Both the natural and the built environments are important, and we must win the hearts and minds of people everywhere if we are to be successful in both areas. The greater attention being given by people the world over to environmental issues is encouraging, even if it has required a Chernobyl to bring it into focus. The enormity of the ecological problems confronting humankind is daunting. The task of achieving a sustainable society, with a human face, an ecological heart and an egalitarian body, requires a massive joint effort by environmentalists and the organized working class.

Cryin' Out for Land Rights

HEATHER GOODALL

Uncle Jacko Campbell, a Dhanggati man, was telling me about the camp of Aboriginal people at Salt Pan Creek in south-west Sydney, where he had lived as a boy in the late 1920s. Many people had settled there after conflicts with the Aborigines Protection Board in other parts of the state: it was a camp of political refugees. They still stood up for themselves. Many of the Salt Pan residents would go into the city to sell gum tips and wild flowers, and they would 'spruik' at the same time, talking to the crowds in Paddy's Market and the Domain.

'They'd only be spruikin' on land rights,' Jacko told me, 'that's all, on land rights!' I was unclear about the words and asked him, 'But they wouldn't have called it "land rights" then, would they?' I was sure I knew how the land rights movement had begun. It had started in the Northern Territory in the 1960s when the Yirrkala and the Gurindji peoples had demanded their land back. Then Aboriginal people in the south-eastern states had taken up the struggle and added the call for land rights to their earlier calls for equal civil rights. Wasn't that how it had been? But Jacko was insistent:

> Of *course* they was callin' it land rights. 'Why hasn't the Aboriginal people got land rights?' they said. 'The Aboriginal's cryin' out for land rights.' They was askin' for Aboriginal land, for the land they was *on*! That's when them whites was chuckin' 'em off. There was places around, thirty-five or 40 acres, 60 acres, that Aboriginal people was on, growin' potatoes, pumpkin, corn, stuff like that. But the white settlers went into 'em, they'd just run their cattle through their crops, knock it down, destroy it! ... Those old fellas, they was pushin' Lang, at that time, for land rights ... and to break up the Aboriginal Protection Board.

Jack Campbell was an acutely observant man with an extraordinary memory. He would recall fine details of events and people from the 1920s and 1930s, then wait with relish to see what pattern emerged from the jigsaw pieces of documentary records. It always corroborated his accounts. So I went looking for traces of the political movement that Jack remembered and found that it was not an isolated event but one episode in the long Aboriginal struggle for land and justice.

This struggle had begun, of course, with the British invasion. In this first land rights campaign, Aboriginal armed resistance continued in the west and on the north coast of New South Wales until the 1860s. Yet when Aboriginal people were no longer able to continue the guerrilla war, they did not give up; they just altered their tactics. They tried to make a place for themselves in the new circumstances, interacting with the whites but still maintaining connections with their traditional values. This was not only a continued resistance but a struggle to create a future for themselves.

Despite the appalling effects of invasion and warfare, Aborigines became workers in both pastoral and agricultural industries, sometimes for cash wages, sometimes for food. This was so even before the 1850s. More were recruited with the labour shortages during the gold rushes. Where there were big pastoral properties, camps of Aborigines were actively encouraged to stay on the sheep runs because the pastoralists wanted an experienced, accessible and cheap labour force. Aborigines were subsidizing the pastoralists by continuing to build their own shelters and harvest their own food. But there was some advantage to the Aborigines as well, because they had relatively easy access to their own traditional country.

A few attempts were made to set up 'reserves for the use of Aborigines' in the early days of the colony around Sydney and, later, with the Protectorate in Victoria. These were white initiatives, intended to fulfil the settlers' aims: to cut Aborigines off from their wider territory and confine them to a small area where they would be 'cured' of their 'nomadism' and taught to be useful to white employers. Aboriginal people were not very interested. Settlers put this down to an inability to understand agriculture and to hopeless 'nomadism'. Yet Aborigines were already showing that they understood the concepts and practice of agriculture: the main reasons for their lack of interest were the disruptive effects of invasion and the fact that they could still get some access to their country.

By the 1860s, however, the rural industries were changing in quite a few areas. The south coast of New South Wales, for instance, was switching from timber cutting to agriculture, growing food for the goldfields. Then the south-west region moved from grazing towards growing wheat. These changes squeezed Aborigines off the land, wiped out even more of their traditional food supplies and made it much harder for them to keep their economy going. Another important change was the introduction of fencing. Aborigines who had worked as shepherds found there were no more jobs for them, and access to the land became much more difficult. The growing use of machinery such as mechanical strippers and harvesters also cut the amount of labour needed in rural industries. Over the nineteenth century, the whole rural economy moved increasingly towards part-time or seasonal employment. It was hard for anyone to find stable, full-time work, but especially hard for Aboriginal workers. Employers labelled them as 'unreliable' and argued that they did not need jobs because they could support themselves by 'hunting and gathering'. These changes generally happened first in Victoria and the south-west of New South Wales, then spread to the north and east. The areas where Aborigines were under greatest pressure were the south-west and south coast of New South Wales, then up the central and north coast.

This was the situation that gave rise to the second land rights campaign in south-eastern Australia, which occurred during the 1870s and 1880s. It was not an organized, formal political movement, but Aboriginal people were well aware of what was happening outside their own areas. Community after community in the south-west and on the coast chose similar solutions to the pressures they all faced. Aborigines began to re-occupy their land. They 'squatted' on small areas, built shelters, planted crops and then demanded that the government give them secure tenure. Using the populist ideas then circulating among whites about 'free selection' to 'unlock the land', they argued that they should have enough land to guarantee them employment and housing. But the land had two sets of meanings for them. They wanted it, not just for economic reasons, but also to secure their access to areas that were within their traditional country. William Cooper of Cumeragunja chose Christian language in 1887 when he petitioned for land, but his argument was based on the prior rights of traditional ownership when he asked for 'this small portion of a vast territory which is ours by Divine Right'.

Aborigines were often able to recruit white supporters to help them with their demands for small pieces of their land. At Coranderrk in Victoria, the official guardian of Aborigines, William Thomas, conveyed the requests for land made in 1859 by a deputation of Taungerong and Woiwurrung Aboriginal farmers. In the south-west of New South Wales, it was the missionary Daniel Matthews who was recruited by the Joti-Jota and Pangerang in the 1870s and 1880s to help them gain land at Cumeragunja. On the southern slopes and on the coast, the police, as 'protectors', often passed the Aboriginal demands for land to the government, reporting them 'very proud to call a piece of ground their own' to 'cultivate', as 'a homestead' and 'to meet for the purpose of holding corroborees'. By far the most successful recruitment occurred west of Sydney in 1876, when the Burragorang Valley people convinced the local Catholic Church to buy a 78 acre farm and hand it over to them to cultivate independently from then on.

Aborigines were asking for full freehold and independent ownership, although they sometimes pointed out that they did not want the power to sell the land. What they received instead were 'reserves for the use of Aborigines'. As was to happen all too often, an Aboriginal demand was watered down and distorted by the government so that the end result benefitted the government as much as, if not more than, the Aborigines. At the time, however, Aborigines were told that the reserves would be secure as long as they continued to live there and farm the land.

Through the 1870s to 1884, twenty-nine Aboriginal reserves were created, all in the south-west or along the coast. Twenty-five of these were created on Aboriginal initiative. Sometimes a reserve was created to give legal recognition to the fact that Aborigines had already re-occupied the land and were farming it. Other reserves were responses to Aboriginal demands for land in specific areas. These Aboriginal re-occupations and demands continued strongly through the next decade. By 1895, another eighty-five reserves had been created, forty-seven of them on Aboriginal initiatives. The Aborigines Protection Board, set up in 1883, had begun to respond to demands by white townspeople and employers for new reserves to be set up to confine Aboriginal populations or secure a labour force. But most of these first 114 reserves were created because of the Aboriginal pressure for land in areas where they were under pressure. There were few demands for land from Aborigines in the north-west and far-west pastoral areas at this time. This was not because they were less

Aboriginal farmers tending their hop plantations hop plantations at Coranderrk.

attached to their land, but because they were not yet being squeezed off it. The pressures in the south-west and on the coast did not ease during the 1890s depression, and there was no falling off in Aboriginal calls for land. But the Protection Board was becoming reluctant to respond to Aboriginal initiatives. This was not because Aboriginal tenure of the reserves had been unsuccessful but because the board had changed its policy.

Aboriginal landholding had been very successful in European terms. At Coranderrk, Aboriginal farmers had pioneered the growing of hops, showing their white neighbours that it was profitable. But the Coranderrk community faced a problem, as did the Cumeragunja people in New South Wales. They did not have enough land. The 27½ acre family farm blocks at Cumeragunja were not large enough to provide a living for a family in that area and climate. Aboriginal farmers were also short of capital; and most Aboriginal communities had to care for large numbers of sick and elderly people who were put on the reserves by the board. Nevertheless, the Cumeragunja farmers consistently got yields of wheat per acre that equalled or bettered the district's average. The reserves of the southern slopes and coast faced similar problems. Farms were small and undercapitalized. They produced a fair living but during lean years the

Aborigines had to earn extra money from grazing other farmers' stock or taking jobs outside.

West of Sydney, however, the Burragorang land was flourishing, with Aboriginal farmers such as the Anderson and Shepherd families continuing to support about fifty people. One problem at Burragorang was that there was heavy pressure from a white man who was determined to acquire the land. This had led the Protection Board to 'protect' the land in 1891 by converting the title to a 'reserve for the use of Aborigines'. This did not at that stage affect the farmers' independence or productivity, and they carried on until well into the 1920s.

The most economically viable of all the reserves were those on the north coast, particularly around the Macleay valley. Here the slower rate of white settlement had given Aborigines time to re-occupy some of the most fertile river flat land. Their reserves of 30 or 40 acres could produce crops such as maize and pumpkins, enough to support their extended families and often produce a profit, which they used for equipment or household goods, or sometimes to make the expensive shift from farming to dairying. These farms looked so 'European' that many white settlers were unaware that their Aboriginal neighbours and their children still spoke their own languages at home and maintained an extensive ceremonial life.

Major changes occurred at the beginning of the twentieth century. At federation, the country had proclaimed its racism as a 'White Australia'. Aborigines in New South Wales found that they were more often facing segregation in country town hospitals, schools and hotels; and their attempts to live inside town boundaries were being blocked with increasing violence. They had suffered more than their share of unemployment in the 1890s depression and drought. Then, just as their employment was starting to recover, Aborigines were hit by changes in Protection Board policy. The board believed mistakenly that the high Aboriginal unemployment of the depression was permanent. It also knew that the Aboriginal population was increasing and was afraid it would have to support a permanently impoverished group. It was even more alarmed, however, by the fact that the 'non full-blood' section of the Aboriginal population was growing and at the same time maintaining its identification with Aboriginal culture. Fostering racial and cultural minorities was contrary to all Australian governments' policies, and the New South Wales Board felt it had to act. It decided to take aggressive steps to disperse Aboriginal communities. It expelled Aborigines from the reserves, over which it had legal control. And it took Aboriginal children away from their families, supposedly to 'train' them as 'apprentices', but really to lower the birth rate by removing young women from the communities.

As early as 1906 the board had started to do this in its longest established stations in the south-west. At Cumeragunja, it began by resuming the family farm blocks and smashing independent Aboriginal agriculture. There was bitter resistance: each community tried to defend its children and its right to farm and live on reserve land. At Cumeragunja, there were long legal battles when Aborigines refused to accept the board's expulsion orders. At times there was literally hand-to-hand fighting over land, farms and children, with both board managers and, less frequently, Aborigines themselves firing guns. The resistance was so strong at Cumeragunja that police were stationed there for three months early in 1922, after a decade of persistent and severe disturbances. By that time, many of the station's residents had been 'dispersed', although they had not lost their identification with Cumeragunja or their determination to get their family farms back again. Other reserves faced struggles almost as violent throughout the 1910s as the board implemented its 'dispersal' programme. The board's intervention was heaviest in the south-west at first, then extended across the state to the north and east. It was not until the late 1910s and early 1920s that the Aborigines of the north felt the full force of the changed policy.

Yet there was a much wider change occurring. As well as more frequent exclusion from town facilities, Aborigines faced a new wave of closer settlement from 1905. First of all, the economy picked up after the depression and drought. Then, from 1916, there was a spate of soldier settlement. Whites were casting hungry eyes on the reserves, especially in view of the proven productivity of the Aboriginal-settled reserves. Coranderrk in Victoria was eventually lost by leasing to soldier settlement after 1918, although intense pressure in the earlier wave of closer settlement during the 1880s had already taken an enormous slice of the land. The New South Wales board's 'dispersal' at Cumeragunja could not have been implemented if white neighbours and soldier settlers had not been so eager to take over leases of the land after 1918. The highest quality north-coast land was not under immediate threat, because the Aborigines Protection Board wished to take these reserves over itself, to gain income by leasing the land to whites to fund its homes for 'training' the Aboriginal children it had taken away. But soon the pressure of white farmers through

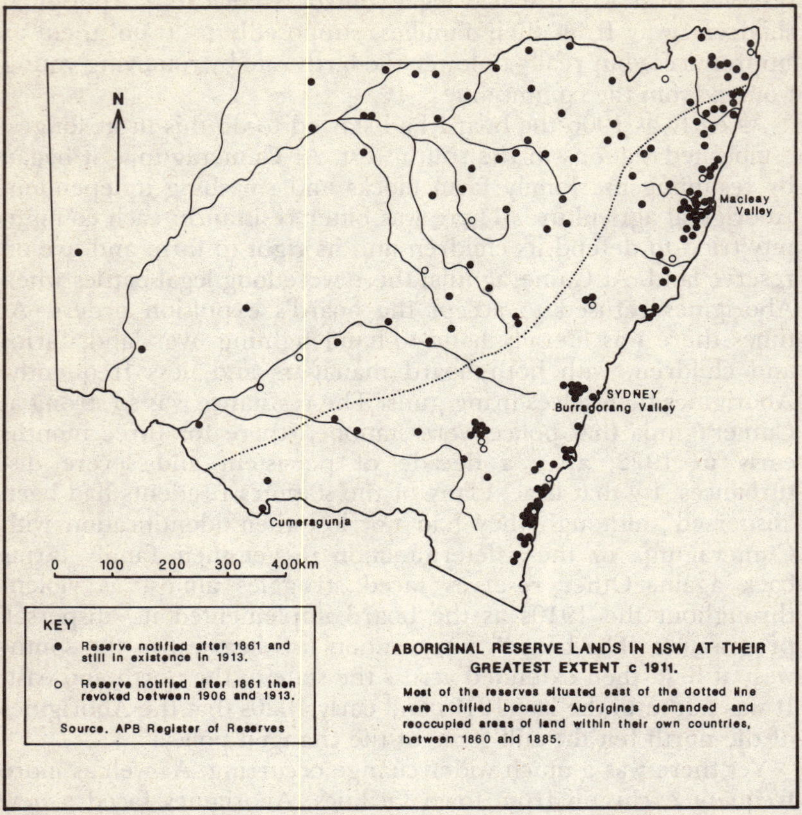

ABORIGINAL RESERVE LANDS IN NSW AT THEIR GREATEST EXTENT c 1911.

Most of the reserves situated east of the dotted line were notified because Aborigines demanded and reoccupied areas of land within their own countries, between 1860 and 1885.

the Lands Department became so intense that the Protection Board gave in, acting against both its own interests and those of the many Aboriginal farmers who were working these reserve lands. Aboriginal reserve area had been greatest in 1910 at around 26,000 acres. White demand ate that land away so that by 1928 it had been halved to 13,000 acres. Three-quarters of the loss was from the north coast: that rich gain from the second Aboriginal land rights campaign had been taken out of Aboriginal hands in another dispossession. Aboriginal farmers were dragged off their land by police, sometimes in mid crop, always under protest. Hardly surprisingly, these individual and community protests soon came together in the third major south-eastern land rights movement.

This was a formal political campaign. At first the communities of the north coast and the metropolitan area, then the south coast, linked themselves in an organization called the Australian Aboriginal Progressive Association (A.A.P.A.). There was activity from 1922 on, but in 1925 the organization became public with a series of large north-coast community meetings, which revealed the dual values Aborigines associated with the land. The speakers were often the Aboriginal farmers from the reserves that had been taken or were under threat. They described how the land was being stolen again, 'legally' or by whites encroaching and destroying their crops to try to drive them away. They used the continuity and productivity of Aboriginal farming to show the justice of their occupying the reserves. But they did this in their own languages, in symbolic assertion of their traditional rights to hold the land. There were parallels with the recent land claim hearings in the Northern Territory, where Aboriginal people have sung the songs of their country as unarguable proof of ownership. These community meetings developed a platform of demands focused on defence of the reserve lands and of the children threatened by the Protection Board. The defensive needs were then developed to become broader, positive calls for the future: land rights for all Aboriginal people in New South Wales, meaning enough land in their own country so that they could be economically independent; cultural independence, with Aboriginal language schools and an Aboriginal staff for any administration of Aboriginal affairs; a guarantee of the full rights of citizenship for all Aborigines.

This was the movement that Jack Campbell remembered, with its Sydney meetings in the late 1920s, 'when they were pushin' Lang for land rights'. The Anderson brothers spoke regularly: they were by then living in the Salt Pan Creek camp because their Burragorang farm had been revoked from under their feet in 1924. Eventually, Joe Anderson claimed the attention of the media. In 1933 he was able to state his manifesto on the Cinesound News:

> I am calling a corroborree of all the natives in New South Wales to send a petition to the king, in an endeavour to improve our conditions. All the black man wants is representation in federal parliament. There is also plenty fish in the river for us all, and land to grow all we want. One hundred and fifty years ago, the Aboriginal owned Australia, and today, he demands more than the white man's charity.
>
> He wants the right to live!

The A.A.P.A. wrote letters to the press, organized petitions and deputations to politicians, called for a royal commission and debated publicly with white missionaries who called themselves reformers but did not wish to listen to Aboriginal people themselves. White support for the organization came from nationalists, of both left-wing and right-wing political parties. They were usually racist, but they saw Aborigines as symbols of a genuine, Australian national identity. Despite this growing support and the way the A.A.P.A. was able to embarrass the Protection Board about 'apprenticeships', the movement was not able to retrieve the land that was being lost. From 1928, rural industries began the slide into severe depression, and the course of the Aboriginal political movement was disrupted. Aboriginal organizing became informal once more, with only occasional public statements.

During the 1930s depression, Aborigines again suffered more than their share of unemployment, although this varied depending on the industry. For the first time, there was a standardized unemployment benefit paid by the state governments, but in rural areas Aborigines were excluded. Instead, they were issued only with Protection Board 'Aboriginal rations', which were about half the value of the 'sustenance' for white workers. Before the depression, the government had defined many Aboriginal people as *not* Aboriginal, despite their active identification as members of the Aboriginal community, because the Protection Board wanted to save money by forcing them off reserves and reducing ration issues. The depression reversed this situation: the government defined *more* people as Aboriginal, to cut costs, because Aboriginal rations were less expensive than the ordinary dole issues. So it was the hard economic times that forced a change to the Protection Board system. The board finally gave in to white demands of the last twenty years and began a policy of segregation, re-location and 're-education'.

Thus in the 1930s there was a major loss of Aboriginal civil rights. Many more people than before were classed by officials as 'Aboriginal' and under the Act this meant they were excluded from the 'dole' and from child endowment. They were also likely to be rounded up, moved around the state, detained on the Protection Board's manager-controlled stations and have their children taken away from them.

When the Aboriginal political movement re-emerged in the mid 1930s, its most pressing concern was with the civil rights strand of the A.A.P.A. platform. This was not a new movement, although as people looked back from the 1960s they sometimes mistook this for the beginning of Aboriginal political struggle. Most Aborigines at the time saw the 1930s movement as a continuation of the

1920s A.A.P.A., which had simply been forced underground during the depression. This time, however, the movement was not confined to one geographical area. A coalition was formed between three regions. The first region to move was the south-west, where in 1934, Cumeragunja residents or exiles in Melbourne formed an organization called the Australian Aborigines' League. Then the coastal network of the old A.A.P.A. and the newly organized western Aborigines formed a New South Wales body called the Aborigines' Progressive Association (A.P.A.). Aboriginal people in all three regions had suffered similar losses of civil rights and so their interests were close enough to make a coalition effective.

Yet the timing of events in relation to land had differed from region to region. Victorian Aborigines at Coranderrk had begun to suffer their second dispossession in the 1880s. For the Cumeragunja and south-western people it had been in the 1910s; for the New South Wales coast, the major loss had come in the 1920s. In the 1930s, it was the turn of the western people. The western pastoral industry was changing. The size of properties was being reduced and mechanization was increasing. This meant that western Aborigines were now being squeezed out of the pastoral camps, off their land and out of work, just as Aborigines in other regions had been before them. But in the economic and political climate of the 1930s, there was no opportunity to force the creation of reserves, and small-scale landholding was in any case uneconomic in the far west. This was when the board decided to enforce re-location and segregation. It took action in precisely those areas where rural industries were changing: the far-west cattle and sheep areas, the north-western sheep industry and the far north-coast cattle runs of the Clarence and Richmond rivers.

Aborigines called this policy the 'Dog Act'. As Henry Hardy, a Yualiai man from Angledool, explained: 'The board treated you just like a dog. They'd get hold of the chain and lead him over there, tie him up over there. They could send you anywhere, do what they liked with you.'

Aboriginal people from many communities, such as Angledool and Tibooburra in the west, were forced to make unhappy treks to be confined on stations hundreds of miles outside their traditional country. Those who resisted were intimidated by police or threatened with losing their children. As a result of these removals, the land rights campaigns of western people have not always been focused on specific patches of reserve land but on their right to live *within* their traditional lands. This was often stated by the A.P.A. in the 1930s as the *civil* right to live where they chose, free of board control. But the central issue was the right of association with traditional country.

The battles over land continued on the coast as well. By 1937, Jack Campbell had returned to his mother's Macleay Valley home at Burnt Bridge, one of the few remaining Aboriginal-settled reserves. He found that the farm had become the focus of one of the Protection Board's 'concentration' programmes, with Aborigines from other areas dumped on adjacent land and the new board manager trying to bring the Aboriginal-settled area under his control. Jack's aunt, Rachel Mosely, wrote letters to newspapers and to old nationalist allies to try to save the land, and his uncle, Percy Mosely, and his brothers barricaded the gates against the manager and police who came to tear down their tanks and farm buildings. When that failed, Percy Mosely began firing shots over the heads of the Aboriginal workers who had been ordered to fence the Moselys off their own land. The family's battle was at least partly successful: the Moselys to this day retain a corner of their land. But their struggle had wider effects. This was the time when the speeches that Jack Campbell had heard at Salt Pan Creek really made their impact on him, their meaning brought alive as he became caught up in his own family's resistance to dispossession.

Nevertheless, the depression had moved the pressures and the 1930s movement had to present civil rights as its urgent demand and defer land rights to a long-term goal. Yet the movement's view on civil rights had broadened. The A.A.L.-A.P.A. coalition took a national position and tried to propose solutions that were applicable to all Aboriginal people, regardless of whether whites defined them as 'full-blood' or 'traditional' or neither. The movement's allies had also broadened, to include not only some far-right nationalist groups but also some left-wing organizations. The unions were involved and, especially in Melbourne, the Communist Party gave sustained support. The coalition had a national perspective. It paid a lot of attention to Aborigines' conditions in other states and the Northern Territory. But in practical politics it is necessary to have an immediate goal, and the coalition's main goal in 1937–8 was to get rid of the New South Wales Protection Board. Gradually this proposal was watered down. The aim became to change the board rather than to abolish it. And even this campaign was taken over by white anthropologists, who wanted to use Aboriginal criticisms of the board to help them enter the

New South Wales administration. The board's staff, in turn, were quite happy to use the anthropologists' terminology to justify their old policies. Segregation became 'education' under the guidance of 'progressive' anthropology. The intention, however, was always to keep the reins of power in white hands.

In 1939 the Protection Board became the Welfare Board, and anthropologists gained a say in its administration. But only the name had changed. The Aboriginal movement rejected the outcome, saying it was a sham. It made no difference who exercised the power – bureaucrats, anthropologists or teachers. It was still power, and Aborigines still had none of it. The Aboriginal campaign to change the Protection Board had left them with nothing but more entrenched white control.

The frustration felt by Aborigines across the south-east exploded in two incidents of community action. The first was a strike at Cumeragunja in 1939. The intensity of feeling was revealed when 200 residents of the reserve walked *away* from the land they had fought so hard to defend. Only the failure of years of 'constitutional' action could force such desperate steps. The strikers set up camp on the Victorian side of the Murray River and stayed there, through a bitter winter, refusing to return until the New South Wales government responded to their demands to sack the manager and give them their land back. They succeeded in forcing the sacking of the manager. But the Victorian government stopped dole payments to the strikers and turned their children away from school, eventually breaking the strike. Still the strikers' resolve was not broken. Many of them moved to other parts of Victoria to continue their political work.

The Cumeragunja people were forced to walk away from their land, but the Tibooburra people walked home. Taken by force from their country in far north-western New South Wales in 1938 and dumped at the Protection Board's station at Brewarrina, the Wanggumara of the corner country stayed there unhappily for three years. In 1941, they decided to defy the board and the police, and go home. They did not reach Tibooburra, but they did return to their traditional country, finding work on the western side of the Paroo out of Wanaaring. Eighty strong, some of the children and old people riding on buggies, the rest on foot, they had walked 190 miles to reach their land.

The Second World War and the long boom afterwards brought rapid economic change in the south-east. Manufacturing grew, and employment needs in rural industries fell further. After the war, Aborigines found that much of their white support had slipped away. The New South Wales government was boasting that it had changed to a policy of 'assimilation'. What this actually meant was that, instead of focusing on segregation in rural areas, the Welfare Board attempted to move Aboriginal people to the industrial cities and towns where it hoped they would disappear into the factory workforce. Persuasion and intimidation were used to pressure Aboriginal people to move away from their own areas. The board's actions, of course, reflected the general situation: mechanization was rapidly reducing the need for rural labour, and many white rural workers were moving to the cities and their factories. Unlike white workers, however, Aborigines had strong motivations to remain close to their own country, even when employment opportunities were drying up.

Through the 1950s and 1960s, the Welfare Board closed down reserves to remove Aboriginal communities' rural residential bases. It had already encouraged local councils and police to take aggressive measures to 'discourage' Aborigines from living in or near country towns. There were confrontations between Aborigines and local authorities over continuing unofficial segregation of schools, residential areas and town facilities as well as the imposition of illegal but effective curfews. These struggles reveal the tenacity with which Aboriginal communities clung to the right to live in their country. The freedom rides and early television documentaries of the 1960s were eventually to show whites something of the living conditions and segregation faced by New South Wales Aborigines. Aborigines had to pay a high price to live where they chose. The pressures to migrate to urban areas were intense, and many people did move to the cities to find work or relatively desegregated schooling. Others kept their home base in their own country but spent many months away on the seasonal agricultural circuit, digging potatoes at Dorrigo, chipping cotton at Wee Waa, then peas on the south coast, asparagus at Cowra and grapes at Mildura. The circuit kept growing longer, as mechanization eroded this form of employment too.

Political organization of all types was constrained in the conservative atmosphere of Menzies' post-war Australia. At the community level, Aboriginal people in New South Wales kept up their calls for full civil rights, which included access to town facilities, an end to board interference and the right to live where they wished. Aborigines became more involved in the union movement in the north-west pastoral industry and in the manufacturing and maritime industries of the south coast. They solidified their alliances and gained more political experience.

As far as formal organizations were concerned, south-eastern Aboriginal politics still had a strong awareness of national issues. An important goal was seen as getting the federal government to intervene to guarantee equal civil rights. Since the war, the south-eastern Aboriginal movements and the movements emerging in other states had begun to interact. The south-eastern groups could call up some urban white support, from liberal or left political organizations, unions or churches, to counter the rural-based elites that were most often in conflict with Aborigines. The northern pastoral industry was still heavily dependent on Aboriginal workers, so industrial demands such as equal wages were often raised. Partly because of increased union involvement, the movement still used the language of the civil rights campaign to express all its demands. South-eastern support of the Pilbara strike in 1946 and the Palm Island strike in 1956 was expressed in terms of civil rights. So was the campaign that led to the apparent success of the 1967 federal referendum, which meant that Aborigines would at last be included in the census and made the responsibility of the federal government.

A change in the thrust of national Aboriginal demands began in

A picket at Aurukun in the early 1970s during the northern land rights campaign.

1963. The Yirrkala people sent a bark petition demanding an end to Nabalco's mining of their land at Gove, where a 'reserve for the use of Aborigines' had proved to be no protection against the miners' intrusion. Their position was similar to the south-eastern Aborigines' in the 1880s or the 1920s. A relatively stable situation had been disrupted by increased pressure and interference, and the Aboriginal people involved asserted themselves in terms that related to their rights to their land. The Yirrkala action was reinforced when the Gurindji walked off Wave Hill in 1966 and demanded their land back.

The civil rights and land rights campaigns are often said to have been separate but complementary. It has been argued that the civil rights demands flowed from the south-eastern Aboriginal experience, while the land rights demands are seen as having been initiated by northern, 'traditional' Aboriginal communities. But, as Jack Campbell had insisted, this analysis is too simple. The Yirrkala and Gurindji land struggles were entwined with issues of labour exploitation, neo-colonialism and the right to equal wages. The south-eastern movement had been built on and continued to foster the south-eastern Aborigines' assertions that they had the right to live on their own country. It was not at all surprising that the south-eastern Aborigines not only supported the Northern Territory peoples' demands, but also tried to draw on the good-will shown in the referendum by urban whites to re-open the campaigns for their own land in Victoria and New South Wales.

The fourth south-eastern land rights campaign was under way from the early 1970s. It was able to draw added strength from the northern campaign, and it gained urgency from the changed economic conditions in the south-east after 1975. Manufacturing slumped badly, creating severe unemployment and reversing many of the pressures that had forced Aborigines to move to the cities after the war. Rural employment for Aborigines had also almost disappeared, but many of the people who had lived in Sydney over the last decade began to move back to the land they had always thought of as home.

This fourth land rights campaign has been marked by the passage of a 'Land Rights' Act in New South Wales in 1981. The Act has severe limitations and fundamental problems. It must be seen, not as meeting Aboriginal demands, but as suiting the interests of a government trying to deal with urban and rural unemployment. Ironically, it was used to distract attention from a bill passed at the same time that validated retrospectively all the closing down of reserves carried out since 1913. The great loss of the Aboriginal-settled reserves had turned out to have been technically illegal.

Rural whites have responded aggressively to the changes of the last decade, reflecting their own economic insecurity and falling numbers and their anger at the assertion of Aboriginal legal rights through community-controlled legal services. Intensified violence, deaths in police custody and vigilante attacks are becoming more common, with more frequent white calls for 'law and order'. But whenever there is violence, Aborigines are the first victims. Aborigines continue to pay a high price for living on their own country. Despite legislative sleight of hand and increased violence, south-eastern Aboriginal people are continuing their demand for land. The struggle is already 200 years old, but it is far from over.

The experience of urban living during the 1960s widened contacts. Many young Aborigines now draw parallels between their situation and the decolonization and liberation struggles of the Third World. These new perspectives have broadened their alliances and added to the tactics available to the Aboriginal movement. Nevertheless, the political experience and the toughness developed among older generations during the earlier south-eastern campaigns have been crucial in building the current one. Many of its major activists experienced the 1930s 'Dog Act' concentrations and segregations when they were adolescents, and the intense struggles since then to stay in the rural town of their community's choice. A central figure has been Jacko Campbell, who brought to his contemporary role all the knowledge he had built up since the 1920s. Through the 1970s until his death in 1983, Jacko travelled and talked and travelled again to meeting after meeting, fighting tiredness, and eventually ill health, but always driven by his purpose of sustaining the land rights movement. He watched, analysed, generated strategies and explained the conflicts by scanning the rich fund of his memory for parallels, examples and lessons. Jacko gave to the younger people with whom he worked the ideological sources of their struggles, spending long nights yarning, recalling those old days when 'they'd only be spruikin' on land rights'.

Teaching Whites a Lesson

GARY FOLEY

It is important that all Australians have some understanding of what the Aboriginal people's movement is about. You need to understand that our movement is no threat to your property: to your swimming pools or your flash buildings in town. And we Aboriginal people need you to understand it because, as far as I can see, we will not achieve what we want without the support of others. Your society has too successfully subjugated us; we are now too weak, numerically, economically and socially to be able to win political battles on our own. The black movement, however, also has positive things to offer the white Australian community. You can do something for us, and we can do something for you. Aboriginal people in the last twenty years have shown the rest of society how to overcome some of the problems we all have in common. Aboriginal people set up the first women's refuges in this country. They also set up the first free legal-aid centres and the first community-controlled health and child-care centres. All of these new concepts have been adopted and adapted by other groups in the Australian community to meet *their* needs and overcome *their* problems. So Aboriginal people are showing and will continue to show other Australians the way to a better, more humanitarian society.

To understand what the land rights movement is all about you have to know a little about the true history of Australia. Most Australians know very little of it, because what they teach you in the schools bears very little relationship to the truth. When I went to school, about twenty years ago, all I was ever taught about my people was that we threw boomerangs and had woomeras, and that the Tasmanian Aborigines 'died out'. Nothing else we had done was worth mentioning.

Fortunately, in some areas, things are slowly beginning to change. You can see the difference in attitude among young non-Aboriginal Australians when they have been taught the truth. A few years ago I had the privilege of talking to a bunch of twelve-year-old non-Aboriginal Australians in the Melbourne suburb of Hawthorn who had done some Aboriginal studies over the previous two years, and I believe the political discussion I had with them was the most intelligent, logical and rational that I have ever had with any group of Australians. You only have to look at the Bruce Ruxtons, the Hugh Morgans and the Joh Bjelke-Petersens to see the other extreme. This is why I think that the real hope for the future rests with the young people, for they are beginning to be told a little of the truth of what happened in their country.

My comment that the hope for the future rests with the young people is deliberately ironic. For many years (and still today, in some parts of this country), there were people who said that there was no hope for older Aborigines, but that the young ones could be educated, especially if they were taken away from their parents and indoctrinated with white values. My argument is the opposite. I say that we should concentrate on teaching the young people the truth, so that they will change their attitudes and help create a better society for all of us.

Aboriginal people have been part of this continent for at least 50,000 years. It is only recently that the great white 'experts', the self-proclaimed authorities on Aboriginal Australia, have acknowledged this, although Aboriginal people had always insisted they had been around for much longer than the archaeologists and anthropologists used to believe. Our oral history always told us that we'd been here a lot longer. Now the experts' research techniques have caught up with the teachings of Aboriginal oral culture. They are no longer telling people that Aborigines have only been living in Australia for 15,000 years and that we came across the land bridge from Asia before the end of the last Ice Age. In the 1970s, at Lake Mungo in the south-west of New South Wales, archaeologists found evidence of a burial site about 30,000 years old. This means that Aboriginal people had a relatively organized, sophisticated society long before anything that looked like civilization had emerged in Europe.

It has been estimated that something like 800 million Aboriginal people lived and died in Australia B.C. – (Before Cook) – before any non-Aboriginal person set foot on this land. That must be difficult to comprehend for people whose history only goes back a couple of hundred years, for a couple of hundred years compared with over 50,000 years is nothing. This is one of the problems people have when the issue of sacred sites comes up. They don't understand that thousands of generations of Aboriginal people lived and died here, to the extent that virtually every square inch of this continent was of some significance to the Aboriginal people who lived here. It's not a question of Aboriginal people today, for convenience's sake, 'discovering' a sacred site where some mining company has just found uranium or diamonds. Aboriginal people have radically different concepts of the land.

Ten-year-old Aboriginal children in the Northern Territory or central Australia know an amazing amount about botany. They know the different sorts of plants, which are edible, what time of the year to find them, what food sources are available, where the water is. Aboriginal people have such total knowledge of their surrounding environment that they can survive in areas where white people would die – white people *do* die there. Had the so-called explorers of Australia bothered to ask Aboriginal people when they were in strife, in what they thought was a desert, they would have found that Aboriginal people, looking through different eyes, with 50,000 years of accumulated experience, could see an abundance of food and water. That's why the mugs on the Burke and Wills expedition died, and many other white explorers. When I went to school, I was told that Blaxland, Lawson and Wentworth discovered the route across the Blue Mountains; they neglected to tell us that an Aboriginal person showed them the way across, because Aboriginal people had been doing it for thousands of years.

Aboriginal society B.C. was and is far more compassionate and humane than white Australian society. Too many people think that the problem is just one of race – our skins are darker than theirs. But if every Aboriginal person in Australia turned white tomorrow, we'd still have a problem, because it has nothing to do with skin colour. It's got to do with what's inside our heads. Aboriginal society and European society are diametrically opposed. European society, if you want a really simplistic analysis, is essentially competitive. It is laughably referred to as a free enterprise society. It holds up materialism and individualism as being the great things to aspire to. And its basic unit is the nuclear family. Aboriginal society is different at all levels. Aboriginal people reject the concept of individuality, of materialism. Ours is a non-competitive society; for want of a better term, it is a socialist society. And the basic unit of our society is the extended family. As far as we are concerned, we lived here in perfect harmony with each other and with the total environment.

Aboriginal people B.C. understood that if you are going to ensure the survival of your own people, you do *not* go out and destroy the environment that gives you food and water. Aboriginal society B.C. was the most stable human society on the face of this earth. Then something went wrong. The British wanted somewhere to dump the victims of their society, the people who didn't count. So they came out here and took over our land. It must have been an amazing thing for the Aboriginal people who were here at the time. They would have realized at once the type of people they were up against, when they saw how the British who came out here treated their own people – putting them in chains, with 500 lashes, and so on, for stealing a loaf of bread.

There is clear evidence these days to show that what has happened in this country since the arrival of the First Fleet is one of the greatest crimes ever committed in the history of humanity. At first, Aboriginal people were shot down whenever they tried to resist the invasion. Then, about the beginning of this century, the whites realized that shooting human beings wasn't a very Christian way to act. Instead, they began to round up the Aboriginal people and stick them in places that were euphemistically called reserves or mission stations. In reality these were concentration camps, designed to bring the Aboriginal people together, out of the sight and minds of white Australians. The theory was that if you isolated Aboriginal people in these places, with luck they would all die out, and there would be no more problems; everything would be sweet. What happened to the Aborigines stuck in these concentration camps? If you've seen the film 'Lousy Little Sixpence', about the enforced separation of children from their parents to work for white people in the towns and cities, and the misery and degradation of these camps, then you've got some idea of what happened to Aborigines in these places, at least on the east coast. They used slightly different techniques in central Australia, where the missionaries started going berserk. There is a great African saying: 'When the white man came, we had the land, and he had the Bible; now we've got the Bible, and he's got the land.' It applies here too.

Every Aboriginal family suffered in some way from the policies that existed up until 1967 in most parts of Australia. Proportionately, more Aboriginal people died as a result of the crimes committed against us over the last 200 years than Jewish people were exterminated in the holocaust. Hitler's concentration camps only lasted about a decade; some of the concentration camps that Aborigines were kept in here lasted for over a hundred years. People don't seem to understand that. What happened to the Jewish people after the holocaust? The whole world reacted in shock and horror. The great powers said, 'These people need a homeland where they can be safe.' So they took over the Palestinian people's land and made refugees of the Palestinian people.

But what happened to us? When we talk today about minuscule bits of land that are not of much consequence to anyone, except perhaps mining companies, people are angry and accuse us of wanting to be a privileged elite, of wanting something that no one else has got, if you believe Joh Bjelke-Petersen. It irks me that Aboriginal people have to spend so much time justifying their insignificant claims. We're not dispossessing anyone in our land rights. Our land rights claims, if you look at them carefully, involve no land that is currently legally occupied by non-Aboriginal Australians. We are being very reasonable, considering what has happened to us. It just shows again what a humane and compassionate people we are.

The history of Aboriginal people since the British invasion is not all bad, however, not all oppressive. There are some positive stories to tell. Something that gives me some hope in white Australians is the referendum result in 1967. Before 1967 this country had a system of apartheid. I spent the first seventeen years of my life under laws that deprived me and all my people of the right to vote, to freedom of movement, to drink, all the basic civil and human rights enjoyed by all other Australians. We were denied those by law. But in 1967 there was a referendum that in essence asked whether Aboriginal people should come under commonwealth jurisdiction. Aboriginal advocates interpreted that as meaning: 'Do you believe that Aborigines should have equal rights?' An amazing thing happened: more than 90 per cent of the population voted Yes. There was a basic reservoir of goodwill among white Australians.

This result had an extraordinary effect on the Aboriginal people where I come from, on a reserve in New South Wales. Suddenly, one day, the big boss, the white manager – he used to be God on the reserve – came up and said, 'Okay, you blacks, you're all free, go and make your way in the white man's world, no more hand-outs, no more tea, flour, sugar, go out and work like everyone else, and earn money to buy tucker to put food in your gut.'

There was only one thing wrong with that. In 1967 there wasn't even any work for white people in the bush, where all the reserves were. And so Aboriginal people were immediately faced with a dilemma: they either went where they could get work or they starved.

The effect was dramatic. The Aboriginal community in Sydney, not including the reserve at La Perouse, consisted of about 2,000 people at the most before 1967; twelve months later, the Aboriginal population of Sydney was 35,000. Almost overnight the population skyrocketed, as people came to Sydney in a mass exodus from the reserves. They didn't go there by choice. It wasn't possible any more to go hunting in the traditional way and live on bush tucker. The land had already been ruined. The only way they could survive was to move to the cities. So 35,000 blacks, none of them educated enough to be brain surgeons or nuclear physicists inevitably wound up together in the poorest parts of Sydney – Redfern, Alexandria and Newtown – in the inner city.

That created enormous problems for us and for the other people in those suburbs. The most obvious reaction came from the police. For some reason, the New South Wales coppers decided that the only way to react to this influx of poor blacks from the bush was to begin a campaign of intimidation and harassment. It was police harassment of the Redfern Aboriginal community that sparked off the second major change in black Australia.

Ever since Captain Cook's arrival, there had been organized resistance by Aboriginal people to the invasion of their land. You've all heard of Sitting Bull and Geronimo and some of the great American Indian leaders, but how many of you have heard of Nemaluk and Musquito? For these are the equivalents, despite the myth that has been deliberately created in this country that Aboriginal people passively accepted the invasion of their land.

But it was the action of the Gurindji people in the early 1960s that first created widespread public awareness of Aboriginal resistance. Vincent Lingiari, a leader of incredible brilliance, took his people, the Gurindji people, off Wave Hill Station in the Northern Territory. They went on strike, first because the people weren't being paid equal wages – they weren't really being paid wages at all – but also because the Gurindji people wanted to go back to their own land. For nine years they stayed on strike – nine years! Lingiari showed Australians that Aboriginal people could stand up. Not only that, he showed black Australians that if they stood up for themselves, it didn't matter how long it took or how much struggle they had to go through, they could win. The

Gurindji land rights struggle was a great inspiration for Aboriginal people all over this country.

Lingiari came and visited us in Sydney and talked to many of our people in Sydney and inspired us to do more to help ourselves. What grew out of that was the first free legal-aid centre in this country. It was set up by Aborigines, for Aborigines, to overcome a specific problem that we saw in our own community.

A few months after the legal service was established, another group of people in the Aboriginal community got together and started a health service. The legal service people were out seeing one of their clients, and they found a man nearly dead in an old abandoned car where he was living in Redfern. They said, 'Why don't you go to hospital? You're sick, you're dying,' and he said, 'No, I'm not going to go to hospital; they treat you like shit there. If you're black, you can be the first person there in the morning and still be the last person treated there at night. I can't stand the people staring at you in the waiting room and calling you "boong". I don't like the way the staff treat you. I don't want to go.' 'What about a doctor?' they asked. He laughed and said, 'You know as well as I do that if you're black, they want money up front first, otherwise you don't get treated, and what blackfellow in Redfern got money?' And these people thought, Why can't we use the same basic concept as the legal service to set up a community-controlled, community survival organization? Why can't we set up a medical service, using volunteer doctors? And they did.

If there's one area where we really are re-writing the rule books it's in these health centres, which are run by Aboriginal people according to their own values. The concept is brilliant, and people are now recognizing that it also can be applied to white society. As well as giving better health care than other systems, the community-controlled centres are more cost-effective, and that's what matters to the white man. In 1983 the South Australian Minister for Health said he believed that community-controlled health centres were the way forward, not only in Aboriginal health but also in developing a whole new approach to health care for everyone in this country.

Meanwhile, back in Redfern, soon after the establishment of the medical service, a group of black women set up a breakfast programme for young Aboriginal kids in that area, and soon they were feeding about 500 kids every morning. It was chaos. But, through the hard work of Norma Williams, Lyn Craigie, Isabel Coe, Barbara Flick and many other Aboriginal women, the break-

The Aboriginal Embassy was set up on the lawns of Parliament House in Canberra. It was removed by police on the orders of the conservative McMahon government in 1972.

fast programme developed into a comprehensive child-care centre and women's centre, the Murraweena Aboriginal women's and children's centre in Sydney, which is one of the more remarkable organizations that exist in black Australia.

Things like this gave confidence to Aboriginal people. After generations under the thumb of the white man's law, under the administration of the managers on the concentration camps, subject to a hand-out system, an artificial dependency on the white man, it was psychologically extremely important for the Aboriginal people to solve their own problems. They discovered that they were capable of doing it in a far more efficient, logical and intelligent way than anybody who'd come along with a fistful of sociology degrees. The thing we really proved was that the only people who are really expert on Aboriginal communities are Aboriginal people. You can go to university for ten years and get all the degrees under the sun, but it doesn't make you understand what goes on inside our heads; and you can be a blackfellow who doesn't speak English but still know more about what goes on in your own community than any of these parasites that hang around us.

That's what these medical and legal services and all these community-controlled, community survival programmes are about. They are called 'community survival' because we have never said that any of these things are the long-term answer to the problems that confront us. They are just organizations that will ensure that we survive until the answer to our problems becomes reality.

That answer is land rights, because land rights mean economic independence. We don't kid ourselves about what surrounds us in Australia. A lot of your mob say this is a Christian society; but we watch what you do, and there is no doubt in our minds that your society worships one thing – money. So if we are to have true control over our own lives today and our children's in the future, we have to be on equal terms with the white man's society. The only way we can achieve that is through economic independence. That's what land rights mean to me.

My people on the reserve could become self-sufficient within five years if we were given two things. The first is the two blocks of land that we want up there – we're claiming the present reserve and the original reserve, where my grandmother was born, an island in the river. The second is one million dollars – which is chickenfeed compared with the land rights settlements in North America. Just one million dollars would give my people, the Gumbangerri people on the north coast of New South Wales, absolute economic independence within five years. And then we wouldn't have to go cap in hand to some Aboriginal Affairs bureaucrat in Canberra so we can do a few things to solve some problems in our community. We won't have to go begging to anyone, and we will cease to be a 'burden' on the Australian taxpayer, which is what everyone keeps telling us we are.

We would also be able to get rid of the parasites that infest our communities. I reckon that if every Aboriginal person in Australia dropped dead tonight, there'd be about 100,000 white people out of work tomorrow – all the sociologists, anthropologists, archaeologists, bureaucrats, head-shrinkers; the head-measurers would have no one whose lives they could interfere with; they'd be out of work. In 1983, in central Australia alone, there were 238 separate research teams studying varying aspects of Aboriginal society, and they were all white, and they were all financed from Australian taxpayers' money. People complain about us getting too much money, but that's where it goes. In 1972, Nugget Coombs, who should know a bit about money, because his name was once on our money as governor of the Reserve Bank, said that three-quarters of all the money allocated to Aboriginal Affairs went into white pockets. We are one of the biggest growth industries in Australia, and that's why our health isn't better. Very little of that money filters through to the Aboriginal people who need it. So give us economic independence, and we don't need to come back to you and ask for anything else. Give us economic independence, and we will then be able to decide for ourselves the direction our communities should go in, what sort of society we want, without any interference.

I believe that, ultimately, when white Australians see the way in which we re-construct and re-build our society, they are going to realize a lot of things about their own society. When people realize how terrible white society is, they will come to us, and we will teach them how to live in a better way. If Ronald Raygun pressed the button over there, and all the capital cities in Australia got wiped out, if it was possible to survive at all, the people who would survive would not be your mob, but the old blacks in Central Australia who would know where the food was and how to survive without fancy four-wheel drive vehicles and other bits of white man's technology.

We have done enormous things to transform the face of Australia. Australia is isolated enough for us to begin a new experiment. There is no need for us to become a plastic, second-hand America; we don't have to try to be like China or Russia; there's no need for us to try to be like anything else. We should create our own society, one that is based on egalitarian principles, one that puts people before money and material possessions. If you want to create a more egalitarian society, come and talk to us. You'll find us most reasonable people, and we'll show you how to do it.

War Against War

CHRIS HEALY

War is an important part of our culture. Books, songs, films, images and stories remind us of past wars. We all know something about the enemies, the battles and the heroes. But those who oppose war have not been remembered in the same way. Today, we may remember the anti-Vietnam movement or turn up to nuclear disarmament marches. There are few people left, however, to tell the story of the anti-war movements that went before: the struggles in Australia against war in the Sudan and in South Africa, against the First World War, and against the rising menaces of war and fascism in Europe during the 1930s. In a sense, these were all struggles at a distance. Most of them were unsuccessful. Yet all touched people's lives and carved out political space for themselves, sometimes in unexpected ways. War is not an isolated phenomenon: its causes run deep. So, apart from opposing particular wars, Australian anti-war movements at different times found themselves in opposition to the state, to militarism in general, to patriarchy and to capitalism. They drew on wider discontents, mobilizing more than just their own members. Their successes and failures have a lot to tell us.

The cause of the Sudan war has been evaded by the platform, the pulpit, and the press.

Anti-war speaker Aitkin, Paddington 1885

Do we regard ourselves as part of the English nation or as mere hewers of wood?

Recruiting speaker, Edmund Barton, Sydney 1885

In February 1885, the Sudanese people of north Africa stormed and held their British-occupied capital. Three weeks later 700 men from New South Wales were shipped to the Sudan – colonial troops sent to aid the empire in reclaiming another colony. Although these soldiers were given an impressive send-off, within four months they had only torrential rain and a gaggle of civic officials to welcome them home. They were lonely 'heroes' who had scarcely seen the 'enemy'. During these months, opponents of the war established a strong public presence in and around Sydney, even without the help of any coherent anti-war organization. The pro-war *Sydney Morning Herald* admitted that: 'The struggle in the Sudan has come to be regarded with something like disgust. Hardly a voice has been raised in its favour.' The campaign against New South Wales's involvement in Britain's war against the Sudanese was the first of many attempts to oppose Australia's involvement in war.

The movement against the Sudan war stands out for its spontaneity, class consciousness and thorough-going radicalism. From the outset the anti-war forces were on the attack. New South Wales' offer of troops had been arranged very hurriedly through an old boy network of retired British army officers. In order to despatch the soldiers quickly, the government spent public money illegally, without parliamentary approval. At first this tactic worked. Parliament, when it met, dutifully supported the government's action. But, in the long run, the government had to go to the people in search of political and financial support. This meant that the pro-war and anti-war cases were argued out in the patriotic rallies that were designed as military fund-raising events. These rallies provided unusually democratic forums within which the war was debated.

In general, the patriotic rallies proved to be disastrous for the war's supporters. Premier Dalley and the chief justice presided over the first meeting, which was held in Sydney's Exhibition Building. Twelve thousand people, overwhelmingly hostile to the war, made such an uproar that the speakers were drowned out and the rally was abandoned. Many similar meetings throughout the colony condemned the New South Wales involvement. Usually only small rallies supported the war effort. A government minister who arrived at a crowded Town Hall would know he was in for a rowdy meeting and could take heart only in the police presence. The anti-war movement was highly decentralized, because it was a movement without an organization. In some areas, for example, the northern coal towns, local mayors provided the focus of opposition by calling anti-war meetings. In other instances, trade unions, local councils or members of parliament established themselves as rallying points for anti-war activity.

The anti-war movement was an alliance of two groups: one expressed its opposition in nationalist terms, the other in class terms. The nationalists were the ones who spoke in parliament, wrote letters to newspapers or later wrote autobiographies, so historians tend to discover them easily. Henry Parkes was representative of the nationalists. Parkes saw the anti-war movement as a force that might bump him back into parliament. Equally, however, it was a forum in which he could argue for 'true patriotism'. When Dalley asserted that to fight was one's patriotic duty to the empire, Parkes retorted that the colonies of Australia also deserved loyalty. Here the question of 'soil' became very important. The Sudanese were on their own soil, the British on another's. Parkes and other nationalists believed Australians should keep their feet firmly planted in their own dust. Though Parkes shared Dalley's loyalty to England, he insisted that loyalty to Australia was more important.

This was not true of the working-class opposition to the war. The working-class mobilization was more concerned with who owned the soil than where the soil was. This section of the anti-war forces was represented by the *Bulletin*, *Liberator*, and the trade unions. Their critique of the war was clear and concise: the British were fighting to protect the 'money lenders and bondholders' (usually couched in anti-Semitic terms); the Sudanese were fighting for liberty against domination. So, unlike the nationalists, they argued that the British deserved to lose. Despite their differences, the combined forces of nationalists and radicals opposing New South Wales's participation eventually won considerable support. But the dramatic position taken by the working-class radicals at that time was not paralleled on a wide scale until Vietnam, when a 'New Left' again argued that Australia ought to be defeated in an imperialist war.

This is a raid by capitalists on a self-governing country.

Cardinal Moran on the Boer War, Sydney 1899

The minority against the war is very great.

Professor G. A. Wood writing against the Boer War, Sydney 1901

The campaign against the Sudan war was immediate and short-lived. Opposition to the Boer war, on the other hand, developed slowly, never assumed a mass public presence, but did generate specifically anti-war organizations. Before looking at the movement that eventually took shape, the absence of any significant initial mobilization needs to be explained.

AN OMINOUS START

Federated Australia "And so my first national act is to back up a wanton deed of blood and rapine!"

In the case of the Sudan war, the initiative came from the Sudanese people, so the British and colonial governments were caught off balance. The Boer war, however, was planned, organized and orchestrated with considerable care by a coalition of pro-war forces stretching from South Africa to Britain and the colonies. The ground was well prepared long before this classic war of economic interests was begun. Cecil Rhodes and his cronies had made flying raids into sovereign territory; British Secretary of State for the Colonies Chamberlain had delayed until potential domestic opposition had been minimized; the large newspapers in Britain and the colonies had been building the case against the Boers; and negotiations with the colonial governments had made certain that 'spontaneous' offers of troops would eventuate. Of course, these preparations did not always turn out as planned. There was a distinct lack of popular enthusiasm for the war spirit. And those who did become excited tended to ignore the parliamentary procedures for involving troops in wars. One sergeant in Adelaide took it on himself to pledge his machine gun regiment for active service. Nevertheless, the conditions on which the war would be fought, both in southern Africa and on the home fronts, had been prepared in advance.

The potential for an anti-war campaign in Australia was influenced by two other factors. During the 1890s, economic depression and industrial defeat had profoundly disorganized the labour movement. This meant that the working-class base for anti-war activity was very weak. And the Sudan campaign had not generated any permanent anti-war organizations that might have provided a focus for a new campaign. Although imperialist expansion was crucial for Britain in the last quarter of the nineteenth century, in 1899 a movement against the Boer war had to begin from scratch.

The first public signs of opposition came from the radical press, some sections of the country press, the trade unions, a few isolated labor politicians, the socialist parties, and a Melbourne-based, middle-class organization called the Peace and Humanity Society. The *Bulletin* led the attack, and was soon joined by a new anti-war journal, *Grip*. Their condemnations of the war were mixed with a strong sense that the British would win a quick and easy victory.

The trade unions argued that the war was drawing attention away from urgently needed social legislation. The socialist parties asserted that the Australian worker had no interest in a war over which group of capitalists would own the gold mines. Unfortunately this class consciousness was also bound up with racism. The socialist parties claimed that the British would try to replace the white workers with 'cheap' black labour. In some colonial parliaments, the troop commitments were only narrowly approved, as doubt about the wisdom of Australian participation was so great. Mostly, however, the debate centred on whether Britain really needed help and not on whether the war should be opposed. So when the consensus of loyalty to England was challenged, as when Labor's W. A. Holman said he hoped England was defeated, the uproar was enormous.

The situation changed drastically when it became clear that the imperial forces would not have an easy victory. In 'Black Week' in December 1899, 3,000 British soldiers were killed or captured. This was the most dramatic of several English defeats. In Australia it hardened pro-war feelings. A second colonial contingent was raised with the almost unanimous support of the various parliaments. At the same time a privately sponsored 'Bushmen's Contingent' was put together. Employer groups and others began organizing attacks on anti-war public meetings so that it became increasingly difficult for activists to speak in public. They were no longer considered an eccentric marginal force but dangerously disloyal.

After January 1900, the British recovered militarily and overran most of the independent southern African states. The commander of the imperial forces returned home, press coverage declined and the adventures seemed all but over. The war then entered its second stage. The Boers broke up their forces and began a guerilla campaign that was to last two and a half years. In vicious desperation, the English responded by burning every farm in areas known to be occupied by guerillas and interning everyone who might possibly have supported the Boers. Twenty thousand non-combatants died in these internment camps.

Reports of these and other war atrocities filtered through to Australia. Labor politician William Holman and liberal intellectual G. A. Wood set up an Anti-War League in 1901. The league was an extraordinary collection of Labor supporters, Irish and Australian nationalists, European radicals and non-conformist Christians. After months of debating its constitution, the Anti-War League began a campaign early in 1902. A petition was sent to every shire in New South Wales calling for Australian withdrawal and an end to the war. An accompanying letter asked that the petition be displayed so that people could sign it. Few shires supported the petition. One council considered the petition so evil that it was ceremonially burnt in the council chambers. On the other hand, the league did collect many signatures – 1000 in one particularly good week. Women, who made up one-third of the league's membership, were largely responsible for this work, though men were almost always the public face of the group. This was to become a familiar pattern in anti-war movements. Before the negotiated peace of June 1902, the Anti-War League gained the support of the New South Wales Labour Council and the 21,000 strong Australian Workers Union, but was not able to organize mass opposition.

At the same time, those who supported the Boer war were unable to arouse much enthusiasm in Australia. Although governments devoted considerable energy to manufacturing support for the war, recruiting was difficult; most of the 16,000 who joined up were land-owners, clerks and unemployed workers. The only large public displays of support for the war were at the troops' send-offs, and these rituals of farewell were more a matter of collective entertainment than shows of enthusiasm for the war. Similarly, opposition to the anti-war movement was sporadic, small and clearly orchestrated by employer groups. Both pro-war and anti-war politicians were returned in elections held in Victoria and New South Wales during the war. In general it seems that neither the supporters nor the opponents of the war out-mobilized the other. For the anti-war forces this was, in part, an organizational failure and, in part, an inability to work out clear reasons for opposing the war.

Only in New South Wales was a viable anti-war organization created. In South and Western Australia, the weakness of organized labour, in Victoria the moralism of the Peace and Humanity Society and elsewhere the fragmentation of oppositional forces all contributed to the lack of effective anti-war organizing. Within the labour movement generally, both pro-war and anti-war unions, politicians and labour councils went to great pains to play down the importance of disagreements over the war. In the process, they pushed the issue to the back of the political stage.

There was, however, considerable passive support for the anti-war movement. Meetings in mining towns and the industrial areas of the major cities nearly always gave a sympathetic hearing to anti-war speakers. But the anti-war organization's concern with nationalism and morality found little support in these audiences. Wood, for instance, saw anti-war activity as true loyalty because the war was bringing shame upon the empire, and some businessmen in the movement asserted that Australia should look after its own interests first. Neither of these two dominant positions in the anti-war organizations had much in common with the perceptions and needs of working people. They were not a sufficient basis for a successful movement.

Wanting an everlasting peace without making any differences between nations, freedom and rights for every nation, all the misery to end. Down with militarism which has taken millions of lives.

Resolution of the Finnish Club to the 1917 Australian Peace Alliance Conference

Pacifists must work hard to remove the causes of war and thus must contribute to the class struggle because until workers are free from industrial slavery they cannot free themselves from war.

J. D. Robertson, in a (love?) letter to Isabell Swan, 1920

Vivid memories of the First World War survive in Australia. Nourished by books, films, monuments and oral traditions, the 'Great War' is represented and remembered as a moment of history. This is what history is really about: men in battle, shedding their ordinariness to emerge as heroes. It is a highly selective memory of a nation united in victory and the continuing glory of the Anzac tradition.

Such a national adventure story excludes many other stories. Among these is the memory of large, organized anti-war movements. By 1916, in the midst of attempts to gain total Australian commitment to the fighting in Europe, anti-war movements had established themselves as a challenging force. Within a year, however, they had been greatly weakened by massive state repression, the exhaustion of two conscription campaigns, internal splits, and isolation from the labour movement. Those who had opposed the war were all but invisible by 1918.

During the war an array of diverse anti-war organizations emerged across Australia. There was not one coherent movement. Two bodies, the Women's Peace Army (W.P.A.) and the Australian Peace Alliance (A.P.A.), provide examples of how anti-war organizations were created in such difficult times.

The declaration of war in 1914 threw pacifists and socialists into confusion. Internationally, socialist groups abandoned the cause of the workers of the world in favour of a war of nations. In Australia, working-class organizations did not take a strong stand against the war, with the exceptions of the Industrial Workers of the World and several socialist parties. The general reaction of most people ranged from 'Rule Britannia' patriotism through to sadness, disbelief and confusion, tinged with a resigned acceptance of the inevitable. Vaguely anti-war organizations, such as the Australian Freedom League and the various peace societies, collapsed. The war brought an entirely different political framework, which initially drove opposition underground.

The Australian Peace Alliance was created only days after the outbreak of war on the initiative of the Victorian Socialist Party, Quaker groups, the remnants of the Peace Society and Freedom League. At first it aimed cautiously to 'safeguard the interests of peace during the current European conflict'. This soon became a call for an immediate end to the war and a negotiated peace. The alliance stuck to this platform throughout the war and established itself as an umbrella group that linked other organizations.

After an impressive first meeting of 500 people in Melbourne's Athenaeum Hall, the A.P.A. grew rapidly during 1915. Within eighteen months it was established in four states. Most of the active members were feminists, socialists, pacifists or disgruntled Laborites. They organized lunchtime meetings at factory gates, evening meetings in the suburbs, and sponsored resolutions in Labor Party and trade union branches. All this was co-ordinated by paid and unpaid workers in central city offices. The alliance and its affiliates also made contact with people across the country through speaking tours and a complex literature distribution network designed to evade government censorship.

Despite state repression and violent attacks by soldier and recruiting groups, by 1916 there was considerable popular opposition to the war. Slowly and painfully, anti-war sentiment came to occupy public space. Fred Riley, Victorian secretary of the A.P.A., wrote to his mother: 'Twelve months ago we were ridiculed, laughed at, and scoffed at, but in spite of all we have not changed our opinion and the great mass of the working people are with us.'

The Women's Peace Army was formed in 1915 as a distinctly feminist group, which also drew upon strands in Christianity and socialism. It was an off-shoot of the Women's Political Association, which argued that the age of consent should be raised to twenty-one, campaigned against male venereal disease, supported equal pay for women, and opposed men's privilege in the legal system. Throughout the war, Adela Pankhurst wrote a W.P.A. column, 'We War Against War', for the association's newspaper, the *Woman Voter*. Pankhurst was the educated and articulate daughter

A cartoon by Syd Nicholls in the I.W.W. newspaper *Direct Action* pillories the pro-war lobby

of British feminist Emmeline Pankhurst. She became known as a powerful critic of war soon after arriving in Australia in 1914.

Her column drew links between war, capitalism and the oppression of women, and she constantly put forward the particular interests that women shared in opposing war.

The Women's Peace Army also organized some of the most provocative anti-war activities on the streets of the cities. Where other more respectable groups hired halls, the Peace Army held women's counter-demonstrations at recruiting and pro-conscription meetings. These confrontations led to vicious attacks on W.P.A. members, who were commonly assaulted and threatened with rape. During the 1916 anti-conscription campaign, 10,000 women marched through the streets of Melbourne led by Cecilia John upon a white horse under a banner that read: 'Gentle Maiden Trust Him Not'; they were greeted by tens of thousands at the Yarra Bank. Through such propaganda by words and deeds, the W.P.A. gained both popularity and notoriety. But this was not marginal politics. Women were being appealed to *as women* by both pro-war and anti-war forces. Though most women would not have supported the anti-war activity of the Peace Army, the autonomous women's anti-war movement was very strong nonetheless.

As well as organizing independently, the Peace Army worked with mixed groups such as the Peace Alliance. Initially, the

An anti-conscription rally on Melbourne's Yarra Bank in 1916

W.P.A. used the Peace Alliance to call upon women to organize politically and industrially to avoid the exploitation and horror of war. There was a problem with this. Within the mixed groups, although women's support and hard work were crucial, they were never given the same status as men. Women were assigned a place 'suited to women' and subservient to men. As the anti-war activity became more intense, W.P.A. and A.P.A. members increasingly worked together. In the process, the three most prominent women activists – Vida Goldstein, Cecilia John and Adela Pankhurst – were set apart from other women as 'the exceptional ones'. These three monopolized the public speaking, criticism and praise. The peace organizations elevated Adela Pankhurst to radical sainthood with the issue of a sepia-tinted postcard bearing her likeness; pro-war forces called the *Woman Voter*, 'Miss Goldstein's rag'. Both sides restricted most women to 'feminine' roles: typing and filing, feeding and supporting men. This co-option, however, was never complete, because the Women's Peace Army was unrelenting in asserting the strength of women to combat their own oppression. Their double attack on war and on patriarchy brought forth a brutal response. These women were the first to suffer mob attacks from men, they were constantly maligned in the press as spinsters, traitors to both womanhood and the nation. They were beaten up, arrested, censored and banned. At the same time, the Industrial Workers of the World had been suppressed just as ruthlessly. This revolutionary socialist organization opposed both war and capitalism, and had built a power base within the trade union movement. However, as Peter Love's chapter on radicalism describes, it was crushed spectacularly by the Hughes government.

The anti-conscription campaign of 1916 brought the anti-war forces into an alliance with those who supported the war but opposed conscription. Yet it was the anti-war movements, and particularly the A.P.A. and the W.P.A., that provided the organizational basis, the best publications, and the most influential speakers for the new campaign. This was largely because neither the Labor Party nor the trade unions had the experience to function as the focus for a mass movement. The anti-war movements were at the centre of the action across most of the country.

But this alliance was an uneasy one. After the first conscription referendum was defeated, conflicts developed between the pro-war anti-conscriptionists and those who were opposed to the war itself. At this point the Labor Party desperately wanted to take the initiative from the anti-war forces, which had gained so much support in the anti-conscription campaign. They were given a perfect excuse when most of the anti-war organizations tried to insist that their 'peace candidate', Vida Goldstein, should replace a Labor candidate on the 1917 Victorian Senate election ticket. This allowed the Labor Party to bar its members from joining the anti-war groups, and this in turn caused splits within the anti-war organizations. Most trade unionists, socialists and Labor members stuck with the Labor Party, which by this stage had expelled its pro-conscription members, including Prime Minister Billy Hughes. Those who stayed in the party saw the most important task as working to change Labor policy on the war. This meant that throughout 1917 the anti-war organizations were cut off from the mainstream labour movement and the working class, where opposition to the war was growing as the fighting dragged on and the point of the war remained unclear. By the second conscription referendum, the Labor Party was firmly in control of the 'no' campaign. The left wing of the anti-war movements worked hard within the party. 'Peace resolutions' were passed by a number of state branches and only narrowly defeated at the 1918 federal conference. The leadership, however, managed to maintain control and ensure that the party stood by its support for the war.

The anti-war movements were battered by the end of the war. They had been attacked by the state and conservative forces, outflanked by the Labor Party and torn apart by internal divisions. Although the conditions for anti-war groups were difficult (with the nation pledged to 'the last man and the last shilling'), the organized movements also made two crucial mistakes.

The first was in the structure of the major national group, the A.P.A. Though the Peace Alliance was at the centre of the anti-war activity, it never became a membership organization. It remained throughout the war an umbrella body, which drew its 'membership' from other organizations: trade unions, Labor Party branches, women's organizations, socialist parties, religious and pacifist groups. When the Labor Party and trade union affiliates pulled out, the alliance had no way of appealing directly to a membership for support. The strength of the major anti-war organizations depended on other groups incorporating opposition to the war as one of their own principles. No major autonomous anti-war organizations were established over and above the religious, feminist and socialist anti-war groups.

Because of the absence of any such organizations, the various separate movements never reached effective agreement about what opposing the war really meant, let alone on how concrete aims could be achieved. This was the second mistake. There were clear contradictions between the policies of the revolutionary socialists, pacifists and liberals. These were recognized but never thrashed out as a basis for producing a dynamic movement. Instead they relied on British pamphlets rather than developing their own responses to the war; they naively trusted that they could 'change bad laws through the courts', even though the state was ruthlessly repressing them; and they generally dissociated themselves from the more radical feminist and socialist anti-war action. Without coherent, understandable and politically relevant arguments to bring people together in opposing the war, the movements were not as effective as they might have been, considering the powerful opposition to the 'Great War' that existed within the trade unions, and feminist and socialist groups.

The aim of the leaders of the anti-war movement is not pacifism but the fomenting of class warfare (the most dreadful strife known to mankind).

Sydney Morning Herald, 1933

And as Comrade Stalin had said: 'Peace is indivisible!'

A young Protestant Minister speaking
from the floor at an International
Peace Campaign meeting, 1936

In the 1920s many people believed that the 'Great War' had established a lasting peace, which would be guaranteed by the League of Nations; others felt that new wars were inevitable. So the tiny peace organizations were either pessimistic or inactive. In 1932 the New South Wales Peace Society debated the question, 'Is there any hope?', and promptly decided there wasn't. The anti-war campaigning that existed was passive and bureaucratically 'official' rather than popular and based on a movement. The Labor Party maintained its dominance in most areas of progressive politics throughout the 1920s. Labour radicalism after the war was limited, and neither the establishment of the Communist Party of Australia nor the beginning of the depression revived mass activism. Despite some small anti-imperialist campaigns organized in the labour movement, the prevailing feeling was that Australia should stand aloof from world affairs. This isolationism was compounded by the immediate hardships of the working class after 1929. At the same time, the feminist movement had been driven

Egon Kisch, second from right, on tour around Australia in 1938.

from the sphere of public politics. The Women's International League for Peace and Freedom was the only anti-war group formed during the war to last through the 1920s.

During 1933 the Movement Against War, later to become the Movement Against War and Fascism, was founded in Melbourne. It was largely a Communist Party initiative intended to undermine popular support for the League of Nations, because the Soviet Union (and hence the Communist Party) regarded the League of Nations as anti-communist. The Movement Against War and Fascism (M.A.W.F.) was a small but active organization that aimed to create the conditions for mass popular action against the threat of imperialist war. It attracted a following beyond the Communist Party, because it seemed a fresh response to the imminent danger of war, and it was imaginative and theatrical in style. It marked the beginnings of new political alignments.

Members took bold and provocative public actions, for example, laying anti-war wreaths during Anzac Day ceremonies. The second national conference of M.A.W.F. was held in Melbourne during the military pageant of Victoria's centenary celebrations. The main international guest at the conference was to have been Egon Kisch, a man with a proud record of anti-fascist activity in Hitler's Germany. The government refused him permission to land in Australia, but Kisch jumped ship – literally. There followed a chase of several months as the broken-legged Kisch tried to avoid the police while continuing to speak in public. It caused havoc for Menzies, the attorney-general of the time. Kisch's visit was important: largely because of the government's ban, he received a lot of press publicity and free speech sympathy, which opened up a new audience to the anti-war movements. And Kisch argued throughout his tour that fascism, already entrenched in Germany and Italy, was a threat to which opponents of war must respond. This helped the movement fight against isolationism and establish an international perspective. But the theatre of Kisch only provided a temporary boost to the young anti-war movement.

Throughout this period, M.A.W.F. was involved in a long and bitter struggle with the Labor Party. Although the communist activists of the anti-war movements were now trying desperately to establish good relations with Labor people, the Labor Party members remembered the days not long gone when communists abused and insulted them at every turn. So it became a question of whether the Communist Party or the Labor Party would 'control' the movement. The pattern of the struggle is familiar. The Labor Party refused to allow its members to join M.A.W.F. and instead established its own communist-free anti-war committee. At first this was of little importance. The Labor committee was never a real force but simply added weight to the growing balance of those who feared another war. In the longer run, however, the anti-war cause was weakened by the two political parties struggling for leadership.

The Labor Party was interested in the anti-war movements as an arena of progressive politics that reached beyond the usual territory of parliament and trade union. In this sense, the movements were both potential rivals and potential sources of support. The Communist Party played a more complex and changing role in the movements of the 1930s. Party members were among the most dedicated and energetic workers for the movements. Yet the Communist Party as a whole drew its policies and political directions from the Communist Party of the Soviet Union. As a result, Australian communists made absurd policy shifts, condemning Hitler one day and supporting the Stalin's pact with Germany the next. The battle over the leadership of the anti-war movements was only resolved in 1941 when the west and the Soviet Union united against Germany. From that point, both the C.P.A. and the Labor Party encouraged anti-war campaigners to support the war. What little opposition there was to Australian involvement in the Second World War was conducted by the minuscule Trotskyist movement.

In 1936-7, most of the anti-war groups coalesced as the Australian branch of the International Peace Campaign (I.P.C.). Like many of the anti-war groups formed in Australia, the campaign came from a European initiative. It was an attempt to bring together the labour/socialist groups around the Movement Against War and Fascism and the liberal anti-war groups around the League of Nations Union. This group was both the high point and the beginnings of collapse for the 1930s anti-war movements. The I.P.C. focused on the threat of war in Europe. In the three years it was active, the campaign had to contend with and respond to the turmoil of a continent in which wars proliferated. From the start, pacifists refused to join the campaign because they did not support its policy of using sanctions to prevent war. Differences over support for the republican forces' fight against fascism in the Spanish Civil War soon brought a rift. The I.P.C.'s main aim was to argue that the collective actions of nations not involved in hostilities could be used to deter or halt aggression on the part of individual nations. This became increasingly unrealistic during 1939. Most of Europe showed no desire to co-operate while the German army invaded Austria, Hungary, Czechoslovakia and Poland. Finally, the I.P.C. coalition fell apart with the communists urging non-intervention, labour supporters and liberals encouraging support for the allies, and pacifists isolated in complete opposition.

That the 1930s movements were able to generate such opposition to the possibility of war is in itself remarkable. But parts of the campaign went a step further. Some actually gave practical shape to the vague demand for peace by supporting boycotts, sanctions and collective resistance to aggression. The most spectacular example of this was the Port Kembla 'pig iron' strike in which waterside workers blocked the shipment of iron to Japan. The waterside workers' opposition eventually spread right across Australia. But this is just one example of many. This was only possible because the dominant view in the anti-war movements was internationalist. Australia, already breaking away from Europe, and not yet tied to the United States, was not seen as an adjunct to a great power but as a potentially independent actor in international politics.

All sections of the movement agreed that a 'broad coalition of anti-war forces' was the way to achieve these ideals. Yet the participants were determined not to sacrifice their own principles for a single coalition. Sometimes this strengthened the movements – it prevented their being submerged by the Labor Party, for

example. But it also led to disunity – as when pacifists refused to support the anti-fascist forces in Spain. Yet this disorganization is hardly surprising. Only a tiny minority of those involved in the anti-war campaigns opposed all wars. Most were opposed to particular wars or the preparations for a more general war. Because of this the movements through the 1930s were constantly having to define and then argue their case as new situations arose. Nevertheless, anti-war movements kept going from the time of the Japanese invasion of Manchuria in 1931 through to the Soviet occupation of Finland in 1939.

WAR AGAINST WAR
PEACE
PUBLISHED FOR THE VICTORIAN COUNCIL OF THE INTERNATIONAL PEACE CAMPAIGN
AUSTRALIAN PEACE CONGRESS, SEPTEMBER 16-19, 1937
WAR
Articles by
W. Macmahon Ball
Dr. C. E. W. Bean
Rt. Rev. E. H. Burgmann
Judge Foster
Katharine Susannah Prichard
Sir David Rivett, Etc.
Price, 6d.

These anti-war mobilizations have been fleeting moments of activity and energy, laboriously created and then fairly quick to disappear. Although there is an anti-war tradition in this country, it is not continuous. Because absolute pacifism has been such a tiny force, opposition to war has been developed in relation to particular wars in particular conditions. So the composition and nature of anti-war movements has varied from one situation to the next. The movements have depended on linking a popular set of anti-war beliefs with effective political organizing. For this reason, it is difficult to draw general conclusions.

Yet there are common elements. All the movements have faced state repression, have had to negotiate and establish a basic programme, and have had ambivalent and fraught relationships with the labour movement and Labor Party. Each has also raised the issues of nation, gender and class. Wars involve people making a peculiar link between their own interests and those of a nation-state. Support for war usually requires the citizen to identify with the nation's duty. One common feature of all the anti-war movements here is that they have tried to redefine the link between citizen and nation. At times this has taken a nationalist form, but more commonly it has been an internationalist perspective that has given the movements their coherence and challenge.

The second issue is the distinction between men and women in relation to wars. It is men who are urged to fight and to believe in war as the ultimate adventure story. Women have been encouraged to breed the boys for the front, sustain the economy in the absence of men, keep the home fires burning and service the men who manage to return. For the most part the anti-war movements have recognized that the issues are different for men and women only to the extent that they have established *new*, male-defined ideas about sex roles. Yet it has been when women have established for themselves autonomous space in which to initiate and control their own anti-war activities that the movements have prospered most.

Finally, to occupy public space, and to achieve such small successes as they have, anti-war movements have always needed to establish alliances across class lines. The links between anti-war activists and the organized labour movement have been consistently important. At the same time, a broad base of working-class support, not only within the labour movement, has been essential. Without it, anti-war groups have remained intellectual and moral debating societies. Yet these alliances have been precarious; they have given rise to dissension and to strength. The anti-war movements of the past offer no simple models for dealing with the dilemmas of today. But then, the lessons of history are never simple.

Power to the Young

BARRY YORK

During the early 1980s, when the peace movement began its great revival over the issue of nuclear disarmament, the press remarked on the large number of 'moratorium veterans' in the ranks. The word 'moratorium' comes from the Latin 'mora', meaning 'delay'. In legal usage it means an authorization to delay payments. Yet the word brings to most people's minds the huge and spectacular protest marches against the Vietnam war in the late 1960s and early 1970s.

The word became a part of everyday language because of the extraordinary success of the Vietnam protest movement. Never before had such a vast number of people taken to the streets against Australia's involvement in a war. Between 120,000 and 150,000 Australians 'stopped work to stop the war' on each of the moratoriums in 1970 and 1971, and many more joined them on the streets. The Australian protests were part of a worldwide anti-war movement. Millions around the globe participated in 'international days of protest'.

The 'moratorium veterans' were in their thirties or forties by the early 1980s. They were, as the commentators noted, rather easy to identify. Protest badges seemed to rest easy on their chests. And they carried their placards with a certain world-weariness born of waving so many banners in the 1960s. Babies in prams, or young children on shoulders, completed the picture of their parents as a generation that was growing up but remaining radical. These veterans represent a generation that has its own distinctive style and outlook.

The Vietnam protest movement is best undertstood in terms of the rebellious aspects of the 1960s youth culture. Although the movement included diverse groups – ranging from trade unionists to priests – it was given cultural shape by the participation of the so-called baby-boomers: those born after the Second World War, who were in their teens by the mid 1960s. To a larger extent than any previous Australian protest movement, the anti-Vietnam movement was a youth movement.

The protest movement against the Vietnam war went through three distinct phases. It began with a period of weakness, cautiousness and development between 1964 and 1967. There was a period of spectacular success and militancy between 1968 and 1971. Then came a period of dramatic decline as many of the movement's aims were achieved in late 1971 and 1972. The Vietnam war began well before Australian or even American involvement. The Vietnamese people had fought the Japanese occupation forces during the Second World War. After the war they successfully resisted the French troops who attempted to regain control of Vietnam, a former French colony. The Americans then moved in to try to fill the power vacuum left by the French. As United Nations secretary-general U Thant declared in 1967, the Vietnamese struggle was 'not a war of communist aggression but a war of national independence'.

Australia became involved in the war from 1962, when the Liberal-Country Party government sent military equipment to Saigon, then capital of South Vietnam. Two months later, the first Australian soldiers were sent as a small 'jungle warfare' advisory team. These 'advisers' took part in combat duties. Warrant Officer Kevin Conway, one of thirty Australians in Vietnam, was killed on 6 July 1964. By the end of 1964, Australian 'advisers' numbered one hundred. This was the prelude to the large-scale involvement of Australian combat troops.

The war began officially for Australia on 29 April 1965, when Prime Minister Menzies informed parliament that 1,000 troops would be sent in response to a request by the South Vietnam government. By 1968 Australia had sent 8,000 troops to Vietnam. Whenever the U.S. stepped up the war, Australia sent more troops. The first battalion was sent, for instance, after U.S. President Lyndon B. Johnson had launched the first major U.S. intervention: the bombing of North Vietnam in February 1965 and the introduction of ground-combat troops in March 1965. By the end of 1965, American troops numbered 148,000, and the Australian government had doubled its troop numbers. By 1968, the U.S. force was almost half a million. The logic of the politics underlying Australia's commitment was expressed, infamously, by Prime Minister Harold Holt: 'All the way with L.B.J.'

The campaign for the withdrawal of U.S. and allied troops was begun by a very small, isolated minority. Not surprisingly, the first organized protests were responses to the initial intensification of U.S. involvement. The turning point was the Tonkin Gulf incident of August 1964, which resulted in the first U.S. bombardment of North Vietnam. The U.S. destroyer, *Maddox*, on intelligence patrol in the Gulf, and later joined by the *C. Turner Joy*, were allegedly attacked by North Vietnamese torpedo boats. Within twelve hours, U.S. bombers were launching a reprisal raid. The U.S. used the incident as an excuse to begin all-out war against North Vietnam. As the 'Pentagon Papers' published by the *New York Times* in 1971 were later to prove, the attack had been provoked; the U.S. had been making secret military assaults against North Vietnam for six months before the incident.

In response to the Tonkin Gulf incident, 200 protestors gathered at the U.S. consulate in Melbourne for a silent vigil. These were mainly Old Leftists, centred on the Communist Party of Australia (C.P.A.) and some religious activists who had been prominent in the 'Ban the Bomb' movement, the 'Hands off Indonesia' and anti-Korean war campaigns of the late 1940s and 1950s. In Sydney, the banners at the annual Hiroshima Day commemoration included one declaring 'No War in Vietnam.'

The C.P.A. warned that Australia was becoming involved in a war of aggression. The Eureka Youth League, the C.P.A.'s youth wing, also predicted that conscription would be introduced. They were laughed at. Yet their claims were vindicated by events. On 11 November 1964, three months after the Tonkin Gulf incident, parliament passed a National Service Act. Liberal member and later prime minister, William McMahon, predicted that conscription would 'meet with the warm approval of the Australian public'. The small anti-war forces thought otherwise.

Opponents of the Act promptly dubbed it the 'National Servitude Act'. It required all twenty-year-old men to register for national service. A ballot was held to choose who would be conscripted: all those whose birth-dates were selected at random were subject to conscription. This was about one in six of those who registered. There was also provision for conscripts to be sent on overseas service. The first conscript-soldier left for Vietnam in April 1966. One month later the first conscript-corpse was flown back home.

The first demonstration against the National Service Act appears to have been in London, outside Australia House, on 26 February 1965. The first organized protest in Australia took place outside the Melbourne office where the first conscript 'marbles' were drawn. The dubious distinction of being the first selector in the lottery goes to Don Chipp, then a member of the Liberal government. In Sydney the event was marked by a street procession of university students. In both protests, however, the numbers were less than fifty.

Around this time, in 1965, 240 academics sent a petition to prime minister Menzies protesting against the Vietnam war. In the same year the Student Labor Federation made the radical decision to aid the Vietnamese National Liberation Front (N.L.F.) against the U.S. This decision was implemented by the Monash University Labor Club in 1967, when it started collecting money for the N.L.F. As a result, the movement's thinking was pushed to the left. The movement not only opposed the U.S. and allied involvement, but also supported the Vietnamese struggle for national independence.

It was the National Service Act, however, rather than the war itself, which aroused the strongest and widest opposition. While the key activists had various socialist, pacifist, and religious beliefs to provide a perspective on the war, most of its opponents simply did not like the idea of young men being conscripted for overseas service by a lottery system. Conscription brought the war home, making it a real, life-and-death issue for many young people and their friends and families. Within three months of the first selection, the seeds of defiance were sown. One hundred and forty-four 'young Australian males of military service age' declared their opposition to the Act in a signed newspaper advertisement. Many were university students. And a fair few surnames of the old peace activists were discernible. In moratoriums, and other important protests, the demand for the withdrawal of U.S. and allied forces was raised quite naturally, along with the demand for the ending of conscription.

Few people quarrelled with this connection, as 'conscription' meant 'Vietnam'. Although there is little evidence to suggest widespread public opposition to compulsory military service as such, there is no doubt that selective conscription for Vietnam had more opponents than supporters. And the opponents were more confident, and more righteous for that matter, than the supporters. In November 1964, when conscription was introduced, a Gallup Poll found 71 per cent in favour and only 25 per cent opposed. When, in April 1965, Menzies committed the first battalion to active service, public opinion did not change much: 69 per cent still favoured conscription, and 23 per cent opposed it. The critical change in public opinion came with the government's decision, in December 1965, to send conscripts to Vietnam. From then on, the polls consistently found more people against conscription than for it. A poll in February 1966 found 57 per cent against and 32 per cent in favour. The stage was set for the movement to take off.

During this early period, the movement was dominated by an alliance of Old Left forces and church people. It combined the moralism of religious opposition to war and the caution of the Old Left, who were always anxious to avoid doing anything that might jeopardize the election of a Labor government. It was not until 1966-7 that the movement began to analyse seriously why the war had come about and how it could be ended. Only after these questions were settled could the moral and political opposition come together, taking an anti-imperialist perspective on the war and developing militant forms of protest without being overly concerned with the short-term electoral results of their activities.

The young man who did not want to fight in Vietnam had two options under the Act. He could file a case for exemption on the grounds of conscientious objection. The exemption, however, would only be granted to those who expressed an opposition to *all* war under any circumstances. As most opponents of conscription acknowledged that there were such things as just wars, the conscientious objection provision did not have much appeal. The other option was simply to refuse to register. The first young man to receive the maximum two-year jail sentence for refusing to comply with the National Service Act was John Zarb, a Maltese-Australian, in 1967. By 1970, 215 men had publicly refused to comply with the Act in any way, and probably many more quietly and secretly failed to register. By 1971 nearly 12,000 had not complied with the National Service Act. In other words, there were more non-compliers in Australia than there were Australians in Vietnam. The National Service Act was rendered almost farcical by the strength of the draft resisters. In Melbourne alone, in 1969, there were twenty-eight suburban draft resisters' support groups functioning quite openly in defiance of the Act. And in early 1970, a hundred public non-compliers formed the Draft Resisters' Union.

Although the Vietnam protest movement was by no means made up exclusively of young people, it nonetheless owed much of its style and popularity to the youth culture from which it emerged. The post-war years in Australia, as elsewhere, witnessed the birth of the 'teenager' as a social force and not just a biological grouping. The 'baby boom' had produced a gigantic army of young people during the 1960s, and many embraced ways of living and values that were sharply different from those of their parents.

Young people were organized, educated, and affluent as never before. In Victoria in the early 1960s, more than a quarter of all people aged between ten and thirty belonged to some kind of youth club. With full employment and a labour shortage, Australia's youth were becoming a significant market. In the early 1960s, 900,000 unmarried people aged under twenty-five were earning between 500 million and 700 million dollars each year and spending at least half of it. The baby boom also nourished the rapid growth of the universities. Students became the most dynamic element in the protest movement.

The values that were sometimes promoted as being those of 'youth' were based on independence, permissiveness, anti-authoritarianism, and a romantic quest for peace. The advent of portable radios and transistors enabled young folk to develop separate tastes and fashions. The youth culture found expression in music. From 1965 on, when an anti-war rock song 'Eve of Destruction' became an international hit, protest became an important component in youth culture. The newspaper *Go Set* attained amazing success, catering for the new 'teen and twenties' market. Commenting on a particularly brutal anti-war demonstration, *Go Set* offered a classical generational analysis:

> The police and other officials made it clear they saw this battle as Them versus the longhairs ... all those old men in power think longhair means rock music, freewheeling sex, dope, and socialism. The symbol of everything that threatens their scene. They're right! Keep on growing that hair everyone ...

Such views were, of course, over-generalized and simplistic. But because youth had most to lose from the commitment in Vietnam, young people were the shock-troops of the anti-war movement.

Many young people's ideals were impossible to reconcile with the horrific reality of Vietnam. Scenes of the war, in graphic and ugly detail, entered people's daily lives through television. By the mid 1960s, an event from anywhere in the world could be reported in Australia. T.V. news services attracted well over three million viewers each night, and 6 per cent of peak viewing was of news or current affairs programmes. People aged between ten and seventeen were the largest single television-viewing audience. There is no doubt that television brought the Vietnam war into people's living-rooms. Who could forget the images of napalmed flesh, or the Viet Cong suspect being summarily executed in a Saigon street?

The combination of 'awareness' and 'youth' exploded, not surprisingly, on university campuses around the world. But students and the other young people were not alone. Trade unionists, church people and women developed their separate ways of campaigning for peace in Vietnam.

'Save Our Sons' was an important women's peace group, arising from the mothers' concern for their conscriptable sons. It was one of many new groups to spring up in the course of protest activity and to develop initiative outside of the traditional left-wing organizations in Australia. But unlike the 1980s, nuclear disarmament campaign, women did not play a central or leading role during the Vietnam period. All too often women activists were given little more to do than type broadsheets or stitch flags. Feminism didn't really get off the ground until the 1970s in Australia. And, when it did, it was largely a separate political movement. The leading role played by women in initiating the 1980s peace movement vindicates those who argued in the 1970s that women should be able to work through their own groups.

The activism of religious folk was nothing new. Such groups as the Quakers had a long history of opposition to war. What was new, by the late 1960s, was the formulation of a 'liberation theology' that crossed denominational lines. Groups such as 'Pax Christi' were influenced by the liberationist trend. They saw Jesus Christ as a saviour of the oppressed, whether in Vietnam or America's Deep South. Then, as now, the regular and prominent participation of ministers, priests and rabbis created a big problem for those who wanted to dismiss the large peace movements as 'communist fronts'.

Although the religious contingent played an invaluable role in developing a moral perspective against the war and conscription, moral outrage alone was not enough. The religious opponents of the war tended to be idealistic, not only in their opposition but also in their ideas about how the war could be stopped. They blamed the individual, the evil within each of us, for war and conflict in the world. So war would not cease until all individuals

CONSCRIPTION IS WRONG

BECAUSE it is against our democratic tradition—it has been introduced without a referendum—it selects SOME 20-year-olds to kill and be killed by means of a marble in a barrel.

Conscription for Vietnam without voice or choice is a denial of freedom and a crime against the right of the individual.

A 1966 pamphlet of the 'Save Our Sons' group in Sydney

had a change of heart. In the words of the Quaker slogan: 'Wars will cease when men refuse to fight.' Such abstract idealism could not solve the Vietnam protest movement's principal problem: how to bring an end to conscription and to U.S. and allied involvement in Vietnam. This could only be solved by trying to grasp what caused the war, and by understanding the political processes by which it could best be ended.

In 1968 a 'New Left' generation had taken a large share of the reins of the peace movement. In late 1966 the Labor Party under Arthur Calwell had been thrashed at the polls. Gough Whitlam's rise as the new Labor leader the following year brought a weakening of the A.L.P.'s Vietnam policy. From favouring a prompt withdrawal of all Australian troops in consultation with the Americans, the A.L.P. moved to a policy favouring 'holding operations' as a means of pressuring the U.S. to halt the bombing of North Vietnam. The first violent clashes between police and protestors occured during President Johnson's 1966 visit to Melbourne and Sydney and the visit soon after of South Vietnam's ruler, Air Vice-Marshal Ky. The movement began to display a revolutionary tendency. With the A.L.P. reneging on its previous principled policy, a parliamentary solution to the war seemed impossible; and with the vocal support of some government members, the police and courts were cracking down on legitimate forms of dissent. Even the Australian Vice-Chancellors' Committee was provoked to protest when the government tried to force university officers to provide information on students who were eligible for national service.

Looking back on this peak period of the movement, one is struck by the highly politicized climate. Activism seemed a daily occurrence. There were so-called wild riots in Melbourne, Adelaide, Brisbane, Melbourne, and even Canberra! It was a time of 'street theatre', public meetings in suburban halls, petitions, letters to editors, draft-card burnings, rallies, all the protester's stock-in-trade. What was extraordinary was that these were occurring constantly, at all levels, all over Australia and the world.

Undoubtedly, the movement's greatest success was the first moratorium, held from 8 to 10 May 1970. It was not just an unexpected numerical success but a bigger political victory. Supporters of the war tried as never before to deter people from marching, or 'occupying the streets' as they liked to call it. Government speakers warned of 'blood in the streets'. But, to their credit, 120,000 Australians refused to be cowed. They were more concerned by the blood already spilled in Vietnam than veiled official threats to their own safety. They thought of the three and a half million tons of bombs dropped on Vietnam by the world's greatest military power; the one and a half million people killed or injured; the 400 dead Australians, 250 of them conscripts. They thought of the continued growth of U.S. aggression in Indo-China. Though it talked of withdrawing and ending the war, the U.S. had placed 47,000 troops in Thailand and was conducting daily bombing raids over Laos. America was spending 80 billion dollars a year on its military machine. It had one and a half million uniformed staff troops in 119 different countries and more than 400 military-related bases abroad.

The moratorium's success also lay in the countless discussions and arguments it provoked at all levels of society: from the family dinner-table and the local pub to the commonwealth parliament, where the debate ran hot for seven hours. Moratorium committees sprang up in suburbs and country towns.

Teachers, doctors and trade unionists organized groups against the war. The truly inspiring thing, however, was that people were not deterred by the government's law-and-order campaign, which over the years had seen scores of protesters arrested, some imprisoned, and many injured by police batons and boots. The then Minister for External Affairs, William McMahon, made it clear how far the government was prepared to go to suppress the moratorium movement. In parliament, McMahon refused to condemn the shooting of four students during an anti-war protest at America's Kent State University. He warned sternly: 'This lesson ought to be taken to heart by all those who are taking part in the moratorium marches.' This was, in effect, a warning that moratorium marchers could be shot by police. The N.S.W. police commissioner refused to guarantee that police supervising the demonstration would not carry guns.

Tempers grew short during the moratorium campaign. The then Attorney-General, Tom Hughes restrains Ian Macdonald, president of the Australian Union of Students, with a cricket bat.

With the movement growing rapidly, repression and resistance fed off each other. Despite some disgraceful examples of police brutality, the demonstrators continued to take to the streets. The dispersal of a small protest march would only result in a much larger rally in defiance. During the peak years of the movement, Australia witnessed police behaviour expected only in societies with one-party dictatorial systems: houses and offices of dissidents were raided, activists harassed and bashed, journalists assaulted at demonstrations, provocateurs employed by police to disrupt protest meetings, and so on. The mentality of the top police was summed up in the words of one senior officer, who was to become an assistant chief commissioner. Writing in the journal of the police union, he declared:

> The day or night must inevitably arrive when, by shrewd planning or accident, these unruly lawbreakers turn up en masse at a vital spot when police are elsewhere ...
>
> [It is] like playing with a mad dog or baiting a tiger. On the law of averages, the day must arrive when you drop your guard and he severely mauls you.

Too many police shared these sentiments. The anti-war marchers were 'animals', threatening the fabric of society. Little wonder that some police seemed to relish restoring law and order with their boots and fists.

The Vietnam period taught many lessons, and some of them remain relevant today. Australians still lack any guaranteed right of free speech or free asssembly codified in a bill of rights. Many anti-war activists learnt the lesson the hard way, especially on the more militant demonstrations such as those held outside the American consulates in Sydney and Melbourne each 4 July from 1968 to 1970. Prime Minister Gorton had warned: 'We will tolerate dissent so long as it remains ineffective.' Many activists interpreted state repression as proof that the movement was being effective.

Although the Vietnam protest movement had assumed huge proportions by 1970, it was nevertheless composed of innumerable factions and splinters. The most cohesive, determined, and influential of these forces in Melbourne and Sydney were revolutionary socialists, who won wide support for their anti-imperialist perspective on the war. These revolutionaries included the Old and New Lefts. Their analysis of the war was summarized by a 1971 pamphlet entitled, 'Vietnam is a Bosses' War':

Mounted police during the 1971 moratorium march in Melbourne

The war in Vietnam is not an isolated mistake but part of an overall strategy for economic domination by the United States. Similar struggles are being waged all over south-east Asia, Africa, Latin America and the Middle East. The huge corporations and financial institutions which control the US economy see south-east Asia and other undeveloped areas as a source of raw materials and as highly profitable investments. At all costs, they want to stop the spread of socialism which would prevent such economic exploitation.

Having identified imperialism as the cause of the war, the socialist activists, who all drew their inspiration from Marxism in one form or another, argued for a strategy of aligning the working class as the main force of the peace movement. The more orthodox Marxists saw the middle-class, student domination of the peace movement as a significant weakness. But how could the war be made meaningful to workers in this relatively privileged country? Workers Action, the Sydney group who published 'Vietnam is a Bosses' War', argued:

Australia has come under the economic control of the big U.S. corporations, and this is reflected in our involvement in Vietnam.

While the majority of Australian workers pay for the war through taxation, a handful of big businessmen profit from war contracts and from rapidly increasing investment in Asia and the Pacific, especially Papua-New Guinea.

Only socialism will convert production for war into production for the benefit of the workers.

Australian government expenditure on war and defence had increased greatly as a result of the Vietnam war. Between 1959-60 and 1968-69, it had nearly trebled from 376 million dollars to 1,077 million dollars. In 1970/71, it stood at $1,337 million. During this period, other expenditure had only doubled. The money came mainly from taxation, which meant that much of it came out of workers' pay-packets.

A few unions (usually communist-led) were active against the war. The Seamen's Union, for example, had taken action in 'blacking' two ships carrying supplies to Vietnam, the *Boonaroo* and the *Jeparit*. The Building Workers' Industrial Union and the Waterside Workers' Federation had promptly condemned U.S. involvement in Vietnam. As early as 1954, on the eve of the battle of Dien Bien Phu (which marked the collapse of the French in Vietnam), Sydney wharfies had protested against the French supply-ship *Radnor*, on its way to Vietnam. The maritime unions had a tradition of internationalism. Most workers, however, considered that political matters were not the proper concern of trade unions, unless they affected working conditions or pay in some way.

This separation of trade unionism from political affairs was an obstacle to working-class participation in the anti-war movement. Trade union leaders did not always support the peace movement as fully as they could have. The Victorian Trades Hall Council, for example, refused to support the first moratorium in May 1970. The Labor Party, which controlled most of the unions, viewed the peace movement cautiously, at best as a mixed blessing. It was seen as potentially a great electoral base, but the Labor Party leadership always sought to contain it and to channel it into conventional parliamentary avenues. There was never any effort by the Labor Party leadership to arouse rank-and-file unionists into action. Where workers did take action to oppose the war in Vietnam, and many did, they were following the lead of the young people who by this stage provided the core of the protest movement. In this period of militant youth leadership, the movement began to succeed. The politicians started to respond.

It is ironic that Whitlam, who had sold out the peace movement in 1967, came to power in 1972 largely on the backs of the Vietnam activists. It is equally ironic that he should be popularly regarded as the prime minister who withdrew our troops from Vietnam. The troops had been withdrawn by Liberal Prime Minister McMahon in late 1971 and early 1972.

The fact that Australian troops were withdrawn under a Liberal-Country Party government testifies to the effectiveness of the Vietnam protest movement within Australia and overseas. Acting as a mass movement outside parliamentary politics, it applied enough pressure to force the government to announce that no further combat troops would be sent and that Australian forces would be withdrawn by Christmas 1971. At the same time, the government also assured the public that no conscripts would be sent to Vietnam, though draft resisters still faced arrest and possible imprisonment. It was the Labor government elected in December 1972 that 'saved' the draft dodgers, as it promptly released the seven who were serving prison sentences, quashed all charges against others, and suspended the National Service Act.

Of course, there is another side to the Australian withdrawals. Quite aside from the mass movement, the Australian withdrawals may be seen as part of the continuing relationship with the U.S. Although the U.S. troop commitment reached its peak under President Nixon (540,000 troops in March 1969), Nixon also began the process of withdrawing U.S. troops. In June 1969 he had announced the first two withdrawals of 25,000 troops. This policy was designed to take the heat out of the U.S. peace movement, which, in the President's words, had brought America to the brink of disaster and chaos. It was also part of a 'Vietnamization' programme. U.S. troops were to be replaced by trained Asian troops to carry on the combat war the U.S. was losing, while the U.S. would concentrate on using the terrible technological weapons of destruction to bomb, napalm and defoliate. At any rate, it was only a matter of months after Nixon's announcement of the first U.S. withdrawals that Australia's prime minister, John Gorton made it clear that he intended to withdraw Australian forces gradually, as the U.S. did so. In April 1970 Gorton had announced that 900 would be back home by December. In early 1971, when Nixon had withdrawn thousands of troops and had announced another withdrawal of 70,000, McMahon announced Australia's biggest withdrawal, of 1000 troops.

From 1968, the morale of the peace movements had been high. In that year the Paris Peace Talks had begun, and the Vietnamese National Liberation Front won a victory in the heart of Saigon, called the 'Tet Offensive'. The initial announcements of withdrawals were met with scepticism, but by August 1971 it was largely acknowledged that Australia was more or less out of the war. It was now an 'American' war. With conscription no longer a life-and-death matter, the Australian peace movement dwindled and shrank to its activist core. It was natural that this should have happened, but many hard-core activists found it hard to comprehend why the vast numbers could not be mobilized when the U.S. was still dropping so many bombs on North Vietnam. The lesson was that people do not respond exclusively in moral terms but primarily when their own lives are touched.

The U.S. intervention in Vietnam did not end until 1975. Between 1965 and 1971 the U.S. dropped 5,693,382 tons of bombs on Indo-China, three times as many as it had used in all of the Second World War. It levelled much of Indo-China, especially North Vietnam, creating ghastly ecological and human problems that will take generations to remedy. It was fitting that such modern barbarism should have been unleashed by the superpower that had used the first atomic weapons back in 1945.

It is equally appropriate that the Vietnam protest generation – 'moratorium veterans' – should be playing a leading role in the anti-nuclear peace movement of the 1980s. They have brought to this movement many of the skills they developed during the earlier campaigns in organizing demonstrations, dealing with the media and publicizing their activities. With luck, they will also bring to this movement, the success or failure of which determines the future of this planet, the knowledge that, properly aroused, people have the power to stop warfare.

Stop the Drop

BRENDAN CARINS

Mass peace movements had emerged in the United States, Canada, Japan, Western and Eastern Europe by the early 1980s. These movements arose in response to several forces. The earlier efforts of East and West to live together peacefully under the policies known as 'detente' had broken down from the late 1970s. The United States and the Soviet Union had acquired nuclear weapons of greatly increased range and accuracy. The Soviet Union had occupied Afghanistan. In military planning circles there was a growing attachment to 'counterforce' doctrines, which stressed the need to wipe out the other side's nuclear arsenals before they had a chance to wipe your own side out. And the Reagan administration in the U.S. was voicing stridently anti-Soviet rhetoric. These added up to what was termed the 'second Cold War'.

The re-birth of nuclear disarmament movements on an international scale was essentially a response to these developments. Australia followed a similar path. Here, the official beginnings of the peace movement were at a public meeting in Melbourne in October 1981, which formed People for Nuclear Disarmament (P.N.D.). In other states, the movement adopted the same structure. P.N.D.'s three major aims were: a halt to the mining and export of uranium; the establishment of a nuclear-free zone in the Pacific Ocean and a zone of peace in the Indian Ocean; and withdrawal from A.N.Z.U.S. and removal of United States bases.

The movement, however, was not homogeneous. It was a loose coalition of state organizations that differed significantly among themselves.

The movement succeeded in arousing public concern about disarmament. But its potential to achieve social and political change was limited by its narrow, middle-class support base, which was reflected in its strategies and relationship with the main party of reform, the Australian Labor Party.

The main organizational focus of the movement was a mass rally on Palm Sunday, just before Easter each year. The first big rally in 1982 drew a modest turn-out. The rallies increased in strength and size each year until 1985, then steadily declined. This was a problem, because P.N.D. was obsessed with numbers, and this guided its strategy. Clearly, a major, yearly rally served an important function, but P.N.D. had little to offer on the other 364 days of the year. This day of protest is becoming institutionalized, something that is expected each year. Its political impact is reduced as a result.

The basis of P.N.D.'s appeal is abhorrence of nuclear weaponry. This 'moral' approach is an important dimension, but it has been the only one. The implications for the movement are clear. The peace movement is strong on moral outrage but lacks a political strategy that can really hope to achieve nuclear disarmament in our part of the world. What strategy it has can be put into effect through the existing political parties, particularly the Labor Party, without any effect on other political developments. But questions of defence and foreign policy cannot be isolated from other issues.

The 'moral' approach also tends to make the movement over-optimistic about the possibilities of success, just because opinion polls show that most people are concerned about issues of disarmament and peace, even though many of them are concerned to maintain Australia's defence links with the U.S., contrary to P.N.D. policy.

One of the most striking features of the contemporary Australian peace movement was the extent to which it was based on local, regional groups. The peace movement was also made up of affiliated groups, such as A.L.P. branches, professional organizations, religious bodies, and women's groups. Altogether, there were close to 500 active local and affiliate peace groups in 1985. The ecology and land rights movements are also working alongside the peace movement.

Banners at a Palm Sunday demonstration suggest the diversity of the peace movement at its height in 1978.

Nevertheless, the movement remains narrow at all levels. For instance, the Victorian leadership of P.N.D. has largely stemmed from four organizations – the Victorian Association of Peace Studies (V.A.P.S.), the campaign for International Co-operation and Disarmament (C.I.C.D.), the Movement Against Uranium Mining (M.A.U.M.), and Pax Christi. Furthermore, only a core group of activists sustain the movement throughout the year; most supporters do little more than participate in the Palm Sunday rally.

A large proportion of the major affiliates to P.N.D. throughout Australia are trade unions and trades and labour councils, particularly in Sydney and Melbourne. In New South Wales, thirty-three out of ninety-two affiliates are trade unions and one is a trades and labour council. In Melbourne there are twenty-six unions out of a total of 112 affiliates. These figures do not represent significant working-class participation in or support for the immediate goals of P.N.D. They reflect a general concern about nuclear war on the part of the trade union hierarchy, rather than a deep commitment by workers to anti-nuclear policies.

Victoria P.N.D. is distinct from the rest of the Australian peace movement in that its affiliates include a large number of A.L.P. organizations: twenty-three branches and one Federal Electoral Assembly in 1985, for instance. By contrast, P.N.D. had only three A.L.P. branches in New South Wales, two in South Australia and none in Queensland or Western Australia. These figures indicate that support within the Labor Party for a 'nuclear-free' Australia is confined mainly to the left of the party, which is strong only in Victoria.

The composition of P.N.D. is similar to Britain's Campaign for Nuclear Disarmament (C.N.D.) in the 1960s. Commenting on C.N.D. in the 1960s, Frank Myers noted:

> Members of the movement were overwhelmingly middle class, and their policy focus upon moral rather than economic issues was thoroughly consistent with this class composition. C.N.D.'s middle class supporters showed greater support for humanitarian and moral policy issues ... than they did for class issues related to unemployment, nationalization and legal protection for trade unions. The issue of nuclear disarmament was seen primarily in a moral context by C.N.D. members, a context not likely to attract the continuous and lasting working-class support that was necessary.

This also is the nub of the problem facing P.N.D. The terms in which it sees the problem, and the strategies it adopts, are not compatible with a wide support base within the working class.

The peace movement was greatly cheered by the A.L.P.'s victory in the federal election of March 1983. The Labor government's foreign policy, however, has oscillated between attempting to appease an increasingly vocal peace movement and trying to please the United States.

On the one hand, the A.L.P. retains a strong commitment to the idea of deterrence, the idea that you can scare off enemies by building up arms. This belief is used to justify Australia's nuclear connections with the United States. At the same time the A.L.P. has tried to win support on the issue of nuclear disarmament. This two-faced position has posed grave problems for P.N.D.

On the positive side, the movement's influence accentuated the minor, though by no means unimportant, foreign policy differences between the conservative and Labor parties. These differences have arisen out of the climate of opinion and public pressure that P.N.D. has generated. The differences are evident in two areas: the level of support for President Reagan's 'Star Wars' programme and the question of regional arms control.

The Hawke Labor government has stated its hostility to the 'Star Wars' programme and has been active in fostering regional arms control. These developments have largely centred around

May Day in Melbourne, c. 1960

the South Pacific forums of 1983–5, culminating in the Rarotonga Treaty of August 1985. The treaty, initiated and drafted by Australia, reflects the selective nature of the Australian proposals. It is aimed essentially at opposing French nuclear testing in the South Pacific, while condoning American nuclear activities in the region. The Hawke government perceived correctly that any constraints on United States ship movements through the region could be viewed as an implicit threat to the United States alliance, which is already shaken by the Lange government's prohibition on United States nuclear ship visits to New Zealand.

The peace movement was quick to realize the potential intent behind the treaty, sensing that it could act as a means of demobilizing anti-nuclear opinion. Jo Vallentine, the Nuclear Disarmament senator from Western Australia, attacked the treaty as a useless exercise that legitimized American involvement in the South Pacific. The Australian Democrats, with Vallentine, asserted that no treaty at all would be better than the one negotiated at Rarotonga.

It is not surprising that the movement is harshly critical of a treaty that claims to be all-embracing but is really rather meek. Yet there is a danger in the movement blindly criticizing any A.L.P. initiatives. The movement can easily become dominated by an absolute set of moral values and condemn any proposals that

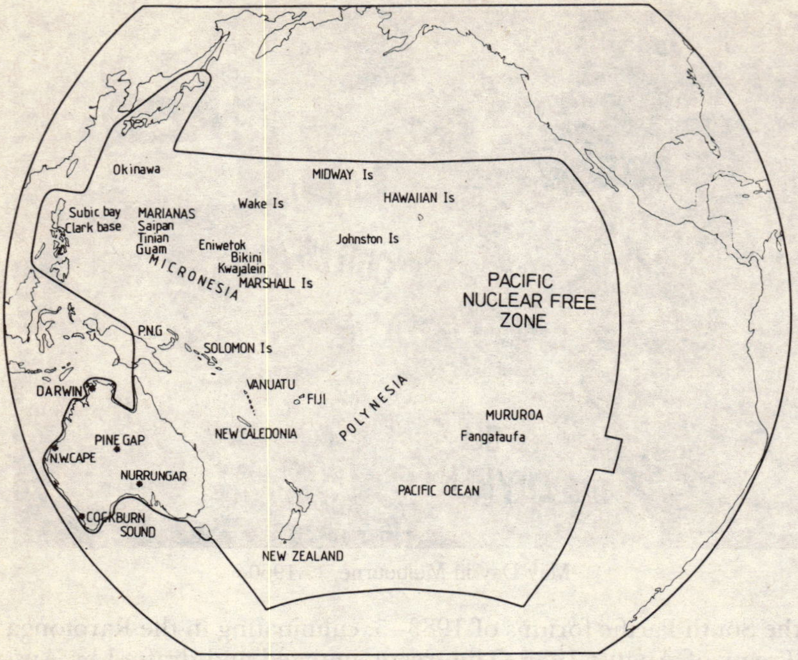

Figure 1. Map of the Pacific Ocean, showing some nuclear facilities and the Nuclear-Free Zone proposed at the 1980 Nuclear-Free-Pacific Conference. It includes Japan, the Philippines and Hawaii. This proposal is more extensive than the recent Australian Government proposal.

The Hawke government's policy for the Pacific fell short of this proposal from the Nuclear Free Pacific Conference of 1980.

fall short of the major objectives as futile and of little significance. Any successful political strategy should be willing to make compromises or tacit approvals without resorting to the 'all or nothing' position so frequently adopted.

Apart from the Rarotonga Treaty, the Labor government has taken a number of other initiatives. It has appointed an ambassador for disarmament, supported a conference on an Indian Ocean zone of peace, tried to strengthen the Nuclear Non-Proliferation Treaty and attempted to secure a comprehensive nuclear test ban. It has also encouraged peace studies throughout the education system and tried to have continuing discussions with peace and disarmament groups.

On close analysis, however, the concessions to the peace movement are limited. Richard Butler, the disarmament ambassador, cannot promote unilateral action on Australia's part. The proposed Indian Ocean zone of peace, like the Rarotonga Treaty, will not be allowed to interfere with United States security interests.

The funding for the Peace Research Institute, established at La Trobe University, will be meagre; and consultation did not emerge between the government and peace groups until late 1985.

In spite of these initiatives, the Australian/American nuclear alliance remains unaltered even though A.N.Z.U.S. is currently annulled by the actions of the New Zealand Lange government. The Labor government will not sever the alliance for fear of the electoral consequences. The peace movement has been reluctant to address the disturbing questions this raises: is the A.L.P. capable of carrying out the movement's major demands? It would seem not. The movement has to a large degree misunderstood the nature of the A.L.P. and, more broadly, the capacity of social democratic governments to institute significant social change. This has led to a deep conflict over strategy resulting in sharp divisions amongst the movement's leadership.

Social democratic parties in Australia tend to be elected in times of crisis. This limits their capacity for social reform. Two types of response to these crises have emerged. The first is a commitment to basic labour policy: the expansion of social services and employment opportunities, financed by progressive taxation on both income and wealth. The other response is characterized by the 'rational economic managers', the technocrats, who go to great lengths to appease capital and to assist its restructuring in the hope of achieving electoral success. This second option is clearly the path taken by the Hawke government.

Previous attempts by Australian Labor governments to nationalize industries or to pursue economic reforms have met with concerted resistance. The fall of the Whitlam government, the controversial circumstances surrounding its dismissal and the massive electoral defeats the party incurred in 1975 and 1977 ensured that any future Labor government would be cautious and conservative. These expectations were realized when Bob Hawke overthrew Bill Hayden as parliamentary leader, signalling a further shift to the right for the A.L.P. Since in office, the A.L.P.'s economic and social policies have reflected this orientation – disciplining the workforce and keeping down real wages, cutting back on public expenditure, deregulating the finance sector and reducing restrictions on foreign investment in Australia and Australian investment overseas.

The Hawke government's policies tempered the optimism of

the peace movement. Questions of strategy came to the fore within the movement. The leadership is divided over its attitude to the Labor Party, and this has sapped the movement's dynamism. These divisions are made worse by the lack of political options outside the A.L.P. It is not surprising that conflicts have developed over strategy and tactics, in view of the feeble nature of an 'alternative political culture' in this country. Dennis Altman aptly notes the dilemma that faces the peace movement:

> Any strategy for real change in Australia need bear in mind the importance of coming to terms with both the state and the Labor Party, which is after all, the only mass-based force for political change, and which is extremely unlikely to be dislodged from this position ... the critical problem is how to prevent that party being totally incorporated into the defence of the existing system ...

Altman adds that the importance of the new social movements lies in their capacity to alter the dominant conservative political culture, even if only in small ways. The ecological, peace and feminist movements can therefore play an important role in society by providing completely different visions and solutions from those normally offered. The clearest example of this development in the peace movement is the formulation of alternative defence policies.

The movement has successfully formulated some defence alternatives for Australia. Four positions have been outlined – non-nuclear A.N.Z.U.S., non-alignment, armed neutrality and social defence. But so far it has failed to sell any of them to the public. Blind opposition to A.N.Z.U.S. is not enough; alternatives have to be suggested. This is even more urgent now, with the vacuum in the A.N.Z.U.S. alliance which has led to discussions between the Australian government and the United States. Unfortunately, the peace movement has failed to exploit these opportunities. Until it can, the alternative options it has on paper will remain unheard.

Here the movement badly needs access to the mass media. The movement's own journals and newsletters reach a limited audience, and it is unlikely that the movement can start a mass circulation journal. Unless the movement can develop ways of overcoming the suspicion of the mass media and gain a sympathetic coverage, the all-important foreign policy debate will remain a fringe issue both in public life and within the Labor Party.

The rise of the Nuclear Disarmament Party (N.D.P.) brought to the fore a number of questions concerning the relationship between a social movement and a minor party. Minor parties in Australia have often held the balance of power in the Senate and have therefore been able to influence the government of the day. The Democratic Labor Party in the late 1950s and 1960s remains the foremost example. The N.D.P., in alliance with the Australian Democrats, had similar aspirations of bringing pressure to bear on A.L.P. foreign policy.

The N.D.P. had a 'single-issue' platform: opposition to uranium mining, closure of United States bases and Australian withdrawal from the A.N.Z.U.S. alliance. It was ill-equipped to deal with the broader issues of state power and the need for governmental reform. It naively assumed that defence and foreign policy could be altered fundamentally by the people's representatives in parliament, not recognizing that the really important decisions are not made in parliament but behind the scenes.

Nonetheless, the N.D.P. did provide a focus for disillusionment and protest against the nuclear policies and conservative orientation of the Hawke government. The selection of Jean Melzer, Peter Garrett and Jo Vallentine to head the N.D.P. ticket in 1984 was a publicity coup. They symbolized the peace movement's bases of support – youth, disaffected parts of the labour movement, ecological, pacifist, religious and women's groups. Undoubtedly, the N.D.P.'s appeal lay in the successful combination of these groups. The recognition and strength the N.D.P. gained in a short period of time was largely a result of the previous hard work of many activists in constructing a support base.

Most important, foreign policy became a major issue in the 1984 election because of the intervention of the N.D.P. The question of Australian initiatives for nuclear disarmament was forced into public debate. The major parties were forced to respond, particularly the A.L.P., which was losing support to the N.D.P. in the pre-election polls. And the Democrats were appalled at having to share the peace vote with the N.D.P. In New South Wales and Western Australia, the last Senate vacancy was a contest between the N.D.P. and the Democrats. After the election, the Democrats tried especially hard to pose as the party of anti-nuclear policies, to ward off future electoral competition.

The relationship between P.N.D. and N.D.P. remained strained throughout the election. The dominant faction of the P.N.D leadership had a pro-Labor strategy: they vehemently denied that the N.D.P. was the political arm of the peace movement. On another level, some activists were disillusioned with the peace movement's entry into electoral politics and were worried that the development of a grass-roots mass movement would be threatened by the overwhelming influence of a handful of individuals. But at the rank-and-file level, among the local groups, there was clear support for the N.D.P., and the local groups' resources were brought to bear on the campaign.

In 1985, both the N.D.P. and the Australian anti-nuclear movement held their first national conferences. The former ended in tragic, even farcical, circumstances; the latter emerged with some positive initiatives.

The outcome of the N.D.P.'s inaugural conference in April 1985 severely discredited the peace movement. Melzer, Vallentine and Garrett, the three Senate candidates, accused the Socialist Workers' Party of manipulating the N.D.P. The candidates and their supporters left the party in protest. Whether the charges were true or not, one thing that was clear was the haste in which the party had been established. If more consideration had been given to the party's structure before the election, the bad publicity and the split might have been avoided. The breakaway group established an organization called Peace and Nuclear Disarmament Action (P.A.N.D.A.), which was intended to lay the basis for a new party. To prevent 'manipulation' and 'takeover', it prohibited members of other political parties from joining.

By late 1985 there were at least four tendencies within the anti-nuclear movement, ranging from the Australian Democrats to the N.D.P., which was dominated by Socialist Workers' Party activities. This is confusing to the electorate and politically disastrous. While in the 1987 election an N.D.P. senator was elected in N.S.W. and Vallentine was returned. The effectiveness of the movement is severely limited by these divisions; the peace movement is in a quagmire from which it seems unwilling or unable to extricate itself.

The second event of significance in 1985 was the first Australian Nuclear Disarmament Conference held in Melbourne in August. This conference at least managed to work out what aims and objectives should be given priority. It recognized that planning and organization were necessary before the movement could hope to change policy and ideology.

With this in mind, the conference recommended that the United States base at North-West Cape, whose lease comes up for renewal in 1988, become a major rallying focus. This base is the most vulnerable to pressure from the movement as it has a clear war-fighting function. Its sole purpose is to provide communications for the United States submarine fleet, and U.S. Trident submarines have a first-strike capability.

For the peace movement to attain its major objectives it will have to transcend the politics of 'life and fear'. No movement can hope to change society without facing up to the question of where power really lies. In the case of the peace movement, it has to locate and challenge the forces that make for war and militarism.

Political domination and oppression take many forms, and no single social movement can hope to end them on its own. Alliances are therefore of vital importance for progressive groups, as they provide the opportunity to link up and co-operate in the struggle for the democratization of society at large. Yet mistrust, suspicion and antagonism all too often keep the different social movements apart, undermining their potential for joint action. Hoping to end this problem, a number of activists in the peace movement have proposed the formation of an umbrella organization for ecological, feminist and peace groups.

In spite of the aspiration of activists and sections of the leadership, it is unlikely that the peace movement will lead to the radicalization either of Australian political life or of the A.L.P. One important and realizable goal of the movement, however, is the removal of the U.S. base at North-West Cape after 1988. If the movement can overcome its self-destructive tendencies and deep divisions, North-West Cape could become a major political issue by the next federal election. Its removal would require massive organization and political courage, but it would be the first important step towards a nuclear-free Australia.

Fragmented Visions

JOHN MURPHY

Between late 1982 and March 1983, the campaign to prevent the damming of the Franklin River in south-west Tasmania was at its peak. Over 2,000 people took part in a blockade of construction work at the dam site, and each morning the workers found new blockaders chained to their construction machinery. One morning, an old woman, 'she'd have to be sixty, a grey-haired old piece,' was found attached to a crane; she had not chained herself but tied herself with string. As the worker who found her (himself a strong Liberal supporter) described it: 'When I got up there she said, "You don't have to worry about the welder on me, just a sharp pocket knife."' For some, the story might seem a metaphor for the frailty of single issue politics, yet it also indicates the moral and political strength of the commitments that bring together the unlikely coalitions of single-issue politics. The problems involved in such movements raise urgent questions about the viability of progressive coalitions for social change. They are particularly urgent given that the greatest question of our age – that of disarmament – boils down to a matter of coalitions that transcend the boundaries of class politics.

In constructing a single-issue political movement, the issue is always crucial, yet in a sense it is never single. If we look at the contemporary Australian peace movement, with its three primary concerns – uranium mining, U.S. bases and nuclear disarmament – can we identify the issue that is most important to it? There are many issues involved, ranging from nuclear radiation, arms proliferation and the environment, to foreign relations, capitalism's social irresponsibility and radicals' attitudes to the Soviet Union.

Even to pose the question reveals the ambiguity involved. A single issue inevitably spills over into other concerns, connects with other social problems. If this seems to confirm the old leftist wisdom that everything is connected to everything else, it is still a problem, since obviously not everybody involved in the movement will make the same connections and draw the same political conclusions. Usually, they do not, and this is because, typically, a single issue movement is made up of a coalition of people who may have little in common other than their concern for the immediate issue.

Fundamentally, a single-issue political movement is a defensive and temporary organization of a coalition of people who can come together and stay together only on the tacit understanding that, in the interests of unity, they will confine themselves to a narrow interpretation of what is at stake. If the issue is kept single enough, then the coalition can continue to work together; with too many interpretations drawn out into the public domain, the differences between actors will also be drawn out, weakening the movement's unity and cohesion. A limited issue makes it possible to concentrate the energies of divergent interests. A single-minded attention to the issue becomes the focus and the symbol of the movement. Yet the limited issue also weakens the movement's capacity to make history radically; for with the issue resolved, perhaps decisively won, perhaps only diverted or

Blockaders on board their boat, the J-Lee-M, at the River Base Camp during the Franklin campaign in 1983.

appeased, there is little to hold the movement together. Different political interests then don't so much confront each other as quietly fragment, media attention is switched to another channel, and public support for fund-raising or demonstrations wanes. Although the activists of the movement normally intend to continue the struggle into other related areas, the absence of a focused issue inhibits the formation of coalitions.

The Franklin dam campaign illustrates this process of a coalition fragmenting after the issue is defused. For some core activists, the campaign had its origins in the flooding of Lake Pedder in 1972. From 1979, when the Hydro-Electric Commission (H.E.C.) announced the damming of the Franklin, a campaign was built that concentrated, with consummate skill, on media manipulation. The campaigners' use of television was outstanding. Well-dressed, well-informed and polished, their television spokespeople were hard to dismiss as 'ratbags'. This campaign had riveted national attention by late 1982, but was clearly not without its contradictions. As Bob Brown explained the strategy:

> We've always put forward a positive, non-threatening type of advertising that people can easily digest ... if you had a television camera aimed at you, a lot of the viewers at home wouldn't be able to communicate if people looked strangely dressed ... You get into more difficulty when you're doing something that's always contentious. The blockade presented this problem *par excellence*: how was it going to go down? But when you get to the stage where you haven't got an alternative, then you take risks.

This is not primarily a problem of dress sense, nor even of presentation, but rather one of the pragmatic strategies that eventually meant that the question was reduced to an election issue within the mainstream political sphere. The professional image, backed up with efficient information releases, doubtless made the campaign acceptable to the broadest range of people – including some very conservative supporters – but it also obscured the cultural and political divisions within the campaign. Some saw the dam as a classic case of inappropriate technology; for others it was an example of the manipulations of international capital, particularly in the aluminium smelting business; some defended the wilderness as an absolute value in itself, which ought to remain untouched for posterity; for others another dam was symptomatic of a patriarchal desire for domination over nature, and for more unthinking 'boom or bust' development.

With the issue meaning all this to different people, it is even more remarkable that the campaign maintained its single-minded efficiency. Many involved were, at least potentially, out of sympathy with an exclusive strategy of lobbying within an election campaign, even if they held their peace in the interests of unity. There were active campaigners who rejected strategies involving either confrontation or manipulation, and who placed much greater emphasis on the development of strategies of non-violent direct action, based around affinity groups and emphasizing communication and conflict resolution. Almost in spite of such diversity, the Tasmanian Wilderness Society had established an impressive structure for capturing and holding public attention – it was, for example, much more efficiently organized than the moratorium campaigns of 1970–1 – but it was one that was effectively diverted into electoral channels.

This diversion also meant that what had been perhaps the most important political implication of the campaign was lost: that the Franklin dam was a perfect example of political decision-making behind closed doors, without free and public discussion. The campaign raised, but then failed to tackle, the question of the public accountability of bureaucracies such as the Tasmanian Hydro-Electric Commission. Despite being a statutory authority, the H.E.C. – which had already given Tasmania thirty-six dams, twenty-six power stations and one of the highest per capita energy consumption rates in the world – acted as an apparently autonomous power beyond the control of parliament. Between 1929 and 1980, every H.E.C. proposal for development had been approved by parliament 'usually without even a perfunctory debate'. The H.E.C. was the state's largest employer, which may explain both its political power and its paternalistic attitude. The events of 1979, when the Tasmanian government had attempted to make the H.E.C. somewhat more publicly accountable, only revealed the difficulty involved. As the H.E.C.'s chief commissioner told A.B.C.'s *Nationwide*: 'If the parliament tries to work through popular decisions, we're doomed in this state and doomed everywhere.'

Such notions of being above politics and popular control are radically anti-democratic. They are also reinforced by a belief that the H.E.C.'s technical expertise allowed it alone to decide what was best for Tasmania. In this framework of technical rationality, public discussion of the ends of bureaucratic action is only a hindrance. The point here is that the H.E.C. was not a dinosaur, but a highly developed combination of technical rationality and political power. The opportunity afforded by the Franklin campaign to

How many issues can you fit on one jacket?

challenge this nexus, and to argue for public, democratic accountability was lost in the understandable rush to save the wilderness. The movement was outflanked by existing party politics, and the emphasis on electoral strategies not only made the immediate issue too easily solvable, but also made it impossible to re-open and expand the question of what was really at stake.

Again, this is part of the fragility of alliances built on a common interest in a limited issue. If the argument cannot be extended to related issues, the usefulness and permanence of gains made in the original struggle may be limited. In this case, the Franklin issue was at least temporarily resolved: the Liberal government had earlier declared the Franklin River a World Heritage area, and then the High Court ruled that the international obligations this involved were also binding on state governments. Soon after, with the election of a Labor government that had briefly made the issue its own, the coalition of campaign forces collapsed. The limited aim of stopping the dam was achieved, yet the status quo was scarcely ruffled. As many pointed out at the time, there was an irony in the movement relying so heavily on centralized federal power to resolve the issue. This was part of the reason why the H.E.C. could survive without change. The Franklin issue illustrates the dilemma of coalitions built solely on a narrowly defined issue that cannot – for fear of alienating support – be extended to encompass, and tackle, the political core of the problem.

A second problem of single issue politics is the tendency to fall into narrow patterns of resistance. Most issue politics are characterized by a tendency to defend values and interests against a particular threat, the encroachment of industrial capitalism on the wilderness being a powerful and symbolic example. Movements of resistance attempt to block the otherwise unrestrained exercise of power. In doing this, they assert other social values, those of co-operation and communication against those of domination and profit. But they rarely set the terms of the issue itself.

The environmental movement, for example, is capable of providing an extended critique of the rationality of development and of the untenable consequences of 'man's' domination over nature, but more usually its political impetus is limited to resisting the effects of this rationality. It tries to save a river rather than rebuild a society. Other recent movements, such as the anti-Vietnam war movement and the movement against uranium mining, also tended to be reactive against the actions of capital or the state. Perhaps of recent movements only feminism has the universal relevance to assert new values and set out to conquer new territory;

in this, feminism is comparable in historical significance to the classic traditions of bourgeois and socialist liberation and can hardly be contained within single-issue politics. Although many movements, particularly the peace and ecology movements, are concerned to defend the organic foundations of life, they are nevertheless reactive; feminism, on the other hand, has the initiative, since it is concerned, in Habermas's terms, with 'the grammar of forms of life'.

A third problem concerns the relation between single-issue or social movements and the traditional working-class movement. This is a difficult area that few claim to have untangled. Many socialists continue to adopt contradictory positions: while arguing that social movements must, in order to be meaningful, attach themselves to the working-class movement, in practice they appear ready to support social movements on the principle of 'if it moves, support it'. But this support often takes the form of 'parachuting' into the movement, and pointing out its 'real' importance as a challenge to capitalism.

There are two principal problems with this. On the one hand, as a socialist strategy, it devalues the actual motivations and commitments of those already involved, and hence devalues their own experience of the issue. People's support for an issue grows out of their own experience as parents, unemployed, trade unionists, gays, and so on. For a strategy to be democratic and popular, it has to assume the authenticity of such diversity and be based on the lived experience of everyday life. The Green Bans of the New South Wales Builders Labourers' Federation, for example, could only be imposed if local community groups voted for the bans – which was both strategic commonsense and sound democratic practice. Yet too often socialist support for social movements is based on the tacit assumption or reservation that people's everyday experiences and commitments are actually a form of 'false consciousness'.

The second problem is related: this 'false consciousness' is measured against a dubious theory of history that assumes that the working class is necessarily *the* representative of the interests of humanity in general. This position, first put by Marx in the mid nineteenth century, assumes the working class has the mission of emancipating society, and that this mission is built into the logic of history. It is against this logic that social movements are judged and often found wanting. This mode of thinking requires that ecological, feminist or peace interests must be read back to those of class, relations of production and the capitalist state.

Clearly the motivation, organization and support of most social movements cannot be reduced to class models, but this does not mean they lack authenticity or are peripheral to the 'real' movement of history. Nor does regarding such groups as progressive necessarily mean assuming the end of class society. It means, rather, assuming the end of class as the representative of general interests, and the recognition of plural interests as and where they are articulated.

For some post-Marxist theorists such as Rudolf Bahro, associated with the German Green movement, the working-class movement (as trade unionism) has proved to be a single-issue movement of disappointing proportions, concerned only with wages and conditions, unable or unwilling to take on the task of representing general interests and little concerned with social questions of growth and its limits, of technocratic rationality, of patriarchy and of peace. For many in the Green movement, these latter questions are of more urgent importance than traditional class concerns. There are plentiful local examples, such as the Green Bans and union support for the peace movement, to show that the divide drawn between working-class movements and social movements need not be so final; but equally, the problem – that of who represents whose interests – remains.

The union movement has often given only equivocal support for single issues. The support for the moratorium movement against the Vietnam war is a prime example. Here was an issue which had, by the first moratorium of May 1970, generated wide public support, and which exhibited all the characteristics of a single-issue movement. As Barry York has already outlined, the interpretations of the war were legion, from the somewhat demure opposition of the Save Our Sons movement to the consciously outrageous support of the Monash Labor Club in raising money for the N.L.F. war effort. The war was seen, from different angles, as everything from an immoral exercise of the government's conscription powers to the ugly face of American imperialism. But, for the union movement, the issue was largely read through a grid of pre-existing left-right divisions, principally those generated out of the Labor split in 1955–56.

Called upon to support the 1970 moratorium march, the executive of the Australian Council of Trade Unions (A.C.T.U.) was unable to formulate a statement that would command wide support in the union movement, although it had voted – by a majority of only one – in favour of the protest. So the question was referred to the state Trades and Labour Councils for their individual decisions. New South Wales, Victoria and Tasmania opposed the moratorium, with the other three states supporting it. The general pattern of individual unions' and unionists' support was disappointingly meagre, both publicly and financially. The one exception was in Victoria, where dissent was focused around twenty-six left-wing 'rebel' unions that had not been affiliated with the Trades Hall Council since 1967 and hence could not influence the right wing's decision to oppose the march.

This more substantial union support in Victoria in turn exacerbated tensions between the left and right wings, with the result that Melbourne became the centre of both union opposition and union support for the anti-war movement, with unions such as the Australian Workers' Union particularly vocal in the campaign against the moratorium. Here, then, the issue had been refracted through internal union political divisions, which had their own history in the bitter divisions growing out of the A.L.P. split. The issues of conscription and the Vietnam war could not be approached on their own merits, in a political vacuum. The A.C.T.U. executive, for example, was hesitant to oppose involvement in the Vietnam war when some of the larger right-wing unions in the country – such as the Australian Workers' Union, the Federated Ironworkers' Union and the Federated Clerks' Union – actively supported the war from their own anti-communist positions.

If this is another way of saying that single-issue politics always takes place within the total history of its society, that it occurs within a pre-existing cultural framework, the same could be said of other groups involved in the movement. The involvement of what became a student movement in the anti-war and anti-conscription campaigns of the 1960s and 1970s clearly took place against the backdrop of an atmosphere of cultural revolution as the children of the baby boom came of age. Activism in these campaigns was the focal point of a political re-awakening that stood in marked contrast to the cultural and political stagnation of the post-war years – Manning Clark's 'years of unleavened bread'.

If single-issue politics take place, and have effect, within a pre-existing historical framework, and if we must do without the comforting certainty that the working class has the logic of history on its side, then we need to examine the relations between class and single-issue politics, and ask what are the pre-conditions for a wide-ranging and successful single-issue movement. For some sociologists of social movements, such as Alain Touraine, class and movement are different orders of phenomena: class is a relation,

The children of the baby boom on the march in Melbourne in the early 1970s.

while the movement is action. Only a movement can possess what he calls 'historicity', the consciousness of attempting to divert the course of history. So 'the social movement ... is never a response to a social situation. On the contrary, the social situation is the result of the conflict of social movements'.

This relates to the question of representation of interests. Certainly, despite some honourable and consistent traditions, such as that of the Seamen's Union, there is little reason to assume from Australian experience that the working-class movement necessarily represents the interests of other progressive groups on an issue such as peace. This may be unfortunate in that it means the single-issue movement is robbed of the political and industrial strengths of the workers' movement, strengths of tradition, and of cultural and organizational focus. And, partly because of this lack, the single-issue movement may be frail when confronted with technocratic capitalism. Class is a structured relationship that can demand solidarity regardless of the issue, while the actors in a social movement may have only the issue in common, and this as a largely symbolic affair. The class, however, may have little direct interest in acting; the movement may be able to act only peripherally.

Political movements organized around a 'single' issue, then, have some marked contradictions. They generally face the dilemma that the more widely and radically they define an issue, the narrower their support is likely to be. When the issue is kept minimal and 'acceptable', as with the Franklin campaign, it may gain wide popular support, and have some immediate political impact; yet its narrowness is also its weakness if the issue can be resolved by 'fine tuning' action without major social change. If, on the other hand, the issue is widely defined, and the connections with other issues militantly drawn out, popular support may be less forthcoming. The movement may retain its purity of intent, but fail to get wide support.

This may not apply so much, however, for movements around issues that are too expansive for either narrow definition or easy solution. The contemporary peace movement is an example; one can hardly compromise about nuclear annihilation, nor hope to effect bilateral disarmament without radical changes to the political and economic structures of both east and west. The problem for socialists is to think through how to foster a movement that is both militant and far-reaching in its influences yet commands the active sympathy and democratic allegiance of the mass of the people. It would have to begin with supporters as they are, articulating and radicalizing the felt concerns of everyday life, yet it would have to be able to broaden these concerns into radical demands. For this, neither the Vietnam moratorium movement nor the Franklin campaign provides blueprints, but each does provide some pointers and some cause for optimism. They were both, after all, successful in their own terms.

Notes on the Contributors

PETER BEILHARZ has been in and around the Melbourne left since the early 1970s. A co-founder of *Thesis Eleven,* he has worked in Victorian high schools, at Monash University, Phillip Institute and Melbourne University. Presently lecturer in Sociology at La Trobe University, he is author of *Trotsky, Trotskyism and the Transition to Socialism* and co-author with Rob Watts of *Labor's Accord*.

VERITY BURGMANN is a postdoctoral research fellow in history at Melbourne University. She is the author of *'In Our Time': Socialism and the Rise of Labor* and other studies of the labour movement. A former member of the British and Australian Labor parties, and the International Socialists, she now barracks for St Kilda.

BRENDAN CARINS has been an active participant in the anti-nuclear movement. While studying at Monash University, he was elected to a number of student representative positions on a socialist platform. He is still striving for a nuclear-free Australia for his daughter, is employed in the Victorian Public Service and is a member of the V.P.S.A.

ALASTAIR DAVIDSON teaches politics at Monash University. He is the author of *The Communist Party of Australia,* two books on Gramsci, two volumes on the Italian Communist Party and sundry articles. He is a former editor of *Australian Left Review*, *Intervention* and *Thesis Eleven*.

GARY FOLEY is a well-known Aboriginal activist. He was involved in the setting up of the Aboriginal Medical Service in Sydney in the 1960s. Since then he has campaigned on many fronts and has held various positions, including director of the Aboriginal Arts Board, spokesperson for the National Aboriginal and Islander Health Organization and organizer with the Aboriginal Medical Service in both Melbourne and Sydney.

CHARLIE FOX teaches Australian history and social history at Melbourne University. His research interests include the history of work, unemployment and leisure. He is preparing books for publication on the history of work in Australia and the Great Depression in Victoria.

HEATHER GOODALL lectures in Aboriginal history at Macquarie University. She has worked closely with Aboriginal community groups for many years. She was employed by the Pitjantjatjara Council for eighteen months in Ernabella in South Australia to help prepare their case before the royal commission into British atomic testing. She wrote her doctoral thesis on Aboriginal community history in New South Wales.

PATRICIA GRIMSHAW initiated the teaching of women's studies at Melbourne University, where she lectures in history. She is the author of *Women's Suffrage in New Zealand*, and co-editor of *Australian Women: Feminist Perspectives*, *The Half-Open Door* and *Families in Colonial Australia*. She has taken an active interest in state schools and in the A.L.P. for twenty years in the Carlton area where she lives, and has served on various university committees promoting equal opportunity issues.

CHRIS HEALY wrote his chapter while involved in anti-nuclear movements in Melbourne during the early 1980s. He has done postgraduate work at the University of Birmingham's Centre for Contemporary Cultural Studies and has worked at the New South Wales Institute of Technology. He has edited *The Lifeblood of Footscray — Working Lives at the Angliss Meatworks*.

CRAIG JOHNSTON was elected as an openly gay man, and socialist, to the Sydney City Council in 1984. He is now involved in the environmental and housing movements.

ROBERT JOHNSTON has been active in the gay rights movement and regularly contributes articles and fiction to the *Sydney Star Observer* and *Campaign*.

PETER LOVE, who has taught Australian history at Deakin University and Phillip Institute, is interested mainly in the study of labour. His *Labour and the Money Power* explored the contradictions in Australian labour populism. For the pleasures of teaching and writing he does penance through membership of the Labor Party.

CHRIS McCONVILLE lectures in public history at Monash University, after working in various places at different jobs. He is the author of *Emigrant Irish and suburban Catholics* and co-editor of *The Outcasts of Melbourne* and *Families in Colonial Australia*. He is active in public radio broadcasting and local politics, especially on environmental issues.

ELLEN McEWEN, who has two young daughters and lives in Sydney, wrote her doctoral thesis on the Newcastle coalmining district in the nineteenth century. She worked for several years on *Australians 1888*, the third volume of the official bicentennial history. She is co-editor of *Families in Colonial Australia*.

STUART MACINTYRE teaches history at Melbourne University. He has participated in and studied the history of the labour movement in Britain and Australia. He has written *A Proletarian Science*, *Little Moscows* and *Militant: The Life and Times of Paddy Troy*. In spite of all, he is a member of the Labor Party.

ANDREW MOORE lectures in Australian history at Macarthur Institute of Higher Education in Sydney. He is an executive member of the Sydney and federal branches of the Australian Society for the Study of Labour History, and edits the Sydney branch's journal, the *Hummer*. He has a book forthcoming on the Old Guard.

JACK MUNDEY was born and bred in North Queensland and came to Sydney in 1951 to play for Parramatta Rugby League team. He is best known for his years as secretary of the New South Wales Builders Labourers' Federation during its Green Bans period in the early 1970s. Since then he has worked as a freelance writer and propagandist on environmental issues. He is a Sydney City Councillor.

JOHN MURPHY lectures in political history and social policy at Phillip Institute in Melbourne. This, along with a young daughter, helps divert him from his major research interest in the Australian intervention in the Vietnam war. He is an editor of *Thesis Eleven* and has published variously on Australian history, historiography and the Vietnam war.

LIZ ROSS has been an activist around lesbian, gay and women's issues since 1972, and an active socialist since the late 1970s. She is now a member of Socialist Action and union shop steward in the federal public service. She has written extensively for feminist, gay and socialist publications, including pamphlets on industrial democracy, workers' control, the Victorian nurses' strike and the Accord.

BRUCE SCATES was born in Sunshine, Victoria, and now lives in Fremantle. He is a lecturer in history at Murdoch University, the author of several articles and a doctoral thesis on radicalism in late nineteenth-century Australia, and is active in community radio. He shares his lecturing post with Raelene Frances, along with the care of their son, William Morris.

BARRY YORK was born in London and was brought to Australia by his English mother and Maltese father in 1954. He grew up in Brunswick in

Melbourne, and became active in the anti-war movement in the mid 1960s. He is the author of *The Maltese in Australia* and many articles in historical, educational and political journals, and co-author of *The Black Resistance*.

Notes on the Chapters

Big Brother is Watching You
ALASTAIR DAVIDSON

There is no text on the Australian state. Two old works that touch on it from a liberal point of view are W. K. Hancock, *Australia*, Jacaranda, 1961 (first published 1930); and F. W. Eggleston, *State Socialism in Victoria*, S. King, 1932. More recent books and collections of articles from a people's point of view are R. W. Connell and T. H. Irving, *Class Structure in Australian History*, Longman Cheshire, 1980; and Sydney Labour History Group, *What Rough Beast? The State and Social Order in Australian History*, Allen & Unwin, 1982. Worth reading is R. Kennedy, *Australian Welfare History, Critical Essays*, Macmillan, 1982. An essay that helps clarify why the Australian state is under-researched is B. Galligan, 'The State in Australian Political Thought', *Politics*, vol. 29, no. 2, November 1984. A good list of the many works in constitutional history is in W. McMinn, *A Constitutional History of Australia*, Oxford University Press, 1979. There is no history of the Australian administration, but A. Castles has now written a good *Australian Legal History*, Law Book Co., 1982.

On the state and convict society, see C. and M. Schedvin, 'The Nomadic Tribes of Urban Britain: A Prelude to Botany Bay', *Historical Studies*, vol. 18, no. 71, October 1978, pp. 254–76; W. Forsyth, *Governor Arthur's Convict System*, Sydney University Press, 1970; J. Hirst, *Convict Society and its Enemies*, Allen & Unwin, 1983; Alan Atkinson, 'Four Patterns of Convict Protest', *Labour History*, no. 37, 1979, pp. 28–51; E. Campbell, 'Prerogative Rule in N.S.W.', *Journal, Royal Australian Historical Society*, no. 50, 1964. On the state and land settlement, the most useful sources are J. Powell and M. Williams, *Australian Space, Australian Time*, Oxford University Press, 1979; A. Wells and A. Davidson, 'The Land, the Law and the State: 1788–1900', *Law in Context*, no. 2, 1983; Marilyn Lake, *The Limits of Hope, Soldier Settlement in Victoria: 1915–1938*, Oxford University Press, 1987; R. Else-Mitchell, 'The Foundation of New South Wales and the

Inheritance of the Common Law', *Journal, Royal Australian Historical Society*, no. 49, 1963.

On the state and the family, see Portia Robinson, *The Hatch and Brood of Time: A Study of the First Generation of Native Born Australians, 1788–1828*, Oxford University Press, 1985; P. McDonald, *Marriage in Australia*, A.N.U. Press, 1975; Michael Sturma, 'Eye of the Beholder: The Stereotype of Women Convicts, 1788–1852', *Labour History*, no. 34, pp. 3–10; Jill Julius Matthews, *Good and Mad Women, the Historical Construction of Femininity in Twentieth Century Australia*, Allen & Unwin, 1984.

On the nature of opposition to the state, see Eric Fry (ed.), *Rebels and Radicals*, Allen & Unwin, 1983; Adrian Merritt, 'Forgotten Militants: Use of the Masters and Servants Act by and against Female Employees, 1845–1930', Paper presented to the Law and History Conference, La Trobe University, May 1982; Noel Ebbels (ed.), *The Australian Labor Movement 1850–1907*, Lansdowne, 1965; W. Pember Reeves, *State Experiments in Australia and New Zealand*, Macmillan, 1965 (first published 1902); Ann Curthoys and Andrew Markus (eds), *Who Are Our Enemies?*, Hale & Iremonger, 1978.

On Federation and how the Constitution works, see H. Anderson (ed.), *Tocsin, Radical Arguments Against Federation*, Drummond, 1977; H. Scott Bennett, *The Making of the Commonwealth*, Cassell, Australia, 1971; R. Menzies, *Central Power in the Commonwealth*, Cassell, Australia, 1967; Dennis Altman, 'Obstacles to Constitutional Change', *Change*, vol. 1, no. 4, 1979–80.

Conflicting Loyalties

CHRIS McCONVILLE

Anyone interested in the twentieth century history of municipal politics and urban affairs should consult Leonie Sandercock, *Cities for Sale: Property, Politics and Urban Planning in Australia*, Heinemann, 1976. For a similar study of the nineteenth century, see David Dunstan, *Governing the Metropolis, Melbourne 1850–1891*, Melbourne University Press, 1984. Of some relevance to issues of planning is W. G. Osmond, *Frederic Eggleston: An Intellectual in Australian Politics*, Allen & Unwin, 1985. On the distribution of wealth in Australian society, see Stuart Macintyre, *Winners and Losers, The Pursuit of Social Justice in Australian History*, Allen & Unwin, 1985. The origins of the Labor Party are considered in Verity Burgmann, *'In Our Time': Socialism and the Rise of Labor, 1885–1905*, Allen & Unwin, 1985. The character of the Labor Party at local level is considered in D. J. Murphy (ed.), *Labor in Politics: the State Labor Parties in Australia, 1880–1920*, University of Queensland Press, 1975. See also Brian McKinlay (ed.), *A Documentary History of the Australian Labor Movement, 1850–1975*, Drummond, 1979. For a highly coloured version of Richmond and Collingwood politics, see one of the many editions of Frank Hardy, *Power Without Glory*.

The Ties that Divide
ELLEN McEWEN

The critique of the use of 'community' by government bodies is discussed in Lois Bryson and Martin Mowbray, ' "Community", the spray-on solution', *Australian Journal of Social Issues*, vol. 16, no. 4, 1981, pp. 255–67. Thomas Croudace's comments on his workmen are in a letter to R. A. A. Moorehead, 12 January 1886, in Croudace Letter Book, 1875–86, Newcastle Public Library Archives. The single men's quarters at Wittenoom are described in Lenore Layman, 'Work and Workers' responses at Wittenoom, 1943–1966', paper delivered to Australian Historical Association Conference, University of N.S.W., September 1982. Blainey's description of welfare provisions in outback mining towns comes from Geoffrey Blainey, *The Rush that Never Ended: A History of Australian Mining*, Melbourne University Press, 1978 (first published 1963). Comments on B.H.P.'s role at Whyalla are from Roy Kriegler, *Working for the Company*, Oxford University Press, 1978.

Apart from the work of Bryson and Mowbray, the most useful sources on social relations in local areas were A. J. and J. J. McIntyre, *Country Towns of Victoria*, Melbourne University Press, 1944; Ronald A. Wild, *Bradstow, Class, Status and Power in an Australian Country Town*, Angus & Robertson, 1974; Ronald A. Wild, 'Localities, Social Relationships and the Rural-Urban Continuum', *Australian and New Zealand Journal of Sociology*, vol. 10, no. 3, 1974, pp. 170–6, which serves as a useful review of empirical studies and their findings; Claire Williams, *Open Cut, the Working Class in an Australian Mining Town*, Allen & Unwin, 1981.

Few local histories provide the social information found in the sociological and anthropological studies mentioned, but they contain valuable material on various aspects of society at any time. Those most helpful for this chapter were James Jervis, *The Cradle City of Australia, A History of Parramatta, 1788–1961*, Parramatta City Council, 1961; James Steele, *Early days of Windsor N.S.W.*, Tyrells Ltd, 1916; Gordon Harris, *Mudgee Past and Present: an historical guide to the first town of the Central Tableland*, Commonwealth Jubilee Celebrations Committee, 1951; Robin B. Walker, *Old New England, A History of the Northern Tablelands in N.S.W., 1818–1900*, Sydney University Press, 1966; Steven Treleaven Eldred-Grigg, Pastoral Families of the Hunter Valley, Ph.D thesis, A.N.U., 1978; Ellen McEwen, The Newcastle Coalmining District of N.S.W., 1860–1900, Ph.D thesis, Sydney University, 1979; Brian Kennedy, *Silver, Sin and Sixpenny Ale, A Social History of Broken Hill 1883–1921*, Melbourne University Press, 1978; Dorothy Jones, *Trinity Phoenix, A History of Cairns and District*, Cairns and District Centenary Committee, 1978; Mandy Robinson, *Cap'n Hancock*, Rigby, 1978; Terry Birtles, A Survey of Land Use, Settlement and Society in the Atherton-Evelyn District, North Queensland, 1880–1914, M.A. thesis, Sydney University, 1967; E. B. Swanson, 'Chinese Immigrants in New England', *Armidale and District Historical Society, Journal and Proceedings*, vol. 11, 1968, pp. 26–36; Margaret Kiddle, *Men of Yes-*

terday, A Social History of the Western District of Victoria 1834–1890, Melbourne University Press, 1961.

F. A. Larcombe discusses how the N.S.W. government stymied municipal initiative in *The Stabilization of Local Government in N.S.W. 1858–1906*, Sydney University Press, 1976. Solidarity in mining towns is treated in Miriam Dixson, 'Stubborn resistance: The Northern N.S.W. miners' lockout 1929–30', *Labour History*, no. 24, 1973, pp. 128–42; and in P. Deery (ed.), *The 1949 Coal Strike*, Australian Society for the Study of Labour History, 1978. Examples of left-wing historians using 'community' can be found in John Foster, *Class Struggle and the Industrial Revolution: Early Industrial Capitalism in Three English towns*, Methuen, 1974; and in R. W. Connell and T. H. Irving, *Class Structure in Australian History: Documents, Narrative and Argument*, Longman Cheshire, 1980, pp. 189–93, 279–80.

The best way to assess social relations within a locality in the past is to read local newspapers, contemporary directories and the manuals of voluntary associations. Newspapers used for this chapter include *Goulburn Herald* 1859, *Mudgee Liberal* 1861–64, *Mudgee Western Post* 1860–64, *Armidale Express* 1859–60; *Wodonga Sentinel, Warracknabeal Herald, Bairnsdale Advertizer, Alexandra Standard, Colac Herald, Coleraine Albion, Shepparton News, Sydney Daily Telegraph*, all for 1888. Directories used include *Official Post Office Directory for N.S.W.* 1851; *Sands Suburban Directory of Sydney* 1888; *Victorian Country Directory* 1889–90; *N.S.W. Electoral Roll* 1894. Voluntary association manuals used include *Leichhardt Mutual Improvement Association, revised rules*, Leichhardt, 1886; *United Ancient Order of Druids, Report of the Grand Lodge of N.S.W. Annual Session* 1888–89, Sydney.

A Nordenfelt at Every Woolshed

ANDREW MOORE

The title and initial quote of this essay are drawn from Nigel Krauth's award winning novel, *Matilda My Darling*, Allen & Unwin, 1983, p. 133.

For comments on an earlier draft of this essay the author is grateful to the editors and Alan Atkinson, Beverley Burgmann, Drew Cottle, Terry Irving, Peter Love, Humphrey McQueen and John Shields.

An important starting point for this essay has been R. W. Connell and T. H. Irving, *Class Structure in Australian History: Documents, Narrative and Argument*, Longman Cheshire, 1980. Drew Cottle's 'Purging Paradise: Class Struggle, the State and Social Order in British Eastern Australia, 1890–1894', *Radical History Review*, forthcoming, has also been used extensively, as has Michael Dunn's *Australia and the Empire*, Fontana Collins, 1984. Articles in E. L. Wheelwright and Ken Buckley (eds), *Essays in the Political Economy of Australian Capitalism*, A.N.Z. Book Co., 1975–83 have also been drawn upon. Other useful essay collections are Richard Kennedy (ed.), *Australian Welfare History: Critical Essays*, Macmillan, 1982; Drew Cottle (ed.), *Capital Essays*, Panacea Press, 1983; Brian Head (ed.), *State and Economy in Australia*, Oxford University Press, 1983; and Sydney

Labour History Group, *What Rough Beast? The State and Social Order in Australian History*, Allen & Unwin, 1982.

On convict society see Philip McMichael's excellent book, *Settlers and the Agrarian Question: Foundations of Capitalism in Colonial Australia*, Cambridge University Press, 1984; David Denholm, *The Colonial Australians*, Penguin, 1979; Martin Sullivan, *Men and Women of Port Phillip*, Hale & Iremonger, 1985; W. G. McMinn, *A Constitutional History of Australia*, Oxford University Press, 1979; and M. Sturma, *Vice in a Vicious Society*, University of Queensland Press, 1983.

The quotation from Stuart Macintyre about Macquarie's emancipist policy is from his *Winners and Losers*, Allen & Unwin, 1985, p. 8. E. W. T. Hamilton's misgivings about convictism are gleaned from J. M. Ward, *James Macarthur: Colonial Conservative 1798–1867*, Sydney University Press, 1981, p. 149. The sections on public order legislation are derived from Frank Brennan's, *Too Much Order with Too Little Law*, University of Queensland Press, 1983; that on the police from Pat O'Malley, *Law, Capitalism and Democracy*, Allen & Unwin, 1983. Sir Thomas Mitchell's apprehensions are documented in his papers in the Mitchell Library, MSS A292, and his solutions are referred to in Cecil Salier, 'Thomas Livingston Mitchell', *Royal Australian Historical Society, Journal and Proceedings*, vol. 17, 1931, pp. 1–43. On the conflicts within the ruling class about land legislation in the 1860s see D. W. A. Baker, 'The Origins of Robertson's Land Acts', *Historical Studies. Selected Articles, First Series*, pp. 103–26. Chris Coulthard-Clark's article, 'The Military as Strike Breakers', *Pacific Defence Reporter*, May 1981, pp. 72–4, provides the basis for material on the military, supplemented by information on the volunteers in Michael Cannon, *Life in the Country: Australia and the Victorian Age*, Thomas Nelson, 1973, and Heather Ronald, *Wool Past the Winning Post: a History of the Chirnside Family*, Lansvale Enterprises, 1978. J. E. Corcoran, *The Target Rifle in Australia*, Dolphin, 1975, provides technical information about developments in rifle technology. The secret guerrillas at Braidwood in 1867 are mentioned in A. W. Martin, *Henry Parkes: A Biography*, Melbourne University Press, 1980, p. 222. The letter from Streeton to Roberts is in the latter's papers in the Mitchell Library, MSS 2478/9–10, and the article in *Bohemia* is in the issue of 9 July 1891. Points about federation have been drawn from Michael Dunn, 'The Britannic Question: The Empire and the Colonies, 1870–1910', *Bowyang*, no. 1, n.d., pp. 37–62 and Richard White, *Inventing Australia*, Allen & Unwin, 1981. For details about a particular scab union during the Great War see G. D. Patmore, 'The origins of the National Union of Railwaymen', *Labour History*, no. 43, November 1982, pp. 44–52.

Much of the primary research for this essay is included in the author's Ph.D thesis, ' "Send Lawyers Guns and Money!" A Study of Conservative Para-military Organizations in New South Wales 1930–1932, Background and Sequel 1917–1952', La Trobe University, 1982, which provides most of the information about conservative alarm and responses from the Great War to the Great Depression.

For preliminary observations about the Brisbane Line see Drew Cottle, 'The Commanding Heights of Treachery: Sydney's Rich Appeasers 1938–1942', paper presented at the 'Wrong Way Go Back' conference, University of Sydney, February 1979. R. W. Connell's *Ruling Class, Ruling Culture*, Cambridge University Press, 1977 provides valuable theoretical and empirical information about contemporary developments in the ruling class, as do many essays in Greg Crough, Ted Wheelwright and Ted Wilshire (eds), *Australia and World Capitalism*, Penguin, 1980. Chris Cunneen, 'A Garrison State: The Police in Arms', *Arena*, no. 71, 1985, pp. 67–89, documents the recent militarization of police forces.

Only the Chains have Changed

PATRICIA GRIMSHAW

Anne Summers, in *Damned Whores and God's Police*, Penguin, 1975, has written an interesting account of the women's movement, a task attempted more recently by Marian Sawer and Marian Simms in *A Woman's Place*, Allen & Unwin, 1984, and by Jocelyn Clarke and Kate White in *Women in Australian Politics*, Fontana, 1983. First-wave feminism and the period between the wars are discussed in numerous articles and chapters in collections: Dianne Scott's article 'Women Suffrage: the Movement in Australia', *Journal of the Royal Australian Historical Society*, December 1967; Judith Allen's chapter 'Breaking into the Public Sphere' in Judy Mackinolty and Heather Radi (eds), *In Pursuit of Justice*, Hale & Iremonger, 1979; chapters by Susan Magarey, Farley Kelly and Brian Matthews on Catherine Spence, Brettena Smyth and Louisa Lawson in Eric Fry (ed.), *Rebels and Radicals*, Allen & Unwin, Sydney, 1983; Anthea Hyslop and Kate White on female social reformers, and the feminists Bessie Rischbieth and Jessie Street in Margaret Bevege *et al.*, *Worth Her Salt*, Hale & Iremonger, 1982; Anthea Hyslop on Marie Kirk and P. Grimshaw on Bessie Harrison Lee in Marilyn Lake and Farley Kelly (eds), *Double Time*, Penguin, 1985. In addition, Susan Magarey has recently published a biography of Catherine Spence, *Unbridling the Tongues of Women*, Hale & Iremonger, 1985. Feminist journals such as the *Dawn*, *Woman's Sphere* and the *White Ribbon Signal* are central to understanding feminist ideology. For second-wave feminism, Ann Curthoys has discussed her experiences in Robyn Rowland (ed.), *Women Who Do and Women Who Don't*, Routledge & Kegan Paul, 1984, and gave an interview; Joyce Nicholson discussed her experiences in a chapter called 'Sisterhood is Powerful' in *Double Time*; Susan Magarey (Eade) in 'Now We Are Six: A Plea for Women's Liberation', in *Refractory Girl*, nos 13–14, March, 1977; Sylvia Kinder in *Her story of Adelaide Women's Liberation 1967–74*, Salisbury Education Centre, 1980; Zelda D'Aprano in *Zelda: The Becoming of a Woman*, privately printed, 1977.

Further useful accounts of second-wave feminism are Anne Summers, 'The Women's Movement', in Henry Mayer and Helen Nelson (eds), *Australian Politics: A Fourth Reader*, Cheshire, 1976; Anna Yeatman and the

Women's Liberation Movement, 'Women's Liberation', in Henry Mayer and Helen Nelson (eds), *Australian Politics: a Third Reader*, Cheshire, 1973; Helen Glezer and Jan Mercer (eds), 'Blue print for a Lobby; the Birth of W.E.L. as a Social Movement', in Henry Mayer (ed.), *Labor to Power*, Angus & Robertson, 1973; and Ann Curthoys, 'The Women's Movement and Social Justice' in Dorothy Broom (ed.), *Unfinished Business*, Allen & Unwin, 1984. See also P. Grimshaw, 'Tasman Sisters: Lives of the Second Sex', in Keith Sinclair (ed.), *Tasman Relations*, University of Auckland Press, 1987.

The Making of Homosexual Men

CRAIG JOHNSTON AND ROBERT JOHNSTON

The history of male homosexuality and lesbianism in Australia has yet to be written. Fragments of references have been put together in this essay within a framework that has been developed by historians in Britain and the United States, where the research data are more extensive. Press reports and literary references offer the barest of outlines rather than presenting a full picture. Below are some of the books which include useful references to homosexuality.

On Aborigines: Ronald M. Berndt and Catherine H. Berndt, *Sexual Behaviour in Western Arnhem Land*, Viking Fund, 1951; Ronald M. Berndt and Catherine H. Berndt (eds), *Aboriginal Man in Australia: Essays in Honour of Emeritus Professor A.P. Elkin*, Angus & Robertson, 1965; Ronald M. Berndt, *Love Songs of Arnhem Land*, Thomas Nelson, 1976; Phyllis M. Kaberry, *Aboriginal Woman: Sacred and Profane*, George Routledge, 1939; Geza Roheim, *The Eternal Ones of the Dream*, International Universities Press, 1945; Geza Roheim, *Children of the Desert*, vol. 1, Basic Books, 1974.

On lesbians: Marion Edwards, *Life and Adventures of Marion-Bill Edwards*, n.d.; J.K. Kelly, *Rugged Angel*, Angus & Robertson, 1961; Herbert V. Moran, *Viewless Winds*, Peter Davies, 1939.

Novels include: Lawson Glassop, *The Rats in New Guinea*, Horowitz, 1963; Neville Jackson, *No End to the Way*, Barrie and Rockliff, 1965; George Johnston, *My Brother Jack*, Collins, 1964; Kenneth Mackenzie, *The Young Desire It*, Sirius Books, 1937; Elizabeth Riley, *All that False Instruction*, Angus & Robertson, 1975; Christina Stead, *Seven Poor Men of Sydney*, Davies, 1934.

Other useful books are: *The Book of Life*, Health and Physical Culture Publishing Company, n.d.; Michael Cannon, *Who's Master? Who's Man?*, Nelson, 1971; Richard P. Davies, *The Tasmanian Gallows: A Study of Capital Punishment*, 1974; A.E. Debenham, *The Innocent Victims*, Edwards and Shaw, 1969; Robert French, *Gays Between the Broadsheets: Australian Media References to Homosexuality, 1948–1980*, Gay History Project, 1986; Peter N. Grabosky, *Sydney in Ferment: Crime, Dissent and Official Reaction 1788 to 1973*, Australian National University Press, 1977; Vince Kelly, *The Shadow: The Amazing Exploits of Frank Fahy*, Angus & Robertson, 1954; Vince Kelly, *The Bogeyman: The Exploits of Sergeant C.J. Chuck, Australia's Most*

Unpopular Cop, Angus & Robertson, 1956; A. G. L. Shaw, *Convicts and the Colonies*, Faber & Faber, 1966; Robert V. Storer, *A Survey of Sexual Life in Adolescence and Marriage*, Science Publishing Company, 1932; Russel Ward, *The Australian Legend*, Oxford University Press, 1958.

Two important recent books are Denise Thompson, *Flaws in the Social Fabric: Homosexuals and Society in Sydney*, Allen & Unwin, 1985; and Garry Wotherspoon (ed.), *Being Different*, Hale & Iremonger, 1986.

Escaping the Well of Loneliness

LIZ ROSS

In the early twentieth century there was an upsurge in research into the nature of sex and sexuality. This period and its significance for lesbians is discussed in Sheila Jeffreys, *The Spinster and Her Enemies, Feminism and Sexuality 1880–1930*, Pandora, 1985. One of the most famous researchers was Havelock Ellis, whose major publication was *Psychology of Sex*, F. A. Davis, 1901. Ellis, among others, labelled lesbians and homosexual men the 'third sex'. One of the most famous novels to be written about the 'third sex' was Radclyffe Hall, *The Well of Loneliness*, Jonathan Cape, 1928. Other writers such as Gertrude Stein were more obscure in their references to lesbianism. See, for instance, *Selected Writings of Gertrude Stein*, Random House, 1946; and *Fernhurst, Q.E.D., and Other Early Writings*, Liveright, 1971. Renee Vivien wrote haunting poetry about her lovers in French, the Complete Poems being published in French in 1948 (*Poesies Completes*, Paris, 1948, 2 vols). Two very comprehensive books cover the whole history of lesbian literature. The first is Jeanette Foster, *Sex Variant Women in Literature*, 2nd ed., Diana Press, 1975; and the second, a bibliography, is entitled *The Lesbian in Literature*, 3rd ed., The Naiad Press, 1981.

After the heyday of the 1920s and 1930s, it was not until the late 1960s that sex and sexuality were again so widely discussed. Women's liberation and gay liberation were the movements that revived discussion. One of the important books of this time was Germaine Greer, *The Female Eunuch*, Paladin, 1971. This book, with its challenging ideas, had a huge impact on many who read it. During 1973, at the National Women's Liberation conference, a paper entitled 'Sexism and Women's Liberation, or ... Why Do Straight Sisters Sometimes Cry when They are Called Lesbians?' had a similar effect within the movement.

Unfortunately most Women's Liberation and Gay Liberation conferences in Australia have not published their papers. Some may have been deposited at the state and national libraries, and occasionally some are published in the movement's publications, but most are not easily available after a conference is held. Some original documents have been collected by the National Gay Archives in Melbourne and may be read on the premises.

Women's and Gay Liberation magazines and newsletters from each state are supposed to be deposited in the state and national libraries and would be accessible as, for example, 'Adelaide Women's Liberation Newsletter' or 'Women's Liberation Newsletter, Adelaide'. A *Lesbian Newsletter*, the only one in Australia, was first published in Melbourne in March 1976, with the second issue not coming out until May 1977. It has been published monthly since that date. The gay publication *Outrage* was first published as the Fifth National Homosexual Conference Newsletter in 1979, then as *Gay Community News* after the conference, and now as *Outrage*.

The history of radical struggle by gays and their supporters can also be found in publications such as *Socialist Action, Tribune, Direct Action* and the *International Socialist*, formerly the *Battler*.

Specific struggles such as the anti-Festival of Light campaign of 1978 are documented in *Resource Kit* no. 2, published by Melbourne Gay Resource Collective, Melbourne, September 1978. *Resource Kit* no. 1 focused on Anita Bryant and the anti-gay campaigns in the U.S. (Melbourne, June 1978). Both publications are held in the National Gay Archives in Melbourne.

Rights for young gay people was one of the most important issues for the Gay Liberation movement. The publication of *Young Gay and Proud* by a collective from Melbourne Gay Teachers and Students Group (1978) and its acceptance into school libraries was one of the most significant gains for lesbians and gay men.

Divided We Fell
VERITY BURGMANN AND STUART MACINTYRE

The best journal for studying the labour movement is *Labour History*. Important general works include T. A. Coghlan, *Labour and Industry in Australia*, 4 vols, Macmillan, 1969 (first published 1918); Vere Gordon Childe, *How Labour Governs, A Study of Workers' Representation in Australia*, Melbourne University Press, 1964 (first published 1923); Robin Gollan, *Radical and Working Class Politics, A Study of Eastern Australia, 1850-1910*, Melbourne University Press, 1960; Ian Turner, *Industrial Labour and Politics, The Dynamics of the Labour Movement in Eastern Australia 1900-1921*, Hale & Iremonger, 1979 (first published 1965); Joe Harris, *The Bitter Fight, A Pictorial History of the Australian Labor Movement*, University of Queensland Press, 1970. Two essays that survey the field are John Merritt, 'Labour History' in Graeme Osborne and W. F. Mandle (eds), *New History: Studying Australia Today*, Allen & Unwin, 1982, pp 113-41; and Eric Fry, 'The Writing of Labour History in Australia' in Eric Fry (ed.), *Common Cause: Essays in Australian and New Zealand Labour History*, Allen & Unwin, 1986, pp. 139-55. Useful collections of documents are R. N. Ebbels (ed.), *The Australian Labor Movement 1850-1907*, Cheshire-Lansdowne, 1965; Brian McKinlay (ed.), *A Documentary History of the Australian Labor Movement 1850-1975*, Drummond, 1979.

A good summary of trade union theory is Richard Hyman, *Marxism and the Sociology of Trade Unionism*, Pluto Press, 1971. On labour and social democratic parties, see Robert Michels, *Political Parties, A Sociological Study of the Oligarchichal Tendencies of Modern Democracy*, Dover Publications, 1959 (first published 1915); Goran Therborn, 'The Rule of Capital and the Rise of Democracy', *New Left Review*, no. 103, 1977. In the Australian context, an early study is Albert Mitin, *Socialism Without Doctrines*, Alternative Publishing Co-operative, 1977 (first published in French in 1901). See also Stuart Macintyre, 'The Short History of Social Democracy in Australia', *Thesis Eleven*, no. 15, 1986, pp. 3-14; and Don Rawson (ed.), *Blast, Budge or Bypass: Towards a Social Democratic Australia*, Academy of the Social Sciences in Australia, 1986.

On Australian trade unions, see John Child, *Unionism and the Labor Movement*, Macmillan, 1971; Ross M. Martin, *Trade Unions in Australia*, Penguin, 1975; D. W. Rawson, *Unions and Unionists in Australia*, Allen & Unwin, 1986; J. T. Sutcliffe, *A History of Trade Unionism in Australia*, Macmillan, 1967 (first published 1921); Ian Turner and Leonie Sandercock, *In Union is Strength, A History of Trade Unions in Australia 1788-1978*, 3rd ed., Nelson, 1983. On the A.C.T.U., see Jim Hagan, *The History of the A.C.T.U.*, Longman Cheshire, 1981. Individual union histories include John Merritt, *The Making of the A.W.U.*, Oxford University Press, 1986; Tom Sheridan, *Mindful Militants, The Amalgamated Engineering Union in Australia 1920-72*, Cambridge University Press, 1975; Robin Gollan, *The Coalminers of New South Wales, A History of the Union, 1860-1960*, Melbourne University Press, 1963; R. T. Fitzgerald, *The Printers of Melbourne, The History of a Union*, Pitman, 1967; Edgar Ross, *A History of the Miners' Federation of Australia*, The Australasian Coal and Shale Employees' Federation, 1970; Frank Waters, *Postal Unions and Politics, A History of the Amalgamated Postal Workers' Union of Australia*, University of Queensland Press, 1978; Issy Wyner, *With Banner Unfurled, The early years of the Ship Painters and Dockers Union*, Hale & Iremonger, 1983; Wendy Lowenstein and Tom Hills, *Under the Hook, Melbourne Waterside Workers Remember: 1900-1980*, Melbourne Bookworkers in association with the Australian Society for the Study of Labour History, 1982. On strikes, see John Iremonger, John Merritt and Graeme Osborne (eds), *Strikes, Studies in Twentieth Century Australian Social History*, Angus & Robertson in association with the Australian Society for the Study of Labour History, 1973; and D. J. Murphy (ed.), *The Big Strikes, Queensland 1889-1965*, University of Queensland Press, 1983. Studies of individual unionists include Stuart Macintyre, *Militant, The Life and Times of Paddy Troy*, Allen & Unwin, 1984; Victor Williams, *The Years of Big Jim*, Lone Hand Press, 1975.

On the Labor Party, see L. F. Crisp, *The Australian Federal Labour Party 1901-1951*, Hale & Iremonger, 1978 (first published 1955); Brian McKinlay, *The ALP, A Short History of the Australian Labor Party*, Drummond/Heinemann, 1981; D. W. Rawson, *Labor in Vain? A Survey of the Australian Labor Party*, Longman, 1966; D. J. Murphy (ed.), *Labor in Politics, the State Labor Parties in Australia 1880-1920*, University of Queensland Press, 1975; Bruce O'Meagher (ed.), *The Socialist Objective, Labor and Socialism*, Hale & Iremonger, 1983; Verity Burgmann, *'In Our Time': Socialism and the Rise of Labor, 1885-1905*, Allen & Unwin, 1985. There is an annual collection of *Labor Essays*, first appearing in 1980, published by Drummond.

State-based studies of the labour movement include N. B. Nairn, *Civilizing Capitalism: the Labor Movement in New South Wales, 1870-1900*, A.N.U. Press, 1973; Jim Moss, *Sound of Trumpets, History of the Labour Movement in South Australia*, Wakefield Press, 1985; John Wanna, *Defence Not Defiance, The Development of Organised Labour in South Australia*, Adelaide Centre of the Arts and Education, 1981; D. J. Murphy, R. B. Joyce, Colin A. Hughes (eds), *Prelude to Power, The Rise of the Labour Party in Queensland 1885-1915*, Jacaranda, 1970, and *Labor in Power, The Labor Party and Governments in Queensland 1915-57*, University of Queensland Press, 1980; Richard Davis, *Eighty Years' Labor: the ALP in Tasmania, 1903-1983*, Sassafras Books, 1983.

There are many biographies of Labor leaders, for example, Lloyd Ross, *John Curtin, A Biography*, Macmillan, 1977; H. V. Evatt, *William Holman, Australian Labour Leader*, Angus & Robertson, 1940; John Robertson, *J. H. Scullin, A Political Biography*, University of Western Australia Press, 1974; L. F. Fitzhardinge, *William Morris Hughes*, 2 vols, Angus & Robertson, 1964; Bede Nairn, *The 'Big Fella', Jack Lang and the Australian Labor Party 1891-1949*, Melbourne University Press, 1986.

The story of Bill Morrow is told in Audrey Johnson, *Fly a Rebel Flag, Bill Morrow 1888-1980. In and out of the Labor Party – Politics with Principles*, Penguin, 1986, especially pp. 14-15. The Shearers' Union Rules are in R. N. Ebbels op. cit., p. 110. Marx and Engels' comment about capitalism encouraging trade unionism is quoted in Michael Poole, *Theories of Trade Unionism: A Sociology of Industrial Relations*, Routledge & Kegan Paul, 1981, p. 12. The striking shearers' diet is described in Julian Stuart, *Part of the Glory, Reminiscences of the Shearers' Strike Queensland 1891*, Australasian Book Society, 1967, p. 145. The article by Jenny Lee and Charles Fahey is 'A Boom for Whom? Some Developments in the Australian Labour Market, 1870-1891', *Labour History*, no. 50, May 1986, pp. 1-27. The 1888 spokesman is John Norton, 'The Status of Labour' in John Norton (ed.), *The History of Capital and Labour*, Oceanic Publishing Company, 1888, p. 304. Jemima Jorkins' letter to the *Worker* is quoted in W. Nicol, 'Women and the trade union movement in New South Wales: 1890-1900', *Labour History*, no. 36, May 1979, pp. 18-30. Sara Lewis's activity is related in Melanie Raymond, 'Sara Lewis: Trade Union Activist 1909-1918', *Lilith*, no. 3, Winter 1986, pp. 45-60. The story of Brodney and Harford is gleaned from the Brodney Papers, Box 3, La Trobe Library, Melbourne. The comments by striking nurses and by Irene Bolger are on tapes in possession of the authors. The comment on women in the A.L.P. is from L. F. Crisp, op. cit., p. 71. George Black's speech is in McKinlay, *A Documentary History*, pp. 17-18. The *Australian Workman*'s comment on the election was 20 June 1891. *Tocsin*'s observation was made on 5 November 1903. George Dale's comment is in his *The Industrial History of Broken Hill*, Fraser & Jenkinson, 1918, p. 14. The premier's private secretary was Vere Gordon Childe, whose *How Labour Governs* is a classic study of the Australian labour movement; the quotations are from p. 31 and p. 80. George Petersen's comment is in his foreword to Burgmann, op. cit.

The Beat of Weary Feet

CHARLIE FOX AND BRUCE SCATES

For the discussion of the early period, quotations are taken from Melbourne Trades Hall Council, *Report of the Unemployed Committee*, 1892; T.A. Coghlan, *Labour and Industry in Australia*, Macmillan, 1969 (first published 1918), vol. 4, p. 2183; *Age*, 17 March 1892; *Argus*, 13 April 1893; *Register*, 17 February 1894; Victorian Police Records, report by Constable Geelan, 18 September 1892; *Australian Workman*, 27 February 1892; *Age*, 28 April 1892; Victorian Police Records, Stokes, 4 September 1892; Victorian Police Records, Wardley, 25 June 1892; *Age*, 17 June 1892; Victorian Police Records, Geelan, 4 September 1892; Speech by W. Maloney, *Victorian Parliamentary Debates*, Legislative Assembly, 31 May 1892, vol. 69, p. 230; Victoria Police Records, Wardley, 1 June 1892; *Hard Cash*, September 1893; *Bulletin*, 21 October 1893; *Justice*, 31 March 1895; E.J. Brady, 'The Red Objective', Australian National Library manuscript; *Justice*, 10 February 1895; Australian Order of Industry, *Objectives*, Sydney, n.d.; *Justice*, 17 February 1894; H. Lawson, 'The Drover's Wife'; *Tocsin*, 31 March 1898; Speech by J. Hancock, *Victorian Parliamentary Debates*, Legislative Assembly, 20 August 1896, vol. 82, p. 1379; Speech by Levian, *Victorian Parliamentary Debates*, Legislative Assembly, 20 August 1896, vol. 82, p. 174; *Bulletin*, 13 July 1895; *Justice*, 10 March 1894; *Worker*, 26 March 1896.

For further reading, see Verity Burgmann, *'In Our Time': Socialism and the Rise of Labour 1885–1905*, Allen & Unwin, 1985; T.A. Coghlan, *Labour and Industry in Australia*, Macmillan, 1969 (first published 1918); Graeme Davison, *The Rise and Fall of Marvellous Melbourne*, Melbourne University Press, 1978; John Hirst, 'Keeping Colonial History Colonial: The Hartz Thesis Revisited', *Historical Studies*, vol. 21, no. 82, April 1984, pp. 85–104; Bob James, *Anarchism and State Violence in Sydney and Melbourne 1886–1896*, Bob James, 1986, ch. 8; Ernie Lane, *Dawn to Dusk: Reminiscences of a Rebel*, William Brooks, 1939, ch. 3; Jenny Lee and Charles Fahey, 'A Boom for Whom? Some Developments in the Australian Labour Market 1870–1891', *Labour History*, no. 50, May 1986, pp. 1–27; Ellen Ross, 'Survival Networks, Women's Neighbourhood Sharing before World War I', *History Workshop*, no. 15, Spring 1983, pp. 4–27; Bruce Scates, ' "Wobblers": Single Taxers in the Labour Movement, Melbourne, 1889–1899', *Historical Studies*, vol. 21, no. 83, October 1984, pp. 174–1899; Gareth Stedman Jones, *Outcast London: A Study of the Relationship between Classes in Victorian Society*, Clarendon Press, 1971, ch. 19; Bertha Walker, *Solidarity Forever*, National Press, 1972.

On the Great Depression, the following books are useful: G.C. Bolton,

A Fine Country to Starve In, University of Western Australia Press, 1972, is an elegant and sensitive study of Western Australia in the depression, which first posits then tries to explain the absence of political tensions in that state. C. R. Broomhill, *Unemployed Workers: A Social History of the Great Depression in Adelaide*, University of Queensland Press, 1978, is the only book that deals exclusively with unemployed workers in Australia, and he argues forcibly that unemployment causes withdrawal and passivity. R. J. Cooksey (ed.), *The Great Depression in Australia*, Australian Society for the Study of Labour History, 1970, is a collection of articles on a wide variety of subjects, from Perth to Queensland, and from economics to politics. Alastair Davidson, *The Communist Party of Australia*, Stanford University Press, 1969, is a thorough and wide-ranging history of the Communist Party, from its birth to the 1960s. Ralph Gibson, *The People Stand Up*, Red Rooster Press, 1983, is a massive account of the 1930s by a leading communist activist, who also refers to people's struggles the world over. Frank Huelin, *Keep Moving: An Odyssey*, Australian Book Society, 1973, is an account of life on the track, which celebrates the spirit of the bagmen against a background of brutality and indifference. L. J. Louis, *Trade Unions and the Depression, A Study of Victoria 1930–1932*, A.N.U. Press, 1968, is the only book dealing particularly with Victoria, and Louis exposes the inability of the trade union movement to comprehend or cope with the depression. Wendy Lowenstein, *Weevils in the Flour, An Oral History of the Depression*, Hyland House, 1978, is famous, and justly so, for it captures the spirit of the depression as no academic work can ever hope to. Judy Mackinolty (ed.), *The Wasted Years? Australia's Great Depression*, Allen & Unwin, 1981, is another collection of essays dealing with a wide range of subjects, including an article by Nadia Wheatley on the politics of the unemployed.

From Convicts to Communists

PETER LOVE

The substance of this chapter is based on the following works: Verity Burgmann, *'In Our Time': Socialism and the Rise of Labor, 1885–1905*, Allen & Unwin, 1985; Vere Gordon Childe, *How Labour Governs: A Study of Workers' Representation in Australia*, Labour Publishing Co., 1923; C. M. H. Clark, *A History of Australia: From the Earliest Times to the Age of Macquarie*, vol. 1, Melbourne University Press, 1962; R. W. Connell and T. H. Irving, *Class Structure in Australian History: Documents, Narrative and Argument*, Longman Cheshire, 1980; Alastair Davidson, *The Communist Party of Australia*, Hoover Institution Press, 1969; Frank Farrell, *International Socialism and Australian Labour: The Left in Australia, 1919–1939*, Hale & Iremonger, 1981; Eric Fry, 'A Hundred Years of Socialism in Australia', *Australian Left Review*, no. 80, June-August 1982, pp. 44–51; Eric Fry (ed.), *Rebels and Radicals*, Allen & Unwin, 1983; Robin Gollan, *Radical and Working Class Politics: A Study of Eastern Australia, 1850–1910*, Melbourne University Press, 1960; Robin Gollan, *Revolutionaries and Reformists: Com-*

munism and the Australian Labour Movement, 1920–1955, A.N.U. Press, 1975; E.J. Hobsbawm, *Revolutionaries: Contemporary Essays*, Quartet Books, 1977, especially ch. 1; T.H. Irving, '1850–70' in F.K. Crowley (ed.), *A New History of Australia*, Heinemann, 1974, pp. 124–64; M.J.B. Kenny, 'Edward Smith Hall' in Douglas Pike (ed.), *Australian Dictionary of Biography*, vol. 1, Melbourne University Press, 1966, pp. 500–2; Peter Love, *Labour and the Money Power: Australian Labour Populism, 1890–1950*, Melbourne University Press, 1984; Ian Turner, *Industrial Labour and Politics: the Labour Movement in Eastern Australia, 1900–1921*, A.N.U. Press, 1965; Ian Turner, *Sydney's Burning*, Heinemann, 1967; and Ian Turner and Leonie Sandercock, *In Union is Strength: A History of the Trade Unions of Australia, 1788–1983*, 3rd ed., Nelson, 1983.

Readers who wish to read further on any of the issues raised in this chapter could begin by consulting the notes and bibliographies in the works listed in these notes. For information on people, the best general source is still the *Australian Dictionary of Biography*. Since most of the radical activity discussed in this chapter has been conducted in or around the labour movement, readers may wish to consult some of the numerous union histories published in the last twenty years. Two informed and perceptive essays that survey the field are Eric Fry, 'The Writing of Labour History in Australia' in Eric Fry (ed.), *Common Cause: Essays in Australian and New Zealand Labour History*, Allen & Unwin, 1986; and John Merritt, 'Labour History' in G. Osborne and W. F. Mandle (eds), *New History: Studying Australia Today*, Allen & Unwin, 1982.

A Hundred Flowers Faded

PETER BEILHARZ

The standard reference in this area is Alastair Davidson, *The Communist Party of Australia*, Hoover, 1969. The intervening period is discussed by Winton Higgins, 'Reconstructing Australian Communism', *Socialist Register 1974*, Merlin, 1974; Peter Beilharz, 'Australia', *Yearbook on International Communist Affairs 1976*, Hoover, 1976; Andrew Milner, *The Road to St Kilda Pier: George Orwell and the Politics of the Australian Left*, Stained Wattle Press, 1984; and Peter Beilharz, 'The Australian Left: Beyond Labourism?', *Socialist Register 1985/1986*, Merlin, 1986.

Important lengthier analyses include Robin Gollan, *Revolutionaries and Reformists*, A.N.U. Press, 1975; and Tom O'Lincoln, *Into the Mainstream*, Stained Wattle Press, 1985. The pro-Soviet view is given by Bill Brown, *The Communist Movement and Australia*, Australian Labour Movement History, 1986; the pro-Chinese view by E. F. Hill, *Reflections on Communism in Australia*, n.d.; and one version of the Trotskyist view is given in *Betrayal: A History of the Communist Party of Australia*, Allen, 1981.

There is now a series of biographical and autobiographical works on the left, all worth reading. See, for instance, Ralph Gibson, *My Years in the Communist Party*, International Bookshop, 1965; Ralph Gibson, *The People Stand Up*, Red Rooster, 1983; Ralph Gibson, *One Woman's Life: A Memoir of Dorothy Gibson*, Hale & Iremonger, 1980; Edgar Ross, *Of Storm and Struggle*, A.P.C.O.L., 1982; Len Fox, *Broad Left, Narrow Left*, A.P.C.O.L., 1982; John Sendy, *Comrades Come Rally*, Nelson, 1978; Roger Milliss, *Serpent's Tooth*, Penguin, 1984.

On the New Left, see for example, Alan Barcan, *The Socialist Left in Australia 1949–1959*, A.P.S.A., 1960; Ian Turner, *Room for Manoeuvre*, Drummond, 1982; D. Bridges (ed.), *Helen Palmer's Outlook*, Helen Palmer Memorial Committee, 1982; Rowan Cahill, *Notes on the New Left in Australia*, A.M.R.F., 1969. Especially significant are Jack Blake, *Revolution from Within*, Outlook, 1971; and Dennis Altman, *Rehearsals for Change*, Fontana, 1979. On the immediate period and its problems for the left, see David McKnight (ed.), *Moving Left*, Pluto, 1986; Peter Beilharz, 'The Left, the Accord and the Future of Socialism', *Thesis Eleven*, no. 13, 1986; Frank Stilwell, *The Accord ... and Beyond*, Pluto, 1986; and Peter Beilharz and Rob Watts, *Labor's Accord*, forthcoming.

Preventing the Plunder
JACK MUNDEY

The issues discussed in this chapter are explored in greater detail in the author's book: see Jack Mundey, *Green Bans and Beyond*, Angus & Robertson, 1981. Also on the Green Bans period of the New South Wales Builders Labourers' Federation, see Meredith Burgmann, 'A New Concept of Unionism: The New South Wales Builders Labourers' Federation 1970–1974', Ph.D thesis, Macquarie University, 1981; Richard J. Roddewig, *Green Bans, The Birth of Australian Environmental Politics*; and Pete Thomas, *Taming the Concrete Jungle*, New South Wales branch of the Australian Building and Construction Employees & Builders Laborers' Federation, 1973.

Cryin' Out for Land Rights
HEATHER GOODALL

The sources for the Aboriginal views discussed here are interviews with Jack Campbell, Henry Hardy, Eddie Edwards, between 1976 and 1982; Cinesound News Review, no. 100, 1933, for Joe Anderson, described as 'King Burraga, Chief of Thirroul Tribe'; letters and statements of Mosely family in New South Wales Aborigines Protection Board Minute Books, 1914, 1915, 1937 and New South Wales Premier's Department Correspondence, 1937–8; Australian Aboriginal Progressive Association statements in *Sydney Morning Herald*, 15 November 1927, *Voice of the North*, 1925–7, Premier's Department Correspondence, 1927; Aborigines Progressive Association and Australian Aborigines League statements in *The Australian Abo Call*, edited by Jack Patten, 1938, and Premier's Department Correspondence, 1937–40; William Cooper's letters to the N.S.W. government, also in Premier's Department Correspondence, 1936–40. Some of Cooper's letters are now published in Andrew Markus (ed.),

Blood From A Stone, Monash Publications in History, Monash University, 1986.

Useful information can also be found in *Report of the N.S.W. Protector of Aborigines*, 1882; New South Wales *Aborigines Protection Board Reports*, 1884 to 1838–9; New South Wales Aborigines Protection Board Register of Reserves, 1861 to 1904; and New South Wales Department of Education School Records. A more complete list of research material can be found in Heather Goodall, 'A History of Aboriginal Communities in N.S.W., 1909–1939', Ph.D thesis, University of Sydney, 1982.

For further reading, there have been important contributions made towards regional histories of some south-eastern Aboriginal communities. These include the work of Dianne Barwick, writing about the Goulburn Valley confederation in, for example, 'Coranderrk and Cumeroogunga: Pioneers and Policy' in Scarlett Epstein and David Penny (eds), *Opportunity and Response: Case Studies in Economic Development*, Hurst and Co., 1972. Barry Morris has written about the Macleay Valley and surroundings in, for example, 'From Underemployment to Unemployment: The Changing Role of Aborigines in a Rural Economy', *Mankind*, vol. 13, no. 6, April 1983, pp. 499–515. James Miller has written about his community's history in the Hunter Valley in *Koori, A Will To Win*, Angus & Robertson, 1985. Peter Read's work has focused on the south-western plains land of the Wiradhuri, including Yass and Cowra, in 'A Double-Headed Coin: Protection and Assimilation in Yass 1900–1960' in Bill Gammage and Andrew Markus (eds), *All That Dirt: Aborigines 1938*, Research School of Social Sciences, 1982, pp. 9–28, and ' "A Rape of the Soul so Profound": Some Reflections on the Dispersal Policy in New South Wales', *Aboriginal History*, vo.l7, no. 1, pp. 23–33.

Teaching Whites a Lesson
GARY FOLEY

The observations in this chapter are based on the author's life experience in general and, in particular, on more than two decades of campaigning for Aboriginal rights in this country. They are the personal reflections of one black activist; they are not intended as a representative statement of any Aboriginal group.

War Against War
CHRIS HEALY

The first general history of peace movements in Australia has been published since the completion of this chapter: it is Malcolm Saunders and Ralph Summy, *The Australian Peace Movement: A Short History*, Peace Research Centre, Australian National University, 1986. Brief though it is and overly concerned to establish a lineage of peace movements, this should be the starting point for those who wish to read further.

In the course of preparing this chapter I have drawn mainly on archival material, journal articles, theses, unpublished papers, biographies, and peripheral mentions in accounts of the labour movement. More extensive arguments and lists of research material can be found in W. A. Wood, 'The Sudan Contingent of 1885 and the Anti-War Movements', *Labour History*, no. 3, 1962, pp. 52–69; M. J. Saunders, 'Australia's first peace movement?', *Labour History*, no. 49, 1985, pp. 38–50; L. M. Field, 'The Forgotten War, Australia in South Africa, 1899–1902', M. A. thesis, A.N.U., 1973; R. M. Crawford, *A Bit of a Rebel. The Life and Work of George Arnold Wood*, Sydney University Press, 1975; C. N. Connolly, 'Class, Birthplace, Loyalty. Australian Attitudes to the Boer War', *Historical Studies*, vol. 18, no. 71, pp. 210–35; P. Gowland, 'The Women's Peace Army' in E. Windschuttle (ed.), *Women, Class and History. Feminist Perspectives on Australia, 1788–1978*, Fontana, 1980; E. M. Moore, *The Quest for Peace As I Have Known it in Australia*, Wilke and Co., 1949; Chris Healy, 'The Australian Peace Alliance, 1914–1918', B.A. hons thesis, University of Melbourne, 1982; Paul Scales, 'Pacifism in Australia 1912–1918', B.A. hons thesis, Flinders University, 1971; C. A. Rasmussen, 'Defending the Bad Against the Worse; The Peace Movement in Australia in the 1930s. Its Origins, Structure and Development', Ph.D. thesis, University of Melbourne, 1984; Frank Farrell, *International Socialism and Australian Labour. The Left in Australia 1919–1939*, Hale & Iremonger, 1981; Ralph Gibson, *The People Stand Up*, Red Rooster Press, 1983; D. Rose, 'A History of Anti-war Organizations in Victoria, 1933–1939. A Study of the Movement Against War and Fascism, the Labor Anti-War Committee, and the International Peace Campaign', M.A. thesis, Latrobe University, 1976.

Power to the Young

BARRY YORK

The following is a selection of primary sources used: Victoria Police Department, *Annual Reports*, 1961–73; *Police Life*, 1963–73; *Police Journal*, 1963–73; Australian Vice-Chancellors' Committee, *Chairman's Report*, 1967–70, 1970; David Myers, *A New University in a Changing World*, Cheshire, 1967; Melbourne University student newspaper *Farrago*, 1967–72; Monash University student newspaper *Lot's Wife*, 1967–72, La Trobe University student newspaper *Rabelais*, 1967–73; Worker-Student Alliance, *Struggle*, 1970–73; Radical Action Movement, *Troll*, 1971–73; Monash University Students Representative Council, *Facts About the Anti-LBJ Demonstration*, November 1966; John Fox, *Free Fergus! Free Brian! Free Barry!*, Melbourne, 1972; Brian Pola, Fergus Robinson, Rodney Taylor and Barry York, *Statement to the Supreme Court*, 7 April 1972.

Some secondary sources used are Barry York, 'Sources of Student Unrest in Australia, with Particular Reference to La Trobe University, 1967–73', M.A. thesis, Sydney University, 1983; Barry York, 'Police, Students, and Dissent: Melbourne 1966–72', *Journal of Australian Studies*, 1984, pp. 58–77; Barry York, 'Sources of Student Dissent', *Vestes: the Australian Universities Review*, vol. 27, no. 1, 1984, pp. 65–75 ; Barry York,

'The Sixties Revisited', *Melbourne Journal of Politics*, no. 16, 1984–5, pp. 102–17; R. Aldridge, 'Campus Revolution Takes a New Turn', *Age*, 22 August 1972, p. 9; Dennis Altman, 'Students in the Electronic Age', *Arena*, no. 21, 1970, pp. 3–18; Coral Bell, 'Oedipal Politics? An Interpretation of Student Insurgency', *Current Affairs Bulletin*, vol. 43, no. 12, 5 May 1969; J. Edwards, 'The Conscription Battle', *Australian Financial Review*, 18 November 1971; H. Frizell, 'Student Power', *Sydney Morning Herald*, 3 December 1970; Michael Hamel-Green, 'The Resisters' in Peter King (ed.), *Australia's Vietnam*, Allen & Unwin, 1983; Malcolm Saunders, 'The Trade Unions in Australia and Opposition to Vietnam and Conscription, 1965–73', *Labour History*, no. 43, pp. 64–82; November 1982; Henry Albinski, *Politics and Foreign Policy in Australia: the Impact of Vietnam and Conscription*, Duke University, 1970; Jim Cairns, *Silence Kills: Events Leading up to the Vietnam Moratorium on May 8*, Melbourne, 1970; R. Forward (ed.), *Conscription in Australia*, Queensland University Press, 1968; Richard Gordon (ed.), *The Australian New Left: Critical Essays and Strategy*, Heinemann, 1970 ; Stewart Harris, *Political Football: The Springbok Tour of Australia, 1971*, Gold Star, 1972; Donald Horne, *Time of Hope: Australia 1966–72*, Angus & Robertson, 1980; Michael Hyde, *It is Right To Rebel*, Free Association Press, 1972; J. M. Main, *Conscription: The Australian Debate, 1901–70*, Cassell, 1970; Dan O'Neill, *The Student Movement: Analysis and Strategy*, Queensland Radicals Conference, 1 September 1968; Theodore Roszak, *The Making of a Counter Culture*, Anchor Books 1969; H. Zinn, *The Politics of History*, Beacon Press, 1970.

Stop the Drop
BRENDAN CARINS

The strategy and class composition of the contemporary Australian peace movement is similar to Britain's C.N.D. movement 1958–65. On the British movement, see Frank Parkin, *Middle Class Radicalism: The Social Bases of the British Campaign for Nuclear Disarmament*, Melbourne University Press, 1968; Richard Taylor and Colin Pritchard, *The Protest Makers*, Pergamon Press, 1981; Frank Myers, 'Dilemmas in the British Peace Movement since World War 2', *Journal of Peace Research*, March 1983, pp. 81–90. See also Nigel Young, 'Why Peace Movements Fail: an Historical and Social Overview', *Social Alternatives*, vol. 4, no. 1, 1984. For an excellent account of social movements and contrasting viewpoint on the importance of moral discourse, see Belinda Probert, 'Social Movements and Socialism' in David McKnight (ed.), *Moving Left*, Pluto Press, 1986, pp. 47–79.

Other works of interest include Dennis Altman, *Rehearsals for Change: Politics and Culture in Australia*, Fontana, 1980; J. Andrews, J. Powels and J. Ward, 'Medicine and Nuclear War', *Peace Dossier*, no. 5; D. Ball, 'Comprehensive Test Ban Treaty: A Role for Australia', paper presented to the Future of Arms Control Conference, Strategic and Defence Studies Centre, A.N.U., August 1985; D. Ball, *A Suitable Piece of Real Estate –*

American Installations in Australia, Hale & Iremonger, 1980; M. Braid and P. Rothfield, 'Women's Actions for Peace', *Arena*, no. 66; Robert Catley and Bruce McFarlane, 'Labor and Economic Crisis – Counter Strategies and Political Realities' in E. L. Wheelwright and Ken Buckley (eds), *Essays in the Political Economy of Australian Capitalism*, vol. 4, A.N.Z. Books, Sydney, 1980; J. Camillieri, 'Neutrality of Non-Alignment', *Arena*, no. 67, 1984; J. Camillieri, 'Labor's Disarmament Policy', *Arena*, no. 64, 1983; J. Camillieri, 'The Australian Peace Movement: The Next Phase', *Flashpoint*, April 1985; J. Camillieri, 'After the A.L.P. Conference, the Anti-War Movement', Arena, no. 68, 1984; Joe Camillieri and Harry Redner, 'Debate on the ANZUS Alliance', Peace Dossier, no. 7, October 1983; R. Eason, 'The Peace Movement, the A.L.P. and MX', *Flashpoint*, April 1985; J. Falk, *Global Fission – The Battle over Nuclear Power*, Oxford University Press, 1982; Jim Falk, 'A Colour-coded Future? Towards an Alternative Australia' in David McKnight (ed.), *Moving Left*, op. cit., pp. 117–35; G. Fry, 'Regional Arms Control in the South Pacific', paper presented to the Future of Arms Control Conference, Strategic and Defence Studies Centre, A.N.U., August 1985; Michael Hamel-Green, 'South Pacific: A Not-So-Nuclear-Free-Zone', *Peace Studies*, October 1985, pp. 6–8; Joel Kovel, *Against the State of Nuclear Terror*, Pan, 1983; R. Leeks and M. Hayes, 'Uranium and Labor', *Australian Left Review*, no. 87, Autumn 1984; Brian Martin, *Uprooting War*, Freedom Press, 1984; David Martin, *Armed Neutrality*, Dove Communications, 1984; T. Matthews, 'Australian Pressure Groups' in H. Mayer and H. Nelson (eds), *Australian Politics: A Third Reader*, Cheshire, 1973; Andrew Milner, *The Road to St Kilda Pier: George Orwell and the Politics of the Australian Left*, Stained Wattle Press, 1984; B. Overy, *How Effective Are Peace Movements?* Harvest House, 1982; A. Barrie Pittock, 'Nuclear War: The Threat to Australia', *Peace Dossier*, no. 4; A. Barrie Pittock, 'Nuclear Winter: Implications for Australia and New Zealand', *Peace Dossier*, no. 2, H. and J. Redner, *Anatomy of the World – The Impact of the Atom on Australia and the World*, Fontana, 1983; G. Scholes, 'The Strategic Outlook: The View from Canberra' in D. Ball (ed.), *The Anzac Connection*, Allen & Unwin, 1985; R. Sharp (ed.), *Apocalypse No – An Australian Guide to the Arms Race and the Peace Movement*, Pluto, 1984; J. Wiseman, 'New Hope or New Problems – Some Reflections on the "Nuclear Election" and the rise of the N.D.P.', *Flashpoint*, April 1985; J. Wiseman, 'Out of the Swamp? Some Thoughts on P.N.D. Strategy', *Flashpoint*, August 1984; interview with Renee Leon, 'Sound Women', *Flashpoint*, vol. 2, no. 1, April 1985; interview with M. Kaldor, *Telos*, no. 52; *Report of the Australian Nuclear Disarmament Conference*, R.M.I.T., August-September 1985.

Fragmented Visions
JOHN MURPHY

For the details of the Franklin River campaign, including the quote from Bob Brown, see Roger Green, *Battle for the Franklin*, Fontana and the

Australian Conservation Foundation, 1981; on the H.E.C., see R. A. Herr and B. W. Davis, 'The Tasmanian Parliament, Accountability and the Hydro-Electric Commission: the Franklin River Controversy', in J. R. Nethercote (ed.), *Parliament and Bureaucracy: Parliamentary Scrutiny of Administration; Prospects and Problems in the 1980s*, Hale & Iremonger with the Australian Institute of Public Administration, 1982, pp. 268–79; Ariel Kay Salleh puts the argument for the Franklin campaign as a radical prototype in organization in 'Whither the Green Machine?', *Australian Society*, vol. 3, no. 5, May 1984, pp. 15–17. The argument about the distinction between resistance and emancipation in social movements is put by Jürgen Habermas in 'New Social Movements', *Telos*, no. 49, Fall 1981, pp. 33–7. Alain Touraine has written variously in anti-nuclear, French regional and other social movements: for the quoted sections here, see his 'Social Movements: Special Area or Central Problem in Sociological Analysis', in *Thesis Eleven*, no. 9, July 1984, pp. 5–15, and also his *The Voice and the Eye: An Analysis of Social Movements*, Cambridge University Press and Editions de la Maison des Sciences de l'Homme, 1981. For a collection of Bahro's speeches and articles on these issues since arriving in the West in 1979, see Rudolph Bahro, *Socialism and Survival*, Heretic Books, 1982. On the Vietnam anti-war movement, see Malcolm J. Saunders, 'The Vietnam Moratorium Movement in Australia: 1969–73', Ph.D thesis, Flinders University of South Australia, 1977 and his 'The Trade Unions in Australia and Opposition to Vietnam and Conscription: 1965–73', *Labour History*, no. 43, November 1982, pp. 64–82. See also the contribution by Barry York in this volume. On the student movement, see Richard Gordon (ed.), *The Australian New Left: Critical Essays and Strategy*, Heinemann, 1970, and Michael Hamel-Green, 'The Resisters: A History of the Anti-conscription Movement, 1964–1972', in Peter King (ed.), *Australia's Vietnam: Australia in the Second Indo-China War*, Allen & Unwin, 1983, pp. 100–28, which is also a useful source for other aspects of the Australian involvement.

More recent Australian work dealing with social movements and single-issue politics includes Drew Dutton (ed.), *Green Politics in Australia*, Angus & Robertson, 1987 and Belinda Probert, 'Social Movements and Socialism', in D. McKnight (ed.), *Moving Left: the future of Socialism in Australia*, Pluto, 1986.

Picture Sources

7 From the *Bulletin*, 5 May 1881; **9** From the Small Picture File, La Trobe Library; **11** From the Bishop collection, University of Melbourne Archives; **16** From the *Bulletin*, 13 March 1880; **39** From the Broken Hill South collection, University of Melbourne Archives; **42** From the CRA photograph collection, University of Melbourne Archives; **43** From the CRA photograph collection, University of Melbourne Archives; **45** From the Commercial Travellers' Association collection, University of Melbourne Archives; **57** Courtesy Frank Strahan; **61** From *Labor Daily*, 1932; **62** From the Rotary Club of Melbourne collection, University of Melbourne Archives; **75** From *The Peaceful Army, A Memorial to the Pioneer Women of Australia, 1788–1938*, Sydney, 1938; **80** From the Communist Party of Australia collection, University of Melbourne Archives; **83** Courtesy David Spratt, Melbourne Media Services; **97** Courtesy David Spratt, Melbourne Media Services; **104** Courtesy David Spratt, Melbourne Media Services; **110** From *Direct Action*, 28 April 1917; **116** From Edward Stokes, *United We Stand, Impressions of Broken Hill 1908–1910*, Sydney, 1983; **119** From the Female Confectioners' Union collection, University of Melbourne Archives; **124** From the R.S. Ross collection, National Library of Australia; **134** From the *Sydney Mail*, 23 July 1892; **144** Courtesy the Communist Party of Australia; **148** By permission of Herald and Weekly Times Ltd; **157** From *Socialist*, 23 April 1909; **159** From *Direct Action*, 1 May 1915; **161** From *Worker's Voice*, 16 November 1934, reproduced by kind permission of Pat Counihan; **166, 167** Courtesy the Communist Party of Australia; **168** Courtesy Barry York; **176** Courtesy Pat Fiske; **178** Courtesy Pat Fiske; **179** Courtesy Alban Johnson; **185** From the Small Picture File, Mitchell Library; **188** Supplied by author; **195** Courtesy David Spratt, Melbourne Media Services; **205** Courtesy David Spratt, Melbourne Media Services; **211** From the *Bulletin*, 1899; **217** From *Direct Action*, 4 December 1915; **218** From the F.J. Riley collection,

National Library of Australia, MS 759/5 (Box 51); **222** From the Communist Party of Australia collection, University of Melbourne Archives; **225** From the International Peace Campaign collection, University of Melbourne Archives; **235** From Miscellaneous Publications, Vietnam file, in the Mitchell Library; **237** Courtesy David Spratt, Melbourne Media Services; **239** Courtesy Barry York; **245** Courtesy David Spratt, Melbourne Media Services; **247** courtesy David Spratt, Melbourne Media Services; **248** From *Peace Dossier*, 8 December 1983; **255** Photograph by Judith Bryce, reproduced by permission from the Tasmanian Wilderness Society, *Blockade*, Hobart 1983; **258** Courtesy David Spratt, Melbourne Media Services; **263** Courtesy David Spratt, Melbourne Media Services.

Index

A.C.T.; *see* Australian Capital Territory
A.C.T.U.; *see* Australian Council of Trade Unions
A.I.D.S.; *see* Acquired Immune Deficiency Syndrome
A.N.Z.U.S. agreement, 123, 243ff
A.P.A.; *see* Australian Peace Alliance
A.S.I.O.; *see* Australian Security Intelligence Organization
Abbott, W.E., 55
Aboriginal culture, homo-eroticism in, 89–90
Aboriginal women and feminist movement, 86
Aborigines, 3, 35, 181–207
  and A.L.P., 130
  and mining companies, 199, 201
  as pastoral and agricultural workers, 182
  'assimilation', 194
  autonomy, early demands for, 189
  children, taken away from families, 186–7, 189–91, 201
  child-care programmes, 204–5
  'community survival', 206
  'concentration' of, 192
  dairying, 186
  deaths in police custody, 197
  discrimination against in country towns, 33–4
  dispersal, 187
  expulsion from reserves, 186–8, 202–3
  farming, 183ff
  foods, traditional, 200
  freedom rides, 194
  health centres, 198, 204
  in gay culture, 98
  insecurity of employment, 183
  lack of capital, 185
  land rights movement, 181–207
  legal services, 197, 198, 203–4
  missions, 182ff
  Murraweena Aboriginal centre, Sydney, 205
  part-, 186
  police and; *see* police
  political movements, 188–207
  population increase, 1890s, 186
  Protection Board, N.S.W., 181ff
  Protectorate, Victoria, 182ff
  rations, 182, 190
  recruitment during goldrushes, 182
  referendum concerning, 1967, 202
  relocation in cities, post-war, 194
  re-occupation of land, 1870s and 1880s, 183
  requests for freehold title, 184
  reserves, 182ff
  resistance to expropriation, 1900–, 187ff
  resistance to white rule, 49, 182
  sacred sites, 199–200
  sedentarization of, 182
  segregation of, 186, 194
  sick and elderly, placed on reserves, 185
  Sydney population growth, 1960s, 203ff
  trade union movement, involvement in, 194
  unemployment among, 147, 186, 190, 196
  vigilante attacks on, 197
  violence against, 201
  wages, 182
  Welfare Board, 193;
  see also Aborigines, Protection Board
  see also under names of particular groups
Aborigines' Progressive Association, 191–2
abortion action groups, 84
abortion law reform, conservative reactions to, 105–6

academics, involvement in anti-conscription movement, 231
accidents at work, 109
Accord, A.L.P.-A.C.T.U., 126, 128, 170–71
Acquired Immune Deficiency Syndrome, 99
Active Service Brigade, Sydney, 1890s, 137–9
Adelaide
  Beef Riot, 1931, 143
  unemployed camps, 1930s, 140
Age, 132
agriculture; *see* farming
Albury, N.S.W., race relations, 34
alcohol, temperance movement's attacks on, 71–3
Alexandra, Vic., 33
Alexandria, N.S.W., 203
Althusser, Louis, 170
Altman, Dennis, 249
Amalgamated Miners Association, 41–2, 128
anarchism
  in unemployed movement, 1890s, 135, 137
  in women's movement, 67, 107
Anderson family, 186, 189
Angledool, N.S.W., 191
anthropologists, and Aborigines, 192–3, 199, 206
anti-Catholicism, 55
  see also religious denominations; relations among
anti-communism, 63, 164–5
anti-conscription campaigns
  in 1916–17, 23–4, 219–21
  in Vietnam period, 64, 230–237
anti-discrimination legislation, Vic., 85, 99
anti-imperialism, 22–3, 169
anti-transportation movement, 152
anti-uranium movement, 108
anti-urbanism, 19–21
anti-Vietnam war campaign, 167, 228–41
  influence on women's movement, 81, 83–4
  women in, 66–7, 234
Anti-War League, 1901, 213
anti-war movements, 208–253
Antill, J.M., 61
Anzac ethos, appropriated by ruling class, 58, 215
Apex Clubs, 35
apprenticeship, 113–14
Aranda tribe, 89
Arbitration Act, attacked by Bruce Government, 59–60
arbitration, 140
  and women, 80, 120
architecture, Georgian, 52
Arena, 166
Armidale, N.S.W.
  local politics, 30–31
  treatment of Chinese on Rocky River goldfields, 33
arms control, regional, 247ff
Arndell, Dr. Thomas, 29
Arnhem Land, Aboriginal people, 90
Arthur, Lt-Governor George, 3
asbestos mining, 44–5
Ashfield, N.S.W., 38
Ashton, Julian, 56
Askin, Robert, 175–7
assignment system, 3
  abolition of, 1839, 53
Australasian Lesbian Movement, 96
Australian Aboriginal Progressive Association, 189
Australian Aborigines' League, 191–2
Australian Agricultural Company, 38, 51–2
Australian Capital Territory Law Reform Society, 95
Australian Council of Trade Unions, 121, 125
  Accord with A.L.P., 126, 128, 170–71
  and Vietnam Moratorium, 261–2
  working women's charter, 85
Australian Democrats, 247, 251
Australian Federation of Women Voters, 79
Australian Freedom League, 216
Australian Labor Party, x, 126–31, 155–6, 169–72
  developmentalism in, 25–6
  in municipal politics, 13, 17–19, 42, 126
  in rural politics, 20–21
  isolationism, inter-war, 221
  Members of Parliament, 125–9, 139
  relationship with anti-war movements, 216–20, 221, 223, 236
  relationship with environmentalist movement, 260–3
  relationship with nuclear disarmament movement, 244–9
  relationship with unemployed movements, 139, 142
  rise of, 56, 126–7
  socialists and, 130, 155
  Socialist Left, 171
  'socialization objective', 156
  split over anti-communism, 1955, 165
  split over conscription during First World War, 59, 158, 220
  support for compulsory military training, 123
  women and, 75–9, 122
  women's auxiliaries, 79
  Women's Organizing Committee, 76, 122
  see also under names of particular Labor governments
Australian Left Review, 168
Australian Legend, The, 90
Australian Magazine, The (A.M.), 93

INDEX

Australian Order of Industry, 137
Australian Peace Alliance, 215–221
Australian Security Intelligence Organization, 65
Australian Social Welfare Union, 107
Australian Socialist League, 154
Australian Socialist Party, 156
Australian Women's Magazine and Domestic Journal, 76
Australian Women's National League, 79
Australian Workers Union, 20, 45, 156, 214, 262
Australian Workman, 126

B.H.P.; *see* Broken Hill Proprietary Co.
'baby-boomers', in anti-Vietnam War campaigns, 229ff, 262
Bahro, Rudolf, 261
Bairnsdale, Vic., 32–4, 37
Balmain, N.S.W., 17, 34–5, 37–8
Balmain, William, 52
'Ban the Bomb' movement, 230
banks
  crashes, 1893, 20
  nationalization, campaigns for, 143
Bankstown, N.S.W., 144
Barrier Truth (Broken Hill), 42–3
base metal industry, links with German capital, 58
Bathurst, N.S.W., convict rebellion, 48
Bayley, Nicholas Paget, 30–31
Bear-Crawford, Annette, 73
'beats', homosexual, 97
beauty contests, protests against, 108
Beccaria, Cesare, 2
Beddek, Francis, 29
Bennett, Harry Scott, 155
Bentham, Jeremy, 2–3
Berndt, Catherine, 90
Betts, Josiah H., 29
Bigge report, 51
birth control, 78, 82
  pill, subsidization of, 85
Bjelke-Petersen, Joh, 22
black power movement, influence on women's movement, 81, 84
Black, George, 126
blacklisting of employees, 46
Blainey, Geoffrey, 3, 45
Blake, Audrey, 171
Blake, Jack, 162, 171
Blamey, Sir Thomas, 59
Bligh, William, 51
Boer War, opposition to, 210–14
bohemian subcultures, 92–3
Bolger, Irene, 121–2
Book of Life, The, 93
booms, long
  first, 116, 132
  post-war, 24–5, 64, 82, 165, 233
bourgeoisie; *see* capitalist class
Bourke, Governor Richard, 53, 113
bowling, as middle-class sport, 34–5
Bowral, N.S.W., 35–6
Braidwood, N.S.W., 55
Brewarrina, N.S.W., 193
Brazill, Mrs, 137
Brisbane
  general strike, 1912, 58
  unemployed agitation, 1890s, 135
Brisbane line, 63
Britain
  capital investment, 51, 132, 174
  in Boer War, 210–14
  in Sudan War, 208–10
  Labor seeks closer ties with, 1910s, 123
  nomadic population of, 1
  relations with Australian colonies, 6, 8, 10–11
Broadsheet (W.E.L.), 69
Brodney, May, 121
Broken Hill, N.S.W., 41–4, 139
Broken Hill Proprietary Co., 42–3, 45–7, 58–9, 63
Brown, Bob, 256
Bruce, S.M., 59–60
Brunswick, Vic., 143
Builders Labourers' Federation, 108
  Green Bans, 169, 173ff, 260–61
building societies, 31, 114
Building Workers' Industrial Union, 240
built environment, necessity of conserving, 180
Bull Ant, 132
Bulletin, 138, 210, 212
Bunch, Charlotte, 102
bureaucratization of union movement, 125
Burke and Wills expedition, 200
Burnt Bridge Aboriginal reserve, N.S.W., 192
Burragorang valley, N.S.W., Aboriginal settlement, 184, 186
Burrendulla station, N.S.W., 30
Burwood, N.S.W., 37
'bush unions', 55
  see also 'new' unions
Bushmen's Contingent, Boer War, 213
bushrangers, 8, 48–9, 55

C.S.R.; *see* Colonial Sugar Refining Co.
Cairns, Qld, Chinese in, 33–4
Cairns, Jim, 169
Calwell, Arthur, 235–6
Camp Ink, 96
Campaign Against Moral Persecution, 96
Campaign Against Repression, 106
Campaign for Nuclear Disarmament, Britain, 246
Campbell, Jack, 181–2, 189, 192, 196–7
Canberra
  feminist group, 83–4
  lesbian movement, 101

Cannon, Michael, 54
capital
  concentration of, 154
  investment in property development, 1960s and 1970s, 174–5
  shortage, 50
capitalist class; *see* landowners, pastoralists, ruling class
Carmichael, Laurie, 171
carnal knowledge, 90
Carson, Rachel, 174
Casement, Roger, 95
Castle Hill, N.S.W., convict uprising, 48, 51–2, 150
Catholic Church, 151
  support for Burragorang Aborigines, 184
  working class in, 35
Catholics, permitted to be married by own clergy, 4
censorship, 3–4, 61, 95, 100, 158, 216
Centennial Park, Sydney, 178
Central Australia, Aborigines of, 89
Central Unemployed Committee, 1930s, 142
Chamberlain, Joseph, 212
chambers of commerce, 56
  representatives harassed by unemployed, 1890s, 136
chambers of manufactures, 56
charities, 28, 34, 56, 136, 138, 139–40
Chernobyl, 180
Chifley government, 111, 127
child endowment, 122
child care
  funding cut under Hawke government, 127
  in Townsville, 1940s, 18
  women's campaigns for, 85
Chillagoe, Qld, 109
China, People's Republic, influence on Australian left, 165
Chinese, 33–4, 136–7
  calls for exclusion of, 153
Chipp, Don, 231
choirs, 36
church attendance of convicts, 3
Church of England, 4, 28, 31, 35, 151
churches, 114, 151
  attacks on homosexuality, 1980s, 99
  dominated by bourgeoisie in nineteenth century, 34–5
  in anti-Vietnam War movement, 232ff
  sponsorship of voluntary associations, 36–7
  targets of unemployed agitation, 1890s, 136
  see also under names of particular denominations
Cigar Makers' Industrial League, N.S.W., 120
cities, 180
  expansion, 1960s and 1970s, 174–5
  lack of 'community', 27–8
  role of local government in service provision, 15
civil liberties movement, 95, 164, 169
civil rights
  Aboriginal demands for, 181ff
  granting of, 1830s, 113
  movement for, 105, 152–3
  women's campaign for, 70ff
Clancy, Pat, 171
Clarence river district, N.S.W., 1930s, 191
Clarke gang, 55
class awareness, first-wave feminists' lack of, 78
class question, gay liberation and, 103
Closing Circle, The, 174
clothing industry, as employer of women, 118–9
coal mining, 38–9, 40–41
co-operative stores, 39, 40, 114
Colac, Vic., 32
Cold War, 63, 164–5
  second, 243
Coleraine, Vic., 32
Collingwood, Vic., 16, 18–19
Collins, Tom; *see* Furphy, Joseph
Collins House Group, 63
  German connections during First World War, 58
Colonial Office, 15
colonial helpmate, myth of, 77
Colonial Sugar Refining Co., 60, 62, 63
Comintern, 158–63
Commoner, Barry, 174
Commonwealth Aircraft Corporation, 63
Commonwealth Employment Service, 147
Commonwealth Public Service, equal pay in, 122
communism, 140, 156–71
  'national roads' to, 165
Communist Party of Australia, 63, 141, 158–71
  and peace movements, 222–4, 230
  attempts to ban, 63–4, 164
  banning, 162–3
  defeat in N.S.W. elections, 1925, 160
  formation, 1920–22, 158
  front organizations, 162, 222
  in local politics in Townsville, 18
  industrial tactics, 1950s, 165
  (Marxist-Leninist), 165–6
  membership, 1945, 163
  relations with reformist movements, 158–63
  ruling class views of, 60
  splits, 1964–84, 165–6
  support for Aborigines, 1930s, 192
  'ultraleft' phase, 168
  unemployed movement and, 1930s, 141–2

united front policy, 158, 162
Communist Review, 168
Community Employment Scheme, 147
community, ideology of, 27ff
community radio, gay liberation programmes, 103, 105, 106
compulsory military training, 123
compulsory unionism, Broken Hill, 42–3
conscientious objection, 232–4
conscription, 64, 123, 167, 230–37, 261–2
referenda, 156–8
see also anti-conscription campaigns
consensus, x
conservation movement; *see* environmentalist movement
conservative political parties
in rural areas, 20–21
women and, 85
see also under names of particular parties and governments
conservative opposition to gay liberation, 105–6
constitutional crises
in colonial period, 7–8
constitutions
colonial, 6–8
federal, 23
consumer capitalism, 64, 148, 169, 173–4
women's movement and, 82
Contagious Diseases Acts, 78
contraception; *see* birth control
contract work, in mines, 44
convict transportation, opposition to; *see* anti-transportation movement
convicts, 3ff, 112–13
disciplining of, 51–2, 151
encouraged to marry, 4–5
homosexual activity among, 87, 90
rebellions by, 48, 51–2, 150
resistance by, 150
secondary punishment of, 5
weakness of kinship ties among, 28
Conway, Kevin, 229
Coogee, N.S.W., 38
Coombs, H. ('Nugget'), 206
Cooper, William, 183
copper mining, 39–40
Coranderrk, Vic., 184–5, 187, 191
Cornish miners, Moonta, 39–40
corruption, inner-suburban Labor councils and, 19
council employees, wages and conditions, 18
Council of Unemployed and Relief Workers, Sydney, 142
counter-cultural groups, 1970s, 27
Country Party, 20–21
diversion of state funds from inner suburbs, 21
country towns
ascendancy of local middle class in, 33–6
discrimination against Chinese, Aborigines, 33–4
politics, 30–34
courts, 52
British, in eighteenth century, 1
use of against strikers, 1890s, 55, 118
Cowra, N.S.W., 194
Cox, G.H., 30–31
Cox, William, 29
craft unions, 113–15, 154
credit squeeze, 1961, 63
credit unions, 46–7
crime, 1–2
Crimes Act, amended by Bruce Government, 59
Criminal Law Amendment Act (Britain), 91
crisis, commercial, 1810–11, 50
cronyism, in Labor Party, x
Croudace, Thomas, 41
Cudgegong N.S.W., 31–2
Cumeragunja, N.S.W., 183–6, 191
strike, 1939, 193
curfews
applied to Aboriginal people, 194
in convict period, 52
Curthoys, Ann, 66–7, 86
Curtin Government, 63, 122, 127, 163
Czechoslovakia, Soviet invasion of, 1968, 169

Dale, George, 128
Dalley, William, 209–10
Daly, Mary, 84–5, 107
damming of rivers, 180, 254ff
Darling, Governor Ralph, 4, 14
Daughters of Bilitis, 96
Dawn, 74, 76, 120
debating societies, 36
decriminalization of homosexual acts, 95–6
Delaney, C.J., 94
Democratic League, 153
Democrats, Australian; *see* Australian Democrats
Denison, Governor William, 6
deportation of 'troublemakers', 59
depressions, 130
1840s, 152
1880s, in South Australia, 41
1890s, 9, 20, 56, 117–8, 132–9, 155, 185–6, 212
1919–20, 59
1930s, 139–46, 190–91
1970s-80s
Aborigines and, 196
adverse effects on environmentalist movement, 169
deregulation, financial, 249
'detente', 243
deterrence, theory of, 246
developmentalism, 24–5, 173ff
environmentalist critiques of, 25

Dialectic of Sex, The, 81
differentials within working class, 112, 116–17
dignity of labour, 117
'discouraged workers', 1970s and 1980s, 147
discrimination
against homosexuals, 91ff
against women, 67ff, 118–22
racial, 33–4
dissenting churches, 28, 213
see also under names of particular denominations
division of labour, by gender, 79–80, 118–22
divorce, women's movement and, 77
doctors
and Aborigines, 204
in Whyalla, 46
'Dog Act', N.S.W., 191, 197
Dole and Relief Workers' Council, 142
Dole Workers' Union, 142
domestic servants, 70, 118–19
Dorrigo, N.S.W., 194
Douglas Credit Party, unemployed and, 142
draft resisters, 232–3, 241
Draft Resisters' Union, 232–3
Dredge, James, 89
drought, 1890s, 133
Dugdale, Harriet, 73
Duncan, George, 96
Dunstan, Albert, 21

Earley-Wilmot, Lieutenant-Governor, 90
early retirement schemes, 1980s, 146
East India Company, 50
Easter rebellion, Dublin, 156
economic conditions, influence on ruling-class strategies, 49
economic crises; *see* depressions
economic subordination of women, 74, 79–80, 118–22
education of women, first-wave feminists and, 78
'effeminacy', 93
Ehrlich, Paul and Ann, 174
Eight Hour Day, 112, 115, 152
elections, 60, 68, 129, 137, 160, 170, 214, 246, 251, 256ff
see also municipal politics; voting rights; and names of particular political parties
Ellis, Havelock, 100
emancipists, 51, 53
establishment of voluntary associations, 28–9
in politics, 5–6
Emerald Hill; *see* South Melbourne
Empire, 153
employers, 'fair' and 'unfair', 117
employers' federations, 56
pro-Boer War activities, 213–14
employment conditions, 113–14, 115–16
employment of women, 79–82, 118–22
Engels, Friedrich, 74
entertainment, commercialization of, 38
entrepreneurs, in early colonial period, 50
Entwistle, Ralph, 48
environment, Aborigines and, 200–201
environmental protection, deficiencies under Hawke govt, 127
environmentalist movement, 25, 169, 173–80
and A.L.P., 127, 130
and trade unions, 179–80
Franklin River campaign, 254ff
Green Bans, 169, 173ff
middle class in, 179
preoccupation with wilderness, 180
equal pay, 76–7, 119, 121–2
for Aborigines, 195–6
in Commonwealth Public Service, 85
equality of women; *see* feminist movements; women
ethnic divisions within working class, 112
Eureka rebellion, 8, 49
Eureka Youth League, 230
Eurocommunism, 165
Evatt, H.V., 164
eviction, 39, 136, 142–5
ex-convicts; *see* emancipists
exclusives, 51, 53
in politics, 5–6
exploration, 50
export industries, problems in 1890s, 117

Fadden government, 164
Fahey, Charles, 116–17
Falleni, Eugenia, 96, 99
'false consciousness', 260
families, 5
limitation of, 78
structure of early Australian, 29
unimportance of, in eighteenth-century Britain, 4
family migration, 5, 29
family relationships, feminists' attitudes to, 78, 83–4
'family wage', 120
farmers
demands for Aboriginal land, 187–8
political activity, 20, 32
farming
Aboriginal, 182ff
governors' assistance to, 5
increasing use of machinery in, 183, 194
rise of, on N.S.W. coast, 183
fascism, 160, 162–3
opposition to, 222–3
'social', 160
support for, 1930s, 60–61
Faust, Beatrice, 68

Federated Clerks Union, 262
Federated Ironworkers Union, 262
federation, 9–12, 56–8
Female Eunuch, The, 68, 81
Female Factories, 4, 28
Female Hotel, Club, Restaurant and Caterers' Employees' Union, 120
Feminine Mystique, The, 81
femininity, radical feminist critiques of, 81
feminist movements, 66ff, 99ff, 118–22, 259–60
  during World Wars, 79, 216–20
  first-wave, 69–78, 100
  influence on homosexual subculture, 91
  labour-oriented, 74, 118–22
  lesbians and, 99ff
  liberal, 82–6
  links with temperance movement, 71–4
  second-wave, 80–86, 167
Fenians, 48
Festival of Light, campaigns against, 105–6
films, images of homosexuality in, 95
finance sector, 51
Firestone, Shulamith, 81
First World War, 58–9, 123
  homosexuals during, 91–3
  opposition to, 215–221
  political impact of, 23
  social tensions arising from, 156
  socialism during, 156
  see also anti-conscription campaigns
first-wave feminists; *see* feminists; first-wave
Fisher government, 122, 127
Fitzgerald, Robert, 29–30
Fitzpatrick, Brian, 164
Fitzroy, Vic., 16
Fleming, 'Chummy', 135
flogging, 52, 53
food laws, first-wave feminists' campaigns to reform, 77
Footscray, Vic., 17
force, state use of in 1890s strikes, 55–6
foreign ownership of Australian businesses, 64
forests, destruction of, 173
France
  nuclear testing in Pacific, 247
  Pacific expansionism of, 9
Franklin River campaign, 1982–3, 254ff
Fraser government, 107
free settlers, 113
  establishment of voluntary associations, 28–9
  in politics, 5, 30ff
free speech, 113
freedom rides, 194
Fremantle, W.A., 112
French Revolution, 48
Friedan, Betty, 81
friendly societies, 28, 29, 33, 35–6, 114
Friends of the Soviet Union, 162
fringe dwellers, 33
frontier, homosexuality on, 90
funeral benefits, 114, 127
Furphy, Joseph, 23
fusion of conservative political parties, 1907, 58
Gallagher, Norm, 171
Gallipoli, 58
gambling industry, links with Labor, 19
Game, Sir Philip, 61
Garden, Jock, 160
garden suburbs, 24
Garran, Sir Robert, 58
Garrett, Peter, 251–2
Gay Community News, 106
gay liberation movement, 95–9, 101–3
Gay Teachers and Students Group, 106
gender differences within working class, 112
gender identity and sexual practice, 87ff
General Labourers' Union, 75
General Motors-Holden, wartime production, 63
gentry, colonial, 50
Germany
  invasion of Russia, 163
  Pacific expansionism of, 9
Gibson, Ralph and Dorothy, 171
Gillies, Duncan, 132
Gladstone, W.E., 50
Glassop, Lawson, 92
Glebe, N.S.W., 67
Go Set, 233
Gold Coast, Qld, 17
gold rushes, 8
  and politics, 30
  mateship during, 90
Goldfinch, Sir Philip, 60, 62
Goldstein, Vida, 73, 77, 219–20
Gorton, John, 238
Goulburn, N.S.W., 31
Gove, N.T., 196
government employees, working hours, 115
governor-general, powers of, 10, 64
governors, powers of, 3ff, 14, 48, 53, 61
Green Bans, 25, 169, 173ff, 260–61
Green Party, West German, 170–71, 260
Greer, Germaine, 68, 81, 101
Grey, Earl, 15
Griffith, Samuel, 9
Grimshaw, Pat, 29
Grip, 212
Guevara, Che, 169
Gumbangerri people, N.S.W., 206
Gurindji people, Northern Territory, 181, 196, 203–4
Gyn/Ecology, 107

Hall, E.S., 150–51
Hall, Radclyffe, 100
Hamer government, Vic., 85

Hancock, Captain, 39–40
hanging as punishment, 1
Hardy, Henry, 191
Harford, Lesbia, 121
Hawke government, 65, 123, 127–8, 170–71, 246–51
Hawkesbury and District Benevolent Society, 29
Hayden, Bill, 249
hegemony, state, 2ff
helpmate, colonial, myth of, 77
Herberton, Qld, 33
Higgins, Justice H.B., 120
higher education, women's moves to enter, 70
Hill, Arthur, 151
hire purchase, 64
  effects of debt in company towns, 44, 46
History of Labour and Capital, 117
Hobart women's liberation movement, 101
Hobsbawm, Eric, 158
Holman, W.A., 213
Holt, Harold, 230
home ownership, 24
homosexual clubs, 1950s, 9
homosexuality, 87ff
  homo-eroticism and, 88ff
  in literature, 92, 95
homosexuals, police harassment of, 91–5
hops, Aboriginal pioneering of, 185
Hordern family, 51
hospitals, 34, 37–8, 186
hotels, 19
  as homosexual meeting places, 97
  as masculine domain, 73
  segregation of Aborigines, 186
hours of work; *see* working hours
housing
  in mining towns, 39, 40
  need for, in Sydney, 1970s, 175
  public, 127, 177
  see also eviction
Hughes, Billy, 17, 59, 156, 220
hulks, as prisons, 3
Hunter, Governor John, 52
Hunter Valley, N.S.W., 32
Hunters Hill, N.S.W., 175–6
Hutton, Major-General E.T.H., 56
Hydro-Electric Commission, Tasmania; *see* Tasmania, Hydro-Electric Commission

immigrant women
  no gains from feminist movement, 86
  wages and conditions, 112
immigrants, 82
  in Whyalla, 46
  in Wittenoom, 44–5
  unemployment among, 147
  see also free settlers
immigration laws, 59
  campaigns for restriction, 133, 152–3
  see also White Australia policy
Imperial Chemical Industries, 63
Indonesian independence movement, trade unions' support for, 123
industrial capitalism, rise of, in Britain, 112
industrial suburbs, politics in, 16–19
industrial unions; *see* 'new' unions
Industrial Workers of the World, 23, 58, 156, 170, 215–16, 219
industrialization
  after First World War, 59
  after Second World War, 174–5
  effects on women's lives, 70
informers, 3
initiation rites, Aboriginal, homo-eroticism in, 89
insecurity of employment, 116, 118
insurance, friendly societies', 114
intelligentsia, gay movement and, 96
inter-colonial trades union congresses, 115
International Peace Campaign, 221, 224
International Women's Day, 102
International Year of the Child, 106
internationalism
  in anti-war movements, 224, 226
  in labour movement, 23–4, 123
invalid pensions, 127
inversion, theories of sexual, 88
Irish , 52, 55, 150–51, 156, 213
Iron Knob mines, 45
Italian immigrants, as asbestos miners, 44
itinerant workers, 43
jails; *see* prisons

Japan, 63, 174, 225
  capital investment, 174
Jennings, A.V., 176–7
job protection, 75
John, Cecilia, 218–19
Johnson, L.B., 229–30, 236
Johnston, William, 150
Joti-jota people, 184
judicial process; *see* courts

Kelly's Bush, Sydney, N.S.W., 175–6
Kerr, Sir John, 64
Khrushchev, Nikita, 165
Kimberleys, W.A., Aboriginal people, 89
Kings Cross, N.S.W., 95, 97
Kinsey, Alfred, 94
kinship
  importance of, in traditional societies, 27–8
  migration and, 29
Kirk, Marie, 74
Kisch, Egon, 222–3
Korea, 124
Kriegler, Roy, 46
Ky, Air Vice-Marshal, 236
Kyabram movement, 21

La Perouse, N.S.W., 203
Labor Call, 121
Labor Party; *see* Australian Labor Party
labour colonies, Victoria; *see* Victoria, labour colonies
labour discipline, x, 3
  changing techniques from 1850s, 53–4
  tightening during and after First World War, 58–9
labour exchange, Active Service Brigade, 137
labour history, 112
labour movement, x, 109–131, 154–6, 161–2
  activists' relationship with A.L.P., 127, 130, 155–8
  attacks on by Bruce government, 59
  attempts to regulate labour market, 152
  nationalism and, 123–4
  reaction to First World War, 215–6, 219–20
  radicals' teetotalism, 19
  relationship with single-issue movements, 260–63
  unemployed and, 133, 139, 140, 142–3
  see also Australian Labor Party; Communist Party of Australia; trade unions
labour process
  introduction of 'scientific management', 58–9
  reorganization of, 1890s, 118
labourism, 155ff
Lake Pedder, 256
Lambing Flat, anti-Chinese riots, 53–4
Lambton colliery, N.S.W., 41
land
  aboriginal, 181ff
  associations, 17
  boom, 1880s, 17, 120
  boom, 1960s and 1970s, 174
  control of by legislatures from 1852, 14
  offered to married convicts, 5
  ownership, 39–41, 50
  policy, 8
  soldier settlement, 187
  unemployed demand for, 1840s, 152
Land Convention, 1857–60, 153–4
landowners
  in Methodist Church, 29
  in rural politics, 21
  in town government, 15–17
Lane, William, 49, 153, 171
Lang, J.T., 60–61, 143, 160, 181
Lange government, New Zealand, 247, 249
larrikins, 19
law, ix, 1–11
Lawson, Henry, 23
Lawson, Louisa, 74, 120
lawyers, role in federation movement, 9–10
Layman, Lenore, 44–5
League of Nations, 221–2
  Union, 224
League of Women Voters, 79
Lee, Jenny, 116–17
legal status of women, 69ff, 85
legal suppression of homosexuality, 94
legislative councils, 6–8, 14, 52–3
Leichhardt, N.S.W., 36
leisure activities, changes in, 36, 146
Lesbian Action Group, Melbourne, 105–6
lesbian feminists, 84, 101–4
Lesbian Newsletter, 106
lesbian separatism, 102–4, 106–7
lesbianism, 96, 98–9, 100–108
Levy, Barbara, 84
Lewis, Essington, 59
Lewis, Sara, 120–22
liberal feminism; *see* feminism, liberal
liberalism
  influence, 1890s, 56
  political expression, 31, 133, 152–3
  rise of from 1840s, 53
  support for Aborigines, 195
Liberal-Country Party governments, 229–41
liberation theology, 234
Liberator, 210
libraries, 114
Libya, 171
Lindsay, Jack, 92
Lingiari, Vincent, 203–4
liquor industry, links with Labor, 19
literary portraits of homosexuality, 92, 95
literary societies, 29, 36
living standards
  during first long boom, 116–17
  during second long boom, 174
  reduction under Accord, 1980s, 126, 249
local councils; *see* municipal politics
localism, 13–26
Lockwood, Rupert, 171
lodges, Masonic, 36
'Lucky Country', image of Australia as, 24
Lyons, Enid, 79
Lyons, J.A., 60
Lyons, Myles Hartle, 30–31

Macarthur, John, 50
Macintyre, Stuart, 51
MacKay, W.J., 59
Mackenzie, Kenneth, 92
Macleay valley, N.S.W.
  Aboriginal agriculture, 186, 192
Macquarie Harbour, 90
Macquarie, Governor Lachlan, 3–4, 51, 53
Magarey, Susan, 83–4
magistrates, pastoralists as, 30
Malaya, 124
Mallee district, Vic., 143
Mann, Tom, 155–6
manufacturing industry

relocation of, post-war, 64
seasonality of employment in, 116
women's employment in, 82
Mardi Gras, Gay, 98
marginal electorates, 129
maritime strike, 1890, 55
marriage
first-wave feminists and, 77–8
official encouragement of, 4–5
marriage laws, campaigns for women's equality under, 70
married women in workforce during post-war period, 82
Marsden, Samuel, 50
martial law, use of in convict period, 52
Martin, James, 31–2
Marxism, 154ff, 260–61
radical feminist critiques of, 81
masculinity, homosexuality and, 91
masculinity, relationship with drinking, 73
mass production, 82
Master Builders Association, 177
Masters and Servants Act, 1828, 54
maternity allowance, 122
maternity leave, 85
mateship, homo-eroticism and, 88, 90
Matthews, Daniel, 184
McAuley, Andrew, 32
McIntyre, A.J. and J.J., 35
McMahon, William, 230, 237, 241
McNamara, Bertha, 75, 111
mechanics' institutes, 31, 37, 42, 114
media
coverage of W.E.L activities, 69
nuclear disarmament movement's need for access to, 249
ownership, concentration of, 127–8
use by environmentalists, 256
Medibank, 127
medical profession; *see* doctors
Mejane, 67
Melbourne
Aboriginal movement, 191
and Metropolitan Board of Works, 37
City Council, 15
Club, 149
Eight Hour movement, 115
feminist movement, 67–8, 84
formation of suburban councils, 15–17
lesbian movement, 96, 103–6
local politics in inner suburbs, 18
National Gay Conference, 102
New Left, 166
Peace and Humanity Society, 212–14
Stock Exchange, 149
trade societies, 113
Trades Hall Council, 115, 121–2, 142, 240
Women's Suffrage Society, 73
Melzer, Jean, 251–2
Members of Parliament, 7–8, 30, 125–7
men
dominance in labour market, 79–80
in anti-Vietnam movement, 67
trade union officials, 121
'men's work', exclusion of women from, 119–20
Menzies, R.G., 63–4, 223, 229, 231
Menzies government, 162, 164, 194
metal trades unions, 171
Methodist Church, 28–9, 35, 39, 151
middle class
achieves voting rights, 1858, 30
A.L.P. reliance on support of, 129
dominance of gay movement, 98
in environmental movement, 179
in federation movement, 10
in First World War, 58
in homosexual subcultures, 91
in local politics, 17
in nuclear disarmament movement, 244
see also liberalism
middle-class women in temperance movement, 73
Mildura, Vic., 194
military bases, United States, 123
military coup, 1808, 51
military forces, 53–6, 123
British withdrawal of, 53
changing class composition of, 55–6
reorganization of, 1850s, 54–6
use of, against strikers, 41, 111, 118, 127
use of, in wars, 208–242
military officers, status of in convict period, 50
militia units, private, 54–5
Mill, John Stuart, 70, 76
Millett, Kate, 81
Miners' Advocate (Newcastle), 42
miners' strikes
1888, 41, 118
1949, 64, 111, 127
Miners' Union, communist influence in, 162
mining towns, 38–44, 214
missionaries, and aborigines, 189–90
Mitchell, Juliet, 81
Mitchell, Thomas, 52
modernism, influence of, on homosexual subcultures, 91
Monash University, 231
money power, Labor attacks on, 60, 153–5, 160
Monitor, 151
Moonta, S.A., 39–40
miners leave for Broken Hill, 41
moral conservatism, 24, 105–6
in rural areas, 21
'moral reform' of convicts, 3–5
moral superiority of women, Victorian ideal of, 76
Moratorium, Vietnam, 236–40, 261–2

Moran, Bill, 99
Moran, Herbert, 96
Moran, Cardinal Patrick, 210
Morrow, Bill, 109–11
'mortgage belts', political importance of, 24
Mosely, Percy and Rachel, 192
motor car, growth of use, 64, 174
Movement Against War and Fascism, 19, 162, 222–3
Ms (U.S.A.), 68
Mudgee, N.S.W., 30–31
Mungo, Lake, N.S.W., 199
Municipal Corporations Acts, 15
municipal politics, 13–19, 30ff
  and anti-war movements, 209–10, 213–14
  landowners in, 29–31
  unemployed and, 143
Murraweena Aboriginal centre, N.S.W., 204–5
music, state provision of, 28
musical clubs, 29
Musquito, 203
Mussen, Gerald, 43
Mutual Protection Association, 152
Myers, Frank, 246

Nabalco, 196
Nambutji tribe, 89
National Council of Women, 79
National Liberation Front, Vietnam, 231, 242
National Organization for Women (U.S.), 80
National Service Act, 230–41
National Trust, 175, 178
nationalism, 22–4, 123–4
  in anti-war movements, 210, 213
Nationalist Party, 21
nationalization, 143
Nazi-Soviet Non-Aggression Pact, 1939, 162
Nemaluk, 203
New Australia Movement, 155
New Guard, 61–2
New Left, 67, 166, 169, 235–6
  association with Gay Liberation, 96
New South Wales
  aboriginal people, 181ff
  aboriginal reserves, creation of, 184–5
  agriculture, rise of, 183
  anti-Boer War campaign, 212–14
  anti-Sudan campaign, 208–10
  Builders Labourers Federation, Green Bans, 169, 173ff
  Constitution Committee, 153
  constitutional development, 6, 14, 152
  Crimes Act amendments, 1955, 94
  demolition laws tightened, 1970s, 178
  female factories, 4
  government resistance to Aboriginal land claims, 184
  Green Bans 169, 173ff
  government suppression of homosexuality, 90, 94
  Housing Commission, 178
  in convict period, 50–53
  Labor Party permits Communist affiliation 1923, 160
  Land Rights Act, 1981, 196
  Lands Department, pressure for expropriation of aborigines, 188
  north coast, rise of agriculture, 183
  parliamentary representation of labour, 126
  participation in Sudan War, 1885, 208–10
  Peace Society, 221
  People for Nuclear Disarmament, 245
  southern districts, rise of agriculture, 183
  strength of Labor in rural areas, 20
  trade union legislation, 115
  Trades and Labour Council; *see* Sydney Trades and Labour Council
  Typographical Association, 120
  unemployment relief, 1930s, 140
    see also under names of specific localities and individuals
'new' unions, 11, 78, 154
New Zealand, opposition to nuclear vessels, 247, 249
Newcastle, N.S.W., 26, 38–9, 40–41, 144, 209–10
Newtown, N.S.W., 34–6, 144, 203
Nicholls, Elizabeth, 74
Nicholson, Joyce, 67–8, 86
Nixon, Richard, 241
nomadic rural workers, 8
nomadic population, British, 1
non-union labour, 117–18, 177
Norfolk Island, 5, 48
North-West Cape, U.S. military base, 252–3
Northern Territory
  conservatism in, 22
  land rights movement, 181, 195–6, 203–4
  mining, post-war, 44–5
nuclear disarmament movement, 228, 243–53, 254–5
Nuclear Disarmament Party, 251–3
nuclear vessels, 123, 247
nurses' strike, Victoria, 1986, 85–6, 108, 121–2

O'Connell, Geoff, 13
O'Shea, Clarrie, 64
obscenity laws, 92
old age pensions, 56, 127
Old Guard, 60–61
One Big Union, 156
One Big Union of the Unemployed, 142
Orangemen, in military forces, 55

organized crime, camp sub-culture and, 97
Otto, Di, 107
Outrage, 106
outwork, 120
overcrowding
in factories, 120
in prisons, 3
overseas borrowing, decline of, 1890s, 9
overtime, compulsory, 46

Pacific nuclear-free zone, 243ff
pacifism, 79, 215ff, 224
Paddington, N.S.W., 17
Palm Island, strike, 1956, 195
Palmer, Helen, 166
Pangerang people, 184
Pankhurst, Adela, 216–19
panopticon, 2
Paraguay, 155
Paris insurrections, 1968, 169
Parkes, Henry, 55, 151, 153, 210
parliamentary representation of labour, 126–31
see also Australian Labor Party
Parramatta, N.S.W., 29
part-time work, growth of from 1970s, 147
pastoral industry, 51
difficulties in 1890s, 117
fencing, and supersession of shepherds, 183
technological change, 1930s, 191
use of Aboriginal labour, 182–3, 191, 195
pastoralists
alliance with farmers, 20–21
as magistrates, 30–31
in politics, 6–8, 20, 30–32, 152–3
relations with townspeople, 32
role in 1890s strikes, 55
Pastoralists' Review, 20
Pastoralists' Union, 55
paternalism in mining towns, 39
Patterson, J.B., 134–5
patriarchy, radical feminist critiques of, 81
Pax Christi, 234
Peace and Nuclear Disarmament Action, 252
Peace Research Institute, 249
peace societies, 215–6
Pearl Harbour, 63
penal powers struggle, 64
pensions, 127
see also under names of specific kinds of pensions
Pentagon Papers, 230
People, 95
People for Nuclear Disarmament, 243ff
People's Advocate, 153
People's Reform League, 21
Perth, unemployed camps 1930s, 140
perversion, theories of sexual, 88
Petersen, George, 128–9
Petrov affair, 164
philharmonic societies, 33
Phillip, Governor Arthur, 3, 87, 99
picketing, legalized, 115
pig-iron dispute, Port Kembla, 63, 224
Pilbara strike, Aboriginal, 1946, 195
pilfering, 1
pioneer woman, myth of the, 71
Piper, Richard, 42
Pitjentara people, 89
plantation economy, 50
poaching, 1
police, 2–3, 144–5,
and Aborigines, 187–8, 191–2, 194, 203
and anti-Vietnam protestors, 238
attacks on homosexuals and lesbians, 91–5, 106
attempts to change image, 1890s, 56
defending property rights, 53
establishment of, 52
harassment of unemployed, 62, 135, 138, 141, 143
militarization of, post-war, 65
in 1890s strikes, 55, 118
state, in convict period, 3
strength of in nineteenth-century Victoria, 8
violence against strikers, 59
Political Association, 153
political clubs, nineteenth-century, 29
political parties, 17–22
fusion of anti-Labor, 1907, 58
left-wing, and homosexual movement, 105
slowness to emerge in nineteenth century, 7–8
women's role in, 79
pollution, of Yarra in 1850s, 16
Population Bomb, 174
population growth, controlled by marriage, 4
populism
conservative parties and, 1970s and 1980s, 22
labour movement and, 20, 153–5, 160
Port Arthur, Tas., 5, 90
Port Melbourne, Vic., 17
poverty, 133–148
Prahran, Vic., 16
Premiers' Plan, 142
Presbyterian Church, 151
and homosexuality, 95
press
and Boer War, 212–13
and First World War, 219
and Sudan War, 209–10
and homosexuality, 93–8
and inter-war peace movement, 223
radical, 151, 154–5
Price, Colonel Tom, 53
prisons, 2–3

homosexual activity in, 90
'privileges', trade, 113
Privy Council, Britain, appeals to, 11
professionals
in anti-Vietnam movement, 237
in gay movement, 98
in women's movement, 85
in Whyalla, 46
professions, women's moves to enter, 70, 78
progress associations, 17
progressivism, 24
labour movement and, 117
see also developmentalism
property, defence of, as factor in colonial politics, 15
property developers, Sydney, 1960s and 1970s, 175
property owners; *see* landowners
prostitutes, 78
prostitution, male, 94
protective legislation, 75
Protestant ascendancy, in convict period, 50
Protestant evangelicals, in women's movement, 71–3
provocateurs, use against homosexuals, 95
psychiatrists, treatment of homosexuals, 96
psychoanalysis, influence on homosexual subcultures, 91
psychological theories of homosexuality, 93–4
public assets, sale of, 128
public housing, 127
public order legislation, during convict period, 52
public service, women in, 85
public utilities, rising cost and centralization, 37
public works, as unemployment relief, 133–5, 138, 145, 152
Puckapunyal army camp, Vic., 95
punctuality, enforcement of, 3
punishment of homosexuals, 87, 90–91

Quakers, 216, 234–5
Queensland
first Labor government in world, 126
Labor Party, 126
People for Nuclear Disarmament, 246
railways, labourers on, 109
rise of populist conservatism in 1970s and 1980s, 22
trade union legislation, 115
unemployed movement, 1930s, 142–3
unemployment relief, 139, 141

race relations
in country towns, 33–4
racial differences within working class, 112
radical feminists, 81–4
radical nationalists, 22–24
responses to federation, 10
radicalism, 49, 150ff
in anti-Sudan campaign, 209
see also unemployed movements
Rae, Arthur, 49
rail passes, for unemployed, 1890s, 138
railway leagues, 17
rainfall, deficiency of Australia's, 173
rank and file unionists, relations with officials, 125
rape, 90
crisis centres, 84
Rarotonga treaty, 246–8
Raymond, Melanie, 121
Reagan, Ronald, 243, 246
recession, 1970s, impact on women's movement, 85
Redfern, N.S.W., 203ff
referenda
Aboriginal, 1967, 195, 202
conscription; *see* anti-conscription campaigns, conscription
Refractory Girl, 86
regulation of alcohol use, temperance campaigns for, 73
Relief and Sustenance Workers Union, Western Australia, 142
relief works; *see* public works
religious denominations, relations among, 37
religious groups in feminist movement, 79
relocation of industry, post-war, 64
rent allowances for unemployed, 1930s, 145
repudiation of interest payments, 60
reserves, Aboriginal; *see* Aborigines, reserves
Reservoir, Vic., 144
resident action groups, 175
respectability, x
responsible government, 53
lack of under federal constitution, 10
retrenchments, 1970s and 1980s, 146
revolutionary socialists 156ff
revolutions, 48, 58, 130, 158
Rhodes, Cecil, 212
Rich, Adrienne, 84–5
Richmond river district, N.S.W., expropriation of Aborigines, 1930s, 191
Richmond, Vic., 13, 16, 142, 145
rifle technology, nineteenth-century improvements in, 55
'rights of Englishmen', 14
Riley, Elizabeth, 92
Riley, Fred, 216
Rischbieth, Bessie, 79
Roberts, Tom, 56
Roberts, Robert ('Sugar'), 19
Rocks, The, N.S.W., 178
Roheim, Geza, 89
romanticism, nineteenth-century, 19–20
Rotary Clubs, 35
Rothbury lock-out, 1929, 59

Royal Australian Nursing Federation, 121–22
Royal Melbourne Hospital, 122
Rugby Union, as middle-class sport, 34
ruling class, 48ff
ascendancy threatened, 1890s, 49
autonomy in convict period, 50
challenged by liberal bourgeoisie from 1840s, 53
changes in, post-war, 64
dominance in churches, 33–5
dominance of state in convict period, 51–3
Pacific expansionism. 23
pro-imperial sentiments, 22–3
rum trade, 50
rural areas, weakness of environmentalist movement in, 25
rural mythology, 19–22
rural politics, 20–22
rural whites, reaction against Aboriginal reform, 1970s, 197
ruralism, 'new', 24–5
Russian Revolution, 58, 158

sailing, as middle-class sport, 34
Salt Pan Creek, Sydney, N.S.W., 181
Salvage Corps, of Melbourne unemployed, 136
Save Our Sons, 234, 261
schools, 40
discrimination against Chinese in, 34
exclusion of Aboriginal children, 193
segregation of Aborigines, 186
scientific management, 58–9
Scott, Rose, 73
Scullin government, 127
Seamen's Union, 240, 263
seasonal employment, 116, 132–3, 183, 194
Second International, 123
Second World War, 18, 63, 123, 174, 193–4
communists during, 162–3
divides feminist movement, 79
homosexuals during, 92–4
secondary punishment of convicts, 5
sectionalism in trade union movement, 113ff
segregation of Aborigines; *see* Aborigines, segregation
Selection Acts, Victoria, 8
self-government of colonies, 6, 14–15, 53, 153
Senate, federal, 10
Sendy, John, 168
separate spheres, ideology of, 76
separatism, in women's movement, 84–5
service industries, women's employment in, 82
Seven Poor Men of Sydney, 92
severance pay, 1980s, 146
'sex-role conditioning', 68
sexual intercourse, role of in Arnhem Land Aboriginal culture, 90
sexual liberation, gay movement and, 98
Sexual Politics, 811
sexual rights
movement, 100
within marriage, 78
Sharkey, Lance, 164
Sheahan, William, 94
shearers, 111, 117, 139
Shearers' Union, Amalgamated, 110
Shepherd family, 186
Shepparton, Vic., 34
sickness benefits, 127
Silent Spring, 174
six o'clock closing, 19
skill hierarchies within working class 112–14
disruption in Whyalla, 46
skilled workers
early trade societies of, 113, 152
effects of 1890s depression on, 133–4
small businessmen in politics, 17
smuggling, 1
Social Democratic Federation, 75
social mobility
decline of, after 1821, 51
of skilled workers in nineteenth century, 113
social scientists and homosexuality, 88
Social Security, Department of, 147
socialism, 154ff
A.L.P. and, 130
British, women's rights and, 74
in anti-war campaigns, 212–3, 238–40
in mining towns, 41–3
in homosexual movement, 105–8
international influences on, 154ff
nationalism and, 23–4
reaction to First World War, 215–6
relationship with single-issue movements, 260–64
second-wave feminism and, 81
see also under titles of particular socialist organizations
socialist feminists, 74–6, 82–6
divisions among, 75–6
Socialist Forum, 166
Socialist Labor Party, 156
Socialist Labour League, 169
Socialist Party of Australia, 166, 168
Socialist Workers' Party, 108, 169, 252
Society for the Protection of Life and Property, 54
Society of Emigrant Mechanics, 152
soldier settlement, 187
South Africa, Boer War, 210–14
South Australia
constitutional development, 14
decriminalization of homosexual acts, 96
formation of Labor Party, 126

government provision of services in Whyalla, 46
League of Women Voters, 79
People for Nuclear Disarmament, 245
Public Safety Preservations Act, 143
trade union legislation, 115
unemployed agitation, 135, 143
unemployment relief, 1930s, 140
weakness of anti-war movement, 1902, 214
women's vote in, 78
South Australian Housing Trust, 46
south coast, N.S.W., Aborigines, 183
South Melbourne, Vic., 144
South Pacific forums, 247ff
Soviet Union
arms build-up, 243
influence on Australian left, 158–65
Spanish Civil War, 224
Spartacist League, 169
Spence, Catherine, 70
sporting clubs, 29
class composition of, 34–5
multiplication of, 36
role in local politics, 18
sports
Chinese and Aborigines in, 33
squatters; *see* pastoralists
squatting, in mining towns, 40
stagflation, 1970s, 63
Stalin, Josef, 160–64
Staples, Jim, 166
Star Wars, 246
state
aid to religion, 31
development of, in colonial period, 2ff
economic regulation, 127, 139
encouragement of marriage, 4–5
expansion of role from 1890s, 56
funding, women's movement and, 84
repression, 51–2, 58, 138, 215–220
ruling class's dependence on, 53
suppression of homosexuality, 87, 90–91, 93–5
transport, 53
see also constitutional development courts; police
Stead, Christina, 92
Stein, Gertrude, 100
stonemasons, eight hour day campaign, 115
Storer, Richard, 92
Street, Jessie, 79
Streeton, Arthur, 56
strikes
Aboriginal, 195
Broken Hill miners, 1892, 139
coal, 1888, 41, 118
compositors, 1880, 120
denunciation of, by communists, 1941–5, 163
general strike, Brisbane, 1912, 58
Great, 1890s, 55–6, 117–18, 155
Great, N.S.W., 1917, 58, 158
miners, 1949, 64, 111, 127, 165
nurses, 1986, 85–6, 108, 121–2
shearers, 1894, 139
sustenance, 1930s, 142–5
transport, general, 118
wharf, Fremantle, 1919, 112
Student Labor Federation, 231
student radicalism, 1960s and 1970s, 167–8, 262
sub-cultures, homosexual, 88, 91–8
Subjection of Women, The, 70
suburbanism, 24
Sudan War, campaign against, 208–10
suffrage; *see* voting rights
sugar workers, in Townsville politics, 18
Summerfield, Rose, 75
Sunday Schools, 39
superannuation, women's access to, 85
Supreme Court, Sydney, 52
Surry Hills, N.S.W., 136
surveillance of convicts, 3
sustenance, 1930s 140–41, 145–6
strikes, 142–5
swamp drainage, as unemployment relief, 138
swinging voters, 129
Sydney
Aboriginal population, 203ff
anti-war movement, 1885, 209
and Parramatta Loyal Associated Corps, 52
Botanical Gardens, 179
City Council, 15
feminist movements, 66–7, 84
first trade societies, 113
gay movement, 96–8
Gay Mardi Gras, 98
Hiroshima Day, 230
homosexuals in, 91
hospitals, 37–8
lesbian movement, 107
local politics in inner suburbs, 18
New Left, 166
Opera House, 179
redevelopment, 1960s and 1970s, 175–7
Supreme Court, 52
Trades and Labour Council, 115, 120, 126, 178, 214, 261–2
unemployed movement, 135–9, 142
United Labourers Society, 36
Volunteers, 54
Women's Suffrage League, 73
Sydney Morning Herald, 95, 209, 221
syndicalism, 140, 156

Tamworth, N.S.W., 20
tariffs, 133
intercolonial, economic effects of, 9
Victorian, political conflicts over, 8

Tasmania, 14
constitutional development, 14
female factories, 4
formation of Labor Party, 126
Hydro-Electric Commission, 180, 256ff
sex-related crime in convict period, 90
trade union legislation, 115
Tasmanian Wilderness Society, 257
Taungerong people, Vic., 184
Tebbutt, Thomas, 29
technological change
post-war, 173–4
unemployment and, 1890s, 134
temperance movement, women's movement and, 71–4, 76
temperance organizations, 114
tennis, as middle-class sport, 34
Terry, S.H., 30–31, 50
Tet offensive, 242
Thomas, William, 184
Tibooburra, N.S.W., 191–193
Tighes Hill, Newcastle, N.S.W., 144
timber industry, 180, 183
Timor, East, 127
Tocsin, 10, 128
Toennies, Ferdinand, 27–8
Tolpuddle martyrs, 112
Tonkin Gulf incident, 230
Touraine, Alain, 262–3
Townsville, Qld, 17–18
trade policy, dissension over, 53–4
trade societies, 113–14
trade unions, 114ff, 179
arise out of friendly societies, 28
'bogus', 58–9
communist tactics in, 165
conferences, intercolonial, 115
coverage, 117
discrimination against women, 118–122
dues, systems of payment, 125
formation, 114–15
growth of, 29
in anti-war movements, 210–24, 240
in mining areas, 40–43
lack of support for environmentalism, 179
legislation, 115
membership, 126, 139
officials, 121, 125
limited tenure in Builders Labourers Federation, 176
pastoral, Aboriginal involvement in, 194
relations with unemployed, 139–47
relations with single-issue movements, 261–3
rise in women's participation from 1970s, 85
socialists in, 155ff
see also socialism
support for Indonesian independence, 123–4
support of White Australia policy, 123
weakness in Whyalla, 46
weakness in Wittenoom, 44–5
women activists in, 75–6
Trades and Labour Council, Sydney; *see* Sydney Trades and Labour Council
Trades Hall Council, Melbourne; *see* Melbourne Trades Hall Council
training, shortage of opportunities for women, 80
transport strike, 118
transport unions, communist influence in, 162
transsexuals, 94
transvestitism, 91–4
Trotskyism, 142, 168–9, 223
Trozer, Horace, 55–6
truancy, state policing of, 56
Truth, 93
Turner, Ian, 166
Typographical Association, N.S.W., 120

under-employment, 49, 116
unemployed, 49, 112, 132–49
bashing of in 1930s, 62
factionalism among, 142–3
in 1980s, 107
recruited for Boer War, 214
women, neglect of, 133, 140, 147
Unemployed and Relief Workers' Union, 142
Unemployed Workers' Movement, 142–5, 162
unemployment, 116, 132–49
benefits, 127, 147
duration of, 133
during 1890s, 56, 118
during 1980s, 146
rates, 139, 147
relief, 1930s, 62, 139, 140ff
not available to Aborigines, 190
seasonal, 132–3
United Association of Women, 79
United Australia Party, 60
united front policy, in Communist Party, 158–60
United States
as destination for transportation, 3
capital investment, post-war, 64, 174
early comparisons with Australia, 173
feminist movement, influence in Australia, 71–3, 80–81
influence of liberation movements from, 1970s, 6, 7
intervention in Vietnam War, 229–41
I.W.W., influence in Australia, 156
military bases in Australia, 123, 243ff, 254–5
nuclear build-up, 243
revolution, 1770, 3
unskilled workers

effects of 1890s depression on, 133–4
exclusion from trades, 113
formation of 'new' unions, 117–8
upper houses of parliament; *see* legislative councils; Senate
uranium mining, 127, 180, 251, 254
urban planning
as safeguard against rebellion, 52
lack of, 1970s, 174–5
urban areas; *see* cities

vagrancy laws, 143
vagrants, Britain, 1
Vallentine, Jo, 247, 251–2
Van Diemen's Land; *see* Tasmania
Vice-Chancellors' Committee, 236
Victoria
Aboriginal policy, 182ff
Aboriginal Protectorate, 182ff
anti-discrimination legislation, 85
constitutional development, 14
formation of Labor Party, 126
Hamer government, 85
League of Women Voters, 79
Legislative Council, 54
legislative council, 6–8
nurses' strike, 1986, 85–6, 108, 121–2
People for Nuclear Disarmament, 245
police, 8
Selection Acts, 8
trade union legislation, 115
unemployed agitation, 132–7, 142–5
see also under names of specific localities
Victorian Socialist Party, 17, 216
Victorian Trades Hall Council; *see* Melbourne Trades Hall Council
Victorian Women's Suffrage Society; *see* Women's Suffrage Society
Vietnam Moratorium; *see* Moratorium, Vietnam
Vietnam War, 124, 228–41
village settlement schemes, 1890s, 138
Vindication of the Rights of Women, 70
Vivien, Renee, 100
'voluntary motherhood', 78
voluntary organizations, 28ff, 114
voting rights
Aboriginal, 202
manhood suffrage, 30
restrictions on, 54
women's campaign for, 70, 76–8

W.C.T.U.; *see* Woman's Christian Temperance Union
W.E.L.; *see* Women's Electoral Lobby
wage labour, rise of, 113
wages
concessions, post-war, 64
cut in 1930s, 62, 127
fall in late nineteenth century, 41, 118, 154–5
trade societies' regulation of, 114
women's, 118
see also equal pay
Wallis, Alf, 121
Wanaaring, N.S.W., 193
Wanggumara people, N.S.W., 193
War Precautions Act, 58, 156
Ward, Eddie, 63
Ward, Russel, 90
Warracknabeal, Vic., 33
wars; *see* under names of particular wars
waterfront workers, communist influence among, 162
Waterside Workers' Federation, 240
Wave Hill, N.T., 196, 203–4
wealth
accumulation of, in convict period, 50
distribution of, 128, 154
Wee Waa, N.S.W., 194
welfare capitalism, mining companies and, 43, 45
welfare issues, women's movement and, 83–5
welfare state, growth of, 38, 64, 127
Well of Loneliness, The, 100
Wentworth, N.S.W., 137
Wentworth, D'Arcy, 52
Wesleyan Church; *see* Methodist Church
West Indies, as destination for convict transportation, 3
West, D.J., 95
Western Australia
feminist movement, 79
formation of Labor Party, 126
mining in north, post-war, 44–5
People for Nuclear Disarmament, 246
Relief and Sustenance Workers' Union, 142
trade union legislation, 115
unemployment relief, 1930s, 140
weakness of anti-war movement, 1902, 214
women gain vote in, 78
western N.S.W., Aboriginal people
expropriation, 1930s, 191
resistance to white settlement, 182
wharf labourers, 17–18
White Ribbon Signal, 77
White Australia policy, 35, 186
trade union support for, 123
Whitehouse, Mary, 105
Whitford, Lilian, 121
Whitlam, E.G., 85, 165, 170, 236, 241
influence on character of A.L.P., 170
Whitlam government, 101, 122, 127, 170
dismissal of, 12, 64, 249
moderate feminists and, 85
Whyalla, S.A., 45–7
widows
friendly societies' relief of, 114
pensions, 127

Wild, R.A., 35–6
wilderness, conservation of, 180, 256
Willard, Frances, 71
Windeyer, Lady, 73
Windsor, N.S.W., 28–9, 150
Wittenoom, W.A., 44–5
Wobblies; *see* Industrial Workers of the World
Wodonga, Vic., 32, 37
  race relations, 34
Woiwurrung people, Vic., 184
Wolfenden report (Britain), 95
Wollongong, N.S.W., 26
Wollstonecraft, Mary, 69–70
Woman Voter, 216, 219
Woman's Christian Temperance Union, 71–2, 77
Woman's Estate, 81
Woman's Sphere, 73, 76
women, 66ff
  A.L.P. and, 130
  Aboriginal, homo-eroticism among, 89
  as trade union officials, 121
  attempts to discipline, 4
  confinement to home, 76
  convict, 28
  exclusion from public life, 70
  in anti-war campaigns, 214, 216–23, 234, 244
  in unemployed movement, 1890s, 136
  middle-class, in first-wave feminist movement, 70ff
  professional, in W.E.L., 68
  right to work in building industry, 176
  socialism and, 74–6
  unemployed; *see* unemployed women
  work, 118–122
  working-class, movement into factories, 70
  see also under lesbianism and names of specific organizations
women's refuges, 84
Women's Electoral Lobby, 68–9, 83, 85–6, 101
Women's International League for Peace and Freedom, 222
Women's Liberation Movement, 66–7, 101
women's organizations, rise of, 35
Women's Organizing Committee (A.L.P), 76
Women's Peace Army, 215–21
Women's Political Association, 77, 216
Women's Weekly, 164
Women's Service Guilds, 79
Women's Suffrage League, 73
Women's Suffrage Society, Melbourne, 73
women's vote, Labor attempts to mobilize, 122
Wood, G.A., 210, 213–4
wool trade with Japan, 1930s, 62
Woolloomooloo, N.S.W., 92, 178
work gangs, convict, 3
Worker (Sydney), 120
workers' compensation, 46, 109–10
working class
  alliance with liberals from 1850s, 152
  communities, weakening of in post-war period, 146
  cultural traditions, in Labor politics, 19
  dominance in mining towns, 38–44
  exclusion from local politics, 33, 35
  lack of involvement in anti-Boer War campaign, 212
  opposition to Sudan War, 1885, 210
  women taking paid work in post-war period, 82
  see also labour movement; socialism; trade unions
working hours, 115, 118, 120
Wren, John, 19, 21

Yalta conference, 164
Yirrkala people, Northern Territory, 181, 196
Young, Gay and Proud, 106
youth
  culture, and anti-Vietnam movement, 228–9
  organizations, rise of, 35
  unemployment, 147

'zone of peace', Indian Ocean, 243ff
zoning of suburbs, 17, 24

ALSO FROM McPHEE GRIBBLE/PENGUIN

BEYOND A JOKE
An Anti-Bicentenary Cartoon Book
Compiled by Kaz Cooke

Even rough justice is a euphemism for what is endured by Aborigines. Deaths in custody, the fear and loathing of land rights, the deep irony of the Bicentenary, and simple racism have roused many of our best cartoonists.

Fifty of them including Leunig, Cook, Moir, Horner, Gaynor, Tanner, Pryor, Petty and Tandberg have contributed to *Beyond a Joke*. John Clarke and Kaz Cooke have written introductions and Galarrwuy Yunupingu, Chairman of the Northern Land Council has written the foreword.

ALSO FROM McPHEE GRIBBLE/PENGUIN

GENERATIONS
Grandmothers, Mothers and Daughters
Diane Bell with Ponch Hawkes

In their own words and through photographs, the private worlds of women produce memories that go beneath the surface of things. Heirlooms and hand-me-downs, teapots and prayer books, routines and rituals, cuttings from familiar gardens and the Singer sewing machine, make plain the patterns of this place.